The book begins when war is declared and the Territorials of the 50th (Northumbrian) Division are mobilised before their move to France. Many of these men joined the territorials in the 1930s because they could find no work in the depression and the monthly bounty they got paid, plus a good pair of army boots, were worth a lot to men who had nothing. In late 1939 the division was moved to France in one of the worst winters in modern memory. In May 1940 the war began and the 50th were in the forefront of the fighting as they tried to stem the Blitzkrieg. When the situation became untenable the British army found themselves outflanked and in full retreat to the French Coast. The 50th reached the Great War Memorial at Ypres, the Menin Gate, and fought a delaying action here but soon found themselves retreating again, by now they had lost many casualties. By 19 and 20 May 1940 the whole British Army was in headlong retreat and heading towards Dunkirk with the panzers close on their heels, it was decided that a delaying action was to be launched by the 50th Division at Arras with British and French armoured units in support. It was here at Arras that the 50th would meet their future nemesis in the form of Erwin Rommel and his Ghost Division. On 20 May the 50th prepared themselves for battle on and around the Canadian Great War Memorial on Vimy Ridge. On 21 May the attack was launched into some very surprised German formations that were just about to move around Arras. The attack was led by tanks of the Royal Armoured Corps and the Troops of the 151st Durham Brigade, 150th Brigade was in Arras itself along the River Scarpe. The shock of the British assault caught the Germans by surprise and the British tanks caused great slaughter among the German units, especially among the ranks of the SS Totenkopf Division who fled the field in terror. The descriptions of the battle by tank crews and Durhams are outstanding and hair raising, the Germans looked to be close to defeat when Erwin Rommel stepped forward and ordered his 88 mm anti-aircraft guns to lower their barrels and be used in an anti-tank role for the first, but not the last time. The British tanks could not withstand their immense firepower and soon the battlefield was strewn with the smoking hulks of British tanks and the dead bodies of both sides. Rommel had saved the day.

The retreat now continued in a mad dash to the coast. At the town of Dunkirk and along the beaches the whole British Army waited patiently to be taken home, under constant air attack and artillery fire. By 2 June the last troops had been evacuated and a very badly beaten army was brought home, men who were there talk of their shame when interviewed, many were never proud of the fact that they were at Dunkirk. The British populace however were just pleased to have the survivors home and the myth of the miracle of Dunkirk took root. For many it was a time of mourning.

The 50th Division were now reorganised and stationed on the south coast of England in preparation for the invasion that never came. In 1941 the newly reconstructed 50th Division was sent to the Middle East, spending a miserable winter moving about from camp to muddy camp. Finally the 50th was sent to the Gazala Line in May 1942, this line was held by the South Africans, the Free French and three brigades of the 50th Division; 150th, 151st and 69th Brigades, plus all the 8th Army's armoured formations. Rommel needed to break through here and in May began to make his plans. The British Forces were positioned in defensive boxes, each one was supposed to be able to support the other in the event of the expected attack, but most were so far apart that mutual support was out of the question. Lt General Cruwell of the German forces was out reconnoitring the ground in a spotter plane when his pilot got lost and flew over the box held by 150th Brigade, his plane was shot down, his pilot killed and he was taken prisoner. The troops who took him saw only a blood spattered German and had no idea who was in front of them, they handled him roughly and stole his *Pour le Merite* and a gold ring. The young officers did not know the rank of the prisoner they had to interrogate and all snapped to attention when his rank was revealed; interviews with these men are featured in this book. In late May 1942 Rommel assembled his panzers, infantry and support vehicles by night, his attack force covered an area of eleven square miles. The plan was to move across 8th Army's front at night and to swing around the left flank, where the Free French held Bir Hacheim, and to the rear of 8th Army, a classic Rommel manoeuvre. As this happened the men of the 50th Division sat tight in their defensive boxes and waited. Patrols reported large troop and tank movements to the British Front but the commanders would not believe it until it was too late. The Free French at Bir Hacheim were attacked by German and Italian armoured formations and fought a legendary defensive action for over 10 days until they were forced to retire leaving behind them one thousand of their own dead and hundreds of enemy dead, dozens of black smouldering tanks littered the battle-field. The panzers smashed into British armoured units behind the Front Line and still it was not believed by the high command that this was happening, desperate messages came over the air-waves warning of the German assault. Rommel's forces were now in the rear of the 50th Division who could hear the thunder of battle all around them. The British commanders threw their armour in piecemeal fashion at the Germans and suffered horrendous losses, Rommel's timetable was slowing down now and he needed to get supplies and fuel for his hard pressed troops. In the face of ferocious attacks by the British armour he backed his units up to the rear of the Gazala Line and formed a defensive crescent of the dreaded 88 mm anti-tank guns around his panzers to hold off the British armour. Again and again the British commanders threw their tanks at this screen, only to see them knocked out in their hundreds, so fierce was the fighting in this area that it was christened 'The Cauldron'. Rommel now turned his attention to the 50th Division and realised that to get the supplies he so badly needed he needed to destroy the 150th Brigade. His tanks and infantry laid siege to this box and launched fleets of dive-bombers against them, heavy artillery fire, plus tanks and infantry. Day after day the battle raged but the 150th Brigade would not yield. After fighting an unsupported defence for five days the situation became serious for the badly depleted 150th. Rommel was so concerned regarding his supplies situation that he personally led one final desperate assault on 1 June 1942, after a morning of the most vicious close quarter fighting the panzers rolled over this doomed position. In Rommel's diary that night he recalled "The defence was conducted with great skill and determination and as usual the British fought to the last round."

Rommel's now replenished troops burst out of their bridgehead and put the British to flight, the troops in the Gazala Line got away as best they could with many close calls and near misses.

At Mersa Matruh the 50th Division was ordered to make a stand in order that other units could get away and in a very confused situation fought until they could fight no more, Pte Adam Wakenshaw won the Victoria Cross here and lost his life in the process. The Gazala Gallop then resumed until at last the 8th Army arrived at the last defensive line before Alexandria, this was to take its name from an insignificant railway siding called El Alamein.

The 50th Northumbrian Division had suffered grievously in the Western Desert and in May and June 1942 had taken 9,000 casualties. These years of defeat had seen them transformed into a battle hardened legion of the 8th Army who would become internationally famous in the years to come.

This study adds comprehensively to our knowledge of the Second World War in a number of ways:

- Firstly, the views of the men involved throw a bright light on what it was really like to fight in an elite infantry division.
- Secondly, it covers events that have not been studied in detail before and shows in no uncertain way the horrors men endured for years if they survived.
- Thirdly: The testimony of the men describes scenes they would not tell their families, from the deaths of friends in action to the terrible things they personally had to do to survive, to men who returned home and had to tell their parents, who knew nothing, what had happened to their brother.
- Fourthly: the text, illustrations and period maps come together to form a clear view of what the 50th Division really did in those terrible times as seen through the eyes of the survivors.

Barrie Barnes has been interviewing veterans in the 80s and 90s and all of their accounts appear in his books. He was brought up on a North Hull housing estate by his grandparents and left school aged 15 with no qualifications to work in a series of none skilled occupations for 18 years. After this he got his qualifications (BA hons, M/Phil) and worked for 26 years as a school teacher in Hull and Beverley. This will be his seventh book; he has now retired to a little East Yorkshire market town and is working on a number of manuscripts for the future.

**Other books by the author**
*This Righteous War. A history of the Hull 92nd Brigade [Hull Pals] during the Great War* (Richard Netherwood Ltd, Huddersfield, UK, 1990) and (Sentinel Press, York, UK, 2008).
*The Sign of the Double T. A history of the 50th Northumbrian Division in Sicily 1943 and North West Europe 1944* (Sentinel Press, York, UK, 1999 and 2008).
*Known to the Night. A history of Reckitt's Factory of Hull during the Great War* (Sentinel Press, York, UK, 2002).
*Operation Scipio. A history of the Eighth Army in the Tunisian Campaign of 1943, culminating in the Battle of the Wadi Akarit, 6th April 1943* (Sentinel Press, York, 2007).
*Known unto God. A history of the East Yorkshire town of Beverley during the Great War* (Sentinel Press, York, UK, 2014).
*The Infinite Debt. A study of the lives and deaths of Beverley's fallen sons and daughters in WW2* (Sentinel Press, York, UK, 2016).
*Stars in a Dark Night. A history of the east coast town of Hornsea during the Great War* (forthcoming).

# 50th At Bay

*The Years of Defeat. A History of the 50th Northumbrian Division 1939 to September 1942*

---

B.S. Barnes

**Helion & Company**

Helion & Company Limited
Unit 8 Amherst Business Centre
Budbrooke Road
Warwick
CV34 5WE
England
Tel. 01926 499 619
Fax 0121 711 4075
Email: info@helion.co.uk
Website: www.helion.co.uk
Twitter: @helionbooks
Visit our blog http://blog.helion.co.uk/

Published by Helion & Company 2018
Designed and typeset by Mach 3 Solutions Ltd (www.mach3solutions.co.uk)
Cover designed by Paul Hewitt, Battlefield Design (www.battlefield-design.co.uk)
Printed by Hobbs the Printers, Totton, Hampshire

Text © B. S. Barnes 2018
Illustrations © B. S. Barnes 2018
Maps drawn by George Anderson © Helion & Company 2018

Front cover: The 8th Army on the move. Rear cover: Royal Artillery. Camouflaged British Artillery position in action, Western Desert 1942. Both paintings by Captain Cyril Mount, used with permission.

Every reasonable effort has been made to trace copyright holders and to obtain their permission for the use of copyright material. The author and publisher apologize for any errors or omissions in this work, and would be grateful if notified of any corrections that should be incorporated in future reprints or editions of this book.

ISBN 978-1-912174-82-9

British Library Cataloguing-in-Publication Data.
A catalogue record for this book is available from the British Library.

All rights reserved. No part of this publication may be reproduced, stored in a retrieval system, or transmitted, in any form, or by any means, electronic, mechanical, photocopying, recording or otherwise, without the express written consent of Helion & Company Limited.

For details of other military history titles published by Helion & Company Limited contact the above address, or visit our website: http://www.helion.co.uk

We always welcome receiving book proposals from prospective authors.

# Contents

| | | |
|---|---|---|
| List of Illustrations | | ix |
| List of Maps | | xii |
| Other books by the author | | xiii |
| Preface | | xv |
| 1 | Formation of the Territorials | 17 |
| 2 | Mobilisation | 24 |
| 3 | All Quiet on the Western Front | 27 |
| 4 | The Nightmare begins, 10 May 1940 | 36 |
| 5 | The Battle of Arras, 21 to 23 May 1940 | 49 |
| 6 | 150 Brigade, 21 to 23 May 1940 | 71 |
| 7 | 'Come on lads it's Empire Day' | 80 |
| 8 | The Road to Dunkirk | 96 |
| 9 | The 50th at Bay | 133 |
| 10 | The Western Desert. 150 Brigade, December 1941 to March 1942 | 144 |
| 11 | Operation Full Size: 20, 21 and 22 March 1942 | 151 |
| 12 | Disaster at Sidi Muftah: The destruction of 150 Brigade, 26 May to 1 June 1942 | 157 |
| 13 | Aftermath | 200 |
| 14 | The Gazala Gallop | 209 |
| 15 | Mersa Matruh, 26 to 29 June 1942 | 225 |
| Conclusion | | 237 |

| | | |
|---|---|---|
| Appendices | | |
| I | Order of Battle – 7th Panzer (Ghost) Division May 1940 | 240 |
| II | Order of the Battle – 3rd SS Panzer Division, Totenkopf May 1940 | 241 |
| III | Order of Battle – German 90th Light African Division | 242 |
| IV | Order of Battle – 15th Panzer Division, sent to North Africa between April and June 1941 | 243 |
| V | Order of Battle – 21st Panzer Division (formerly 5th Light Division) | 244 |
| VI | Order of Battle – Bir Hacheim. 1st Free French Brigade, May 1942 | 245 |
| VII | Order of Battle – 50th Division, May 1940 | 246 |
| VIII | Order of Battle – 150 Brigade, 26 May to 1 June 1942 | 248 |
| IX | Order of Battle – Panzer Army Africa | 249 |
| X | Order of Battle of Attacking Columns – Arras, 21 May 1940 | 250 |

| | | |
|---|---|---|
| XI | 50th Division Gallantry Awards, France 1940 | 251 |
| XII | 4270383 Private Adam Wakenshaw, VC. 9th Battalion Durham Light Infantry, 151st Brigade, 50th Northumbrian Division | 254 |
| XIII | Numbers of British and Allied troops who were evacuated from Dunkirk and landed in England, 27 May to 4 June 1940: | 257 |
| XIV | 50th Division Honours and Awards 1941 to August 1942 | 258 |
| XV | The British Free Corps | 262 |
| XVI | Chronology of the War 3 September 1939 to 7 September 1942 | 263 |

| | |
|---|---|
| Bibliography | 269 |
| Glossary | 271 |
| Index | 273 |

**List of Illustrations**

Men of the 4th Battalion East Yorkshire Regiment, Territorial Army, at the Hull Cenotaph 11 November 1938. Left to right: Colour Sergeant Wilfred Gilson, Sergeant Alderson, Sergeant Wright and Sergeant Blake, MM. 19
The Gilson family. Top left: Colour Sergeant Wilfred Gilson, 4th Battalion East Yorkshire Regiment, TA. Wounded at Arras, May 1940. Top right: William Maxwell Gilson, Wilfred's father, served in Queen Victoria's Rifles, the Rifle Brigade, in the Great War. Bottom left: Sergeant Major Thomas B Wright, Wilfred's grandfather, served in the Horse Artillery in the 2nd Punjab War of 1849 and the Indian Mutiny of 1857. Bottom right: John Taylor, cousin of Thomas B Wright, served in the cavalry in the Indian Mutiny of 1857. 20
Sergeant Herbert Glenton, 4th Battalion East Yorkshire Regiment. 25
Men of the Green Howards land in France, January 1940. 27
Pte Reg Protheroe, 150 Field Ambulance. 28
Captain Bob Stafford, 4th Battalion East Yorkshire Regiment. 29
Pte Sid Atkinson, 4th Battalion East Yorkshire Regiment. 32
Men of the Royal Northumberland Fusiliers mobile reconnaissance unit, France, May 1940. 34
British troops move into Belgium, May 1940. 35
A German armoured column advances through a French town, May 1940. 37
Sergeant Max Hearst, 5th Battalion East Yorkshire Regiment. 40
A German half-track tows an 88 mm anti-aircraft gun through a French town, May 1940. 41
Pte John Thompson, 5th Battalion Green Howards. 41
Major Peter J Jeffries, DSO, OBE, 6th Battalion Durham Light Infantry. 42
French civilians flee before the violence of the Blitzkrieg, looking for a place of safety in a world gone mad. 43
German Stuka dive-bombers in action, May 1940. 45
Rommel's 7th Panzer Division moves across the Somme valley on its way to Arras, May 1940. A Storch spotter plane can be seen flying overhead. 49
Sergeant George Denis Elliot, 9th Battalion Durham Light Infantry. 51
Lt Colonel Harry Miller, 6th Battalion Durham Light Infantry. 53
A German 88 mm Flak gun in action at Arras, 21 May 1940. Two tanks of the Royal Tank Regiment can be seen advancing. 58
Burning British tanks at Arras, 21 May 1940. 59
Pte Thomas W Jackson, 8th Battalion Durham Light Infantry. 61

| | |
|---|---:|
| Pte John H Clark, 8th Battalion Durham Light Infantry. | 62 |
| Sergeant Charles E. Davis, 4th Battalion Royal Northumberland Fusiliers. | 64 |
| German infantry move to the attack behind a barrage of fire, 22 May 1940. | 66 |
| Captain George L Wood, MC and bar, 6th Battalion Durham Light Infantry. | 68 |
| Troops of the SS Totenkopf Division burying a fallen comrade, Arras, 23 May 1940. | 77 |
| L/Cpl William Ridley, 9th Battalion Durham Light Infantry. | 81 |
| Distraught French civilians on the road fleeing the German assault, May 1940. | 82 |
| Pte Wilf Mooney, 4th Battalion East Yorkshire Regiment. | 85 |
| Corporal Albert Snowdon, 5th Battalion Green Howards. | 88 |
| Captain Douglas King, 4th Battalion East Yorkshire Regiment. | 92 |
| Sergeant Bob Gibson, MM, 151 Brigade Provost Company. | 92 |
| Major C R Battiscombe, 9th Battalion Durham Light Infantry. | 94 |
| German infantry marching along the sun lit roads of France, May 1940. | 96 |
| Pte William Cheall, 6th Battalion Green Howards. | 103 |
| Thousands of British troops waiting on the beaches to be evacuated, 31 May 1940. | 107 |
| Pte Ken Tidball, 4th Battalion East Yorkshire Regiment. | 108 |
| Death in the street, Dunkirk, May 1940. | 110 |
| Dunkirk seen from the sea, blazing oil tanks send plumes of smoke into the night sky as raging fires light up the scene, May 1940. | 112 |
| Pte Roy Walker, 5th Battalion East Yorkshire Regiment. | 114 |
| A causeway of vehicles that was used to evacuate the wounded from the beaches at high tide. Taken by a German photographer on 4 June 1940 after the British had left. | 117 |
| British troops waiting on the Mole at Dunkirk, 31 May 1940. | 118 |
| British troops on the Mole at Dunkirk scramble aboard a waiting destroyer, 31 May 1940. | 120 |
| Mrs Rose Lyon. (ATS) | 121 |
| British troops wading out to a waiting ship, Dunkirk, 30th May 1940. | 122 |
| British dead and wrecked vehicles litter the streets of Dunkirk, 1 June 1940. | 123 |
| British troops on a destroyer crossing the English Chanel, 30 May 1940. | 124 |
| German troops enter the burning ruins of Dunkirk after the British had left, 3 June 1940. | 125 |
| Lt Ian R English, MC and bar, 8th Battalion Durham Light Infantry. | 126 |
| British troops on board a destroyer arrive on the south coast of England, 1 June 1940. | 127 |
| The Green Howards arrive on the south coast, 1 June 1940. On the left with dog is CSM Jack Verity, 7th Battalion Green Howards. | 129 |
| Worn out and tired British troops board a train on the south coast that will take them to their assembly areas for refitting and rest. | 129 |
| Sergeant Arthur Chester, 4th Battalion East Yorkshire Regiment. | 131 |
| Pte John Chester, 4th Battalion East Yorkshire Regiment. Killed in action at Arras, May 1940. | 131 |
| Pte William Gleave, 4th Battalion Green Howards. | 137 |
| Pte Kilgallon, 9th Battalion Durham Light Infantry. | 140 |
| Men of 150 Brigade look out over no-man's land from their slit trench, wondering when Rommel will make his next move, April 1942. | 147 |
| Pte Joe Kneeshaw, 5th Battalion Green Howards. | 148 |

| | |
|---|---|
| Pte Norman Hardy, 4th Battalion East Yorkshire Regiment. | 154 |
| The blazing airfield at Martuba after the raid, 22 March 1942. | 155 |
| Rommel and his generals plan the next move at Gazala, May 1942. | 158 |
| A German half-track tows a large artillery piece into position, May 1942. | 162 |
| French anti-tank gunners in action at Bir Hacheim, 27 May 1942. | 165 |
| Sergeant Buck Kite, MC and bar, 3rd Battalion Royal Tank Regiment. | 167 |
| A British Grant Tank passing a knocked out Italian tank. | 168 |
| Lt John Michael Gregson Halstead, Queen's Bays. | 173 |
| Picture by Cpt Cyril Mount, Royal Artillery. Camouflaged British Artillery position in action, Western Desert 1942. | 182 |
| General Ludwig Cruwell, OC Africa Corps, May 1942. | 184 |
| Pte Herbert Thompson, 4th Battalion East Yorkshire Regiment. | 188 |
| Panzergrenadiers await the order to move off, May 1942. | 191 |
| British troops take cover behind a knocked out vehicle in the Gazala Line, May 1942. | 195 |
| The men of 150 Field Ambulance in the Gazala Line, May 1942. Seated centre is James Keith Kilby. | 200 |
| The Auleb box, 2 June 1942. In the background the men of 150 Brigade queue up for water. | 202 |
| Top left: Soldiers of the French Foreign Legion pause for a bite to eat during a lull in the fighting. Bir Hacheim. May 1942. Top right: Colonel Amilakvari, left, commander of the 13th Regiment, Foreign Legion, in conference with his battalion commander Puchios, right, and other officers. Bir Hacheim. May 1942. Colonel Amilakvari would be killed at Alamein on 24th October 1942. Bottom left: Smiling French survivors of Bir Hacheim heading for Alamein, June 1942. Bottom right: Troops of the French Foreign Legion going out on patrol at Bir Hacheim. May 1942. | 211 |
| The Devil's Cauldron. Knocked out tanks and vehicles litter the landscape, June 1942. | 212 |
| Pte Harry Forth, 5th Battalion East Yorkshire Regiment, and his wife Rene. | 214 |
| Pte Adam Wakenshaw, 9th Battalion Durham Light Infantry. | 227 |
| The battlefield grave of Pte Adam Wakenshaw, next to it is the anti-tank gun he and Mohn operated. | 231 |
| L/Cpl William Taylor, 5th Battalion East Yorkshire Regiment. | 234 |

# List of Maps

| | | |
|---|---|---|
| 1 | The British Expeditionary Force Campaign. May to June 1940. | 47 |
| 2 | The Battle of Arras, 21 May 1940. | 76 |
| 3 | The German plan of attack 1940. | 90 |
| 4 | The Panzer Corridor, 18 to 21 May 1940. | 98 |
| 5 | The withdrawal to the coast. | 106 |
| 6 | Rommel's forces advance and outflank the British line, 27/28 May 1942. | 163 |
| 7 | Rommel's forces turn upon 150 Brigade at Sidi Muftah, 29/30 May 1942. | 179 |
| 8 | The destruction of 150 Brigade, 1 June 1942. | 189 |
| 9 | The Battle of Gazala, May to June 1942. | 207 |
| 10 | The Battle of Mersa Matruh, 26/27 June 1942. | 232 |

For my dear friend Ian S. Davidson who sadly passed away this year, 9 March 2018.

An irreplaceable loss, he will be missed by all who knew and loved him and will live on in our hearts.

Forget-me-not.

# Preface

Thirty four years ago I began interviewing veterans from the First World War and the Second World War, in the intervening years I compiled hundreds of accounts of the men at the sharp end of war. Most of these have appeared in my books that have been published, in particular *The Sign of the Double T* and *Operation Scipio*. The first deals with the 50th Northumbrian Division in their years of victory in 1943 and 1944. The latter deals with the story of the Eighth Army in Tunisia in 1943, culminating in the Battle of the Wadi Akarit on 6 April 1943.

This present study is the prequel to *The Sign of the Double T* and follows the experiences of the famous 50th Northumbrian Division in their years of defeat from September 1939 to October 1942. The men I interviewed have now mostly passed away, in 2017 I interviewed Joe Kneeshaw, ex 5th Battalion Green Howards, who is now in a nursing home and is quite ill. Harry Forth, ex 5th Battalion East Yorkshire Regiment, died recently at the grand old age of 100. I have heard of the deaths of the men I knew with sadness and as I read or listened to their recorded stories the memories of them are still sharp and clear. We would talk for hours as they recounted their exploits, sometimes breaking down as they recalled what they did as young men. They could not remember what they had eaten for dinner the day before they met me but the memories of those terrible times they could recall with a clarity that was deeply impressive and moving. I remember their keen sense of humour and generosity in sharing all they knew with me as we sat and drank tea and chatted.

It has been my aim to make sure that these valuable reminiscences are preserved for posterity and that these men who gave so much should be remembered by future generations. Here I present their testimony warts and all, after over 70 years the impression which remains of them is their easy going good nature and fierce loyalty to each other. They would advance when ordered into the most terrific barrage, when told to stand fast most would stay until told to move. These were kind hearted sociable men who would stand firm while their comrades did the same, no battalion broke in mutiny when they were ordered to advance and martyrdoms were inevitable.

Torn away from the joys of youth they did their duty as they saw it and now their experience has passed into history. When each man spoke of his time with the 50th Northumbrian Division he did so with great pride, their achievements stand for all to see and it has been my privilege and pleasure to have met so many of them.

# 1

## Formation of the Territorials

By the year 1907 the strength of the volunteer infantry was some 221 battalions in England, Scotland and Wales, each regular unit contained a number of volunteer battalions and that number varied from regiment to regiment. Alongside these battalions there also existed a number of cadet units, usually of company strength. Each cadet unit was affiliated to a volunteer battalion which was responsible for providing training and to prepare the younger boys for future enrolment in the volunteer force when they were old enough.

The Secretary of State for War, Richard Haldane, introduced army reforms in 1907. Under these the existing Yeomanry and Volunteer Forces were to be amalgamated into an organisation that was to be known as the Territorial Force. Haldane's Bill, The Territorial and Reserve Forces Bill, brought into being an establishment of 14 divisions, each made up of three infantry brigades of four battalions. The Territorial Force came into being on 1 April 1908, most of the volunteer infantry adapted quickly to the new system, but some of its members could not cope with such drastic surgery and chose not to continue their service.

The new innovative reforms of 1908 established several new regiments made up entirely of territorials and created an officer training corps. These men could not be ordered overseas but were to be used only in defence of the homeland. However the imperial service section gave a man the option of volunteering for service abroad if the situation required it.

On 3 August 1914 regular and territorial units were mobilised, the territorials moving immediately to their wartime home defence stations. The situation in France and Belgium became serious as the British retreated from Mons, the presence of all regular troops was now required in the battle zone and territorial battalions would be asked to serve overseas to replace them. Territorial units volunteered *en masse* to serve abroad and found them being posted to Egypt, India and the Mediterranean. The first territorials landed in France in September 1914.

In April 1915 the 50th Northumbrian Division went to France. Its battalions were made up of the men of:

- The 5th, 6th, 7th, 8th and 9th Battalions Durham Light Infantry.
- The 4th, 5th, 6th and 7th Battalions Royal Northumberland Fusiliers.
- The 1/4th Battalion East Yorkshire Regiment.
- The 4th and 5th Battalions the Yorkshire Regiment.

They took part in many of the bloodiest actions of the Great War and by November 1918 many of these units had lost the bulk of their compliment killed, wounded or taken prisoner. In 1918 the remnants of the 50th Division was inspected by King George V in a field off the Maubeuge-Avesnes Road and in the latter part of November demobilisation began, the Great War had ended.

After the end of the Great War the Territorial Force was disbanded only to be reconstituted in 1920 and as from 1 October 1921 the Territorial Force would be known as the Territorial Army. A number of battalions were not reformed in 1920 as the pre-war compliment of 208 battalions was to be reduced. Some were amalgamated into other units, other infantry battalions became converted to an anti-aircraft roll as the threat of mass attacks from the skies became a growing reality. In 1938 the Territorial Army was reorganised in a major way and each division was reduced from 12 battalions to nine.

As 1938 came to a close the 50th Division was designated to become one of the new motorised divisions, designed to act in close support with armoured forces. 149 Brigade was disbanded, its four battalions of the Royal Northumberland Fusiliers taking on different roles. The 4th Battalion stayed with the 50th Division until after the fall of France in 1940 as a reconnaissance motor cycle battalion, the other three battalions becoming searchlight, anti-tank and machine-gun units.

For the Territorial Army the inter-war years consisted of a set routine of annual camps, social gatherings and training events. On Armistice Day each year they would parade to remember their fallen comrades. Many men in the Territorials had seen service in the Great War and Armistice Day was poignant with vivid memories of the trenches and of missing friends.

During the hard times of the 1920s and 1930s the reasons a man joined the territorials were varied and many. Some felt it a duty that had to be done, others joined because of the annual bounty, the promise of travel and something new. Many men enlisted because of family tradition, in some cases their fathers and grandfathers had served and so the tradition of the volunteers had always been with them. Arthur Chester recalls how he and his brother John joined the Territorial Army in March 1939:

> My father was in the First World War and was killed in the Ypres Salient in 1915 serving with the 1/4th Battalion East Yorkshire Regiment. During the 1930s my brother John and me joined the 4th Battalion East Yorkshire Regiment, TA. It was full of local men, some had served in World War One and it was like a family, I was just a lad at the time but the old hands wore their first war medals ribbons on their chests.[1]

All men that served with the territorials felt this close bond and camaraderie that existed in such local units no matter what part of the country they came from.

In May 1939 Corporal William Ridley joined the 9th Battalion Durham Light Infantry. He was recruited in Gateshead and remembers how close knit the territorials were in that area:

> The bugle bands had served together since they were boys and were a solid group of individuals, all for one like. Friendships were deep and long. On top of that there were a lot of

---

1   Taped interview with author with Arthur Chester (Hull, 1994).

Men of the 4th Battalion East Yorkshire Regiment, Territorial Army, at the Hull Cenotaph 11 November 1938. Left to right: Colour Sergeant Wilfred Gilson, Sergeant Alderson, Sergeant Wright and Sergeant Blake, MM.

dads with their sons and uncles. Many had fought in the Great War and always wore their medal ribbons, which impressed us younger lads. We had one family called Levee; there was four or five brothers, so it was like a family battalion.[2]

Colour Sergeant Wilfred Gilson had been a post office worker in Hull before the war and earned a very meagre wage for his labours. He joined the 4th Battalion East Yorkshire Regiment on 4 December 1931 and became a proficient and enthusiastic young soldier, rising to the rank of colour sergeant. His low wages were not the only reason he enlisted, his family had military traditions going back to at least the 1840s. Wilfred's grandfather, Thomas B. Wright, had been a Sergeant Major in the Horse Artillery, seeing active service in the 2nd Punjab War of 1849 and the Indian Mutiny of 1857. His grandfather's cousin, John Taylor, had served in a cavalry regiment during the Indian Mutiny. Wilfred's Father, William Maxwell Gilson, joined up in 1892 in Queen Victoria's Rifles and served in the Great War. He instilled into his son Wilfred the military virtues of duty and sacrifice, qualities the preceding generation had been raised with all their lives. Wilfred knew war was imminent and heard what the men had to say who had been in the Great War:

> I think everyone knew war was coming and when it did we were called up because we were the TA. We already had two uniforms and were issued with a rifle and bayonet. We also

2   Ibid, with William Ridley at Veteran's re-union (Hull, 1993).

The Gilson family. Top left: Colour Sergeant Wilfred Gilson, 4th Battalion East Yorkshire Regiment, TA. Wounded at Arras, May 1940. Top right: William Maxwell Gilson, Wilfred's father, served in Queen Victoria's Rifles, the Rifle Brigade, in the Great War. Bottom left: Sergeant Major Thomas B Wright, Wilfred's grandfather, served in the Horse Artillery in the 2nd Punjab War of 1849 and the Indian Mutiny of 1857. Bottom right: John Taylor, cousin of Thomas B Wright, served in the cavalry in the Indian Mutiny of 1857.

had our full equipment as we used to drill in it. Two First World War men were in my company, one was called Stan Harper and the other was a fellow called George Greenfield. They used to tell us stories about the hard life they had in the trenches, we all had worries about a First World War type of conflict and hoped it was going to be different this time.[3]

Men like Wilfred Gilson were the backbone of the Territorial Army and served with others who had seen action on the Somme, at Arras and Ypres during the Great War. In February 1939 Lt Douglas King joined Wilfred Gilson's unit and commented on the men he found there:

These men who served in the Territorial Army were very dedicated and their interest in things military was far greater than my own. Some of them had seen service between 1914 and 1918 and knew what it was all about. It was obviously a very important part of their lives. I came in as a raw subaltern who knew nothing and I had a lot to learn.[4]

Those that joined the territorial army during the inter-war years did not all come from one social class, though non-commissioned officers and the other ranks were in the main from the working class which formed the bulk of the population. Reasons why a man joined up varied from individual to individual, the mass unemployment of the 1930s and the financial hardship it caused certainly played its part in drawing men to the territorials. Jack Cavanagh recalled the harsh life people led and how his provision of army equipment helped:

They were hard times, the depression you know, soup kitchens, parish relief and all that. At one time when the miners were on strike there was a police baton charge against the picket lines at Harris Bank just down from our drill hall. Hard times to say the least. The boots I got from the territorials were as good as gold to me, I was out of a job and you had to walk miles looking for work even though there wasn't any. It was as well I had me army boots. None of us had a penny between us, our platoon commander was always good for a few bob, he never asked for it back either. Many a time I've seen lads out of the platoon go up to him and say 'can you lend us a shilling sir?' and they got it from the lieutenant, he was a decent fella and it was from his own pocket, not very military I suppose but that's how it was.[5]

Sergeant James McGarey, MM, 8th DLI, was a miner before the war:

There was a canny few of us pit-men in the TA, a lot of the lads were from the St Anne Pit. Jimmy Alderson was sergeant, he was Overman at the pit shop, and there was Lt Nelson, of course his father's family was coal owners, they owned Pelaw Main Collieries. A good few had been in the first war, CSM Nell, Colour Sergeant Tommy Jackson, PSI Simpkin, Sergeant Ralph Timothy, MM. A lot of the men had served in the trenches, they were old soldiers and knew all the tricks.[6]

3 Ibid, with Wilfred Gilson (Hull, 1994).
4 Ibid, with Douglas King (Hull, 1993).
5 G Purdon, *From Coalfield to Battlefield* (County Durham Springboard Media Project, Durham, 1995), p. 22.
6 Ibid, p. 27.

Pte Bob Fort, 8th Battalion DLI, remembers the day he enlisted:

> There was a recruiting campaign going on in Chester le Street at the time and there was me and Jimmy Hubbick, Billy Cook, George Stevenson and another bloke, we all worked in the store and had been out drinking that night in the Bridge End Pub. Somebody suggested joining the army so we trooped into the drill hall full of beer, once you got in the doors closed behind you, you were there and you couldn't change your mind. The queerest thing about it was the medical, you signed on, got the King's Shilling and they said 'are you fit?' when I said I was that was it. As it happened I'd had bad eyesight all my life, but there I was in the Durham Light Infantry.[7]

Pte Thomas Maher was a pitman before joining up and was one of the youngest men at the enlisting centre:

> We all took the King's shilling and signed on, they had a trestle table set up down the drill hall. Lt Waggett was doing the paperwork, he had a bit of a squeaky voice. He handed me a five pound note when I signed and said 'take that straight home to your mother', I was just a kid really, the youngest in the battalion, it was touch and go whether the 8th Battalion took me on at all. Well I'd never seen a fiver, it was a months wages for a pit lad. Needless to say we were straight into the Bridge for a drink, I still had change in me pocket out of that fiver when we were in Oxfordshire three months later.[8]

Sapper Frederick Carter was unemployed and saw the army as a way out of his predicament:

> When I heard war had broken out I didn't really worry. It was rough in England at that time, unemployment was very bad and I thought maybe if we had a war something might happen. I was out of work and I thought I'd join the Royal Engineers, nobody seemed to be upset about the war starting, I thought it would be over quickly.[9]

Corporal Joss Little was already in the 8th Battalion DLI and was told to report to the local drill hall:

> My brother came up to the pit, he had this card saying I had to report to the drill hall. Why I was as black as the fire-back and straight out of the pit, so I went down to the drill hall and Sergeant Major O'Brian was there, he says 'what the hell are you doing here? We want no black men in here, get away bloody home, get washed and put your bloody khaki on before you come back'. So I went home and got washed like he told me, we lived in Third Avenue then, pit-men had to go home black because there was no pit-head baths in those days. I said to my mother and father I've got to go back to the drill hall, do you know what for?[10]

---

7 Ibid, p. 29.
8 Ibid, p. 23.
9 Taped interview with author with Fred Carter (Hull, 1997).
10 G Purdon, *From Coalfield to Battlefield* (County Durham Springboard Media Project, Durham, 1995), p. 49.

Sergeant John Williams, 6th Battalion DLI, noticed that not all local men were keen to go in the army:

> I noticed that some of my contemporaries suddenly developed asthma and ailments we'd never known them to have before. One or two said 'I wish I was fit enough to join up'. They were as fit as I was, but who would want men like that in the battalion. Before we went out to France my mother said 'don't shoot any of those poor German boys will you', I said 'No mum not unless they shoot me first.[11]

Others wanted something new to do and felt family traditions affecting their outlook. Many felt a duty to their country but would not admit it publicly for fear of ridicule. The comradeship of being part of a close knit disciplined unit was a big attraction to enlisting and all men interviewed for this study speak of the importance of the friends made on active service and how their support saw them through some rough times in the war years. As the 1930s drew to a close events in Europe were on the move and the Territorial Army would soon be called upon to face the might of an army their fathers had thought to be defeated and destroyed two decades earlier.

---

11   Manuscript sent to author, William Ridley (Durham, 1996).

## 2

## Mobilisation

The men of the 50th Division were mobilised before the formal declaration of war which came on 3 September 1939. Units were ordered to report to their respective drill halls to be issued with the necessary equipment and from there to their local billets. Most men remember vividly the day they were called from their homes.

Pte Ken Tidball, 4th Battalion East Yorkshire Regiment, was taking it easy after work when he heard the news:

> I hadn't finished work long and was dozing on the settee listening to the wireless when the news came on. All territorial units were told to report to their barracks at once, I lived in Day Street in Hull, only five minutes away from the barracks. We signed in and were told to report back the next day. Most of us were very worried about what might happen in the future, we thought oh no, Gerry's at it again.[1]

A mobilisation scheme had previously been worked out with the civil authorities and was now being put into force. However much of the equipment needed for full mobilisation did not come to hand for some months, even though the 50th Division was earmarked for the overseas theatre of war. The barrack buildings of individual units could not cope with the numbers of men now called to the colours and many found themselves billeted in dance halls, churches, cinemas and schools. Arthur Chester and his brother John found themselves sleeping on a church hall floor.

Sergeant Arthur Chester recalls:

> For temporary billets C Company, 4th Battalion East Yorkshire Regiment, was told to report to St Columba's Church Hall, Laburnum Avenue, Hull. That was our billet until we were brought up to strength, everything was very hush-hush, sentries had been posted outside the church and rumours flew about regarding our destination. Sweethearts and wives were in tears at the church gates, many of them had lost fathers in the last war, we felt sorry for them but nobody was allowed in.[2]

1   Taped interview with author. Ken Tidball (Hull, 1995).
2   Ibid, with Arthur Chester (Hull, 1994).

Training took place in local parks or any other open ground that was available and marches around the local streets were organised, groups of men could be seen in shorts and plimsolls running along main roads. Any men that could get a leave pass took advantage of that precious time at home to take care of their personal affairs, as soldiers preparing to go off to war had done for centuries.

Sergeant Herbert Glenton:

> We were training in our new billets for about six weeks, the battalion was scattered all around the town of Hull and was none existent as far as we were concerned. While I was on 48 hours leave I got married, possibly that's worth recording.[3]

Lt Douglas King felt totally unprepared for his new role:

> I knew nothing about arms so I had to learn as quickly as I could from the men around me, after the basic infantry training that we all had to do I was put in charge of the gas platoon, it meant dealing with gas masks, mines and that sort of thing. I didn't know much about that either. I can't even remember having a revolver as an officer. The bren-guns were coming in and I learnt how to strip and re-assemble one. Our transport was very limited but we had the odd bren-carrier.[4]

Sergeant Herbert Glenton, 4th Battalion East Yorkshire Regiment.

In October 1939 the men of the 50th Division left their home towns and local areas to move to the Cotswold country of Oxfordshire. Here they were to complete their training and mobilisation. Most troops enjoyed their stay in this pleasant location and were made very welcome by the people of the area who would often invite men into their own homes. Their generosity took some of the men by surprise.

Pte Ken Tidball, 4th Battalion East Yorkshire Regiment, was one such young man:

> The people that lived around that neck of the woods were very kind to us, it was a real nice feeling being among such friendly folk as they made you feel at home, you got that many invites out to tea you could have been out nearly every night.[5]

Training for the whole division continued apace as the time to move overseas drew ever closer. Rumours of the divisions destination began to fly about and many men hoped against hope that the situation in Europe would fizzle out of its own accord, others however felt that war with

3 Ibid, with Herbert Glenton (Hull, 1995).
4 Ibid, with Douglas King (Hull, 1993).
5 Ibid, with Ken Tidball (Hull, 1995).

Germany was only a matter of time. Reinforcements began to pour into each battalion until the whole division was up to strength.

Sergeant Herbert Glenton felt the changes sharply as his once local unit began to fill up with men from West Yorkshire:

> The make-up of the battalion had changed quite a bit since mobilisation, the original lads were still there but men from farther afield had joined us to make up our numbers. It was all still a game to us, we were young and full of beans and had seen very little of the world, we had no idea of what was in store for us, but perhaps that was a good thing.[6]

By the end of 1939 the division was at full strength and fully trained, but equipment was very short in many areas. A shudder of excitement ran through the young men of the 50th Division as they prepared themselves for the move to France. In early January 1940 the King inspected the troops and on 19 January elements of this territorial unit left the shores of England for France.

Pte James Young, 4th Battalion Royal Northumberland Fusiliers, was ready for the move overseas and looked forward to the next stage of this great adventure:

> I'd been on leave to see mam and dad and me brothers and sister, most of my mates had already gone off for training and the whole feeling at home was a bit of an anti-climax after the hard work of the last few weeks. I went out for a pint with dad, we had a long talk, he knew what he was talking about as he had been in the infantry in the last lot, what he told me fair shook me I can tell you and he made me realise it was no game, as he put it 'Gerry was no mug and he knows how to fight'. My enthusiasm wasn't so great after that. When we went home I looked at my family and thought this might be the last time I would see them, there was no more boozing that leave, I spent the rest of it with my family, when it came time for me to leave only mam, dad and my little sister came to the railway station to see me off. It was a grim experience, I tried to reassure mam it would all be over in a short time but I could see in her face she was worried sick, I hugged her and my little sister and shook hands with dad. As the train pulled out of the station I waved and looked back at those three sad figures until they were out of sight, then I sat down with the other soldiers and we shared our fags and chatted, things started to seem a bit better.[7]

The mothers and fathers whose sons were about to leave the shores of England still had vivid memories of the Great War and it was with heavy hearts that they let their young men go to another conflict in Europe with the old enemy, Germany. The 50th Division had trained for this moment and it was with feelings of excitement and trepidation about the future that they boarded their transports and left their homeland with no certainty of when, or if, they would return.

---

6   Ibid, with Herbert Glenton (Hull, 1995).
7   Ibid, with James Young at Veteran's re-union (Gateshead, 1996).

# 3

## All Quiet on the Western Front

---

The advanced guard of the 50th Division arrived at Lens on 27 January 1940, the main body of the division followed and disembarked at Cherbourg in one of the worst winters of modern times, to find roads blocked by heavy snow falls and everything covered in ice. The planned preparations of defensive positions had to wait as the division waited for the roads to be cleared and a thaw to set in.

Pte Reg Protheroe, 150 Field Ambulance, remembers a miserable crossing to France:

> We went across the Channel at night in very rough weather, I remember leaning over the side as the ship rolled back and forth, the sea looked black and scary and I puked my guts up. We were all sick as dogs and I've never known anything like it. When we finally arrived there was no one to greet us, no rousing welcome, we went ashore feeling sick, cold and very

Men of the Green Howards land in France, January 1940.

miserable. The French people we met were alright with us but there was no flag waving or anything like that.¹

Pte Albert Gaskin, DLI, felt very emotional as he left the shores of England for the first time:

> Soon the decks were crowded with khaki clad figures, some very silent, wondering perhaps the same as me, would this be the same as dad's war? Fix bayonets, over the top, barbed wire, water filled trenches, mud and blood. As the troop ships nosed their way into the Channel a friend of mine who had brought along his long silver trumpet stood at the bow of the ship and played Auld Lang Syne. Looking around me on the deck I watched some of the troops for their reaction and like me many were gulping back the tears and some were weeping, as I was, unashamedly.²

Pte Reg Protheroe, 150 Field Ambulance.

Sergeant Alfred Young felt a deep foreboding about the future:

> So far I was not very impressed with what I saw since I had set foot in France. When stepping off the ship we were confronted by numerous French soldiers walking aimlessly along the quayside accompanied by hundreds of horses, some pulling antiquated artillery pieces. There was no mechanised transport of any kind. The French troops looked tired, disorganised and unenthusiastic, totally unprepared for war.³

Sergeant John Williams came ashore with the 6th Battalion DLI:

> The morale of the battalion was high and we were going to that magic place called France where a lot of our parents and uncles had been in the last lot. We landed at Cherbourg and my contemporaries were saying 'you can speak French can't you?' I said I could so we went to this market and there was a stall selling oranges under flickering gas lamps. I said '*combien des* oranges madame?' But I was surprised to see all these glaring lights because we had the blackout in England, all the bars and brothels had lights on. We saw some kids who said '*Ici France! Vous Anglais! Allez!*' cheeky little buggers.⁴

Because of the unexpected situation the officers found themselves in billets were hard to find and men had to rough it in order to escape the elements.

Captain Bob Stafford, 4th Battalion East Yorkshire Regiment, recalled their misery:

---

1    Taped interview with author, Reg Protheroe (Hull, 1997).
2    Ibid, with Albert Gaskin at the Veteran's re-union (Durham, 1994).
3    Ibid, with Alfred Young (Hull, 1997).
4    Ibid, with John Williams (Hull, 1996)

The accommodation we got was bloody rotten, we were stuck in anywhere, our billets were cow sheds or pig sties, they all had one thing in common, they were all filthy.⁵

Pte Thomas W Jackson was with the 8th Battalion DLI, his first night in France was a cold one:

Captain Bob Stafford, 4th Battalion East Yorkshire Regiment.

We made our fires in petrol tins and cooked our meals on whatever we could get hold of. That night it was clear and moon lit when we went to bed, the roof had once been covered with pan tiles but now most of them had gone and we could see the stars. We lay down on straw and put our gas capes on top of our blankets which was lucky for us. During the night there was a snow storm and the next morning we had to dig ourselves out.⁶

Pte John Thompson, 5th Battalion Green Howards, found his new accommodation in poor shape:

We finished up in a little French village and were put in an old barn on the upper floor with cows beneath us. One of our lads found a cap badge in the straw from the First World War and the barn walls were still full of holes where shells and bullets had passed through. The wind howled through them all night long and it was hard to keep warm.⁷

Sergeant Bob Gibson, MM, 151 Brigade Provost Company:

We were in the worst sodding winter you could imagine, the wind was icy and howling around our billets all night, with snow and sleet coming down in sheets and to top it all our beds were straw on a mud floor. What a bunch of miserable bleeders we were.⁸

Despite the appalling weather and poor accommodation the troops still had to carry out all the daily chores required to keep an army in working order. Lt Bob Stafford saw the difficulties the men had doing a simple thing like keeping their clothes clean and dry:

We got snowed in, it was one of the worst winters in modern memory and at one point the fellows had to do their own laundry, no sooner had they hung it out to dry than it was frozen solid. Braziers had to be lit to thaw and dry the laundry out.⁹

5  Ibid, with Bob Stafford (Hull, 1994).
6  Ibid, with Thomas W. Jackson at the Veteran's re-union (Durham, 1994).
7  Ibid, with John Thompson (Beverley, 1995).
8  Ibid, with Bob Gibson (Hull, 1994).
9  Ibid, with Bob Stafford (Hull, 1994).

Men acquired many items that made their lives a bit more comfortable and not always legally, livestock disappeared from farms and was a welcome supplement to army rations. Angry farmers would appear at headquarters demanding action be taken regarding this matter but little could be done to stop the more enterprising scroungers in their search for food. Heat was essential in this icy weather and things to burn were taken from many places.

Colour Sergeant Wilfred Gilson's company was billeted in a dog track and he turned a blind eye to the scrounging activities of his men:

> The main concern on the men's mind was food and how to stay warm, some very tasty morsels turned up on my plate but I didn't ask too many questions, cold makes you very hungry. When the men needed to wash and shave they had to go down to the village pump no matter how cold it was. The company coal allocation soon ran out and fences and railings were torn down and kept us warm, this was not legal but needs must when the devil drives.[10]

The terrible weather and bad accommodation proved not to be their only problem, other unwanted visitors made their lives very uncomfortable indeed. Sergeant James McGarey was with the 8th Battalion DLI:

> As soon as we moved into our billets we got the lice, whoever had been there before must have left it because the place was thick with dirty straw and hadn't been cleaned out. They were old buildings and the lads was full of lice. The sergeant major had two pairs of shears, one was to shave their heads, the other to shave their balls. I mind one lad saying 'I hope you're not getting them shears mixed up Geordie', aye life was pretty grim in that hard winter.[11]

If there was a feeling of adventure at being away from home for the first time it was also tempered by homesickness for many of these young men and in quiet moments thoughts turned to home. Pte George Sandersfield was billeted in the village of Fresney-Sur-Sarthe with the 6th Battalion DLI:

> This small village has a special memory for me about a soldiers feeling of homesickness. On the second night there was a large group of our company who had gathered round a big fire in the brewery yard, after a while of having a chin-wag they started singing as there were some good entertainers among them. Suddenly someone started playing a radio and it was a Vera Lynn show and she sang some songs. Naturally all the men joined in and then at the end Vera sang The White Cliffs of Dover, nearly all of them started to cry. I suppose as nearly all of them were terriers they were missing their wives and children.[12]

---

10   Ibid, with Wilfred Gilson (Hull, 1994).
11   G. Purdon, *From Coalfield to Battlefield* (Durham: County Durham Springboard Media Project, 1995), p. 37.
12   Taped interview with author, George Sandersfield (Durham, 1996).

Food was always on the minds of these healthy young men and the harsh weather made it doubly important that hot meals were provided for the troops after a hard day's work. Pte Alfred Chittock, MM, 150 Field Ambulance, remembers one incident when the distribution of food was seen by the men to be unfair and they were not slow in voicing their grievances. He was working in the sergeant's mess at the time and the meal being prepared for them was hot stew, when the other ranks came to the cookhouse for their evening meal and found only corned beef sandwiches a minor mutiny ensued:

> The lads were fuming and went round to the sergeants mess mob handed and were shouting for the sergeant majors blood, put the fear of Christ up him it did. After a while the officers got wind of what was happening and they had to start a hot meal for the men. I was happy though, I'd had my hot stew in the sergeant's mess.[13]

Pte Thomas Maher felt at home among our French allies:

> Not all the French liked the British but the folk round Gondecourt seemed to like us well enough. It never seemed that foreign to me, a bit like Durham, woods, fields with a colliery here and there, I felt quite at home. There was dances in the town hall, I'd go to Mass on Sunday and drink in the cafes of an evening. I was friendly with a lass there, her parents had a farm just outside of Gondecourt, she was a bonny lass. We'd work together in the fields, heaving stuff we'd gathered onto a big cart. Well we were both young and hot blooded and at the end of the day we usually both ended up on the back of it ourselves, Ala carte you might say.[14]

Food was not the only thing on the minds of healthy young men abroad for the first time, the novelty of legal brothels was something not to be missed for some and no doubt the owners of such establishments rubbed their hands together at the approach of the British Army and the promise of a boom in trade. Sergeant James McGarey, MM, was billeted with a French glazier at St Remy:

> We got to St Remy du Plain and it was only a small village, why there was no brothels there, the nearest one was at Mameuse. Why man if you'd seen the snow, it was a hard winter but they still managed to get there. Talk about dogs serving bitches in all weathers, and they had to walk em after as well. Me and Ikey Mcdermott bunked with this little old Frenchman called Maurice, he was a glazier. He had a limp from being wounded in the first war, he used to ply us with free rum so we would smash windows on a Friday night, he'd go limping along on Saturday morning and put them all back in. By God he hated the Germans and we were telling him how we were going to wipe the floor with them, yer bugger we were back with him within a month.[15]

---

13 Ibid. Alfred Chittock. Hull 1993.
14 G. Purdon, *From Coalfield to Battlefield* (Durham: County Durham Springboard Media Project, 1995), p. 47.
15 Ibid, p. 31.

On 19 February divisional headquarters was established at Que-Vau-Villiers, 15 miles south west of Amiens. During the following week the weather improved and the whole division was able to assemble and begin intensive training. At the end of February the division was ordered to move to the area around Loos, two miles west of Lille, and become part of GHQ Reserve. Here the men would begin work on strengthening the 11 Corps Reserve Line. Training now began in Ernest and the troops spent many hours on the firing ranges making up for time lost during the hard winter. Billets were generally much better here and as the weather improved so did the morale of the men.

Colour Sergeant Wilfred Gilson recalls his time at the little village of Annoelin with fond memories:

> We were posted to a little place called Annoelin and for the first time we got decent billets, they were really nice. We got to know the local people really well and enjoyed our time there. That was our happiest time in France and I believe they still think a lot about us today, the older people that is.[16]

Annoelin is a small town in what was the industrial South-West *of Lille*, when the Tommies arrived crowds filled the streets to welcome them and bonds of friendship were formed between civilians and soldiers that would last all their lives. Many of the population were very poor and would earn extra money by doing chores for the troops. The men of the 50th Division appreciated the lot of these poor people and showed towards them a kindness and generosity that was to endear them to the local population.

Corporal Sid Atkinson, 4th Battalion East Yorkshire Regiment, was billed with a miner's family:

Pte Sid Atkinson, 4th Battalion East Yorkshire Regiment.

> A miners wife used to do all our washing, she looked much older than she was because of the hard life she'd led, her husband was really poor, the wages there was terrible and he suffered with this disease from the mines. At the cinema across the road from us, under the stage, they stored all these army socks, we decided to help the poor chap out and nicked a few pairs of socks for him. His reaction fair took me aback, he couldn't do enough for us and gave us wine saying 'drink, drink' and his poor wife broke down and cried. I wasn't well off but these people had nowt.[17]

The part of the line in which the division was to construct massive defensive positions ran from Loos south east for eight miles through Seclin and Wavrin. 150 Brigade was working in the northern half of this sector and 151

16   Taped interview with author. Wilfred Gilson (Hull, 1994).
17   Ibid, with Sid Atkinson (Hull, 1988).

Brigade on the southern half. This work consisted mainly of the excavation by hand of a wide and deep anti-tank ditch and of the construction of concrete pill-boxes at intervals along the line.

Corporal Sid Atkinson took part in this back breaking work and was not overly impressed with some of the nit picking by certain officers:

> They made us dig these big anti-tank traps about 20 feet deep with one side sloping, we had to scrape the sides smooth, you'd have thought Gerry was coming over to inspect our workmanship not to kill us. When our officer came round to inspect our efforts he would put his stick on the side and if he thought it not smooth enough we had to carry on scraping and smoothing the sides, talk about making work. I wouldn't mind but the Germans never even came that way.[18]

Discipline within the ranks of the 50th Division was very good, though this regimen is not lightly accepted by civilians turned soldier. Certain disciplines enclosed within the military framework contribute to the development of a good and efficient soldier, these include punctuality, cleanliness and obedience. Barrack square drill was a regular event for infantrymen and is often said to produce only automatons. Drill however is the embodiment of military discipline, training soldiers to move as one, as part of a unit, taking pride in that unit and by disciplined reaction enabling men to adapt to changing circumstances on the battle field. A poorly disciplined soldier, as we shall see later, soon becomes a casualty. One incident of indiscipline stands out clearly in the mind of Lance Corporal William Ridley, 9th Battalion DLI, and it was to lead to the implementation of Field Punishment No1. This form of punishment was used during the Great War and involved chaining a man to a wagon wheel crucifix style, in full view of his comrades for four hours at a time:

> It's been said there was no Field Punishment No1 during the Second World War, well I know of two lads who got it, one of them I knew well. His name was Charlie Watson from the Pioneer Platoon, in camp he had a do with one of the bugle boys, one thing led to another and Charlie nutted him. The rest of the bugle lads had been out drinking and returned to find their mate covered in blood. So away they went to where Charlie was billeted and shouted for him to come outside, as soon as Charlie stuck his head out the window somebody clouted him straight away like. Charlie was as mad as hell, got his rifle, put one up the spout and went out threatening to shoot them. He was arrested and got 28 days field punishment. He had to double everywhere he went from the time he got up until late at night and each day for a certain number of hours he was strung up on tiptoe, crosswise like a crucifix you know, with chains.[19]

While the 50th Division continued the work of building a defensive line in front of Lille, plans were being made by the allied high command to contend with a German attack through the Low Countries. The first of these was known as the Albert Canal Plan and this envisaged

---

18 Ibid, with Sid Atkinson (Hull, 1988).
19 Ibid, with William Ridley at the Veteran's re-union (Hull, 1993).

the movement of French forces along the Albert Canal and its fortifications to a destination as far east as possible. The second was the Escaut Plan, this involved moving forward to the river Escaut and so covering Audenarde, Grand and Anvers. The Dyle Plan was a compromise between the two and this would establish a defensive front along the River Dyle to protect Brussels.

The Belgians favoured the Albert Canal plan because it protected nearly all of their country. But the French General Staff rejected it as they considered it to be far too risky. The Escaut Plan was rejected because it pre-supposed the surrender of Brussels and made no provision for a link up with the Dutch defence forces and Holland. General Gamelin favoured the compromise plan, others criticised this choice but their warnings went unheeded and the rest of the allied command endorsed the Dyle Plan and made what preparations they could. While Belgium and Holland maintained their neutral stance all such plans could be no more than theories with no hope of being put into practise, without being invited by the Belgian Government no allied force could enter Belgian territory. This was not the only handicap the allies had to contend with during this period of inactivity aptly called the Phoney War by the American press. Another far more serious problem was the cumbersome and unwieldy system of command and control, under which every one of the three army groups positioned along the Western Front had its own separate headquarters.

Men of the Royal Northumberland Fusiliers mobile reconnaissance unit, France, May 1940.

Hitler's code name for his planned attack on the west was *Fall Gelb* [Case Yellow], many aspects of this resembled the opening moves of the old Schlieffen Plan of 1914 and was rejected as being too conventional, other plans were put forward but were not received well. Finally a much more daring plan was devised in which the main body of attack would pass through the Ardenne. This was the region through which the French confidently predicted no major attack could ever be launched successfully. The whole of the allied defensive strategy was based upon this assumption, so what better place could there be to launch a heavily armoured group in a surprise attack? The flimsy opposition encountered would be quickly dealt with enabling the

British troops move into Belgium, May 1940.

Panzer forces to cross the Meuse and make a thrust to the Channel coast, cutting off the allied forces drawn into Belgium to meet the predicted conventional attack.

The German High Command was by no means receptive to this new audacious plan but fate now took a hand in the affair. Two Luftwaffe officers were flying near the Belgian frontier when they had to make a forced landing due to bad weather, one of them, Major Reinberges, was carrying in his briefcase top secret papers relating to the revised *Fall Gelb* operation. Their plane came down in neutral Belgium and they were promptly placed under arrest, the luckless Major tried to burn his papers but only partly succeeded in the attempt and the details were passed on to the Allied High Command by the Belgian authorities. The plans only reinforced the allied belief that the main attack was to be launched in the north. Germany's interests were served well by this quirk of fate and the anxieties about an apparent serious breach of security were ill founded.

Colonel Schmundt, Hitler's Chief of Staff, paid a visit at this time to Von Runstedt's Army Group HQ. Here he talked with Von Manstein who promptly told him of the new proposals and he was keen to sell them to one of the Fuhrer's inner circle. Upon his return to Berlin Schmundt briefed Hitler and on 17 February 1940 Von Manstein and his corps commanders were invited to present the Army Group 'A' proposals to the Supreme Commander. The next day Hitler gave an outline of the plan to his generals and found them most receptive, agreement was soon reached on all the main points and a fresh mood of confidence replaced earlier doubts. The future path of events in the west would no longer be left to chance, the final plan had at last been decided and the die was now cast.

# 4

## The Nightmare begins, 10 May 1940

On 10 May 1940 at 6:30 a.m. the code-word 'Birch' was received at 50th Divisional Head Quarters informing them of the German invasion of Belgium and Holland. The 4th Battalion Northumberland Fusiliers moved forward to control the advance of the British Expeditionary Force and the 50th Division remained in reserve. From the British Head Quarters at Arras the following message was issued:

> Plan DJ today. Zero hour 1300 hrs. May cross before zero. Wireless silence cancelled after crossing frontier. Command post opens 1300 hrs. Air recess may commence forthwith.[1]

The generals of the allied armies predicted that the main German thrust would come exactly where they had expected it, when Hitler and his generals heard the allied forces were moving into Belgium they were overjoyed that their trap had been sprung and the enemy had been hoodwinked into thinking that the Germans were sticking to the old Schlieffen Plan.

By 1:00 a.m. British armoured car patrols were crossing the frontier into western Belgium reaching the River Dyle that evening. No serious attempts were made by the Luftwaffe to hinder the allied advance and at first the allied staff was not surprised by this as it was thought that the Luftwaffe could not be everywhere at once. In fact German air operations had been planned to enable the allies to advance into Belgium without opposition. This emptied the rear areas through which the German armour could advance when the main attack came through the Ardenne and crossed the Meuse at Sedan. The Belgian Air Force suffered most on the 10 May and half their aircraft were destroyed on the ground by German air attacks

It was believed by the French High Command that the Belgian defence of their frontier would hold up the German advance and prevent them reaching the River Dyle until the allies had completed their move to the planned front line. But thanks to the capture of the bridges over the Albert Canal and the fortress at Eben Emael by the Germans this did not happen and with great speed the Germans established themselves on the western bank of the canal and attacked the Belgian 7th Infantry Division stationed along that sector, in a short time the German forces had reached Tongres. This rapid German advance made the position of the

---

1   E. Clay, *The Path of the 50th* (Aldershot: Gale and Polden, 1950), p. 14.

A German armoured column advances through a French town, May 1940.

Belgian troops still on the canal, and those at Leige, untenable. Combined with the news of the Dutch withdrawals further north this left the Belgian High Command with no alternative but to order a withdrawal to the Dyle Line on the 11 May. The failure to blow the bridges over the Albert Canal had undoubtedly been decisive.

The German breakthrough in Belgium was not the decisive action in the invasion of the west, but its effect on the final issue was paramount. Not only did it draw the allies attention in the wrong direction but in the battle that developed there pulled in the most mobile section of the allied forces, making it impossible for these divisions to be pulled out to meet the greater menace in the south that, on 13 May, suddenly loomed up on the French frontier at its most vulnerable point beyond the western end of the incomplete Maginot Line.

Rundsted's army group spearhead drove through Luxembourg and Belgium towards France after traversing the supposedly impassable Ardenne and pushing aside the weak opposition in the area, they arrived at the banks of the Meuse on 13 May. The first Panzer Division to cross the Meuse on 14 May was Erwin Rommel's 7th Ghost Division, his eight wheeled command vehicle on the first pontoon.

With every step the allied armies took into Belgium their rear became more exposed to Rundsted's flanking drive through the Ardenne and to make matters worse the hinge of the whole allied advance was guarded by low grade French troops that were poorly equipped to deal with an armoured attack. This was the crowning blunder of the French High Command who had based their plans on the assumption that an attack on the Meuse would not materialise until the ninth day, trained in the slow motion methods of 1918 the French commanders could not cope with the helter-skelter pace of the fast moving Panzers and there developed among them a creeping paralysis.

The deciding factor at every turn was speed, French counter strokes were too slow to keep up with the changing situations and that was due in the main to the fact that the German armour moved even faster than the German High Command expected. Late in the day on 16 May the drive westward had penetrated as far as Oise, an advance of 50 miles, the German commanders could not believe their luck and still expected a French counter attack against their vulnerable flank. Hitler was also apprehensive and halted the advance for two days so that the Infantry corps could catch up and form a flanking shield along the Aisne. The shock of the mechanised Blitzkrieg had paralysed the French Army to such an extent that it was incapable of profiting from the opportunity which Hitler's intervention had provided.

Kleist, Panzer Commander, said of the advance:

> Our advance met no serious opposition after the breakthrough, Reinhardt's Panzer Corps had some fighting near Le Cateau but that was the only noteworthy incident.[2]

Lord Gort, VC, Commander in Chief of the BEF began to realise that the lack of German air attacks on the allied advance was not just a matter of good fortune and that what was being described as a bulge was in fact a German spearhead driving for the coast in order to break the allied lines of communications and supplies. The 50th Division was at this time still being held in reserve when on the 16 May things began to move.

Sergeant George Denis Elliot, 6th Battalion DLI, was working in the Head Quarters Company:

> The GSO, Royal Artillery, called me up on the set and asked me to get the general as something important was happening. At the time I could hear aircraft roaring overhead and heading in the direction of Gerry. The General came to the phone and the next day we were on the move into Belgium.[3]

The 50th was to advance to the Dendre and take up a defensive position, on the same day Lord Gort received orders to withdraw from the Dyle Line. The divisional area became a hive of activity as transport was organised and the men prepared themselves for battle.

Colour Sergeant Wilfred Gilson, 4th Battalion East Yorkshire Regiment, noticed increasing activity in his sector:

> It was one afternoon about tea time and there was a lot of activity at company headquarters, a number of cars and trucks passed through us at full speed as they rushed forward. We all knew something was up, we were all feeling a bit windy and knew the war was about to start. My father had told me about the actions he was in during the last lot, not a pleasant thought, the next day we moved a long way into Belgium.[4]

The new positions for the 50th Division extended from Ath on the right to Ninove on the left, the tail end of the division coming into position on the morning of the 17 May. Troops that

---

2     J. Duncan and G. Forty, *The Fall of France* (Kent: Guild Publishing, 1990), p. 38.
3     Taped interview with author, George Denis Elliot at the Veteran's re-union (Durham, 1994).
4     Ibid, with Wilfred Gilson (Hull, 1989).

had been in action began falling back passing through the 50th's positions, the looks on their haggard faces left a deep impression on these as yet untried young soldiers.

Lance Corporal William Ridley, 9th DLI, looked on as these badly shaken troops fell back:

> You could tell the lads falling back had been well hammered, they moved through us like robots without a word and their faces had a terrible grey look, all the colour had left them.[5]

Sergeant Bob Gibson, MM, 151 Provost Company:

> We saw the French falling back, it was a sight I'll never forget, they looked downtrodden and beaten. They had what looked like tar boilers road workers use only these were full of soup and on carts pulled by horses. They didn't look like they wanted war as they hadn't got over the first lot the poor devils.[6]

The plight of the poor animals in the fields that were caught in the battle zone was pitiful to see, Pte Roy Walker, 5th Battalion East Yorkshire Regiment, saw concerned men trying to help them but to no avail:

> During our retreat we took over this deserted farm building, the poor livestock had been left to fend for themselves and the cows was bursting with milk, some of our lads tried to milk them but it was impossible as shells were flying all over the place. It would have been better to shoot them. We had a lad with us called Johnny Dolan who would never see horses or cattle suffering and he'd go and shoot them to put them out of their misery.[7]

Corporal Sidney Atkinson found himself on guard in a factory that night:

> Our officer sent me into a big factory saying 'you go in there Sid, take some men with you and stand guard tonight'. I put two men on guard duty, went inside and sat down on what I thought was an ordinary big long box, it was pitch black and I couldn't see a thing. Morning came and as dawn broke we saw what the long boxes were, the place was full of empty coffins.[8]

The divisional troops dug in quickly and occupied any nearby buildings that were available, the rumble of heavy gunfire could be heard from the east and explosions rent the air as enemy aircraft bombed the surrounding area. Divisional engineers had prepared the bridges on the Dendre for demolition and on the night of 17 May the British troops got orders to withdraw to new positions on the Escaut Canal. As the last troops fell back over the bridges the waiting engineers blew them up, although not without incident for some.

Sergeant Max Hearst, 5th Battalion East Yorkshire Regiment, was on one bridge as they blew it:

---

5   Ibid, with William Ridley at the Veteran's re-union (Hull, 1993).
6   Ibid, with Bob Gibson (Hull, 1994).
7   Ibid, with Roy Walker (Scarborough, 1989).
8   Ibid, with Sid Atkinson (Hull, 1992).

Our Lt Quartermaster Billy Gail, said 'hang on a minute Butch let's have a smoke', so we stopped for a drag and watched the lads dodging and running across the bridge, we finished our smoke and followed. 11 of us were on that bridge when it was blown, we all disappeared in a cloud of smoke and flying debris and ended up in the water. My mother received a telegram telling her I was missing in action believed killed.[9]

The cut off armies in the north fell back to the Escaut Line and the 50th Division began their withdrawal at dawn on 18 May and because their transport was needed elsewhere had to march the whole way to their new positions. Here their right flank was at Pecq and extended northwards for five miles. The Allies found themselves under increasing frontal pressure from Bock's infantry but were spared the deadly stab in the back from the Panzer forces.

Sergeant Max Hearst, 5th Battalion East Yorkshire Regiment.

Pte Roy Walker, 5th Battalion East Yorkshire Regiment, was stationed on one bridge when the Germans turned up downstream:

We was billeted in a school when they asked for volunteers, the volunteers was 'you, you and you go on these bridges over a canal'. There was four of us to each bridge and they said they would pick us up next morning, we was stuck there for three days. We could hear the battle getting closer and closer and it was getting a bit too hot for us so our corporal says 'I'll walk down to the next bridge', so I went with him. We didn't get to the next bridge because as we approached it we saw Germans going across it in vehicles, we went back and informed the RE's the bridge upstream had been captured so blow this one. Before they blew it I saw them drive ten new petrol or water tankers into the canal, they just sank below the surface. They blew the bridges and we began our long march to Dunkirk.[10]

Captain Bob Stafford, 4th Battalion East Yorkshire Regiment, saw tired men falling out at the roadside as they marched long distances overland:

We moved forward into Belgium and dug in quickly because the Germans were shelling us from a short distance away. At 03:00.a.m. the next day we moved back the way we had come, marching 37 miles the first day and 17 on the second day. These forced marches were the reason so many of our chaps were taken prisoner as they were so dog tired they fell asleep in the estaminets and at the roadside and they got left behind. We managed to get a nights sleep in Lille, after that it was a none stop slog to the coast under fire all the time.[11]

9   Ibid, with Max Hearst (Hull 1990).
10  Ibid, with Roy Walker (Scarborough, 1989).
11  Ibid, with Bob Stafford (Hull, 1993).

A German half-track tows an 88 mm anti-aircraft gun through a French town, May 1940.

The pace and violence of the blitzkrieg had thrown the civilian population into a state of panic stricken terror, they left their homes, taking to the roads in their hundreds. The allied armies found themselves with one more problem to cope with, roads blocked by thousands of fleeing civilians. The Luftwaffe used this situation to its own advantage, as troops and civilians streamed along the French country lanes the German pilots showed no mercy as they bombed and machine gunned lines of soldiers and civilians alike.

Pte John Thompson trudged along with the 5th Battalion Green Howards and looked on in disbelief:

> The scenes on the roads were terrible, utter chaos, the Gerry planes were strafing us none stop, then there was the poor civilians, it was a bad experience to see women and children killed like that, I'd never seen anything like it in my life, Gerry didn't give a sod the rotten bastard. The planes would come screaming down very low, we was smart and out of it.[12]

Pte John Thompson, 5th Battalion Green Howards.

12  Ibid, with John Thompson (Beverley, 1990).

Pte Reg Rymer, 2nd Machine-gun Battalion, Cheshire Regiment, was horrified at the actions of the Luftwaffe pilots:

> The Stukas would do their normal circle around above us and one after the other they dived down almost vertically and I thought they must be blind, they're not going after us. The next thing is they let their bombs go in among the refugees, now these are old people, young people and babies, we saw them blown to pieces and not one bomb anywhere along the army convoy. You tell me, who could be that cruel? We were there and being paid to do a job so you expect it, but that? You could see babies' arms and legs and all kinds of bits of people being blown into the air![13]

Pte Alfred Chittock, 150 Field Ambulance, watched the carnage in disbelief:

> The roads were choc-a-block with wagons, prams, carts and people, the Gerry aircraft was just flying down the line of the road and strafing them, it was a terrible sight to see. When they come over we jumped into the dykes at the road-side, one bloke got into a dyke and thought it was one of our blokes he was cuddling, turned out it was a dead civilian.[14]

Major Peter J Jeffries, 6th Battalion DLI, remembers the march as a nightmare:

> The refugee problem was quite awful and there were the cars of the rich covered in their belongings. But what was tragic and unbelievable was the hundreds and hundreds and hundreds of poor people on their feet. '*Ou est les Bosches?*' they cried. Those poor people, they crammed the roads and in addition to this in those days the streets were cobbled and cobbles are a devil to march on. Cobbles full of refugees, it was an absolute nightmare that march, but somehow ones spirits more than being sorry for oneself or ones chap, the whole well of your feelings were full of pity for these poor beggars, women, children, old men, young men, all trudging this way, then trudging that way. You could come to a road junction, a lot of people were coming out that way, a lot of people were going down that way and all they would say was '*Ou est les Bosche?*'[15]

Major Peter J Jeffries, DSO, OBE, 6th Battalion Durham Light Infantry.

Some troops soon learnt it was safer when possible to leave the roads and cut corners, but the Stuka dive bombers, with their wailing sirens fitted to their wings, continued to swoop down on the defenceless refugees.

13  Ibid, with Reg Rymer (Cheshire, 1989).
14  Ibid, with Alfred Chittock (Hull, 1993).
15  Manuscript sent to author by William Ridley (Durham, 1997).

Sergeant Max Hearst was affected deeply by the sights he saw that day:

> It was a pitiful sight to see the women and children screaming and running about as Gerry aircraft roared down on them, they had nowhere to go. I saw one little girl fall over an old fella as she was running and she broke her leg, she lay there howling and nobody seemed to care, it was an army chap who strapped her leg up but he still had to leave her. I had never seen such things before and hoped I would never see them again, it played on my mind for years after the war. Those poor people didn't deserve this. I recall a unit of the Guards coming back, one of the lads shouted out to them 'what's it like mate' and one of them shouted back 'you'll soon find out' and we did, it was pretty grim.[16]

The last elements of the 50th arrived at the Escaut Canal on the night of the 18 May and on the evening of the 19 May Divisional Headquarters were informed that their services were now required at Arras which was being held by a Guards battalion and assorted units. Masses of refugees thronged the roads as the soldiers of the 50th pressed on, Stukas roared overhead bombing and strafing and the terrible sights seen that day left a deep impression on the young men of the BEF.

French civilians flee before the violence of the Blitzkrieg, looking for a place of safety in a world gone mad.

16  Taped interview with author, Max Hearst (Hull, 1990).

General Martel went to Arras on 20 May to ascertain the present situation and the leading troops of the 50th Division arrived at Vimy at noon the same day. The sector to the east of *Arras*, along the River Scarpe, was being held by the French 1st Light Mechanised Division who possessed some 70 Somoa tanks, however the infantry units that accompanied them were weak and exhausted. One battalion of 150 Brigade, one anti-tank battery and one field company of Royal Engineers were dispatched to help in the defence of Arras, while the remainder of 150 Brigade relieved the hard pressed French on the Scarpe. 151 Brigade and various divisional units arrived at Vimy after a very tiring journey by foot having had very little rest for days.

Pte Maher was with the Durhams and remembers well the feeling of apprehension that he and many of his mates felt:

> Lt Regnart came round the platoon and told us we should meet the enemy within the hour, that was to be our first experience of action and as you can imagine it fair shook us up. We'd had boiled eggs and bully beef for breakfast and one of the lads says 'well there's no danger of us shitting ourselves then' which got a bit of a laugh and released some tension. I suppose morale was high enough, although I would say we were all in a bit of a bad way with all the foot slogging. The weather was boiling hot and we were tired out, hadn't had much sleep at all. My feet were that bad blood was coming through the lace holes of me boots, and I wasn't the only one. As our time for action approached we all had that bit of worry at the backs of our minds.[17]

Pte Bob Fort was in reserve with the 9th Battalion DLI on Vimy Ridge and had a grandstand view of events:

> The Germans had pushed through and we were banged into trucks in real British Army style and rushed to where nowt was happening, we were all left sitting on this hill-side just outside of *Arras*. We just lay there and could see the hordes of refugees streaming down the roads, some one way, some another, everything was a mess. Some dive-bombers flew right over us and dropped their bombs, bang-bang, but not on us, we were just lying there getting our grub and watching what was happening while we could as we knew it would soon be our turn.[18]

Lance Corporal Joss Little was marching with the 8th Battalion DLI when they came under attack:

> We was on the march a couple of days and the way we was going Gerry was coming, we marched till we came to Vimy Ridge and we were fell out. This officer comes round and says 'you know what to do lads' I says 'aye sir', he says 'what's that corporal?'. I says 'shoot first and ask questions later', he laughed and said 'that's right'. Anyhow we moved up this road, a section on each side, we'd just passed the big Canadian monument on Vimy Ridge, it'll be still there yet. This village we came to was all boarded up because of the war but there was

---

17  G Purdon, *From Coalfield to Battlefield* (Durham: County Durham Springboard Media Project, 1995), p. 56.
18  Ibid, p. 58.

still a souvenir shop open selling postcards, pens and that. The Canadians had lost a hell of a lot of lads there in the first war and all their names is round that monument. We were just passed it when this aircraft came fleeing over, one of the lads says 'it's alright she's British', that was when it opened up on us. I says 'oh aye? she's a Gerry!' There was a ditch on both sides of the road and I says 'right lads jump for it', one says 'I'm not jumping in there', I says 'please thee bloody self if you wants to get mown down but here's one that doesn't'. The ditch was five or six feet deep, full of carts and it stank, but I couldn't have cared less if it was full of shit you know. At the finish we had to drag this lad into the ditch and hold him down, I says 'listen lad you do what I tell you and you'll not go far wrong, but do as you're told'. I always remember Captain Walton saying the same to me back at the drill hall 'now look you're here to do what your told, do the job and complain later', so I told the lad the same 'when I says get in the ditch I mean get in the ditch not stand there like a scarecrow'. The plane went down the road machine gunning and I said 'that bugger'll be back you know', it turned and came back up the line of the road, but there was this French tank with a Hochkiss machine gun mounted on it hid among the trees waiting. It let fly and the plane was machine gunned by us as well, we heard this roar and I says 'he's had it'. The French tank got it, he had the fire power we hadn't and he put paid to the plane. So anyway we got out of the ditch, reformed and moved up to where the plane had crashed, it was a Gerry

German Stuka dive-bombers in action, May 1940.

alright. We went over and had a look, we got the pilot out but he was dead like, I took off his helmet and he was just a young lad, he looked about 18 years old. There was some photo's in his wallet, must have been his mother, father and sister and another one written on from a young lass. The lads name was Hans and I said 'away Hans you've had it now.[19]

Lt Colonel Harry Miller, Commanding Officer 6th Battalion DLI, had served in this area with the same unit during the Great War and found himself in familiar surroundings a few miles south of Lille at the Butte de Wallencourt. Captain Vernon Ferens was with Colonel Miller and remembers the journey well:

We did a reconnaissance and so we went in Colonel Miller's Humber car with Mike Lockhart, the Transport Officer, QM, the CO and his driver. We went down from *Vimy* Ridge, down into the valley and went up towards the Butte de Wallencourt and quite near it was a war graves cemetery and sure enough we found the graves of four platoon commanders and platoon sergeants. These were the graves of Colonel Miller's former platoon officers and platoon sergeants who had been killed in 1916. I thought to myself 'here's a man with a lifetime of fighting the same enemy on the same ground.[20]

The young men of the Durham Light Infantry got what rest they could as the time for battle drew ever nearer. Last minute cards and letters had been sent home and most men were far too tired to do anything but sleep. The enormous white Canadian monument on *Vimy* Ridge from the Great War towered above them and gave a solemn reminder of what was to come.

Pte Thomas Maher was marching at quite a pace with the 8th Battalion DLI and his feet were in a sorry state:

I remember this train stopping and it was full of American civilians, they were getting out while they could, one said I looked rather young to be a soldier. We'd done a bit of mock action in a wood and had done a lot of marching, the boots I had on were newish and hurt my feet. When we stopped I took my boots off, the blood was drying and making my socks stick to me. Lt Regnart says 'let's have a look at your heel', it was like a raw tomato. I put some powder on it but when I got my boot back on it was agony, when you start walking it's a bit easier but it was still sore. We were walking behind a 15 hundredweight truck, I was carrying the bren-gun and limping a bit. Big Jossie, Joss Little, says 'give us that bloody bren and get a bike off the back of the truck'. The sergeant saw me on it later and went mad, nearly put me on a charge. The first time we saw action was when we went to Vimy Ridge, before that it was just an adventure, we were all very young and didn't know much. When we got up onto the ridge and saw the great white memorial and all the First World War trenches, it brought it back to us really sharp like the seriousness of it all.[21]

---

19 Ibid, p. 61.
20 H. Moses, *The Faithful Sixth* (Durham: County Durham Books, 1995), p. 58.
21 G. Purdon, *From Coalfield to Battlefield* (Durham: County Durham Springboard Media Project, 1995), p. 58.

The Nightmare begins, 10 May 1940 47

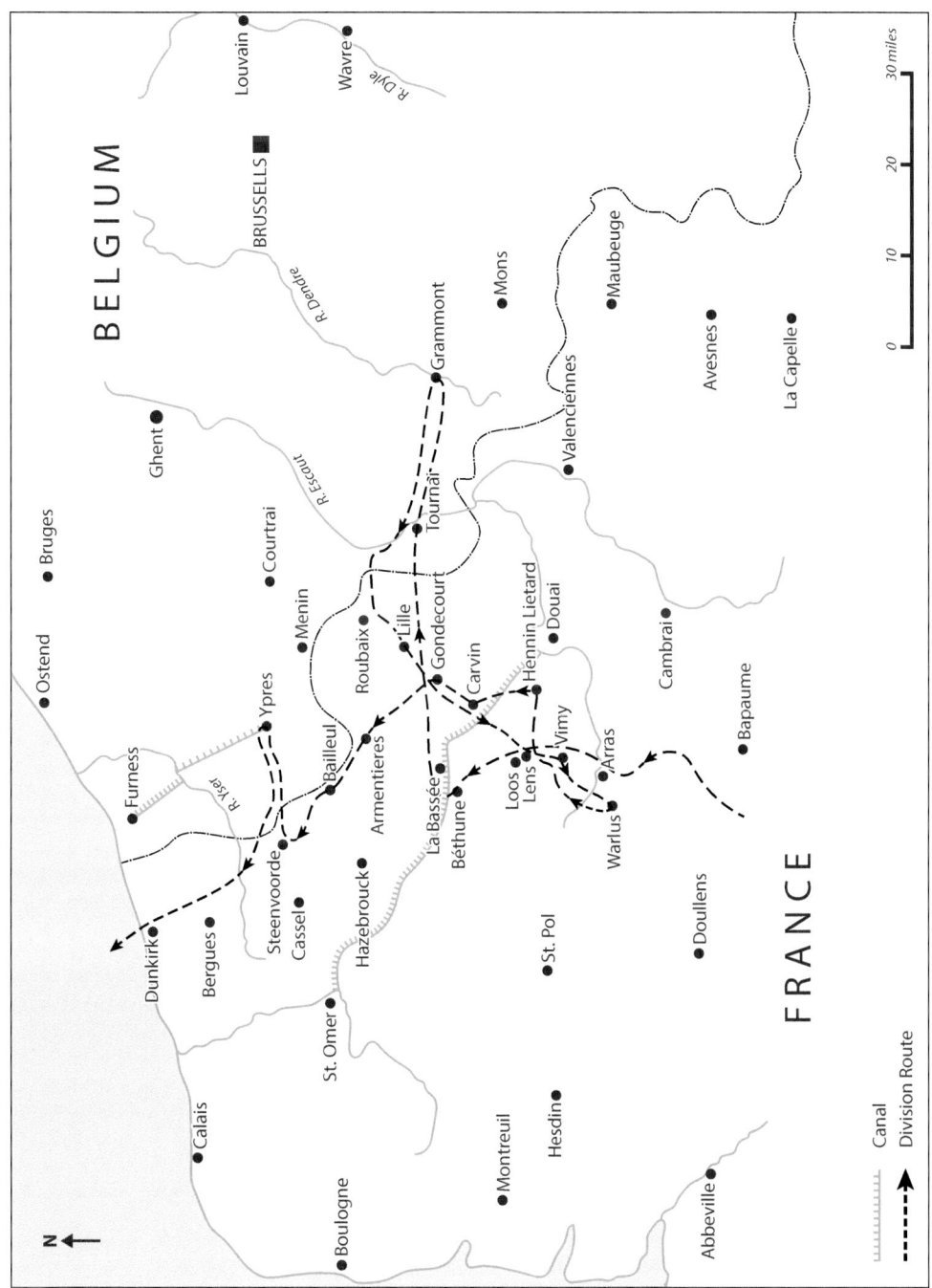

Map 1 The British Expeditionary Force Campaign. May to June 1940.

Not all relics of the Great War were to be found above ground, below the surface lay masses of equipment, ammunition and other grimmer reminders of our own mortality. Sergeant Charles E Davis, 4th Battalion Royal Northumberland Fusiliers, remembers supervising the men digging in on Vimy Ridge as the troops sought safety below ground:

> I sent a couple of men to the highest point on the ridge, they were to let me know if they saw any enemy movement. At the same time we were digging in on the back slope. We only got down about 18 inches when the lads were pulling out relics from the last lot, rifles, bombs, shells and even bones. I was sat on the edge of a trench and held up a skull and said this is obviously German, a lad asked me how I knew. I said just look at the jaw, it was a standing joke with us that all Germans were big jawed.[22]

---

22  Taped interview with author, Charles E. Davis at the Veteran's re-union (Durham, 1992).

5

## The Battle of Arras, 21 to 23 May 1940

---

Lord Gort now organised the kind of counter attack that the German commanders most feared, an attack southward, intended to sever the strung out German advance. The leading elements of Rommel's 7th Panzer [Ghost] Division had reached the outskirts of Arras by the evening of 20 May. The city was defended by Petreforce which consisted of the 1st Welsh Guards and a hastily raised mixed force of base troops, commanded by Major General R L Petre, commander of the 12th Division. The German armoured spearhead took Beaurains and clashed with the Arras defences during the course of the day. The units of the 50th Division that had been allocated reinforced the city's garrison. General Sir Harold Franklin, KCB, DSO, MC, commander of the 5th Division, was ordered by Gort to secure Arras and to launch an attack south of that city to cut the German supply route between the advancing panzers pressing west and north

Rommel's 7th Panzer Division moves across the Somme valley on its way to Arras, May 1940. A Storch spotter plane can be seen flying overhead.

and the motorised infantry and supply columns coming up behind them. For this operation he was given the 50th Division and the 1st Army Brigade of tanks. The troops in Arras and in the villages to the south were putting up a stiff resistance but Rommel was determined to keep up the pressure and made plans for an attack to the south-west of Arras the next day. The German armour paused briefly to refuel and refit.

The two divisions Gort had dispatched to protect the right flank of the BEF, the 50th and 5th, were called Frank Force after their commander Major General Franklyn. The need to reinforce Arras, defend the line of the Scarpe and keep back a reserve meant that Franklyn could muster only Brigadier Churchill's 151 Brigade: 6th, 8th and 9th Battalions of the DLI, for the attack, the men of the Durham Brigade had gone into Belgium in trucks but had returned on foot and were very tired, most of them had never seen a tank before let alone work with one. Franklyn was also allocated Brigadier Douglas Pratt's 1st Army Tank Brigade which was made up of the 4th and 7th Battalions of the Royal Tank Regiment. The Tank Brigade had 72 Matildas, 16 Mk11 and 56 Mk1 tanks, as well as a dozen light tanks. These tanks had driven 120 miles on their tracks in only five days and more than a quarter of their number had been accounted for by breakdowns.

Added support for the assault would be given by 365th Battery, Royal Artillery, with its 18 pounders and 368th Battery, Royal Artillery, with its newer 25 pounders plus the 206th and 260th Batteries of the 52nd Anti-tank Regiment. Reconnaissance was to be provided by the 50th Division's Motor-cycle Battalion the 4th Battalion Royal Northumberland Fusiliers.

The attack would be launched in two phases, the first was to clear the area to the river Cozeol five miles south-east of Arras. Phase two would clear the area as far as the river Sensee a few miles further on. The aim of this attack was to capture the high ground between these rivers, thereby holding up the German advance and giving the BEF a badly needed breathing space. The force intended to achieve this was split up into two columns, the left hand column was made up of the 6th Battalion DLI and the 4th Battalion Royal Tank Regiment. The right hand column was made up of the 8th Battalion DLI and the 7th Battalion Royal Tank Regiment, plus supporting units.

Lt Thomas Craig, MC, was with the 7th Battalion Royal Tank Regiment:

> I arrived at Petit Vimy in my Matilda exhausted and disorganised. I was given a map by my company commander and told to start up and follow him. The wireless was not working and there was no tie-up with the infantry and no clear orders. That was our state as we crossed the start line for our first action.[1]

Franklyn had originally wanted the attack to go in at 5:00 a.m. on 21 May, but as the last tank did not arrive at Vimy until this time it was clearly impossible. Pratt, commanding 1st Army Tank Brigade, and Martel, commanding 50th Division, both agreed an attack was not possible before 3:00 p.m. Franklyn insisted on an earlier start and so 2:00 p.m. was agreed upon. The infantry however did not arrive on time and so the tanks had to be released on their own. The other men of the 50th Division manned the areas on and around Vimy Ridge.

---

1   Taped interview with author, Thomas Craig (Hull, 1988).

Sergeant George Denis Elliot, 9th Battalion DLI, looked on as the Durham's moved to their assembly positions near Neuvile St Vaast and watched events unfold:

> We were in reserve at Vimy village down by the war cemetery when we saw two battalions of Durhams going into action. Gerry was giving us hell with his Stukas, they came screaming down on us with a fearful howl, this being followed by a tearing explosion, we got this all sodding day.[2]

As the tanks advanced the first to come into action were the Matilda Mk 1s of 4th Battalion Royal Tank Regiment. They rumbled through the area between Dainville and Arras and came across enemy motorised infantry packed tightly into soft skinned vehicles. The tanks heavy machine guns slaughtered them as the helpless German soldiers tried to escape the carnage.

Sergeant George Denis Elliot, 9th Battalion Durham Light Infantry.

Captain D Hunt, 4th Battalion Royal Tank Regiment:

> Shortly after crossing the Doullens-Arras line we came across a column of German vehicles and half-tracks towing anti-tank guns, I enjoyed watching my corporal's infantry tank drive down the side of the column firing at each in turn. Most of the vehicles were put out of action and lots were left burning.[3]

Lt Peter Vaux, 4th Battalion Royal Tank Regiment, was in the thick of the action as his unit pressed home the attack:

> We didn't linger and soon we set off across the start-line and met trouble almost from the start because the railway cutting was a great deal steeper than we had anticipated. Two of the lead tanks went down the bank of the cutting and then they couldn't get up the other side and they couldn't get back the way they had come from and so they were stuck on the railway line. The level crossing gates were shut and there was a bell ringing, just as though a train was coming. I remember it took a good deal of effort of will before someone was able to push on and drive clean through the gates and then the whole regiment was over and went one after the other up the hill the other side of the railway where we spread out.
>
> We had come straight into the flank of a German mechanised column which was moving across our front. They were just as surprised as us as we were right in amongst them and for the first quarter of an hour or so there was a glorious free for all. We knocked out quite a lot of their lorries and Germans were running all over the place. I do not know how many Germans we killed or how many German vehicles we set on fire. At that moment I didn't

2   Ibid, with George Dennis Elliot at the Veteran's re-union (Durham, 1994).
3   Ibid, with D. Hunt at the Veteran's re-union. (Hull, 1991).

see why we shouldn't go all the way to Berlin. But even in those early stages there were some scary moments, during our encounter with this column an enemy soldier jumped up on my tank, I was looking out of the periscope and saw him looking in, I suppose he saw me looking out. Then a neighbouring tank very kindly turned his machine-gun on me and that removed my passenger. I remember a motor-cyclist at the side of the road and when he saw the tanks his hair stood on end and he tried to start up his motor-cycle which wouldn't start. There was this fellow with the veins standing out on his neck and his eyes popping out, kicking away at this thing to get it started and the gunners were laughing so much they were unable to take aim and shoot. Eventually he threw the motorcycle into the ditch and ran for cover.[4]

Major John King, commanding B Squadron, 7th Battalion Royal Tank Regiment, came up against some of the lighter German anti-tank units with the second column:

The Matilda Mk 1s had deployed and I followed up at the rear of two parties, suddenly we came under the fire of three or four anti-tank guns about 300 yards to our front. They did not penetrate us so we went straight at them and put them out of action. My tank ran over one and I saw another suffer the same fate, small parties of enemy machine-gunners and infantry kept getting up in front of us and retreated rapidly giving us good machine-gun targets for about ten minutes. There must have been about a 150 altogether.[5]

The infantry of the 6th DLI were not far behind the tanks and Major Peter J Jeffries remembers coming across a scene of carnage:

As we pushed on the shells came down harder and harder, when we got past *Dainville* we saw the tanks in action for the first time. There didn't seem to be many of them about but they were firing and some of them were on fire having been hit. There were dead Germans laid about and a lot of smashed up German vehicles, the route we had come by had these villages on it and open corn fields in between. The tanks had obviously played hell with the German infantry which they had met, part of the 7th *Panzer* Division was moving across our front upon which we attacked and their tanks had gone on past our right as if to go round the flank and what the 4th RTR had run into was the soft skinned infantry vehicles following the German tanks and of course had bashed into them in tremendous form. We found a lot of German dead and took a lot of prisoners. They came forward surrendering and very correct they were, I remember a German officer came up to me and said in broken English; 'are you the senior officer round here? I would like personally to surrender to you' I said 'you can do what you like, throw all your stuff down there and give me your map' and I handed them over to a Lance Corporal to take back and off we went.[6]

Lt Colonel Harry Miller was urging on the tired troops of the 6th DLI as they marched to the sound of the tank battle raging in front of them. He was one of a few officers who had

---

4   Manuscript sent to author from Max Hearst (Hull, 1989).
5   J. Duncan and G. Forty, *The Fall of France* (Kent: Guild Publishing, 1990), p. 61.
6   H. Moses, *The Faithful Sixth* (Durham: County Durham Books 1995), p. 132.

worked with tanks in the Great War and knew the importance of infantry supporting tanks in following up their success. He also knew this area of France having served here in the 6th DLI in April 1917. At this time he was 47 years old but on this day he was to show powers of leadership and endurance which would have done credit to a man half his age. For three days he had practically no sleep and now his weariness was being aggravated by the normal stress of battle and a latent confusion which was taking a mounting toll of the British plan.

Lt Colonel Harry Miller, 6th DLI, recalled:

> The leading company arrived at the forming up point but were 45 minutes behind the time laid down in the brigade commanders orders. At this stage I was very perturbed because I could see by the appearance of the men that they were very tired and footsore. Their spirit was however excellent. Continuing the advance we made good progress in spite of heavy and accurate shelling on the crest of Wagnonlieu, but the effect of this enemy fire on the troops seemed to hearten them. By this time the tanks in front of us were really getting busy and although we could not see much of their activities we could hear their two pounders and machine-guns rattling away.[7]

Lt Colonel Harry Miller, 6th Battalion Durham Light Infantry.

As the tanks of the left hand column pressed on they came across a battery of enemy field artillery and were heavily shelled, the German gunners fired over open sights at the advancing British armour but found they could not penetrate the Matilda's thick shell. Some tanks were hit many times and had great chunks of metal torn from their armour but still overran the German batteries.

CSM Jock Armit, 4th Battalion Royal Tank Regiment, was in a tank that took many hits from the German gunners:

> My 50 calibre machine gun was brought into action and I got two of them before they realised I was on them, the range was approximately 200 yards. The other guns started on me now and one hit the gun housing, this caused the recoil slot pin of my gun to snap and shook the gun back in the turret. I forced the gun back and pressed the triggers of my two smoke mortars but they did not fire. I found out later that they had been shot straight off. During this time, which was only the space of a minute, they hit my tank about ten times but none of the hits did any real damage. I quickly made up my mind that the best way out was to back over the crest until I could get my gun cleared, so I gave my driver the order and we slowly zig-zagged back a distance of about a 100 yards. I got my gun going again and, thirsting for revenge, returned to the attack. They must have thought I was finished for I caught the guns limbered up ready to move to another position and revenge was sweet.[8]

---

7   Teeside Gazette cutting sent to author by Thomas W Jackson (Durham, 1997).
8   R. Kershaw, *Tank Men* (London: Hodder and Stoughton, 2008), p. 180.

Things were not going well with the right hand column, the reconnaissance forces became separated as the scout cars raced ahead and the motor cycles of the 4th Royal Northumberland Fusiliers were not ready on time and were left behind. The tanks soon found they were well ahead of the infantry and elements of the enemy forces were encountered before they reached the start line, to make matters worse the leading tanks turned south east instead of south west and became entangled with the rear of the left hand column. The infantry moved forward well behind the tanks, close to Duisans, crossing the main road they came across a badly shot up battery of the 7th Panzer Division. The surviving Germans had taken shelter in and around Duisans and this area was to be cleared by the 8th DLI aided by French tanks.

Lt Ian R English, MC and bar, 8th Battalion DLI, described the effects of an attack by dive-bombers on his men:

> We came under very heavy fire from German positions on the Arras-Doullens Road itself, especially mortar fire. And then we were attacked by Stukas. Several of our troops were caught in the open just as they were getting into position. This was the first time we'd been directly attacked and the whole thing was very frightening, as they came down in a near vertical dive with a tremendous scream and they appeared to be aiming their bombs right at you. Then they strafed us with machine-guns, this went on virtually unopposed apart from one man firing his bren-gun at them. Then the truck behind him got hit and he went into a ditch. This attack went on for about 20 minutes and there was tremendous smoke, dust and confusion. Everyone was absolutely pinned to the earth. Then the Stukas left, I think we had three trucks damaged and about ten men wounded, the material damage was virtually nothing but the effect on morale was absolutely amazing. Everyone was really shattered. It really took an awful lot of effort by the NCOs and officers to get anyone moving again, they really had to be kicked to get in position. They seemed numbed and absolutely shattered.[9]

Pte Thomas Maher met his first German:

> We took hundreds of prisoners to start with, I remember the first German we came face to face with. He was crouching down behind some bushes with his rifle at the ready and we just walked into him. He could have shot us if he'd a mind to, but he just threw down his rifle and up went his hands. I don't know who was more frightened him or us.[10]

Half a mile west of Duisans, 100 or so Germans had taken refuge in a cemetery to evade the advancing British armour, as the 8th DLI prepared to attack, a group of French tanks moved in and raked the cemetery area with their heavy machine guns, ripping apart men and masonry. Sergeant Alfred Rispin entered the cemetery after the French tanks had done their work:

> When we finally entered the place we found a slaughterhouse, what a fucking mess, we only took about 20 prisoners and we handed them over to the Frogs, they stripped them

---

9   Manuscript sent to author by Ian R English (Durham, 1997).
10  G. Purdon, *From Coalfield to Battlefield* (Durham: County Durham Springboard Media Project, 1995), p. 58.

naked and made them lie face down on the floor. Them Gerries was shitting themselves, the French hated those bastards.[11]

Both DLI battalions pressed forward and air attacks became more frequent as the unopposed Stukas targeted the advancing Tommies, the tired, weary troops found themselves hard pressed and with no information of the whereabouts of the enemy.

Pte Thomas Maher was with the 8th DLI when they met the enemy:

> We marched across open country till we came under strong machine-gun fire from both infantry and tanks. We weren't able to do anything much but keep our heads down, when we finally could see the enemy they was only a few hundred yards away, we opened fire and started to bowl them over.[12]

Pte Steven Barker, 6th Battalion DLI, was taken prisoner:

> I got took prisoner at Wancourt, we didn't know what hit us and the situation seemed chaotic. There were big German tanks all over the place and we got some rough treatment as well I can tell you. It was a forced march off the battle field, some of the lads was wounded and they were falling back but the guards pushed them on with their rifle butts shouting 'raus, raus.[13]

The right hand column advanced as far as Wailly, in the ferocious battle that was now raging the CO and the Adjutant of 7th RTR were both killed, the whole area was jammed with Rommel's guns and vehicles. The British attack had caught Rommel off guard as he was about to push home his own attack around Arras.

Colonel John King, commanding B Squadron, 7th Battalion Royal Tank Regiment, witnessed the bravery of Sergeant Doyle during the action and recommended him for a decoration and he was awarded the Distinguished Conduct Medal:

> Odd groups of the enemy were seen and engaged, but near a main road west of Achicourt we came under anti-tank fire and sustained three direct hits, The effect was that of hitting a large stone at speed and the track on the right hand side was seen a yard or two in front of the tank. Two more shots followed and then the guns were silenced by our fire and that of the Mk 1 tanks which went on without seeing us. We were subjected to intense rifle fire for some minutes and then left alone, apparently in the belief that we were all killed. After five or ten minutes about 30 to 50 Germans were congregated in groups on the road and to the right of us. We estimated the range of each group and then opened fire. Many of the enemy fell but doubtless some were unhurt. Later an abandoned German anti-tank gun was re-manned. Early in the action I and Sgt Doyle's section, four Matilda Mk 11's, became heavily engaged with a German anti-tank battery, all four of the enemy guns and

---

11  Manuscript sent to author by A. Rispin (Durham, 1993).
12  G. Purdon, *From Coalfield to Battlefield* (Durham: County Durham Springboard Media Project, 1995), p. 57.
13  Ibid, p. 35.

two Matildas were put out of action, leaving just Sgt Doyle and myself. Behind this battery small parties of Germans with machine-guns had been maintaining an intense fire on the tanks, they rose from cover and retired as we reached their positions. There must have been about 150 men in all and they were practically all knocked out by the machine-guns of our two Matildas. The two tanks then went to the assistance of five Matilda Mk 1s, which were armed only with machine-guns and were in difficulties with four German tanks armed with cannon. Sgt Doyle and I knocked out these four tanks and left them burning, killing those of the crews who attempted to escape.

A little later we ran up against another four gun German battery and put all those guns out of action, Sgt Doyle, under intense fire, going straight for one gun and running over it. Both our tanks now had fires burning in their forward toolboxes and had repeatedly to open the top covers to avoid suffocation by fumes.

While taking a breather myself I saw Sgt Doyle doing the same thing with smoke pouring out of his top cover. I also noticed that his two pounder gun was pointing at me, that is to his left, and surmised that his turret had been jammed by hits on the turret ring, as had my own. Shortly after this engagement, on reaching the crest of rising ground, I came across a German 88mm anti-aircraft gun 20 yards from the track I was on. He depressed onto me but before he could fire I was able to run between two high banks which bordered the track here for about 200 yards.

My turret was jammed with the gun pointing right rear and the 88mm gun was on the left of the track, as we moved out of cover my driver swung the tank round and brought the gun onto target. Almost simultaneously, Sgt Doyle, who had appeared on the crest behind quickly grasped the situation, swung his tank round and opened fire. He scattered the crew with his machine-guns and then shelled the gun with his two pounder, thus relieving what was for me a critical situation. I halted and opened my top cover and my tank then flared up inside and we had to get out. Sgt Doyle moved up and showed me his right hand which was minus the two centre fingers, these having been shot away on one of the occasions when he had opened the top of his cover to get air. His tank was still emitting smoke and he told me his driver couldn't stick the heat and fumes much longer, he also told me his turret had been jammed in the action with the second anti-tank battery and all his periscopes were shattered. I gave him my map and told him to carry on to the rallying point as quickly as he could and off he went. I met him again two days later as a prisoner in Cambrai.[14]

Sergeant Doyle, B Squadron 7th RTR:

Colonel King called me up and when I got to him his tank was on fire, his exact words were 'Doyle, let's finish the job'. So in again we went knowing we were outnumbered and never had a chance of coming out of it, then the fun started. I know of at least five German tanks he put out of action and a number of trucks, we paid Gerry back for the loss of the rest of the company. At about eight-o-clock I saw him get hit in the front locker but still he kept going. I myself was then on fire but he must have been on fire for an hour or so,

---

14  J. Duncan and G. Forty, *The Fall of France* (Kent: Guild Publishing, 1990), p. 165.

he would not leave his tank because we were surrounded by German tanks so we kept on letting them have it.[15]

The 4th and 7th RTR pushed on against increasing opposition, the 4th reaching Wancourt and the 7th Wailly. The 25th Panzer Regiment had become separated from their infantry support and had passed across the front of the British tank column at Warlus. At 7:00 p.m. they turned to take the 7th RTR and the 6th DLI in flank and rear and a tank battle of great ferocity ensued. *Rommel* was most alarmed by this counter attack and recorded events in his diary that evening:

> Running along behind the battery lines we arrived at Wailly. The enemy tank fire had created chaos and confusion among our troops in the village and they were jamming up the roads and yards with their vehicles, instead of going into action with every available weapon to fight off the oncoming enemy. We tried to create order. After notifying the divisional staff of the critical situation in and around Wailly we drove off to a hill 1,000 yards west of the village, where we found a light anti-aircraft troop and several anti-tank guns in hollows and a small wood, most of them totally under cover. About 1,200 yards west of our position the leading enemy tanks, among them a heavy, had already crossed the Arras-Beaumetz railway and had shot up one of our Panzer 111s. At the same time several enemy tanks were advancing down the road from Bac Du Nord and across the railway line towards Wailly. It was an extremely tight spot, for there were also several enemy tanks very close to Wailly on its northern side. The crew of a howitzer battery, some distance away, now left their guns, swept along by the retreating infantry. With Most's help I brought every available gun into action at top speed against the tanks. Every gun, both anti-tank and anti-aircraft, was ordered to open rapid fire immediately and I personally gave each gun its target. With the enemy tanks so perilously close, only rapid fire from every gun could save the situation. We ran from gun to gun, the objections of the gun commanders that the range was still too great to engage the tanks effectively were over ruled. All I cared about was to halt the tanks by heavy gun-fire, soon we succeeded in putting the leading enemy tanks out of action. About 150 yards west of our small wood a British captain climbed out of a heavy tank and walked unsteadily towards us with his hands up, we had killed his driver. Over by the howitzer battery also, despite a range of 1,200 to 1,500 yards the rapid fire of our anti-tank and anti-aircraft guns succeeded in bringing the enemy to a halt and forced some of them to turn away. The worst seemed to be over and the attack beaten off when suddenly *Most* sank to the ground behind a 20mm anti-aircraft gun close beside me. He was mortally wounded and blood rushed from his mouth. Poor *Most* was beyond help and died before he could be carried into cover beside the gun position. The death of this brave man, a magnificent soldier, touched me deeply.[16]

Lt Rudolph Koch, Flak Battery, 7th Panzer Division, directed the fire of the 88mm guns of his battery at the British tanks that pressed forward and saw the devastating effect they had:

---

15 Newspaper cutting sent to author by A. Curtis (Manchester, 1991).
16 B. Liddle-Hart, *The Other Side of the Hill* (London: Pan Books, 1983), p. 271.

A German 88 mm Flak gun in action at Arras, 21 May 1940. Two tanks of the Royal Tank Regiment can be seen advancing.

If we achieve a direct hit on our targets the penetrative power of our guns is so great that they pierce the armour of the British monsters and send them up in flames. The advancing enemy seems to be in chaos and those coming forward behind them will not be encouraged by the sight of the burning brutes. More enemy tanks appear from the woods, the first is set alight by a direct hit and the second put out of action, the rest move toward us and engage our guns with their main armament. Our infantry falls back through our position, time and time again we throw shells into Tommie's face, there are explosions all around us and shrapnel clatters against the gun barrel shattering the fuse setter. The steel monsters churn on towards us getting closer and closer, three of the gun team are wounded and our commander killed by a shot to the head. The fire of our batteries eventually halts the British attack and the survivors turn back.[17]

Lt Thomas Craig, MC, 7th RTR, could hear the noise of battle all around but he could see no other tanks from his unit:

After a brief halt near Achicourt I was ordered to move to Wailly, I was entirely on my own without any support at all. About 500 yards from the village I was fired on by a large armoured car with a small 20mm gun in it with no effect on my tank. I fired back and the car burst into flames, one of the crew must have had guts as, although wounded, he continued to fire as I closed in and eventually I saw him climb out and fall into the gutter badly burned. As I moved passed the blazing armoured car the village came into view before me and I saw that it was full of German infantry. There was a lot of traffic darting across the cross-roads from east to west and this I engaged with varying success. All of a sudden they tried to push a little 37 mm anti-tank gun round the corner to fire on me, but it had no effect and we drove them back. I got closer into the village near a garden wall and

---

17   Manuscript sent to author by H. Wernaman, Africa Corps veteran (Germany, 1989).

a shower of grenades was thrown over the wall onto the tank. I now felt that as I was alone in the village and vulnerable to this sort of attack, I should withdraw, this I did into a field to the north of the burning armoured car where I stayed until a light tank from the Recce troop came and told me to get back to Achicourt.[18]

On the left of Rommel's 7th Panzer Division the *SS* Totenkopf Division moved forward and ran across the path of the right hand column near Warlus, it has often been stated by historians that at this point the Totenkopf Division panicked and withdrew from the fight and though it is true that parts of that unit did leave their positions it was nothing like the route later claimed. The confusing nature of the battle between tanks, armoured cars and infantry was indeed a great shock to the Totenkopf Division, but luckily for Eicke, the commander, the brunt of the attack in his sector crashed squarely into the tank destroyer battalion that deployed swiftly and began pouring their fire into the wildly careering British armour.

The German gunners watched in amazement as their shells bounced off the thick armour of the Matildas, a number of gun crews were blasted to pieces at close range or crushed to death beneath the tracks of these 30 ton British monsters. Several companies of the tank destroyer battalion abandoned their guns and left the field to re-group, other supply units saw the situation and ran as fast as their legs would take them at the approach of a group of British tanks. After an hours fighting Eicke managed to stall the armoured advance by firing over open sights with his artillery, the timely arrival of Stukas finally drove off the remaining British tanks. The bulk of

Burning British tanks at Arras, 21 May 1940.

18   R. J. Icks, *Famous Tank Battles* (Northamptonshire: Profile Publications 1973), p. 92.

the Totenkopf Division seems to have performed well at Arras and if there was panic amongst its ranks early in the battle it was not nearly as serious as that which prevailed in Rommel's 7th Panzer Division as they absorbed the impact of the centre and left of the British attack.

Pte Thomas Maher:

> We weren't far away from the Germans, we marched down the *Givenchy* Road to this village and I can remember this Gerry spotter plane, it was a *Storch*, flying around. You got the feeling when you were marching with your platoon you were the only ones fighting the war, you thought you were on your own. But I suppose that *Storch* could see the whole brigade, the whole division even stretching for miles. That was the first time I saw proper action, we came to a lot of German transport on fire, the tanks had caught it in the open and really given Gerry what for. One soldier was lying in the middle of a cross road, all his guts was hanging out you know, he must have been SS because he had their two lightning flashes on his helmet. Over the crossroads the order was given to fix bayonets as we were coming up to this wood, I was on the bren and was carrying that. The road went through the wood and as we got to the other side Corporal Hall comes up to me and says 'up here with your Bren Tom', We'd heard machine-gun fire just before that and he said Norman Huscrofts copped it, [killed 21 May 1940]. I says 'what just wounded?' he says 'no killed'. Gerry couldn't have been more than 50 yards away when he opened up but he got clean away, anyway we goes running to the top of this road, Bobby Gordon was number two with me on the bren, we were back of this hedge and just laid there waiting for events. For about half an hour we could hear skirmishing going on around us, then the sergeant came and said right get out of it.[19]

The battle was fast and furious as the 6th and 8th Battalions of the DLI came to grips with the German units, the crews of the 4th and 7th RTR worked feverishly as they came under fire from the German artillery. Shells exploded and machine guns rattled amid the loud roar and rumble of tanks zig-zagging across the battle-field.

Lt Peter Vaux was sent to ask for support but on his return found a terrible scene of destruction:

> Colonel Fitzmaurice on spotting a German heavy tank sent me back to Beaurains to ask the commander of a French tank to come to our aid, but he refused to help, I made my way back to report this to the Colonel. As I went down the hill I saw that some of the tanks were not moving, but by the time I was 50 yards away and I sensed that something was not quite right. As I approached I saw that some of the tanks had their tracks knocked off, some of the turrets were crooked and had smoke pouring out of them and some had chaps hanging out of the turrets dead. There were about 15 to 20 tanks and all of them were dead. I saw the Colonels light tank with its flag on it, the front of the tank was smashed in and the engine was pushed right back. No-one in the tank could have survived.[20]

---

19 G. Purdon, *From Coalfield to Battlefield* (Durham: County Durham Springboard Media Project, 1995), p. 54.
20 Manuscript sent to author by Bob Stafford (Hull, 1991).

Pte Thomas W Jackson, 8th DLI:

> That was the first time we met the German infantry, I was a transport driver and was driving a bren-carrier. We were parked in a wood and saw what happened to the advanced carriers. We lost eight or nine lads in bren carriers that time, the Gerry artillery just popped the front out of them. Our lads were given to understand that ordinary anti-tank guns wouldn't penetrate them, they went through them like tissue paper.[21]

Pte Thomas W Jackson, 8th Battalion Durham Light Infantry.

By early evening the 8th DLI had passed Warlus with the right hand column and the 6th DLI with the left hand column had reached Beaurains, where it sat in a tank proof position. The 8th DLI came under heavy small arms and mortar fire from the German infantry positions on the Arras-Doullens Road and was forced to take cover. The Durhams began to take casualties as things heated up and the Germans closed in on them.

Sergeant James McGarey, MM, 8th DLI:

> A Company was advancing on our left, we'd just got through this village and that's where Norman Huscroft got it, the first to be killed in B Company. It was bad countryside, a wood here, a wood there, but mostly open fields. I remember this old woman with a pram, she was lying on the road all twisted, riddled with bullets, we fell back on this village called Warlus and we had to hold it. The lads was strung out among the houses.[22]

There now commenced, on Warlus and Beaurains, the most intensive air attack yet experienced by the troops of the 50th Division. The sky seemed to be full of aircraft as 100 planes worked in relays to bomb and machine-gun the British positions for 20 minutes without pause. The shrill scream of the Stukas falling out of the sky, the whistle and explosion of bombs and the clatter of machine-guns as planes swooped low to strafe the Tommies made a crescendo of noise unimaginable to those who did not experience it.

Lt Colonel Harry Miller, 6th DLI, felt the full brunt of the air attack:

> By this time we were established at Agny, on the railway and the bridge over it. C Coy was close by and D Company held the eastern edge of Beaurains. Within a short time an exceedingly heavy dive-bombing attack was made on both Beaurains and Achicourt, casualties being very heavy. The enemy had the great advantage of unmolested air co-operation during the whole of the attack, one of their machines hovering overhead continually. Our smallest movements were observed and obviously signalled back to the enemy artillery at once.[23]

---

21 Taped interview with author, Thomas W. Jackson (Durham, 1994).
22 G. Purdon, *From Coalfield to Battlefield* (Durham: County Durham Springboard Media Project, 1995), p.56.
23 Newspaper cutting sent to author by William Ridley (Durham, 1994).

Pte Bert Davies, anti-tank platoon, 6th DLI:

> In an attack like this you felt so helpless, you haven't enough strength left to retaliate. As long as you can retaliate a bit you feel alright, but when you can't retaliate and the dive bombers come over you see, well you can't retaliate against them, you just lie down and take it. It was pretty disheartening as you've no protection.[24]

Lance Bombardier Eric Manley, 92nd Field Regiment, Royal Artillery, wondered why their own aircraft were not opposing the Stukas:

> Where was the RAF? We are obviously at the Germans mercy, no wonder they conquer countries overnight. Where are our planes? Where is the ack-ack? 20 planes pass over us in formation, don't really know what they are but we lie in the grass at the roadside and feel absolutely abandoned. 20 more following them, 15 more and still no British planes to be seen, 18 more followed by a formation of 12. We move off under brutal attack from the air. Enemy planes are so thick and unmolested that we have a very hot time and most of the lads were pretty demoralised.[25]

Pte Thomas Maher felt helpless as the bombs rained down:

> Then the bloody Stukas came, this lad says 'get down' why I went straight down on my face, I didn't hear anything just felt me lugs then this heat and it was over. There was a wump as the truck went up. Then he started machine-gunning, my mouth was hanging open, it shook you that much. This corporal with glasses says 'come on lads give us a hand', on the other side of the wagon these lads were laying among the trees, there wasn't a mark on them, they'd been caught by the bomb blast and they were stone dead.[26]

Pte John H Clark, 8th DLI, was armed with a Piat anti-tank rifle and found that they were pretty ineffective against German armour:

> We saw a lot of civilian casualties clogging the roads up and Stukas kept attacking us, they came down with a terrible shrill howl that went straight through you. The Germans were moving up a road and we were accompanied by some French light armour, we were attacked by German tanks and infantry. All we had was small anti-tank rifles, Piats, I was on one of them

Pte John H Clark, 8th Battalion Durham Light Infantry.

24  Interview with Bert Davies (Durham 1996).
25  Taped interview with author, Eric Manley at the Veteran's re-union (Hull, 1992).
26  G. Purdon, *From Coalfield to Battlefield* (Durham: County Durham Springboard Media Project, 1995), p. 70.

and they were pretty ineffective and I doubt if I knocked any tanks out. Every time I let fly I could hear the shells bouncing off them.[27]

The 6th DLI were forced to extricate themselves from Beaurains and as they did so were attacked by a large enemy tank force in the open. Major Peter J Jeffries saw tanks approaching his position and went to greet them but he was in for a shock:

> I had no contact and nobody to communicate with me, so I went up to Ronnie at the east end of Beaurains and told him he must withdraw. He said he would try, I then went to the other end of Beaurains to D Company and when I got there a runner came back from Ronnie saying there were enemy tanks working round both flanks and he would try to gradually withdraw. There was nothing else he could do as by this time darkness had started to fall. The Intelligence Officer of the 4th RTR came along on a motor-bike, I told him we were going to withdraw to Achicourt, at this moment we heard some tanks coming down the road from C Company on the other side of Beaurains towards us. I said whose tanks are these yours? We could see them up the road after a bit, about 200 yards away. He said 'yes it's alright they're our Matildas'. The leading tank came onto the crossroads, this tank man and I walked up to it and in the gloom at about ten paces I looked at the man with his head out of the top of the tank, he was German! He had these things on his collar, SS Runes. Then he realised I was an Englishman so he shut the top of his tank like hell and I ran across the front of his tank, for I realised what was going to happen, he was going to open up on us. But I thought the thing to do was to get down in the front of his tank so he couldn't depress his guns on me. I nipped across the front of the tank and got into a ditch on the far side of him. There were a couple more tanks behind him and they opened up, but behind us were two or three of our own tanks and they engaged the Germans.[28]

Lt Peter Vaux, 4th RTR, found himself in the sights of a German sniper:

> I told my driver to reverse and I stood up on my seat in the turret so I was exposed from the waist upwards. I was shouting to the driver to do this and that and was shouting at the gunner to do the other. But what I little knew was that behind me a German soldier was lying on the ground with his rifle resting on his kit-bag, drawing a bead on my back. I didn't know this but Captain Cracroft did. It wasn't until we got back to England that his gunner told me that Captain Cracroft drew his revolver and shot this man through the throat before he could pull the trigger, after that we pulled out of what was really a valley of death. We picked up a number of tank crews as we went, there must have been half-a-dozen men clinging to the outside of ones tank.[29]

The 8th DLI was attacked at the same time in front and right flank by the German armour, as evening fell the 8th were still dug in at Warlus. The effects on morale of the bombing was now

---

27 Taped interview with author, John H. Clark (Durham, 1990).
28 H. Moses, *The Faithful Sixth* (Durham: County Durham Books 1995), p. 137.
29 R. J. Icks, *Famous Tank Battles* (Northamptonshire: Profile Publications 1973), p. 201.

being felt, many of the troops were in a dazed condition, a result of sitting amid an inferno of high explosive delivered by a totally unopposed attack.

Sergeant Charles E Davis, 4th Battalion Northumberland Fusiliers, thought his chances of survival were very slim:

> We were in a bad way and Gerry wasn't going to give us a moments peace, my mate Stan was white as a sheet and shaking. As shells struck our positions flashes lit up the darkness and we could hear Gerry's tanks firing close by, tracer rounds flew above and among us. The noise of battle was terrific and Warlus was a grim place, I just hoped I would live to tell the tale and not remain there forever, in the ground.[30]

Sergeant Charles E. Davis, 4th Battalion Royal Northumberland Fusiliers.

French tanks, which had taken a long cast around the right flank of the 8th DLI, suddenly appeared from cover, mistook the Tommies for Germans and opened fire putting one anti-tank gun out of action and killing two men. The anti-tank gunners of the Durhams assumed they were being attacked by German armour and began to return fire, the fire fight that ensued saw four French tanks knocked out amid great confusion.

Sergeant James McGarey, MM, realised his mistake too late:

> We saw these tanks coming at us and all we had was our two pounder anti-tank guns you know. Yah bugger we had two knocked out before we found they was French, what a cock up.[31]

Lance Corporal William Ridley had a close escape:

> We saw some tanks approaching and some silly lad opened fire on one of them with a Boyes anti-tank gun, it was a French tank. He thought we was Gerries and opened up with his machine gun. I got up on one knee and felt something clip the back of my hair and the bloke behind us dropped, he was our first casualty, a bloke called [Mathew] Levee.[32]

Four French tanks had been put out of action and their crews killed or wounded on the Durhams front on the outskirts of Duisans before the mistake was recognised, tank recognition in the BEF in 1940 was not good.

As darkness fell the 8th DLI was attacked by a strong force of enemy tanks and infantry at Warlus. All troops were drawn into the village and a strong defensive ring was formed, German

---

30  Taped interview with author, Charles E. Davis (Durham, 1991).
31  G. Purdon, *From Coalfield to Battlefield* (Durham: County Durham Springboard Media Project, 1995), p. 56.
32  Taped interview with author, William Ridley (Durham, 1991).

mortar bombs rained down on the Durhams setting fire to many of the buildings. The fires and explosions lit up the night as the Durhams fought on amid an increasing rattle of small arms fire and the crack of grenades.

Lt Ian R English, MC and bar:

> A Company had taken quite a number of casualties so the commanding officer pulled them back to Warlus and we took up a position for all round defence of the village. This took a bit of organising because the men were just sitting about after a particularly bad air-raid. The German pressure became more intense as the day went on and there was quite a lot of shelling and accurate mortar fire. We suffered a few casualties and the CO was wounded in the leg, but that didn't seem to make a great deal of difference to him, he just went around a bit more slowly than before as he organised things. Darkness was beginning to come down and the village of Warlus was burning from the shelling, there was a lot of smoke and confusion. We learnt that the commander of A Company had been taken prisoner along with several of his men.[33]

Captain John Charles Austin, Y Battery, Royal Artillery, arrived at Vimy Ridge in the late afternoon and had a long distance grandstand view of the battle as it developed below him. He had no way of knowing this was the Durham Brigade fighting for its life:

> It was four in the afternoon when I put my head over the top of Vimy Ridge for the first time and gazed on the battle in the distance. To the left lay Arras in the middle distance of the plain, but a thick curtain of smoke hung before it. A bombing attack was in progress and the heavy explosions punctuated the continual distant thunder of the gunfire. Now and again the sound of sharp vicious bursts of machine-gun fire mingled with the heavier booms. Night fell and the battle became more visible along the horizon, the whole front was lit up with red flashes of bursting bombs and shells. Two big fires were burning and the glare coloured the clouds in the sky a dirty pink. One bomb had evidently found a petrol store and the flames were ascending skyward in great rolling billows. High in the sky above all of this an incredible firework display went on for hours, tracer shells made wonderful and weird designs in fiery orange loops. Now and again up shot a rocket which burst into a ball of brilliant coloured light that shone for a few seconds then vanished. Less frequently Verey Lights burst of either red, green, blue or yellow, which floated about for a full half minute before expiring. As a spectacle it was tremendous.[34]

As the battle raged in Warlus German armoured patrols struck around the flanks of the village to reach the Duisans-Warlus Road, other enemy patrols secured the Duisans-Maroeuil Road and cut communications between Duisans and Brigadier Churchill's HQ in Maroeuil. The position in Warlus now seemed hopeless as Lt Colonel Beart and his men were completely surrounded. After several abortive attempts were made to make contact with the rear, Lt Potts, Mortar Officer, rode hell for leather on his motor-cycle and broke through the German cordon,

---

33  Manuscript sent to author by Ian R. English (Durham, 1992).
34  J. C. Austin, *Return via Dunkirk* (London: Hodder and Stoughton, 1940), p. 79.

German infantry move to the attack behind a barrage of fire, 22 May 1940.

reaching Brigade HQ in Maroeuil at 2:30 a.m. on the 22 May. He was given orders to the effect that the 8th DLI were to withdraw at once and he then passed through the enemy lines once more to get back to B and C Companies at Duisans. It was however impossible to get through to A and D Companies at Warlus as the battle there was now moving swiftly to a violent climax, ammunition was running short and German reinforcements had been brought up.

In the early hours of 22 May six French tanks broke through the German cordon accompanied by two armoured troop carriers and to the amazement of the hard pressed Durhams they rumbled into the beleaguered village. A break out was quickly planned and at 3:30 a.m. every carrier and truck that had not been hit in the battle was used to evacuate the exhausted troops that had held out for so long and suffered such grievous casualties. With French tanks covering their rear and by the light of blazing fires the vehicles ran the gauntlet of German fire as tracer rounds cut through the black night. Some trucks were hit but this desperate gamble paid off and the surviving overloaded vehicles did not stop until they reached Vimy.

Sergeant James McGarey, MM, managed to climb aboard one of the last vehicles leaving Warlus:

> Word came for the platoon sergeants to meet at the edge of the village for a briefing, we were told we were going to hold the village and the 5th Division was supposed to advance through us. There was me, Ikey McDermot, Ralphy Crowe and a few others at the meeting. When we got back to the square the last trucks were pulling out and we just managed to jump on the back of one. When we were at the meeting word come through that the 5th Division's advance was off and we had to fall back to Vimy Ridge. We got back to the ridge

and Major Clarke was there, he said we'd done well under the circumstances. He ended up as a Lt Colonel of the 9th and was killed in Sicily.[35]

Lt Ian R English, MC and bar:

We were under constant attack and the brigadier ordered that the battalion should withdraw as it was running up against opposition which was very much greater than it could cope with, but it was some hours after that we actually withdrew. We went back the way we'd come to Vimy which we reached around five in the morning. At Vimy we moved further along the ridge to Givenchy, where we took up defensive positions. The next day was fairly quiet and then at about three the following morning we were ordered to withdraw to Carvin. It was extremely slow going as the roads were absolutely packed with vehicles and refugees. We then got word from our signals officer that a French Algerian Division was manning the La Bassee Canal and were very hard pressed. I was sent into Carvin to report to the French at their divisional headquarters, there must have been a dozen or more French officers there all poring over maps on the table and all talking at once. I stood there with the Liaison Officer for a moment, then somebody saw us and there was tremendous excitement. ah bravo les Anglais.[36]

The 6th DLI pulled back to Achicourt and received orders to withdraw during the night, the tanks of the 4th RTR gave invaluable support to the hard pressed Tommies and the anti-tank gunners did the rest. As the Durham's pulled out their retreat was covered by Y Company 4th Battalion Royal Northumberland Fusiliers commanded by Major K A Clark.

Lt Peter Vaux, 4th Battalion Royal Tank Regiment, was caught up in the utter chaos of the retreat and was very nearly taken prisoner when his tank took a wrong turn:

There was absolute chaos as we pulled back because there was a very narrow railway bridge at Achicourt with a bend in it and we went over that, there was unbelievable confusion. There were our tanks, there were bren carriers that belonged to the Durham Light Infantry and there were German motorcyclists. It was dark and it was noisy and we had no ammunition left as we'd used it all up. After a while we reached the Arras/Doullens Road but instead of crossing it we turned left and when I looked out of the tank we were quite alone on a road I didn't recognise. We were heading south-west towards Doullens and a lot of traffic started coming the other way, it was all German. The Germans didn't react to us, it was quite dark and we didn't have insignia in those days. As long as we kept moving there was no reason why anybody should know who we were. Unfortunately we got to a cross roads where a column of German half-tracks were backing out, they were right across the road while an angry German officer directed traffic. I didn't really know what to do. But my driver, Cpl Burroughs, had the answer, he drove quite deliberately and slowly into the back of a lorry. There was an expensive crunch and loud shouts from the soldiers inside the

---

35 G. Purdon, *From Coalfield to Battlefield* (Durham: County Durham Springboard Media Project, 1995), p. 76.
36 Manuscript sent to author by Ian R. English (Durham, 1992).

lorry. The German officer swore at us, told the lorry to pull forward and told us to get the hell out of it. He never knew us for anything but a German tank.[37]

Captain George L Wood, MC and bar, 6th DLI:

> The Fusiliers sat tight in their positions as Major Clark moved from post to post, the German tank attack that came thundering in over-ran our remaining outposts and a heavy barrage fell upon our troops, enemy tanks were seen advancing up a sunken road in single file, Major Clark found an abandoned anti-tank gun and two rounds of ammunition. He at once brought it to bear on the enemy tanks, the first shot just bounced off the thick armour but the second scored a direct hit on the leading tank blocking the road and the Germans pulled back to re-group.[38]

Captain George L Wood, MC and bar, 6th Battalion Durham Light Infantry.

Major K A Clark, Y Company, 4th Battalion Royal Northumberland Fusiliers, was ordered to cover the withdrawal of the 6th DLI:

> I was ordered to reconnoitre the whole enemy position ahead with particular reference to the village of Beaurains, but while these orders were being given the whole force was subjected to heavy dive bombing which caused many casualties and some confusion. At this point the column received orders to withdraw and Major Jeffries, 6th DLI, ordered Y Company forward to a cross-roads ahead to cover the withdrawal of 6th DLI which was to commence at dusk. I deployed two platoons forward, No4 on the right and No5 on the left, and withdrew No6 into reserve some distance behind. A section of scout cars was allotted to each forward platoon. The Germans appeared to be active, not only ahead but also on the flanks. However 6th DLI was able to withdraw leaving only a few outposts until Y Company was firmly established. German artillery fire increased sharply and judging from the wide arc of German very lights it appeared that a counter attack might be imminent. We had not long to wait before the enemy launched a tank attack which quickly overran the remaining 6th DLI outposts. The leading tanks advanced up a sunken road and could not at first deploy out into open ground, or at any rate they hesitated to do so. I had already got my mechanics to explore the possibilities of an abandoned anti-tank gun nearby and with the only two remaining rounds seized my opportunity and opened fire on the leading tank. I secured a direct hit with the second round which disabled the tank and thus successfully blocked the sunken road. Enemy artillery now put down a short concentration which was quickly followed in the failing light by an

---

37  Manuscript sent to author by Eric Manley (Hull, 1994).
38  Ibid, by John H Clark (Durham, 1990).

infantry attack. Company headquarters was forward with the two leading platoons and we held off the enemy in fine style. Abandoned weapons were in abundance and nearly every other man had possessed himself of a bren-gun and a good quantity of ammunition. Heavy casualties were inflicted on the Germans and their attack was stopped. The enemy evidently decided that special measures were to be adopted for now they brought flame-throwers into action and supported this with a further tank attack. This action resulted in the officer commanding the scout car platoon being severely wounded, causing him to die some time later in enemy hands, whilst two other ranks were killed and about 12 wounded. At the same time great destruction was caused amongst our vehicles. I was wounded in the arm while I was visiting the section posts. By now it was evident that the company was surrounded, No4 Platoon was taking the full force of the enemy attacks, its commander firing a bren-gun and in between bursts distributing ammunition to keep the fight going.[39]

Lt Clark Lowes, 4th Battalion Royal Northumberland Fusiliers:

I remember as we went back seeing some anti-tank guns deployed on our line of march and their muzzles pointing to the west. At the time it did not strike me as peculiar, but later I wondered why they were pointed in the opposite direction to where I thought the enemy was. I know now that they were deployed to deal with the enemy armour I had reported to the west which was later to attack from west to east.[40]

Lt Peter Vaux, 4th Battalion Royal Tank Regiment:

This was the end, as evening wore on it became increasingly evident that the Germans were about to attack. Stuka activity increased and ranging shells fell in the neighbourhood of Achicourt where we had to wait at the crossroads for a despatch rider from brigade. The main body moved back 100 yards and Fernie and I stayed by the light tank whilst Robert Cracroft leant against his own running board alongside chatting. Daylight went and a full moon shone. Then we heard tanks close by coming towards us, we hoped they were the Matildas belonging to the 7th RTR and Cracroft walked forward to talk to them. He waved his maps at the drivers visor of the first tank, but to his astonishment some close cropped heads popped out and he realised they were German. Only 12 yards separated us from the Germans and the most attractive 75mm tracer was already sailing over our heads, it hit Armit's tank. Just behind our own tanks were returning fire with enthusiasm. Cracroft beat all records in his dash back to us and then we moved back to join the others. At about this moment an abandoned petrol lorry went up in flames, illuminating the whole scene and this spirited little action went on for the next 10 minutes until Cracroft dropped a smoke candle and the Germans withdrew.[41]

The German 6th infantry Regiment swept into the area held by the Royal Northumberland Fusiliers and a ferocious fire fight ensued, the Fusiliers kept up a murderous fire upon the enemy

---

39  Teeside Gazette newspaper cutting sent to author by Mr Kilgallon (Durham, 1995).
40  Taped interview with author, Mr Clark Lowes (Durham, 1992).
41  Manuscript sent to author by Peter Vaux (1989).

and the ground before the Tommies was littered with enemy dead and wounded. Y Company now began to take severe casualties as German tanks and infantry moved in, the night was lit up by flame throwers but the men hung on with a grim determination. Tank shells cracked over the Fusiliers heads to explode in the rear, setting fire to buildings and lighting up the scene of this desperate struggle. Major K A Clark was wounded in the arm. Corporal T G Winder was badly wounded in both legs but refused to leave his position and fought to the end.

It soon became obvious that the position was totally surrounded and communications with the reserve platoon was lost, Major Clark gave the order to withdraw, each man having to make his own way to the rear as the enemy moved in for the kill. As the Fusiliers tried to make their escape many were shot in the back, the lucky ones were taken prisoner and only the reserve platoon made it back.

Major K A Clark, 4th Battalion Royal Northumberland Fusiliers:

> Now fires broke out behind the company position and I realised there was no hope of an organised withdrawal, nor could I expect to receive any further orders from 6th DLI. I therefore determined to hang on as long as possible, the persistent but receding sound of firing to the flank and rear emphasising the value of such a course. By now light was failing quickly but nearby fires enabled us to inflict severe casualties on the Germans until at last we were overwhelmed. I was hit in the head as I tried to leave and was taken prisoner along with other survivors.[42]

Guide parties went out in the night from the main body to bring in any survivors but they were all in such a shell-shocked state that little information about the action could be gained.

Second Lieutenant J R Baynham, 4th Battalion Royal Northumberland Fusiliers, was captured by two German officers, they put him in the back of their car, took his map, gave him cigarettes and chocolate and carried on. A British tank appeared and opened fire on the car killing both German officers. In the confusion the Lt grabbed the German maps and document cases and ran for his life, he was now totally lost and all that night and most of the next day he stumbled about in French fields hiding from German patrols and trying to find his headquarters. Eventually he found it, but instead of a warm welcome the weary Lt found himself looking down the barrel of a gun.

Lt Colonel Roland Wood, 4th Battalion Royal Northumberland Fusiliers, met Lt Baynham but did not recognise him at first:

> He was so dirty and so disreputable looking that the staff thought he might be a spy, eventually I recognised him through his crust of dirt. Guide parties went out at night to help lead in any returning troops, they were all stunned and exhausted and in a pretty bad way because of what they had been through, it was quite impossible to obtain any coherent account of the operation as a whole until some days later when their minds had cleared. The battalion had more than carried its weight and had made itself felt, it was a fine continuation of the spirit of the battalion in the Great War which had so often made its mark in just such a way.[43]

---

42  Newspaper cutting sent to author by William Ridley (Durham, 1994).
43  Ibid, by Thomas W. Clark (Durham, 1992).

# 6

## 150 Brigade, 21 to 23 May 1940

---

General Martel had sent 150 Brigade to relieve the French on the Scarpe and one battalion of that unit, the 4th Battalion East Yorkshire Regiment, to reinforce the troops holding Arras on the afternoon of 20 May. On the 21st the brigade was shelled and mortared by the Germans, the history of the 4th Battalion East Yorkshire Regiment speaks of huge fleets of enemy aircraft marauding about unopposed in the skies. The men of 150 Brigade dug-in or occupied any buildings that gave some protection and a good field of fire. Across the Scarpe the rumble and roar of the battle being fought by the 4th and 7th Battalions Royal Tank Regiment and 151 Brigade against the German armoured forces could be heard clearly. The transport that had been left on Vimy Ridge was now subjected to an intensive air attack by Stukas and many vehicles were destroyed, adding to the general crescendo of noise. Amid all of this German snipers were very active in Arras and the British troops found it a full time occupation flushing them out and eliminating them.

Sergeant Arthur Chester, 4th Battalion East Yorkshire Regiment:

> A sniper had us pinned down in this barn and the only thing higher than us was a church spire, so we surmised the sniper was there. A section was sent out to the area, the sniping stopped and we heard no more about it, they'd got him.[1]

Sergeant Les Hilton, 4th Battalion East Yorkshire Regiment, was part of one such section actively hunting snipers:

> We were on the banks of a canal with the enemy on the other side and a sniper was picking men off from a factory building. I was in a church doorway trying to see where the sniper was, I turned to speak to my mate when a bullet rushed passed my face and hit the church door and the hole is still there to this day. A party of us put on plimsolls as boots was too noisy, we rushed across the bridge and began searching this building floor by floor, starting at the bottom so as to flush him to the top. When we searched the top floor only one room was left and the only hiding place in it was a big cupboard. We all got our weapons at the

---

1 Taped interview with author, Arthur Chester (Hull, 1989).

ready and one man quickly opened the cupboard door, there he was, crouching down and dressed in civilian clothes, we all opened fire at once and that was the end of him. We spent quite some time every evening searching for fifth columnists, when enemy aircraft were overhead some people used to signal to them with lights, we would watch out for them and try to pin-point the source of the lights. As a result of this two locals were arrested and later shot by the French police.[2]

Patrols were sent out to the south side of the river Scarpe as the enemy was very close and it was not long before the advanced troops of each side clashed.

Sergeant Herbert Glenton, 4th Battalion East Yorkshire Regiment, saw his first action:

Our first action was when we fired on this motorised platoon of Germans, as soon as we realised they were Germans we thought well this is it and we opened fire. Behind us were some machine gunners, Cheshires I think, and they opened up from our rear, that scattered some and killed a lot. At the time the Germans had a three inch mortar that was very accurate and he returned our fire. When it got too hot we pulled out.[3]

It was a frightening experience for the young men of 150 Brigade as for the first time they began to take casualties, shells rained down on their positions and, as the attack by the two DLI and RTR columns ran out of steam, the enemy grew in strength and began to infiltrate their positions.

Sergeant Arthur Chester remembers how close the German troops were:

Imagine being in the city of Hull with the enemy already in the city. We ran from door to door, from street to street, as we dashed from building to building there was a lot of machine gun fire. I remember in Arras, all the shop fronts was blasted in, rubble was all over the place and it was in a terrible state. Well I was company runner to C Company, my officer commanding was Captain Farthing, a TA officer, I was his bat-man. I ran through the area when things was red hot, I used to jump, dive, skip, anything to dodge the fire raking the streets. We happened to get a German prisoner and it was the first prisoner I'd actually seen. We took him down to battalion HQ, I remember one officer saying 'what are we going to do with this fella?' he was only young and we were very bitter. I wouldn't have cared if we'd have cut his throat. To this day I don't know what happened to him, I could imagine what did happen to him.[4]

Captain H D Whitehead, MC, 5th Battalion Green Howards, had a narrow escape as shells fell into the town:

We had barely moved into our Head Quarters, which we shared with the Welsh Guards at the Palais St Vaast, when our attempt to unpack was disturbed by two deafening bangs and a sheet of flame leapt into the sky as four of the battalion's trucks exploded. 11 British

2   Ibid, with Les Hilton (Hull, 1987).
3   Ibid, with Herbert Glenton (Hull, 1995).
4   Ibid, with Arthur Chester (Hull, 1989).

soldiers were killed or injured, I was inside the Palais and was shielded from the blast. The injuries suffered by many of the survivors can only be described as horrific, the blast had stripped off their clothing and flayed them alive. I tramped up the ghostly empty streets with their modern shops on both sides displaying gents' natty suits, shoes, boots and groceries. We passed a dead dog which had its four legs sticking straight up and then a tailors dummy in a shop door-way which made me jump. Broken glass helped to make our tramping almost ear splitting and all the time one felt one ought to be quiet. We passed a house surrounded by a high brick wall and up went a green star shell, I asked what it was and the intelligence officer said 'Oh Fifth Column'. It was the first time I had considered that civilians might still be about, they were though, they used to snipe our sentries at Bn HQ from across the street. We had sniper hunts out every evening. It was not until the third day that I found a cellar full of women and kids in some other large building not one 100 yards away from Bn HQ. What they lived on God knows but few came above ground while we were there.[5]

Captain J M Whittaker, 5th Battalion Green Howards:

The city was an eerie no-man's land between the civilian and the military worlds. The shop windows were full of pre-war goods but the streets were deserted. There was little sign of civilians but there must have been several hundred in the city who, too feeble or too listless to escape, dragged out a miserable existence in the cellars. Some were doubtless there for loot and some for no good at all from the British point of view, judging from the sporadic sniping after dark and the mysterious very lights which went up at intervals.[6]

Hot food was brought to the defending troops from the rear in trucks of varying sizes. This was a hazardous job with Stukas and fighters overhead looking for targets and it became even more so as the German infantry moved in closer. Colour Sergeant Wilfred Gilson, 4th Battalion East Yorkshire Regiment, remembers one such journey to the front line, he and his comrades loaded up their transport, drove to the battalion forward positions and began to discharge their load:

I went with our 15Cwt truck with Herbert Wiles the driver and a fatigue man. We were taking up the meal to the battalion which was in the line and as we got the tea, soup and bread off onto the road there was a rattle of machine-gun fire which got mainly the soup containers and the tea urns, the odd bullet went through my left leg. I didn't know at first I had been wounded, I just fell down and felt it only two minutes later. I didn't see who shot me. Herbert Wiles and the other fella took me to the side of the road to a little ditch and I started to crawl along this ditch and came to a culvert. I chucked my equipment away but kept my rifle and gas mask, I managed to get through this culvert to covered country, I found the handle of a pick axe, turned my rifle upside down and used them as crutches. About a mile down the road I came across a French farmer with a big horse, he offered to

5  Manuscript sent to author by H. D. Whitehead (Richmond, 1993).
6  Ibid, by J. M. Whittaker (Scarborough, 1991).

lift me up on it and send me on my way. But I refused because I knew if I got on I wouldn't be able to get off, so I continued and it was quite a long time before I arrived at the Dunkirk perimeter.[7]

Many of the men of 150 Brigade had been long serving territorials and some joined up in the early 1930s and knew their comrades intimately. The family spirit of such units became even stronger on active service, when, for the first time, friends were being killed and wounded. These deaths were deeply felt by these tight knit territorial units and most men could remember when and where their section or platoon took its first casualty.

Sergeant Herbert Glenton, 4th Battalion East Yorkshire Regiment:

> The first casualty I saw die was a fellow called Bill Robinson, you must remember we had been together before the war had started, we were just a family. We were on this railway embankment looking out across the country side. We saw what we assumed to be Germans in the distance and of course we opened fire on them, they fired back and hit Bill Robinson. When they pulled us out we had to carry him back in a blanket to the company, he went from us but we understood he died of his wounds later. That was the first fella I saw killed, I'd seen plenty of dead civilians but I knew Bill Robinson personally and he was one of the family. He hadn't been married long, poor bloke and his death upset us very much.[8]

By 23 May the position along the Scarpe and at Arras was fast becoming untenable as German troops continued to press forward and infiltrate the area. Frankforce was now practically isolated with the enemy in great strength closing in around the north of Arras. During the day on the 23rd 150 Brigade was ordered to retire.

Sergeant Arthur Chester recalls:

> Captain Farthing told us the position and ordered us to secure all belts, buckles and to tie sacking round our boots, anything that rattled had to be tied secure and we made our retreat out of Arras in the darkness. We were so close to the enemy, we crept out on tip-toe.[9]

Sergeant Herbert Glenton was glad to leave Arras:

> Eventually they blew the bridge over the canal, we had stayed for 48 hrs and were absolutely tired out when suddenly we were told we were moving out. I well remember, they told us to hurry across any streets as snipers and machine-guns were active. I pulled my section out and we ran down the main street where we met the colonel who hurried us on. We got to a park and boarded these trucks, shells were falling all around us, we went on through flattened villages.[10]

---

7    Taped interview with author, Wilfred Gilson (Hull, 1992).
8    Ibid, with Herbert Glenton (Hull, 1995).
9    Ibid, with Arthur Chester (Hull, 1989).
10   Ibid, with Herbert Glenton (Hull, 1995).

Captain John Charles Austin, Royal Artillery, returned to Vimy Ridge to his old gun position to be greeted by a sight he would never forget:

> We were to reoccupy the positions we had left on Vimy Ridge that evening, just passed Givenchy I halted the battery and went forward to the ridge to reconnoitre the gun positions. The sight that greeted me turned my blood cold, heaps of dead and dying men, women and children filled our gun pits. They were refugees who had taken cover there and been literally blasted out of life some hours earlier by German dive-bombers, probably looking for us. From the interior of these piles of torn, limbless, decapitated bodies sounded an occasional groan where some unfortunate still drew breath. A sickening stench pervaded the warm air, upon this spectacle of horror the midnight moon shone brightly from a cloudless sky.
>
> My driver and I stared at each other speechless, our feelings beyond words. The total absence of any sign that these poor wretches had received any assistance accentuated the horror, the mangled piles remained after all these hours in exactly the same state as when the bombers had finished with them. From these ghastly gun-pits I drove over to what had been the battery command post, here another nightmare. The entire front of the house had been blown away and opposite a straw barn blazed furiously, cremating a dozen or so refugees who had been bombed while sheltering there. It was impossible to expect the battery, after their long hours of firing, to enter this charnel house and start clearing away dead bodies to make room for the guns.
>
> Next morning after crossing the Lens-Arras road who should I come across but the 400 German prisoners I had seen brought into Achicourt the previous afternoon. They had been marched all the way back and were now dead beat and lying asleep in a ditch, guarded by a few Tommies with fixed bayonets. Little groups of refugees were prowling around with decidedly hostile intentions, trying to get at the prisoners. If they happened to escape from the shambles at our gun-pits they may be excused their murderous passions, but the Tommies guarded their prisoners like diamonds. It was a whiff of sane old England to hear one calling out 'pass along please, pass along' Just as coolly as a London policeman breaking up a crowd.[11]

For the last divisional troops out of Arras it was a close run thing as the enemy armour and infantry entered the town and hunted down any stragglers. Sergeant Charles E Davis, 4th Battalion Royal Northumberland Fusiliers, was taking his men out of Arras when German tanks appeared in the side streets:

> L/Cpl Crystal had a Piat anti-tank rifle, he believed me when I told him it would stop any known tank, well it would just about stop a truck. He was laid in the gutter taking aim and he fired and hit this tank three times, each time the shells just bounced off. Gerry then opened up on us with his machine gun and bullets flew around us, we got away and he still had this anti-tank rifle, I said 'have you got any ammunition' he said 'no' so I said well throw that bloody thing away it's no use.[12]

---

11  J. C. Austin, *Return via Dunkirk* (London: Hodder and Stoughton, 1940), p. 98.
12  Taped interview with author, Charles E. Davis (Durham, 1991).

76    50th At Bay

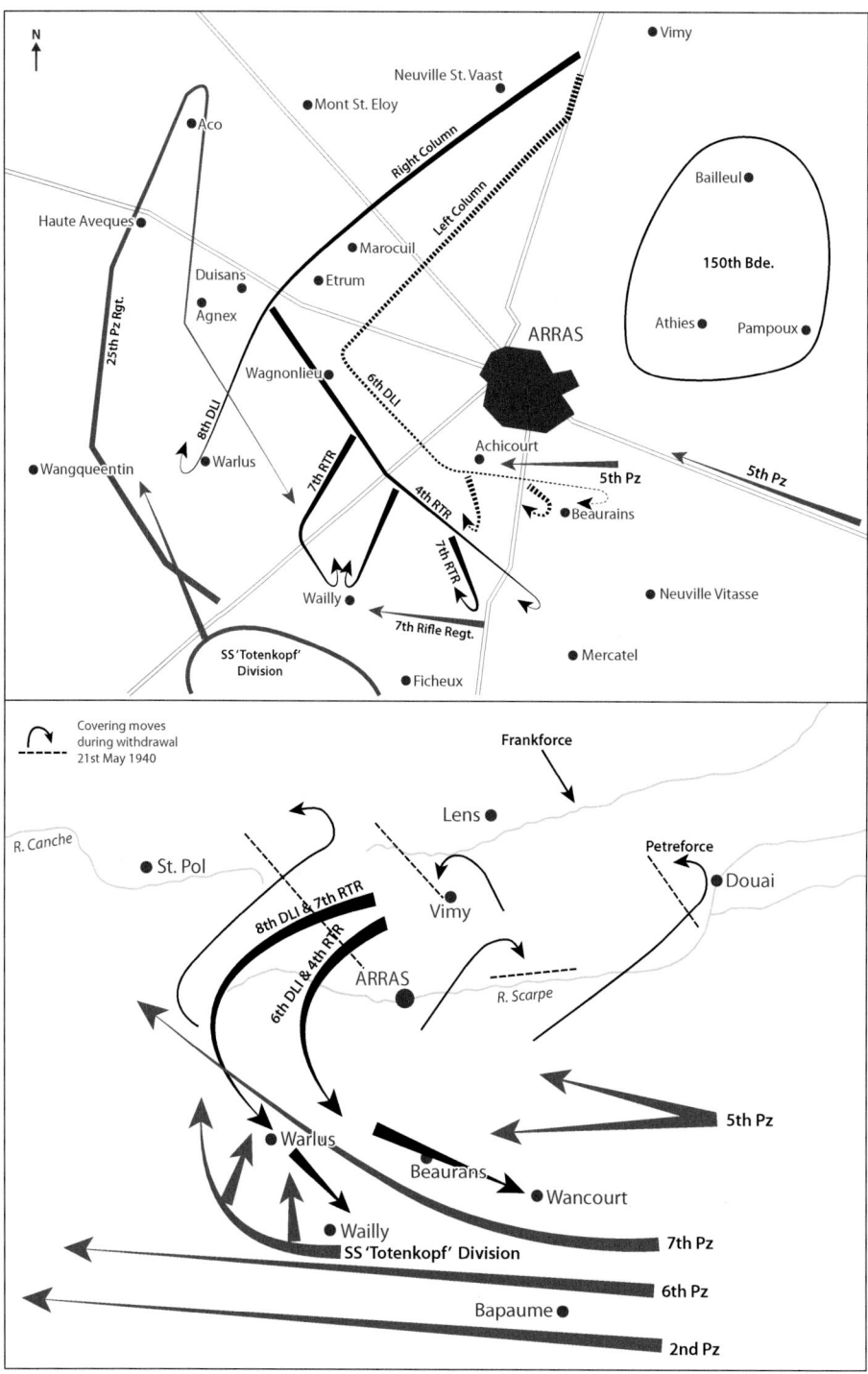

Map 2 The Battle of Arras, 21 May 1940.

This small scale action fought by the British around Arras was meant to ease the enemy pressure on Arras and to delay the German encircling movement round the rear of the British Expeditionary Force. The immediate objective of its first phase was to clear the ground between Arras and the Cojeul River of enemy troops and it had in this a considerable measure of success. The 5th and 7th German Divisions were so busy defending themselves that they could make no concerted attack on Arras that day and Rommel's situation maps show he thought he was under attack from a much larger force of tanks and infantry than those who actually opposed him. On the other hand its immediate objective was bound to fail unless the early successes of the attacking columns could be followed up by a force that was strong enough to occupy and hold such wide a stretch of countryside.

The British inflicted heavy casualties on the German 7th [Ghost] Division: 20 tanks knocked out, 89 men killed, 216 wounded and 173 missing.

The Totenkopf Division must have suffered equally as heavily. Rommel claimed the British force had finally been smashed by the defensive fire of his artillery and anti-aircraft regiments. Looking at his situation maps for that day nothing is more striking than the positions of his artillery units, they were deployed well up with the advanced front line troops and the British formations ran headlong into a gun-line that stretched to the west from Wailly. As Rommel claimed this was indeed the deciding factor in the battle, no comparable support could be provided by the British artillery for their attacking formations.

Troops of the SS Totenkopf Division burying a fallen comrade, Arras, 23 May 1940.

The British casualties were heavy, as is to be expected when a small force attacks a larger one, the lack of experience in the joint use of infantry and tanks no doubt increased them as there had been no time for careful preparation and there were times throughout the operation when the infantry and tanks were out of touch. Both tank battalions had their commanding officers killed and radio communications in the tanks was poor to useless, when Franklyn realised that the ground taken on the first day could not be held and that the enemy was continuing to work round his right flank in great strength, he decided that the operation must be abandoned.

The close and effective collaboration between German land and air forces was exemplified at Arras and the German infantry called in numerous bombing attacks to aid them before they pressed forward. It was very different on the British side as there was no air formation that Franklyn could call upon at short notice to support his troops in action. On 21 May, 57 Blenheims of number two group, stationed in England, attacked targets between Arras and the coast four times, by the time the Blenheims appeared their targets were not always easily identified, enemy columns were bombed when they could be picked out from the streams of refugees fleeing in droves before the advancing Germans. The targets for these attacks were selected in England not France, for by now rapid communication with commanders in the field was impossible.

By the night of 21 May German forces had rallied and restored the situation, but the most important effect of this action was to demonstrate to the German high command and to Hitler that their leading panzer divisions were vulnerable. Many German senior commanders felt great unease during and after this action. Von Rundstedt recalled after the war:

> A critical moment in the drive came just as my forces had reached the channel, it was caused by a British counter stroke from Arras towards Cambrai on May 21st. For a short time it was feared that our armoured divisions would be cut off before the infantry could come up to support them. None of the French counter attacks carried any serious threat as this one did.[13]

The war diary of German X1X Corps related how the British counter attack had made the entire Kleist Group nervous, the German army command sent out orders that an attack by Army Group A, in a northerly direction, was out of the question until the infantry divisions had taken the high ground north-west of Arras. Finally the shock of the Arras attack affected Hitler himself, resulting in a new nervousness that was to lead directly to the Germans greatest failure of the campaign in the west. On the allied side the breakdown of the Arras operation convinced Gort that the only remaining hope for the BEF was to fall back on Dunkirk, rather than to fight its way through to the south as Ironside and Churchill had hoped.

The counter attack at Arras did little more than throw the Germans off balance for a while, but the shock it caused has led to much speculation as to what a strong and well-co-ordinated attack could have achieved. However, even if a strong allied punch had been delivered the Germans were strong enough to recover and come on yet again and by 21 May the French Army had lost too much of its striking force to recover. But there can be little doubt as to what Frankforce did achieve, it upset the German timetable regarding the capture of the Channel

---

13   J. Duncan and G. Forty, *The Fall of France* (Kent: Guild Publishing, 1990), p. 66.

Ports and without this the evacuation from Dunkirk would have been impossible. Gort, on his own initiative, decided to attack on 21 May, and on his own initiative ordered the withdrawal on the 23rd that he knew would lead to evacuation. These were far reaching decisions and Gort knew by the 23rd the French Army was finished and that it was now his duty to save the BEF to fight another day. If the BEF had been wiped out in France it is difficult to imagine a way in which Britain could have effectively carried on the fight. The soldiers of the 50th Division fell back to the coast with the enemy hot on their heels.

7

**'Come on lads it's Empire Day'**

---

On 24 May the 50th Division had set up their Headquarters at Loos as the divisional troops pulled back from Arras. Discussions of a new offensive southward were still underway but came to nothing as both time and resources needed for such an undertaking were in short supply. The roads were by now choked with refugees and these long lines of desperate people became easy targets for the marauding German aircraft as they trudged their way through village after village. Many of their heavily loaded carts received direct hits from bombers, after the smoke had cleared and the dead put to one side they would continue out into the open countryside. These unfortunate people were in dire-straights and had started their flight when the Germans had invaded Belgium only to find their way to the south-west blocked by the German breakthrough to the Somme, day after day they sought some small refuge in a world gone mad.

Pte Reg Protheroe, 150 Field Ambulance:

> I can remember being on a road that was packed with long lines of civvies, Gerry dive bombers came screaming down on us, the civvies dived into the fields but a lot of them got killed. When we got back to England nobody would believe us when we told them about it, they couldn't believe Gerry would do such a thing, but we knew better.[1]

Sergeant Arthur Chester, 4th Battalion East Yorkshire Regiment, was caught up in the long civilian columns seeking safety:

> We got mixed up with all the refugees on the road and this was at a time when things were really starting to hot up. On 28th May we was in the full blast of it and we'd been on the march for days. The refugees were a pitiful sight and we were endangering their lives by being among them, we were all fodder for the *Stuka* dive bombers. They had no respect for civilians that got mingled with the troops. There were lines of bodies at the side of the road, it was a terrible sight having to watch civilians strafed.[2]

---

1   Taped interview with author, Reg Protheroe (Hull, 1992).
2   Ibid, with Arthur Chester (Hull, 1994).

On 25 May 151 Brigade were in positions in the Carvin-Provin area and met the enemy there about noon.

Lance Corporal William Ridley, 9th DLI:

> We went into action again at *Provin*, again we got machine gunned and *Stuka*'d to bits, we moved from place to place. They'd say to us 'right we'll make a last stand here' and we'd tense ourselves up, then as soon as it got dark we'd move out, every day we were on a different front. At *Provin* this sergeant comes up to me an he said 'I want you to take that Boyes Anti-tank Rifle and to place it in the middle of the road there' I thought it was a bit of a stupid thing to do like, I don't know if you know anything about a Boyes Anti-tank Rifle, it's supposed to go through a tank, it wouldn't go through a tin of Heinz Beans you know. I said 'what do you want us in the middle of the road for like?' he says 'there's a panzer division coming up there' I says 'just one like?' he says 'oh aye just the one' so I told him where to stick his anti-tank rifle.[3]

L/Cpl William Ridley, 9th Battalion Durham Light Infantry.

As 150 Brigade pulled away from the line of the *Scarpe* and moved in the direction of Lille they were shelled by the German artillery and bombed constantly by the Luftwaffe.

Company Sergeant Major Jim O'grady, 6th Battalion Green Howards:

> In front of my trench a poor lone bird was hopping about, sure I said to the lads, those fucking Bosches are putting so much stuff up there today that even the fucking birds have to come down and walk.[4]

Pte Ron Railton, 5th Battalion Green Howards:

> It was chaos down the ruddy roads, there was all these refugees and of course as soon as Gerry came with his ruddy Stuka's there was chaos, dead horses, women and kids laid all over the place, I never saw owt like it. They shelled us for about 24 hours, in one position, I always remember this officer stood up waving his revolver about and shouting above the din 'come on lads it's Empire Day, don't let them break you'. He was a brave man.[5]

---

3   Ibid, with William Ridley at the Veteran's re-union (Hull, 1993).
4   Manuscript sent to author by John Thompson (Beverley, 1991).
5   Taped interview with author, Ron Railton (Beverley, 1989).

Lance Corporal Kenneth Carver, Royal Army Service Corps, felt for the plight of the refugees:

> The refugees continued to present a very sorry picture indeed. It was heart-rending to see the people with all their worldly belongings on their carts, shoulders, wheelbarrows and perambulators. You had to push these people aside while trying hard not to cause casualties, but invariably you pushed a cart or wheelbarrow into the hedge, and your instructions were to keep going and not to help people at all. It was heart rending. These people were travelling for miles with no food or water and no accommodation. When I finally got home I said to my parents 'If the Germans arrive here stay in the house, you have a roof, you have somewhere to sleep, once you are on the road you haven't got anything at all.[6]

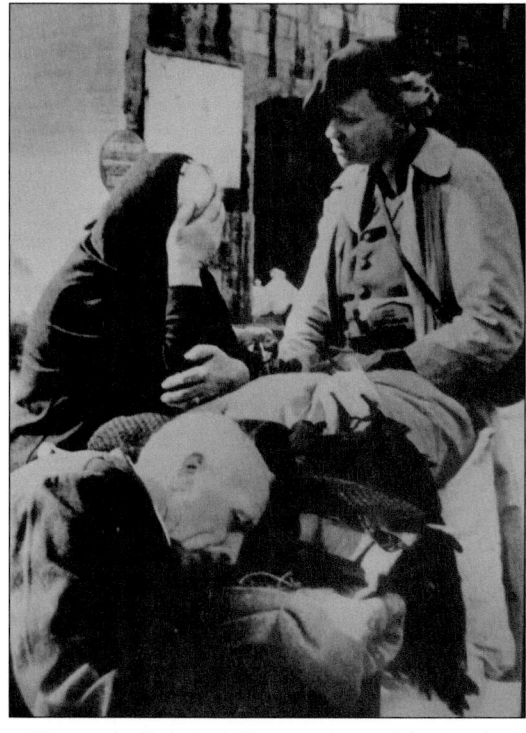

Distraught French civilians on the road fleeing the German assault, May 1940.

Sergeant Max Hearst was given an unusual delicacy on the retreat:

> A woman from a farm called us over and there was these bowls of steaming hot stew and we all dived in. I'm always a nosey so-an-so and I'm looking out of the house across the field, there was a bloody great big horse with its feet in the air and a great lump cut out of its behind. I said 'Madame?' and pointed at the dead horse, she said 'oui oui'. I said 'oh lovely', it didn't bother me, the lads said 'what you on about Butch?' I said 'we've just had horse meat stew' and at least one of them threw up.[7]

On 26 May General Martel ordered all units of the 50th Division to retreat in the general direction of Ypres.

Pte Thomas Maher, 6th DLI:

> We pulled back from Carvin and arrived at a village near Lens that had been badly knocked about, we all settled down for some bully beef and cocoa. Me and my mate thought we would have a look around. There was this hall opposite us and it had been bombed, there

---

6    Manuscript sent to author by Kenneth Carver (1989).
7    Taped interview with author, Max Hearst (Hull, 1991).

was bodies just lying about the place, but it didn't seem to bother you because you didn't have to be in action long before you was in a wild sort of state.[8]

Lance Corporal William Ridley, 9th DLI, was with a section whose job it was to look for casualties that could be saved:

> During an air-raid we went down into the cellar of a house for half an hour and when we came out a sergeant told us to look for any casualties. We found one officer who wasn't dead, but as we lifted him onto a truck his back fell away. I went over to another lad who was down on one knee with his rifle in his hand, 'are you alright son' I asked. He was motionless and as I touched him he fell over. One body was lying face up with tin hat and pack on, his rifle in the crook of his arm, you'd think he was lying to attention. There was another one we couldn't move, so we went to one of the houses and took a window shutter to use as a stretcher. We tried to lift him onto it but when we lifted the top part the bottom part stayed where it was. It was only the buttons of his battle-dress and his pants that were keeping his body together. I went to lift what I thought was the end of the shutter, but it was the bone of his leg. That's the only time I felt as though I was going to be sick. We took and did with him what we did with all the others, we dug a hole in someone's garden and tipped them all in.[9]

Captain John Charles Austin, Y Battery, Royal Artillery, passed through Carvin at night and saw a sight that made his blood run cold:

> On to Carvin and here another petrifying horror, one of those appalling spectacles that, like the shambles in our Vimy gun-pits, strikes the heart cold, something transcending even the normal imagined horrors of war. Behind some railings in the main street stood a red brick convent school that had been badly bombed and spread out on the wide white pavement in front were the bodies of six victims, all girls between the ages of 15 and 17. The corpses had been arranged in regular rows, one behind the other on the broad flags. There they lay rigid and motionless in the moonlight staring up at the sky, exactly like a company that had formed fours and then fallen down flat on their backs. The mathematical precision of the arrangement added to the terror of the scene, to heighten the horrible, inhuman aspect of this pavement mortuary the faces, bare arms and legs were discoloured by a ghastly mauve tint, probably the result of shock or bomb blast.[10]

Sergeant William Bush, Royal Army Medical Corps:

> We was in a school near Lens and it was here we set up a dressing station, on the flat roof was a make shift massive red cross. German and British wounded started to trickle in and Stukas used the red cross as a marker and bombed the hell out of us. The Stukas used to

---

8 G Purdon, *From Coalfield to Battlefield* (Durham: County Durham Springboard Media Project, 1995), p. 82.
9 Taped interview with author, William Ridley at the Veteran's re-union (Hull, 1993).
10 J. C. Austin, *Return via Dunkirk* (London: Hodder and Stoughton, 1940), p. 46.

scream as they came down and so did their bombs, they were part of Hitler's psychological warfare, they made an eerie and very frightening howling sound. During one raid I had a mess tin of chicken and rice, I raced down a passage and jumped down a whole flight of stairs, I didn't spill one drop of food though.[11]

The men of the 5th Green Howards spent a gruesome night in Lens before moving to Ypres, the city had received much attention from the enemy and there had been no time to bury the dead, the weary troops were just glad of a place to grab a few hours precious sleep.
Pte John Thompson:

The dead were laid out in the street as there had been a lot of bombing and shelling. We were so tired we just lay down beside them and went to sleep. When it was time to get up the officer kicked us and we were off again.[12]

The 50th Division pressed on to Ypres, arriving there at dawn on 27 May, the men were now marching over ground hallowed in British military history, known to all troops as the Ypres Salient. That bloody battle ground where their fathers had fought in the Great War and was now dotted with cemeteries. As the young men of the 50th passed them their significance was not lost on them.

The retreat to Ypres was not a peaceful affair, the enemy constantly probed the British rearguard units and harassed them from the air, as the 8th DLI reached Campin the Germans began to break through the French to their front and engaged the Durhams. Troop movements and hoards of refugees blocked up parts of the roads for hours amid great confusion.

Pte Thomas Maher found it impossible to get his ambulance through the mass of refugees:

I was driving an ambulance as we were getting towards Armentiers and the roads was crammed with people, there was these French horse drawn wagons and they were holding everybody up, it was chaotic and we was there three hours. There was a Frenchman with his pistol out and he was shouting at these others, traffic was coming this way and traffic was coming that way, so we just pulled into the roadside. There was rifle fire in the distance, then machine guns, these Frenchmen pulled their horses into this field at the finish, somebody shouted 'motor-bikes!' so we got away quick. There was two roads to take, we bore left, the tracer bullets were flying overhead and a hell of a lot of firing was going on, because when there was motor-bikes tanks weren't far behind. Anyhow those Frenchmen copt it. We got through Armentiers, it was getting Stuka'd to hell, and we were back to more or less where we started.[13]

On 27 May 150 Brigade was at Ypres and were digging in in front of the Menin Gate and along its ramparts, Sergeant Les Hilton was near this famous monument when one of his comrades called him over:

---

11   Taped interview with author, William Bush at the Veteran's re-union (Hull, 1993).
12   Ibid, with John Thompson (Beverley, 1991).
13   G. Purdon, *From Coalfield to Battlefield* (Durham: County Durham Springboard Media Project, 1995), p. 67.

My mate shouted of me to come over and see all the names inside the war memorial, there was row upon row of them and as I browsed through them what a surprise I got, there was my dad's name, he was killed in the first war in 1915 at Zonnebeke serving with the same unit I was in then. It really made me think.[14]

The troops worked hard preparing their defensive positions as an attack was expected at any time, during the day of the 27th, before 151 Brigade was in position, the Germans launched an assault on Ypres. Under the command of Brigadier Haydon 150 Brigade met the enemy with resolution.

Pte Wilfred Mooney, 4th Battalion East Yorkshire Regiment:

> We was in a farm house when we spotted Gerry motor-cyclists, we had the first shot at them. We had a machine gun in the corner manned by a bloke called Richards. It got a bit hot and we were told to withdraw so we came out, a Captain Sharp saw us and said 'fix your bayonets and go back' so we did. I got an eight stone bag of flour and put it against the window and I had my position there, the Germans still had tattie mashers, [stick grenades], you know and was lobbing them at us. I could see their square helmets as they crouched down behind a wall. The officer, Mr Richards, passed me on the stairs, went outside and was hit at once, a lad called Penrose brought him back, by that time three more had been killed. I got shot then, I don't remember much more except I was laid against Captain Rogers. I heard a scuffle outside, the Germans was firing at these medical people, a sergeant called Spooner said 'we're in trouble here' because by now Gerry was firing shells at us.[15]

Pte Wilf Mooney, 4th Battalion East Yorkshire Regiment.

Sergeant Herbert Glenton remembers that day well as he directed the fire of his section upon the enemy, as the battle raged he saw one incident that made his blood boil:

> My section, of which I was then corporal was on the ramparts of the Menin Gate itself, I well remember two soldiers being shot by snipers as they crossed the road not far from us. Our Red Cross men were going to pick them up and if ever I saw an atrocity during the war I saw it then when they shot the two Red Cross people who were only trying to do their job and were no threat to them. We found out the house the snipers was in, we had an anti-tank gun and we pumped shells into the house until there was nothing left of it or them.[16]

---

14  Taped interview with author. Les Hilton. Hull 1987.
15  Ibid, with Wilf Mooney (Hull, 1990).
16  Manuscript sent to author by Herbert Glenton (Hull, 1991).

Henri Braem was a Belgian civilian and was watching the troops of the 50th Division as they repelled German attacks:

> The 50th British Division had been in our area, they had been in the bitter fighting around Arras and arrived in the Zillebeke, Hollebeke and Houthem area of Ypres during 25/26th May. They were attacked by elements of the German 6th Army. The British used the natural defence lines in our area, Hill 60, Hill 62, the Ypres-Comines railway line and the canal alongside it. The main German assault on Monday 27th May went in under a heavy barrage, they advanced from Zillebeke Green and Hill 60 against the railway line. The British slaughtered them and each time the German attack was renewed the British shot them down from their good defensive positions. Although the British were without food, exhausted and outnumbered they held to the last.[17]

151 Brigade arrived at Poperinge on the night of 27 May to take up their defensive positions and play their part in the defence of Ypres, during the retreat the Durham's had been harassed constantly by the enemy and all men had tales to tell of near misses.

Sergeant George Denis Elliot, 6th DLI, was trying to move his men on the packed roads when they were attacked by aircraft:

> We arrived at a small village with a line of three ton trucks, the roads were packed with refugees and they refused point blank to get off the road. I told the first truck to turn right and go through a field to get to the other side of the village, it only got 30 yards when Gerry opened up on it with his machine guns. The drivers turned round and headed for cover under some trees, all the men were told to leave their trucks if the Germans attacked and to shelter in this nearby stream that had high banks. I went over to speak to the refugees again and ask them to clear the road but they wouldn't budge, with that there was a whine of aircraft engines, this signalled an attack, they roared down machine gunning and bombing the line of the road. One woman stood with a tiny baby paralysed, my mate and I went to ground, when we saw her he ran, grabbed the baby off her and threw it at me like a rugby ball, I caught the baby and he brought the woman. As we got down bullets flew just above our heads. The transport that was full of ammunition was hit and burst into flames, the lads grabbed fire extinguishers and tried to put the fires out, under one truck we could see someone trapped, when he was dragged out it was obvious he was dead, riddled with bullets.[18]

To the south of Ypres the Germans were reported to have infiltrated the British line and Brigadier Haydon, CO 150 Brigade, put in an urgent request for a reserve unit to stem any German advance here. The 8th DLI moved forward to occupy the high ground at Dikkebus, scene of much bitter fighting in the Great War, and was heavily shelled by the German artillery but did not suffer a major assault. Even so the day was not without incident.

Lance Corporal Harry Moss, 8th DLI, spent his 20th birthday in action:

---

17 P. Delaforce, *Monty's Northern Legions* (Barnsley: Sutton Publishing, 2004), p. 7.
18 Taped interview with author, George Denis Elliot (Durham, 1994).

I had my 20th Birthday on the battlefield, 28th May 1940, we were holed up in a barn, an old hay loft with half the tiles off the roof. There were cornfields to the front with quite high corn, there was a cow in the field and we were watching that instead of watching for the Germans, they was creeping through the corn. We thought it was over quiet so we fired into the cornfield and the cow went down with the first shot. Anyroad the firing flushed Gerry out, they were there right enough, there was four in the cornfield, well I just give them 10 rounds rapid fire, my rifle bolt was fair fleeing. This German went down badly wounded and he was crying for his mother, *mutter-mutter*. Well we'd got the first of them but they homed in on us quick enough, well we knew what was coming by then and had just got out of the back of the hay loft when it got ripped apart by Gerry heavy machine gun fire.[19]

On 28 May the Germans resumed their attacks on the 150 Brigade front. At midday the whole 50th Division was ordered to pull back to a position between Poperinge and Elverdinghe. The attacking German forces wasted no time and quickly moved in to close quarters as 150 Brigade tried to disengage for the move out of Ypres.

Sergeant Bill Pexton, 4th Battalion East Yorkshire Regiment, was taken prisoner and was expecting to be executed on the spot:

Refugees were still coming through from somewhere. Saw two men running down the road, refugees said they were parachutists. Captain Martin and myself called on them to halt but they didn't, not immediately, we took aim and dropped them both. They were dead when we got to them. At 10:00 a. m. the fun began, Germans came from nowhere, properly surprised us. Got down to it in the open and fought for all we knew how. Thought we were getting wiped out this time alright, got out of the farm buildings and he's sending everything he has at us. At 11:00 a. m. still holding out and there's a bit of a lull. Kid on my right will keep sticking his head up above the clover, he's sure to get his soon I'm thinking. Can't remember much about the next hour but I remember the order to cease fire and that the time was 12 o'clock. Stood up and put my hands up, my God how few of us stood up. A German officer came over and spoke in English, told to pick up the wounded and carry them to the road, there aren't many that need carrying and we had to leave our dead. Took us off the road into another field, I expected my last moments had come and lit a fag, everyone expected to be shot there and then. Patched up our wounded as best we could and we were taken back about two miles.[20]

Captain F W Chadwick, 5th Battalion Green Howards, was also taken prisoner:

I led my own small party in the direction of Lille, the Germans seemed to be all around us and after a while we were put in the bag. I was taken to Lille and questioned by a German intelligence officer who told me he had been a professor of history at Oxford. After being grilled for some time he gave up trying to get any information out of me and said 'you will

---

19 G. Purdon, *From Coalfield to Battlefield* (Durham: County Durham Springboard Media Project, 1995), p. 70.
20 Manuscript sent to author by Bill Pexton (1989).

be taken to Germany where you will have a very good time and be returned to England in September when the war is over', to this I replied 'surely as a Professor of History you must know that the English always win the last battle', the German officer laughed and said 'as a matter of fact you are right, but this is the exception that proves the rule.[21]

Corporal Albert Snowdon:

Corporal Albert Snowdon, 5th Battalion Green Howards.

I was ordered out of my nice safe cellar as I was to take a message to Company HQ, when I got there I found they'd had a direct hit, the company batman was killed, there was a chap called Arthur Howey from Market Weighton, he was killed, the quartermaster had both legs blown off and the company commander had a bad wound on his leg. We didn't know what was happening, it was chaos.[22]

As the last troops of 150 Brigade pulled out of positions in and around the Menin Gate they had to run the gauntlet of heavy machine-gun and rifle fire, their dead comrades littered the ground around their positions and many German dead lay before them, bearing witness to the dogged defence they had put up at Ypres.

Corporal Sidney Atkinson, 4th Battalion East Yorkshire Regiment, was in a position near the entrance to the Menin Gate:

You could see tracer bullets hitting the road and bouncing off, Captain Fields came across, we were in a square next to a church, he said 'come on Sid we're off' and these bullets was bouncing about all over the place, he was a brave man. The kid I was with got panicky a bit because he'd seen these tracer rounds going right across us and clean through the Menin Gate. There was chaps being killed in that church yard, as our carrier left I feel certain we run over one, but you don't think about that, you've got to get away.[23]

The Allied Armies now cut off in the north were falling back closer and closer to the coast and Bock's infantry put them under ever increasing pressure. On 25 May the Belgian line gave way in the centre with no reserves to stem the tide. They were hemmed in on a narrow strip of land that was packed with refugees and with their backs to the sea. Later that same day King Leopold sued for an armistice, it came into effect the following morning, Churchill asked the Belgians to sacrifice themselves and fight on, but the encircled Belgians, who were already aware the BEF was preparing to evacuate, were not prepared to do this. Nor did King Leopold take Churchill's advice and escape himself, but felt he must stay with his people and his army to the end. In the long term this may not have been the wisest decision, but seen in the light of the

21  Ibid, by F. W. Chadwick (1991).
22  Taped interview with author, Albert Snowdon (Beverley, 1992).
23  Ibid, with Sid Atkinson (Hull, 1989).

dire circumstances of that time his actions were an honourable choice. The British withdrawal to the coast now became a race to evacuate before the German trap could snap shut.

Later in the day of 28 May the 50th Division took up new positions, the enemy did not follow up the withdrawal that night but were probing the line by the afternoon of the 29th. The 8th DLI was to join the new defensive line at 9:00 p.m. but 30 minutes before they were due to leave the Germans began to bombard them with artillery and mortar-fire and a heavy attack was launched against C company, the momentum of the attack carried the Germans around the flanks of the hapless Tommies and their line of retreat was swiftly cut. All night the men of C Company fought on against vastly superior numbers until they were finally overrun.

Pte Frank Galloway, 8th DLI, was taken prisoner:

> Gerry came at us in large numbers with a number of tanks, there was all kinds of shit flying about, tracers cut through the night air and we was firing at anything that moved. The German tanks just knocked down houses near us and the next thing I knew there was this big explosion and I was knocked senseless, that was the last I knew of it, next day we was in the bag.[24]

Lance Corporal Joss Little, 8th DLI, and his mate got out by the skin of their teeth:

> Moppy Armstrong goes into this house, takes his gear off and gets into this bed, I says 'Moppy if we've got to get out of here in a hurry you'll be caught with your pants down'. We'd been there two hours when Gerry came, I says 'get out, away man, move Gerries coming'. He says 'eh what? Oh man I need rest'. I says 'Gerry will find you if you don't move, he's coming in the top end of the village and we're going out the bottom'. He got his clothes on, I've never seen anybody put them on so sharp in all my days, he was still lacing his boots up in the back of the truck.[25]

The German follow up was swift and as the carriers of the 8th DLI pulled out of the village of Woesten German vehicles were moving in at the other end. The whole division now headed for the Dunkirk perimeter, all the time being pressed by the enemy forces and continually harassed by mortar fire, shell fire and Stuka raids. The British forces trudged along roads hopelessly congested with army transports, horsed and motor, and civilian traffic of every kind. In the distance Dunkirk was a mass of flames, burning oil tanks emitted dense black clouds of smoke that billowed high in the sky.

Major Cheeseman, 74th Field Regiment, Royal Artillery, told his men to destroy their trucks and guns before they retreated:

> I spent hours collecting my men together, they were all over the place, jammed on the roads, destroying their equipment. When we finally moved off we found ourselves at the head of a nose to tail column in an eight cwt truck when I saw a Stuka dive at us out of the clouds. I told the driver to keep his eyes on the road, not to look at anything else. I saw the

---

24  Manuscript sent to author by Frank Galloway (Durham, 1990).
25  G. Purdon, *From Coalfield to Battlefield* (Durham: County Durham Springboard Media Project, 1995), p. 70

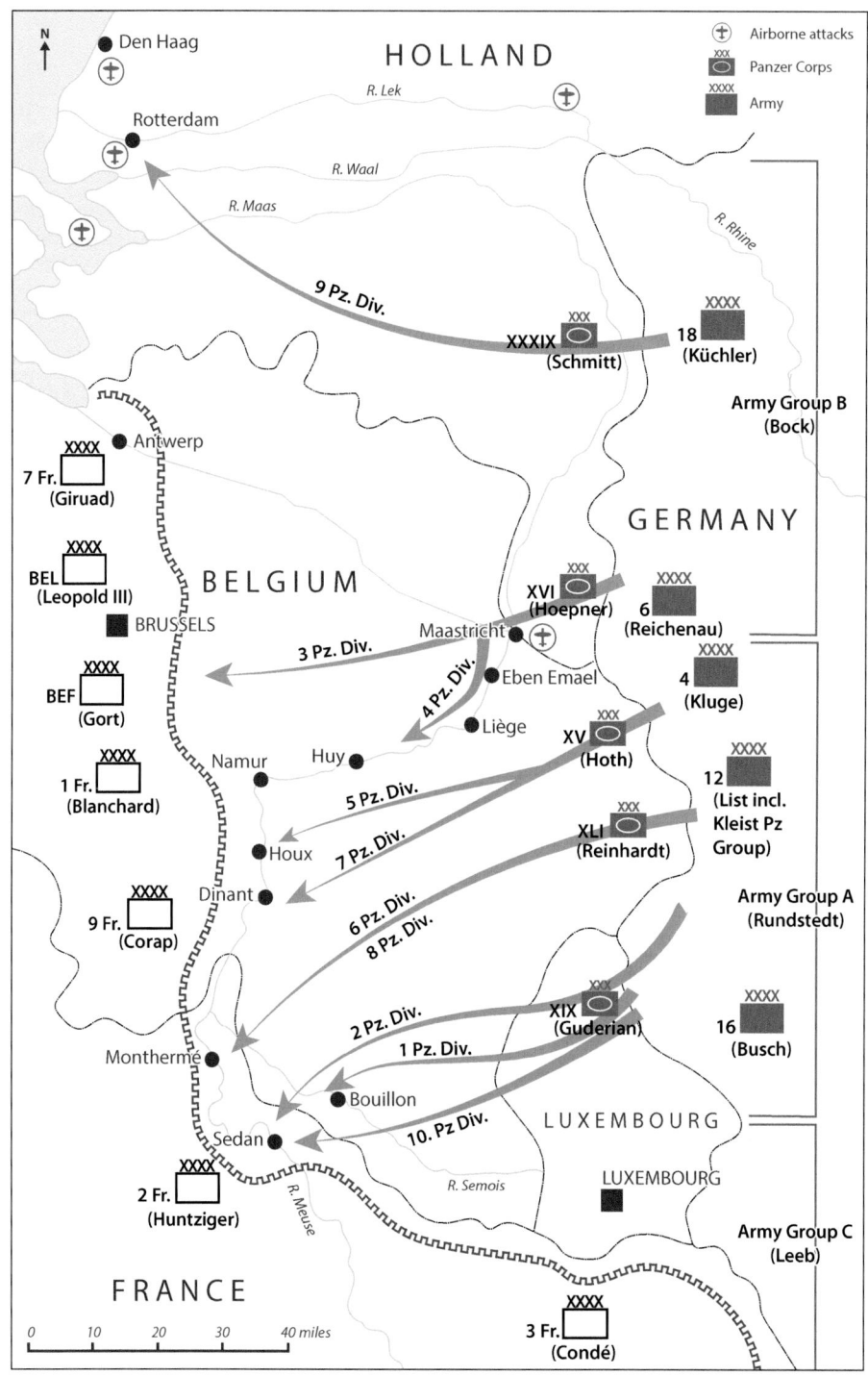

Map 3  The German plan of attack 1940.

Stukas bomb doors open and the bombs dropping straight for us. One came down and hit the ground just 10 yards on our right, I watched it fascinated, we were all going to be blown to pieces. Then a funny thing happened, the bomb just didn't go off, from that day on I was never frightened of bombs. The Germans didn't only drop bombs, they also peppered us with leaflets that tried to appeal to the British cricketing fraternity, it said; 'The game is up, the innings is over! There is no alternative but to surrender', that gave us a bit of a laugh.[26]

Captain John Charles Austin, Y Battery, Royal Artillery, and his men came under attack from German fighters as they tried to get to Dunkirk:

About a mile and a half from the area that was to be occupied by our gun positions two French tanks were drawn up stationary at the roadside near a small copse. As I approached five Messerschmitt fighters wheeled around in the sky one behind the other in preparation to attack them. The tanks had also seen the planes and were just closing their turrets, I guessed what was coming their way and hoped to get passed in time to avoid getting a share of it but it was too late. Just as I came abreast of the tanks the first plane was beginning its dive right overhead, 'Jump for it' I yelled. I shot out of one side of the truck as my driver and radio operator took a headlong leap out of the other. I scrambled into a hedgeless ditch by the roadside just as the German machine-guns began to spray the roadside, my ditch was so shallow that I could only partly conceal my head and bullets whizzed in front of my face. When they smacked the dry earth at the edge of the ditch puffs of dust spurted up half blinding me, every now and then a bullet flew so close the blast hit me in the face like a punch, I touched myself to see if I had been wounded and was quite surprised not to see blood on my hand. For nearly 10 minutes the fight went on, the planes circling about 100 feet up and the tanks firing back at them with their heavy machine-guns. When silence came I poked my head up gingerly out of the ditch, 'Williams! Simson! are you alright?' I called to my two men. 'yes sir' came back the welcome answer in muffled tones, but there was no sign of them anywhere. Shaking the dust out of my eyes and ears I walked back to the truck, Williams and Simson suddenly wriggled out on their bellies like eels from underneath one of the tanks, they had crawled in between the tracks with only a foot of space to do it in. 'Suppose the tank had moved on?' I said with a shudder, 'we didn't have time to think about that sir'. When we came to examine the truck we realised our luck was in, it was riddled with bullets, in the splinter proof glass of the windscreen there were 13 holes.[27]

Lt Douglas King, 4th Battalion East Yorkshire Regiment, recalled the chaos of the retreat:

We had no maps, only knew we were heading for the coast and that was it. Civilians with cattle and carts were going along this road, as were other units, but I can't remember ever seeing an officer senior to myself. Nobody seemed to know what was going on, eventually we came to a wood and there were a few military policemen who guided you. I lost contact

---

26 Manuscript sent to author by Mr Cheeseman (1897).
27 J. C. Austin, *Return via Dunkirk* (London: Hodder and Stoughton, 1940), p. 37.

with my platoon sergeant major and never saw any of the men from the battalion, dawn was breaking and we all got a hot cup of tea, tea had never tasted so good. There didn't appear to be anybody in charge of what was going on, it was quite worrying.[28]

Sergeant Max Hearst was a bit of a joker and came very close to being shot by his own side:

> We had no grub and was starving, when we found a bunch of abandoned wagons we went through them looking for food. I tipped out one kit bag and in it was a French dress uniform, one of the lads says 'what you gonna do with that Hearsty'? So I tries on the hat and coat, I'm going to the lads 'Parlez-vous Anglais?' and they're saying 'shut up you soft bastard'. With that a voice shouts out 'yer French thieving bastard' followed by a click as a rifle bolt is pushed home. I looked up and it was a sergeant major from another unit about to put a bloody round through me, one of our lads yells out 'don't it's just one of our blokes buggering about'. Well did he give me what for, he told me exactly what he thought of me, called me all the useless bastards under the sun and how close I had come to being shot on the spot.[29]

Captain Douglas King, 4th Battalion East Yorkshire Regiment.

Sergeant Bob Gibson, MM, 151 Provost Company:

> It was a rough time the retreat to Dunkirk, I was travelling with a group of military police on motor-bikes, shells were dropping all around the area, we pulled into the yard of a farmhouse and as we got off our bikes one dropped right in the middle of us, hit the RSM and splashed a few of us. We got the wounded into a cellar, I always remember one lad who got hit, they called him Pete Gravill, the shrapnel had torn his arm away and later I found he had a shrapnel wound in his chest which I didn't spot at the time. I don't know if he lived.[30]

Sergeant Bob Gibson, MM, 151 Brigade Provost Company.

28  Taped interview with author, Douglas King (Hull, 1993).
29  Ibid, with Max Hearst (Hull, 1990).
30  Ibid, with Bob Gibson (Hull, 1994).

Lt Colonel Peter J Jeffries, 6th DLI, had his car shot up by German tanks as he headed for the rear:

> The movement back was fraught with difficulty. On my way from Armentieres I was in an unarmed vehicle and I found myself suddenly shot at by some guns which whistled over the car. I told the driver to go faster which he did, only to find some German tanks coming towards us. We jumped out of the car, threw ourselves into a ditch, and hoped for the best. Three tanks came on, as well as some others to our right which put five shells into the car and then moved on. This left me, my driver and the orderly room sergeant on our feet and miles from the Berques Canal. These tanks had just broken through at random, when we walked further up the road we found a battalion of the Sussex Regiment which had been very severely handled by the tanks. They had just driven up the road firing their heavy machine-guns and had inflicted the most dreadful casualties. There were men with terrible wounds lying about the road sides crying out for water and there was nothing we could do. The situation was fairly depressing but by extraordinary luck I came on a vehicle with a sapper captain, and I told him I'd had my car shot up and that I must get to the Burgues Canal. To his eternal credit he agreed to lend me his pick-up.[31]

Sergeant Arthur Chester:

> We weren't told where we were going now, on the roads everything was a shambles, then there was trucks burning and ammunition dumps had gone up. Cattle in the fields had been left by the farmers, their milk sacks were at bursting point. There was trucks and guns all over in the ditches and mingled in with this was the 4th East Yorks. We got orders to make a stand in these fields, the sole object was to sacrifice us to enable the others to get off the beaches at Dunkirk, but soon we was told to fall back again and off we went.[32]

Lance Corporal William Ridley was with the 9th DLI and came in for a hard time as the enemy infantry closed with his unit, his memories of those days are clear and precise and even amid such confusion and chaos the bravery of men around him stands out like a beacon:

> I went into this house with a bunch of Northumberland Fusiliers and this officer says 'I don't want bloody DLI's, I want machine gunners' and just as he said that there was a great explosion and the bloody cottage went up. A lump of shrapnel must have scalped the officer we'd been talking to, his hair was hit from the back and it covered his face, just like a wig. He just pushed it back into place and carried on, I couldn't believe my eyes.
> 
> We walked along the road and I came to our second in command, Major Battiscombe, he was lying down. I says to him 'do you mind if I join you sir' he says 'I'd be glad of your company son'. Up to that time I was never so terrified in all my life, I never used to pray to get us out, I used to pray for courage, please don't let us show how frightened I am like. Once I met Major Battiscombe I was never frightened again, that man he answered my

---

31  H. Moses, *The Faithful Sixth* (Durham: County Durham Books, 1995), p. 138.
32  Taped interview with author, Arthur Chester (Hull, 1992).

prayers and we lay there for about half-an-hour and got mortared. I can tell you now there was one shell went off and I thought Batty had got it like, because he never moved. I said 'are you alright sir'? he said 'yes I'm alright son' when I looked there was a hole not two yards away from our feet.[33]

As the troops continued their slog to the coast enemy snipers picked off men from hidden locations, some of the snipers were fifth columnists, others were German soldiers. Pte Max Hearst and his comrades came under sniper fire as they retreated:

Major C R Battiscombe, 9th Battalion Durham Light Infantry.

I'd had a bit of luck and had won myself a horse and as the others foot slogged their way to the coast I was riding, I passed my mate, Tiny Johnson, who complained about the wasps buzzing around him, I soon realised what was going on and as I dived off the horse I shouted to him you daft bugger it's bullets we're being sniped at. We gets into a ditch and signals for help and along comes a CSM, we pin-pointed this chap and he was behind an old tractor in the corner of a field, we opened fire with brens and rifles but couldn't dislodge him. One bloke says 'I'll sort him out' and he came up with an anti-tank rifle, it went straight through the tractor and through the bloke. When we found him it was a German in civvies, he was searched and we found his Wermacht identification.[34]

Sergeant Leonard Howard, 201st Field Company, Royal Engineers, ran the gauntlet of machine-gun fire as he and his mates tried to cross a road:

We had to cross between two buildings and the Germans had got the road covered with enfilade fire. Only one person could cross the road at a time and you had to pick your spot and take your chance. I crossed behind driver Wheeler and when he was some eight feet in front of me machine-gun fire hit him in the stomach, I had no option but to hold back my run across the road but would try to drag him to safety when I could. As I almost got to him a further burst of fire took the top of his head off right in front of me. Had it not been for him I would have caught that burst. I always think that poor Wheeler, who'd had it anyway, saved my life.[35]

The British Expeditionary Force was now in headlong retreat to the coast, amongst this great throng the men of the 50th Division trudged along doing their best to stay with their units.

33 Ibid, with William Ridley (Durham, 1993).
34 Ibid, with Max Hearst (Hull, 1990).
35 Ibid, with Leonard Howard (1989).

None broke into panic and their discipline held through the most trying of times. Men speak of how their training helped them cope and others speak of the importance of comradeship and the leadership of their officers and NCOs. After the many grim events that had befallen the troops of the 50th and after all the losses and horrors they had seen their fighting spirit was unbroken. It was a tribute to the traditions of the Territorial Army that they had performed so well in battle and to the stoic fighting qualities of the British Tommy.

8

# The Road to Dunkirk

On 20 May 1940 Churchill had given his approval for steps to be taken for the assembly of a large number of small vessels to be prepared to proceed to the French coast with the intention of rescuing stragglers of the BEF who may get cut off. This was to be named Operation Dynamo and sea transport officers from Harwich to Weymouth were ordered to list all ships of up to 1,000 tons. The situation deteriorated rapidly in the days that followed and it soon became obvious that Dunkirk was going to be the only possible route of escape open to the beleaguered BEF.

Operation Dynamo was put into operation on 26 May before even the cabinet had authorised the evacuation, it was expected 45,000 troops would be brought away in two days, only a fraction of the total numbers of the British Expeditionary Force. By the night of 28 May only 25,000 had been landed in England, it was fortunate indeed that the period of grace turned out to be much longer than expected. In the first five days the evacuation was slowed down by an insufficiency of small boats to ferry the men from the beaches to the larger transports waiting off shore, the Admiralty now made strenuous efforts to provide and man them, naval personnel were reinforced by a host of civilians, fishermen and anyone who had any experience of handling boats.

The first heavy air attacks on Dunkirk came on 29 May, it was only by chance the harbour had not been blocked with sunken ships, if this had happened it would have been a catastrophe for the BEF as the

German infantry marching along the sun lit roads of France, May 1940.

majority of troops were embarked from the harbour and less than one third from the beaches. During the three days that followed the air attacks increased and were a severe strain on the waiting troops. The most damage was done at sea where six destroyers, eight personnel ships and over 200 small craft were lost out of a total of 860 British and Allied vessels employed in Operation Dynamo. The German navy, thankfully, made little attempt to interfere in events but most of the air attacks went in unopposed as the hard pressed RAF, operating from the south of England, could not maintain anything like adequate air cover.

The weather had stayed fine and up to 30 May 126,000 British troops had got away and all the rest of the BEF had arrived within the Dunkirk perimeter. The perimeters defence against the encircling enemy advance became much stronger as a result. During the night of 29 May the 50th Division followed the 5th Division into the bridge-head along the Bergues-Furnes Canal. Divisional HQ was established at Adinerke shortly after midnight, with 150 Brigade's right flank on the frontier and 151 Brigade near Bulskamp. The enemy forces closed up on 30 May and began to probe the outer perimeter with light attacks, 200 of the Grenadier Guards were placed under the orders of the 50th's command to help deal with these attacks. The 2nd Northumberland Fusiliers and the 4th Gordon Highlanders, although seriously under strength, also swelled the divisional ranks at this time and fought alongside 151 and 150 Brigades.

Lt Colonel Peter J Jeffries, 6th DLI, was at 6th Battalion Head Quarters when they were spotted by the German artillery:

> We took up our positions on the Furnes Canal with our HQ close to Brigade HQ at Moeres Chateau, Brigade HQ was in the dining room of this Chateau, there were some steps at the end of the office to the cellars and we could hear the farmer's women weeping. Well we had a very unsettling day defending what was the Furnes Canal. The other battalions were also adjacent to the Moeres Chateau, it wasn't tactically very sensible because the German OP [observation post] soon spotted that this Chateau was the centre of communications. There was another battalion attached to the brigade, 3rd Battalion Grenadier Guards, which helped a bit. During the afternoon the Chateau became a target and drew a tremendous amount of artillery fire, I moved my small headquarters out considerably to the right hand side, the shells continued to fall around the Chateau grounds and did a lot of damage. Brigade HQ had a terrible time.[1]

Lt Ian R English, MC and bar, 8th DLI, found the enemy had moved uncomfortably close:

> The first time we knew we were nearly surrounded was at a place called Steenvoorde. We took up positions in a field facing east and we were suddenly fired upon from the west. The next day, 29th May, the brigade withdrew to Woesten, where we were one of the forward battalions. Once again the carrier platoon was sent forward to be the eyes in front and a light screen. Eventually the enemy came up as expected and I withdrew the carrier platoon back to the battalion and from there we were ordered back to the Dunkirk perimeter. Just as we were doing this the Germans attacked and there was tremendous shelling and mortaring, an infantry attack worked its way round us and more or less surrounded our C

---

1  H. Moses, *The Faithful Sixth* (Durham: County Durham Books, 1995), p. 146.

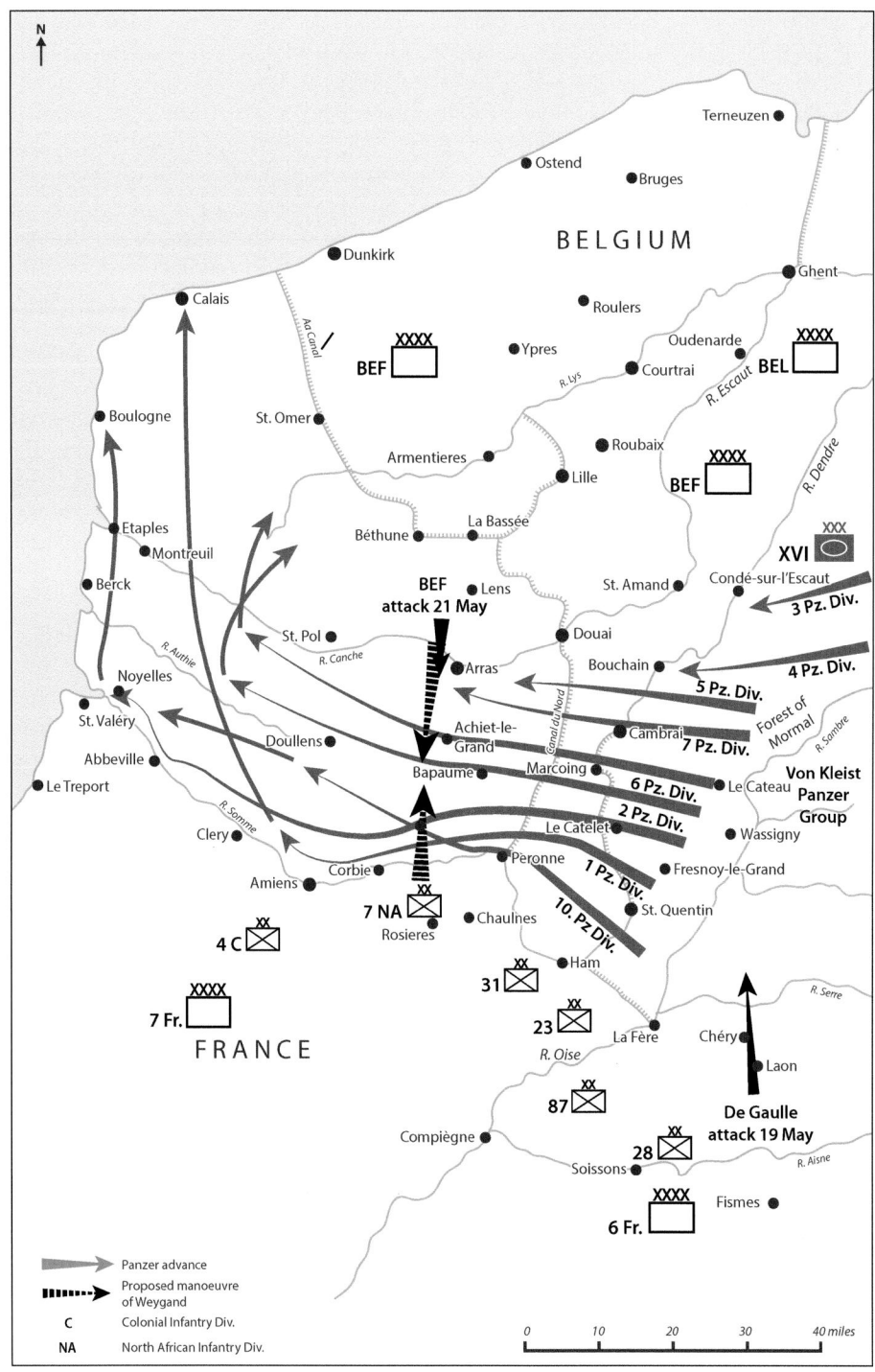

Map 4 The Panzer Corridor, 18 to 21 May 1940.

Company. The majority of them, those that weren't wounded, were taken prisoner, so we lost the majority of one company in one action. At Les Moeres we were told to destroy our vehicles, which seemed the most terrible order. One could see the reason for it later on, Dunkirk was so crowded with troops of every sort that the number of vehicles in the bridge-head had to be kept down to a minimum. The carriers were spared, so we had them with us until we got to the beaches.[2]

Major William Burdon-Taylor, DLI:

The 16 men I had with me had about one cigarette left apiece, they would stop for a few puffs, stub out their cigarettes and march on again. Suddenly we came across a NAFFI truck which had been bombed, you couldn't move for cigarettes. We had plenty of smokes on the way back[3]

Sergeant Leonard Howard, Royal Engineers, witnessed an act of bravery by a friend:

It wasn't until 30th May that we were ordered to make our way to Dunkirk, we abandoned our transport and the boys and I walked and ran, we were being shot at and mortared all the time. At one stage we had to cross a sunken road and the enemy had machine-guns enfiladed down its full length. We were really suffering a terrific amount of casualties. A good friend of mine, George Parks, stood up and threw a mills grenade through the loophole of a pillbox which was machine-gunning us. For some reason they didn't manage to shoot him and he threw the grenade straight through the loophole. I was flat on the deck and so was anyone else with any sense. George said 'how's that for a cricket throw', he got the Military Medal for that and it was one of the bravest things I have ever seen.[4]

Pte Jack Toomey, DLI, came close to meeting his maker but instead he had a lucky escape:

After an hour the wagon we were on stopped and everyone got off and got into a ditch, that is except for another bloke and myself who were left jammed in the back of the lorry. We could hear machine-gun fire and thought it was a shoot up by Gerry planes, but when tracer shells started coming through the roof of our lorry I knew I was wrong. Two shells took a knapsack from the box next to my head and threw it out of the back looking like cotton waste, another went passed my ear so close I felt the wind of it. All the time machine-gun bullets were smacking and ricocheting off the struts. I just sat and gave up all hope of coming out of that lorry alive. I heard the noise of a tank chugging past the lorry and the shooting stopped, the bloke driving the tank saw us in the lorry and calmly tossed a hand grenade under the tail board! After it had gone off we found we were still alive and we came out of the lorry with our hands in the clouds. There are pleasanter ways of committing suicide than fighting five tanks, an armoured wireless car and a plane with a rifle. Well they took us prisoner and while we were looking after the wounded the French opened fire on

---

2    Manuscript sent to author by Ian R English (Durham, 1995).
3    Ibid, by William Burden Taylor (Durham, 1993).
4    Taped interview with author, Leonard Howard (Hull, 1988).

us and we were caught in the cross fire, so back into the ditch we went. The main body of prisoners was run off to a nearby village and we lay in the ditch for two hours and then went back to our own lines. So much for my great escape, more of a case of getting left behind.[5]

Sergeant William Knight, Royal Engineers, recalls one incident near La Panne when he came across some retreating infantry who were on their last legs:

> It was just before dawn when we heard the shuffling of feet coming up the road. We knew that the last of the British troops had gone to the beaches and we were preparing to pull out ourselves. Then we heard this shuffling noise as we were preparing to pull ourselves together. Now the Germans didn't come up with a shuffle of feet, they came up with a whoosh on motor bikes with sidecars followed by tanks. So we knew it had to be the British army, nobody else would be walking. After a while a file of absolutely deadbeat weary chaps came by led by an officer carrying a full pack like his men, trying to cheer them along. When they got to us they saw the lorry, I called out to them 'we're just brewing up sir, would you like a cup of char? He said 'sergeant I'd love a cup of char, but not until my men have had one. Have you got enough for all my men?' I said we had but the latecomers might not have any milk, but we've got tea for them and we've got provisions. We got to talking to them and the officer told me that he had had to leave his wounded behind. His men were so tired that they were absolutely incapable of going any further carrying their wounded comrades, so he'd had to leave them at a farmhouse. He knew the Germans were right behind them and he was very worried about what would happen to them. Like a mug I offered to go back with him and take him in the lorry to the farmhouse. He had a word with his sergeant and saw that his men were alright, they were sitting drinking tea and resting. We got in the lorry and went back down the road quite a distance and then we heard the sound of action up ahead. I decided if we went to the farm we had better go across the fields and approach it from the back. We reached the back of the farmhouse and went in and found his wounded men. Most of them were very badly wounded and they were engaging the enemy with rifles and grenades through the front windows. We got them out the back door one by one, with the others giving covering fire. We got them onto the truck and went like hell out of there. At first we were shielded by the farmhouse, but as soon as we broke cover and started off across the field the Germans opened up with everything they'd got. When we got back to where we'd left our men the truck was a mass of ragged canvas, it was a good job that most of the men in it were lying down otherwise they would have got further injuries. In fact only one bloke had. We decided things were getting hot and as Gerry was coming up the road we thought we'd better get out of there. We'd got the wounded on board and we took them right the way down to the casualty clearing station, but by then things were getting pretty bad. The approaches into La Panne were pretty well blocked but we managed to push a lot of trucks and personnel carriers off the road and into the canals. We unloaded the wounded at the casualty clearing station and said goodbye to them. Quite a few of those poor devils were on their last legs. I'll never forget the officer's last words, he said 'sergeant, you're one hell of a man' and I said 'Sir, so are you'. His men

---

5  Ibid, with Jack Toomey (Durham, 1988).

absolutely worshipped him and he stuck with them through thick and thin, getting them right down to the beaches.[6]

Sergeant Max Hearst was the battalion butcher and found his skills in demand:

> We got to one little spot and the call came out for all battalion butchers to report to 50th Divisional HQ, I left my horse and took my butchers box of tools, which you had to carry as well as your normal gear. We gets to this big château and this RSM says to me 'there you are Yorkie help yourself' and pointed to this enclosure packed with cattle. A fatigue man helped me pull out a cow and I shot it with my 38 revolver, I'd got that one dressed and drawn and I'd started with a second one when all of a sudden this RSM shouts 'come on Yorkie you aint got time to pack your gear, get on the bloody truck'. As we went down the lane I could see German tanks coming up the other end firing at us. When I got back to my unit Billy Gale said 'where's all your gear'? and told me I'd be put on a charge for that. We passed through one village and there was a butchers shop open and deserted, so I went in and got all the gear I wanted.[7]

Before entering the bridgehead most of the artillery and transports had to be destroyed to prevent them from falling into enemy hands, Gunner Peter Stonnard served with the 74th Field regiment that was attached to 150 Brigade and was called upon to help destroy the gun he had spent many months maintaining and polishing:

> The battery withdrew into the corner of a field, all vehicles and surplus equipment was destroyed, the guns fired off the remaining ammunition except two shells. The troop decided to destroy their guns by the traditional method of one down the spout and one in the breach. I volunteered to destroy my gun, feeling that having spent the greatest part of the last six months polishing and cleaning it I was entitled the dubious honour of blowing it up.[8]

The roads to the Dunkirk bridgehead were bordered by fields littered with countless vehicles, some ablaze after having had a grenade put into the engine, but all with their bonnets up. Others had the engines smashed with a sledgehammer, had sand poured into the oil sump as the engine raced, or had a bullet put through the sump allowing the oil to drain out as the engine ran causing it to seize up.

Corporal George Ledger, 8th DLI:

> We got to the outskirts of Dunkirk and came across dumped arms, lorries and equipment, miles and miles of it. Wherever you looked the whole place was engulfed with abandoned weapons and machines. A lot of us were sent out to immobilise some vehicles. We'd put things into radiators or drop a grenade in the engine and smash it.[9]

6   Ibid, with William Knight (1989).
7   Ibid, with Max Hearst (Hull, 1993).
8   Ibid, with Peter Stonnard (Hull, 1991).
9   Manuscript sent to author by William Ridley (Durham, 1992).

Sergeant Leonard Howard, Royal Engineers:

> We arrived at the outskirts of Dunkirk at 17:00 p.m. having run and walked 40 miles in 16 hours. Occasionally we hadn't been able to move because we were being attacked. Survival was the main objective in everyone's mind, but I remember a warrant officer walking down the road, dressed just in knee breeches, service dress jacket and cap. Tears were streaming down his face and he said 'I never thought I would see the British Army like this'. The poor man was absolutely shattered. He was a regular soldier and it moved him to tears. For myself, at 21 years old, one hadn't experienced death close to you and it was all a bit frightening.[10]

Sergeant John Williams, 6th DLI, was sent out on patrol to find out where the enemy positions were but was with an officer who was not up to scratch:

> A captain of the West Kent Regiment told the regular engineer officer to go with me and do a patrol to see how far away the enemy were. It wasn't a very arduous patrol, at the start there was a bridge which had been mined, you had to step on the sleepers to get across it and then lower yourself down into the canal. Before we got to the bridge the engineer officer said 'I'll just stay here and you go up and see how things are, you can pick me up on the way back'. I had the same thing for two nights and the blokes started complaining. The next night I said to the major I wanted a word with him, I said 'on behalf of myself and the men we don't want this officer, he never does the patrols, he's not doing his duty and it's bad for the morale of the men, I'd rather we just did it ourselves'.
>
> The captain called the engineer officer in and said 'this sergeant tells me that you haven't been doing the patrols, you've been waiting for him while he does the patrol and gives you a report and then you've been reporting it to me'. The engineer officer suddenly shouted 'it's suicide! it's suicide! we're all going to die!' and burst into tears. The captain shouted 'shut up you cunt, you're a bloody disgrace, in front of a sergeant, I'll have you court marshalled when I get back to England'. He replied 'I don't care, I don't care' said the engineer officer, 'it's bloody suicide, I don't want to die, I didn't think officers did things like that'. The sequel was rather amusing, the next night, it was just getting towards dusk, the captain said to the engineer officer 'get your kit'. The engineer officer had his batman carrying his kit and we all went to a junction in the road, the captain said 'if I get back to England you're going to be court marshalled because you're a disgrace, now get along that road and get out!' The engineer officer shot along the road with his poor batman and the captain looked at me and said 'well that's that sergeant', I said 'you do know sir that that road leads to the German lines? The other roads lead to Dunkirk'. The captain said 'I know sergeant, I know.[11]

Captain John Charles Austin saw one incident of panic during the retreat and had to take drastic action:

---

10  Taped interview with author, Leonard Howard (Hull, 1988).
11  Manuscript sent to author by John Williams (1996).

Approaching the bridge over the canal we once more found ourselves in a main stream of military traffic, the road narrowed here and to add to the confusion a truck full of Poilus, French soldiers, who seemed to be in a panic to get away, insisted on trying to pass all other vehicles on the road. They were blocking up the whole procession and causing dangerous delays as aeroplanes could be heard overhead. Shouts of 'pull in, wait your turn, what's your hurry' came from the angry British troops, mingled with oaths and curses. But the Poilus took no heed, they insisted on forcing a passage through. At last they endeavoured to pass my truck, I didn't waste any words, I leapt out, drew my revolver and told the driver that if he didn't get back in line immediately I'd shoot him. He got back in line. A few moments later the threatened air attack began, three bombers swooped low over the bridge and dropped their bombs. They missed the bridge but hit the banks, as the bombers swooped everyone leapt from the vehicles and scattered over the fields on each side of the road and I crouched in a ditch. A few yards away a French soldier and a little boy had taken refuge, a bomb had exploded and a fragment of it had sliced the head and shoulders off both of them.[12]

Pte William Cheall, 6th Battalion Green Howards, arrived at the coast and the sight of the beach at Bray Dunes filled with troops waiting to get home was a shock to him and his comrades:

Pte William Cheall, 6th Battalion Green Howards.

> It seemed to have taken a very long time, but after some hours and about 12 miles, we saw a cluster of buildings in the distance and added a little more haste to our walking. We were surprised that our destination seemed no larger than a sea-side village. It was Bray Dunes and we were very pleased to have sight of it but other troubles were very soon to descend upon us. We walked down the sand blown main street and at the end came to a small promenade overlooking the sea, not a soul was in sight apart from our lads, we turned left and walked along this promenade. We stood and looked at the sea which could mean our salvation and on the other side of that water was England, how simple. We walked to the end of the promenade about 200 yards, which led to deep soft sand, followed by huge six foot sandbanks. The sea was about 200 yards away from the high water mark and both east and west the beach was very flat. The accompanying sight which greeted us will forever live in our memories. On the beach, running both ways, there were many tens of thousands of khaki clad figures milling around as far as we could see, but there was nowhere to go. There were columns of soldiers, three deep, going out to sea up to their shoulders trying to get on to small boats to take them to England, it was 30th May.[13]

12 J. C. Austin, *Return via Dunkirk* (London: Hodder and Stoughton, 1940), p. 71.
13 Manuscript sent to author by William Cheall (1994).

On 31 May, near Bulskamp, the troops of the DLI were under terrific pressure as the Germans surged forward seeking a weak point in the line to penetrate, the 9th Battalion DLI was ordered to put in a counter attack commanded by Captain George Wood and was promised other units to support the venture. The only units that turned up were the machine-gunners of the Northumberland Fusiliers.

Captain George L Wood, DSO, MC:

> The Bosche had got across the canal and they had been letting us have it with machine-gun and rifle fire, their patrols had been probing our line constantly always looking for a weak spot in our defences to exploit.[14]
>
> The fusiliers laid down a heavy covering fire on the enemy positions as the attack went in, Captain Threlfall stood upright amid a hail of shells and bullets with his pipe in his mouth, calmly directing the fire of the Northumberland Fusiliers. As the Durham's pressed forward one company tried to cross a field that had in it a very angry bull, crazed by the noise of battle and careering up and down its enclosure. The troops did their best to keep out of its way, Captain Wood recalls: I was more frightened of the bull than anything else.[15]

The Durham's managed to get passed it in one piece and came across a group of buildings from which the Germans had been giving a lot of trouble with small arms fire. By the time the troops entered these buildings the Germans had gone and the men of 151 Brigade now spent a most unpleasant few hours as the enemy rained down mortar and shell fire upon them, when night fell the Durhams pulled back into the bridgehead, passing the positions that had been held by the Northumberland Fusiliers as they did so. Captain Wood recalled: We were on our way back and I came upon the dead body of Captain Threlfall, he had put up a very gallant fight.[16]

The British Artillery near Bulskamp was using a windmill as an observation post and the Germans were using a church steeple to guide their gun-fire upon the Durhams, Captain John Charles Austin was given the job of Forward Observation Officer and was to guide the British guns onto their target, the church tower, before the German observers could bring their guns to bear on the windmill:

> Through the hole in the timbers I took a view of the prospect, in the morning sunshine the country-side lay for miles before me, vivid and distinct. Immediately in front I looked across a series of flat green fields which were neatly bisected by a yellow road running direct into enemy country. In the middle distance I picked out groups of red farms, small clumps of osiers and a level crossing with a halt sign, far away to the left the sunshine glistened on Furnes, as yet un-smashed by bombers. To the right in the far middle distance was Bulscamp just on the other side of the canal that the rear guard of the BEF were holding as a line. In the centre of Bulscamp, from the middle of a cluster of red houses, rose my destined victim, a grey church surmounted by a wooden steeple.
>
> At once I fastened on the two slit windows in the belfry, from these windows we, in our turn, were doubtless being observed by some German OP officer. I wasted no more time, as

14  Newspaper cutting sent to the author by William Ridley (Durham, 1993).
15  Ibid, by William Ridley (Durham, 1993).
16  Ibid, by William Ridley (Durham, 1993).

soon as I had measured the switch, range and angle of sight to the church I sent them and the order to fire down to the guns. I raised my glasses to see the effect of the bursting shells, there it was, a wisp of whitish smoke rising from some houses on the left of Bulscamp, the next round fell just in front of the church. I bracketed the church and went on to fire for effect and saw the shells go tearing through the roof of the church, one more correction and I had the satisfaction of seeing two of the next four shells crash into the windows at the top of the belfry, great lumps of masonry began falling. I was not entirely satisfied so I got the troop to send over another five shells to make sure the Germans couldn't use the belfry again.[17]

Heavy attacks were now made on 50th Divisions front, the right flank of the 3rd Division on the left was driven back and 151 Brigade took heavy casualties and lost some ground. Thanks to the dogged fighting qualities of the men of the 50th their front held, they had been fighting and marching from one position to another since 21 May and as a result of fatigue and lack of sleep many of them began to experience unusual feelings of unreality.

Captain Cheeseman, 74th Field Regiment, Royal Artillery:

For the first two or three days you are horribly tired, then something goes click and you are not tired anymore, you get a sort of second wind but nothing seems quite real. When I did get back home I found I couldn't sleep even when I had the chance.[18]

In the early hours of 1 June the whole division withdrew to a position south of Bray Dunes, just behind the perimeter which was held by a screen of French troops. 150 Brigade held this position and the now badly depleted 151 Brigade dug in behind them. Groups of men were ordered to leave their positions and head for the beaches and evacuation.

Pte Joe Kneeshaw, 5th Battalion Green Howards, and his comrades were told to get to Dunkirk:

A sergeant said 'do you see all that thick black smoke? well head for that, it's Dunkirk'. We split up into twos and walked and hitch-hiked to Dunkirk. When we got to the beaches we saw lots of ships out to sea, some burning, with lines of men wading into the water trying to get on the smaller boats, Gerry was straffing the beach all the time with shell fire and Stuka dive-bombers dropped their bombs all over the place. We couldn't get on a boat and on the last night an officer ordered us to march to the Mole, when we got there we saw it was pretty well smashed up by shell-fire and bombing. Where there were gaps in the gangways ladders had been placed over them and we had to crawl over with our rifles on our backs. We got to this destroyer and the sailors were throwing men on-board, they grabbed our rifles and said 'you won't be needing them now' and threw them in the sea. Once on the ship we went down ladders to the lower levels and I thought if we get hit while we are down here we have no chance of surviving. I had not slept for days and fell into a deep sleep, the next thing I knew we were back home.[19]

17   J. C. Austin, *Return via Dunkirk* (London: Hodder and Stoughton, 1940), p. 85.
18   Manuscript sent to author by Mr Cheeseman (1987).
19   Taped interview with Joe Kneeshaw (Market Weighton, 1995).

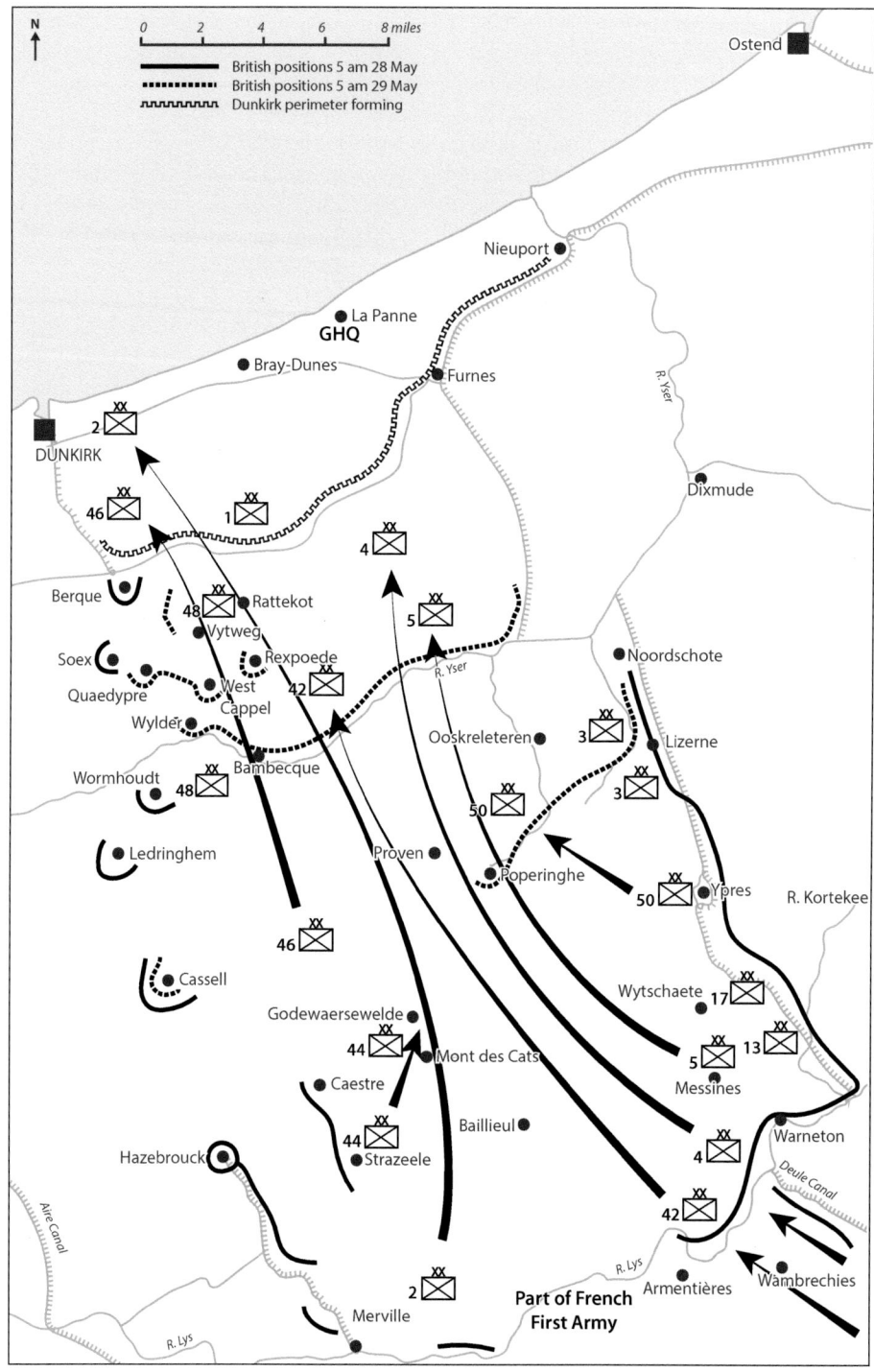

Map 5 The withdrawal to the coast.

Pte James McGarey, MM, 8th DLI:

> We were in our last fighting positions before the beaches, Major Percy of the 9th Battalion came round and he shouts 'come on, get out, get out, I want you lads out'. So we fell back into the sand dunes a few miles out of Dunkirk and we lay there. We didn't know what they were gonna use us for, maybe to put in a last attack to hold up the Gerries. But it fell through and we were told it was our turn next to pull out.[20]

150 Brigade was to embark from the east end of the beaches at Malo-Les-Bains and 151 Brigade and attached troops from the Mole at Dunkirk, in the confusion many men lost their units and many men from 150 Brigade ended up at Dunkirk. This famous pier and its adjoining beaches was subjected to heavy bombing and shelling on 1 and 2 June, because of this the evacuation had to be abandoned in day-light but continued unabated at night. When the troops of 150 Brigade finally arrived at the beaches a terrible sight awaited them, French horse drawn transport had been abandoned leaving the animals unfed and un-watered, many of them had been caught in the enemy shell-fire and roamed about terror stricken with gaping wounds. French and Belgian refugees huddled for safety in any cover they could find and their distress was pitiful to see.

Thousands of British troops waiting on the beaches to be evacuated, 31 May 1940.

20  G. Purdon, *From Coalfield to Battlefield* (Durham: County Durham Springboard Media Project, 1995), p. 73.

Sergeant Arthur Chester, 4th Battalion East Yorkshire Regiment, remembers that in the chaos he and his mates stuck together:

> It was a shocking sight, there was a burning hospital ship turned on its side and ships all over the place out at sea, there was dead horses and dead soldiers on the beach, it was a hell of a mess. These little boats kept coming inshore and blokes waded out up to their necks in water to be picked up. Up to then we was still an organised battalion, we couldn't run off and say blow it I'm going to get this boat, we were still a fighting unit. We were in the sand dunes with Stukas strafing all the time and there was a lot of wounded on the beaches. We all had to muck in and it was a case of one for all and all for one type of thing.[21]

Sergeant Chester speaks with great pride of the fact that discipline remained firm throughout the 50th Division and this strong feeling of comradeship was felt by most men who lived through the 1940 campaign.

Pte Bernard Styles, 4th Battalion East Yorkshire Regiment:

> On the 1st June we were told that if the Guards held the perimeter we could withdraw and arrived on the beaches at Bray Dunes as daylight broke, we could see the deserted beach with the lines of vehicles that had been driven into the sea to form improvised jetties. We slowly moved down the beach to Dunkirk taking cover when German aircraft appeared to strafe the area. I and several other companions gradually moved closer to the eastern Mole of Dunkirk harbour where we helped to bring dead bodies out of the sea as they were being washed up. We arrived at the Mole in the early morning of the 2nd June and started to walk along it in the hope we might find a boat. We were amazed to hear a voice shouting out 'I am not stopping, if you can get aboard jump!' we looked over the side of the Mole and saw a small paddle steamer six to eight feet below us slowly reversing out of the harbour. We leapt onboard, in all I think about 25 to 30 of us. When we spoke to the captain he said that he had come over with only himself and the chief engineer and no crew as they were all shattered by their previous visits and would not come again.[22]

Other men made their way to the beaches only to become casualties of enemy mortar and shell-fire. Pte Ken Tidball, 4th Battalion East Yorkshire Regiment, was caught by mortar fire as he headed for the beaches:

> I was trudging along when we got orders to pull into this open space, the CO wanted to speak to us all, they called him Rough House Martin because his initials were R H, he carried this nickname all his life. We

Pte Ken Tidball, 4th Battalion East Yorkshire Regiment.

21  Taped interview with author, Arthur Chester (Hull, 1991).
22  Ibid, with Bernard Styles (1992).

were told to march along to the beach at mid-night and stop there to be picked up, when we set off again there was these trench mortar shells coming over and one exploded among us, the two chaps beside me got their heads blown off and I felt a queer sensation in my feet, I stamped my foot and carried on for some time until I got to the beach. It was in the early hours of the morning and a field dressing was put round my ankle, a few of the lads carried me on a stretcher to the top of the beach and sat with me. The fit men left us and the last man I saw was Captain Cockin, he shook hands and said: It's alright the ambulance is on its way.[23]

The ambulances arrived and took the wounded men onboard, they were taken inland with the intention of picking them up the following night to be taken to the boats. The next day German troops moved in between the ambulances and the beach, the drivers of the three ambulances now tried to find a way back to the beaches but their luck ran out when they were spotted by the German infantry who opened fire at once killing all three drivers and many of the wounded soldiers being transported. Pte Ken Tidball was on the bottom bunk in one ambulance when machine-gun and rifle fire tore through the vehicle's thin walls killing the two men above him; the living were lifted out of the ambulances and could do nothing now but await the arrival of the enemy troops.

> We lay on a driveway, I think it was the 3rd or 4th June but I'm not sure, it was a brilliant sunshiney day and there was a young Lt from Lincolnshire alongside me, I've never seen him since, he was only 19, a territorial. Somebody said 'do you think they'll shoot us?' I said 'I don't think so, I'm like you I'm scared to death'. The Germans came down the drive, one chap came over to me and said 'my name is Herbert' and shook hands with us, he spoke perfect English. He said 'the war is finished for you' and pulled out a packet of Gold Flake they got out of the Naffi. He was interesting to talk to and said 'we will be broadcasting from London soon' and we said that's what you think.[24]

The Luftwaffe tried to make good Goring's claim that the defenders of Dunkirk would be crushed by the use of air-raids, many pilots were so determined to do this that they repeatedly pressed home attacks against ships marked very clearly with the red cross. Other aircraft went for the men crowding on the beaches but the soft sand lessened the effects of bomb blast limiting casualties. Ships out at sea could be seen burning furiously as the Royal Navy took heavy losses, the stricken vessels were packed tight with men and the surf was soon littered with dead bodies, through these bobbing corpses the living pressed their way out to the waiting rescue vessels.

Captain Elliman, Royal Artillery, remembers the intolerable waiting amid the falling bombs:

> The tide was fairly low and a steamer lay on her side at the waters-edge. The sandy beach was about 100 yards wide and down the centre stood a line of men three abreast. The smoke from the burning oil tanks drifted eastward over the town, a few officers walked up and down, all was quiet. And then it started, a formation of high flyers came up from

---

23  Ibid, with Kenneth Tidball (Hull, 1989).
24  Ibid, with Kenneth Tidball (Hull, 1989).

Death in the street, Dunkirk, May 1940.

the west and dropped stick after stick of bombs. This first attack was most unnerving, you felt completely exposed on the beach and for a time some of us huddled under the hull of a wrecked steamer, but as nothing happened for some time I called in all my men and formed them up in the queue again for fear we should lose our place. Out at sea the destroyers pumped shells into the air and disappeared behind 80 foot high walls of spray thrown up by near misses. While these attacks were in progress Stukas were diving, screeching and wheeling over our heads like a flock of infernal seagulls. By the evening I was dulled by hours of explosions, I heard a Stuka coming down in a vertical dive right on top of me, the imminence of death aroused no feeling of fear, either the bomb would land on me or it wouldn't. I thought of Margaret in those few seconds of suspense and she brought me a sort of peace of the spirit. The next moment Crash! then darkness. And then a vision of falling sand in front of me, I realised I had been missed and I could hear the plane climbing away over Dunkirk. Some of the men had been less fortunate, the medical orderly's cheek had been blown away and two other men had been killed. The telephonist was so shocked by the injuries he saw he went wackers and was carried away laughing uncontrollably. We abandoned our original plan to get on a boat and joined another queue which led to the Mole, thousands of men stretched away behind us but we failed to move forward, only the wounded got away that night. As the hours went by the spirits of us all must have been sinking, mine certainly were. Sleep was impossible, it was just waiting, waiting, waiting.[25]

25  Ibid, with Mr Elliman (1988).

Corporal George Ledger, 8th DLI:

> When we got to Dunkirk on Saturday there was just a feeling of dejection and we were tired and filthy dirty. We were picked up in lorries on the outskirts and taken the last few miles to drive through the people who were guarding the perimeter, you couldn't just walk through. They were fighting a rear guard action, keeping the perimeter open for us. When we got through we got out of the lorries and started walking through Dunkirk. It was one horrific sight with dead men, machines, lorries, guns and armaments strewn both sides of the road. In fact it was that bad in places that it wasn't a case of marching like a disciplined troop, we were straggling through in different directions to avoid the debris.[26]

Captain Stephen Holloway, Royal Engineers:

> As night came on the tide was going out and it became quite evident that loading men into boats would have to be abandoned because it was impossible for small craft such a dinghies to come up to the beach at La Panne. At this time the phosphorescence of the water was quite the most vivid that I have ever seen, so that all the wet ropes were brilliantly illuminated and every footstep one took across the sand was lit up as if by electricity.[27]

Sergeant Leonard Howard, Royal Engineers, saw how men were affected by the strain of what they had been through:

> I saw British troops shoot other British troops. On one occasion a small boat came in and men piled aboard it to such a degree that it was in danger of capsizing, the chap in charge of this boat decided that unless he took some action it would, so he shot a hanger on at the back of the boat through the head. It probably saved those chaps in the boat but I hoped I would never be called upon to do that. I think he did the right thing but it was awful to see, there was no reaction to this at all, there was such chaos that this didn't seem to be out of keeping. There were chaps who unfortunately were going round the bend, I saw chaps run into the sea screaming because mentally it had all got too much for them. During the two days we were on the beach at least a couple of dozen men committed suicide by running into the sea. They were under terrific strain and one couldn't do anything for them.[28]

Sergeant Les Hilton, 4th Battalion East Yorkshire Regiment:

> We walked along the beach to Dunkirk then headed for the sea front houses and saw some French troops were coming out of the basement of the end house of one row, my mate said 'let's get our head down in there I'm beat', so we went in. We slept so hard that night that even the bombing never woke us, when we woke up early next day we walked outside to find the adjoining houses had been blown apart, ours was the only one left standing.[29]

---

26 Ibid, with George Ledger at the Veteran's re-union (Hull, 1993).
27 Ibid, with Stephen Holloway at the Veteran's re-union (Hull, 1993).
28 Ibid, with Leonard Howard (Hull, 1989).
29 Ibid, with Les Hilton (Hull, 1989).

Dunkirk seen from the sea, blazing oil tanks send plumes of smoke into the night sky as raging fires light up the scene, May 1940.

Lance Bombardier Donald Jackson, Royal Artillery:

> My first view of the beach on arriving after an air raid was a bombed out ambulance with the former occupants all dead outside. Looking out to sea we saw chaos, a ship slowly sinking bow first, the next hit amidships was going down in a V-shape, the third was sailing on the horizon blazing from stem to stern, completely in flames. It was now dusk and we joined a queue on the beach but nothing was happening so we came back to the promenade. Wounded men were laid up against a wall, one man was in so much pain he cried out 'for God's sake shoot me' my partner Randolph Cook said to me 'you are the senior', I had one stripe, but I refused, next morning we looked and yes the poor chap had died. To us Dunkirk was just another seaside town and little did we know the part it was to play in history.[30]

Mr Arthur Divine was a civilian boat owner and had volunteered to come over to Dunkirk, as he approached in the darkness he was confronted by a scene from hell:

> We were in a sort of dark traffic lane, full of strange ghost shapes and weird unaccountable waves from the wash of larger vessels. When destroyers went by at full tilt the wash

---

30  Ibid, with Donald Jackson (1991).

was a serious matter to us little fellows. Even before it was fully dark we had picked up the glow of the fires burning at Dunkirk and as we drew nearer we could steer by the glow, it made visible the silhouetted shapes of other ships, the shapes of boats coming home already loaded and low dark shadows that might have been enemy torpedo boats. The enemy dropped parachute flares that hung about us like young moons, the sound of firing and bombing grew steadily louder as we got nearer and nearer. The flames on land grew too, from a glow they rose up in enormous plumes of smoke and fire that roared high into the night sky, as we approached Dunkirk there was an air attack on the destroyers, the night was brilliant with bursting bombs and tracer bullets climbing into the night sky, the noise was terrific. Illuminated by the fires we could see the beach was black with men, that picture will always be etched into my memory, lines of men wearily and sleepily staggering across the beach from the dunes to the shallows and falling into little boats. Great columns of men thrust out into the water among the bomb and shell splashes. The foremost ranks were shoulder deep moving forward under the command of their young subalterns, themselves with their heads just above the waves. As the front ranks were dragged aboard the boats the rear ranks moved up, from ankle deep to knee deep, knee deep to waist deep, until they too came to shoulder depth and their turn. The little boats that ferried from the beach to the big ships in deep water listed drunkenly with the weight of men. The big ships slowly took on lists of their own with the enormous numbers of men crowding on board and always down the dunes and across the beach came new hoards of men, new columns, new lines. On the beach was a burning destroyer that had been caught by the bombers and at the water's edge were ambulances that had been abandoned when their last load had been discharged. The background to all of this was the red glow of Dunkirk, the din was infernal, batteries and war ships shelled ceaselessly lighting up the night, to the whistle of shells was added the scream of falling bombs. Even the sky was full of noise, anti-aircraft shells, machine-gun fire, the snarl of falling planes and the angry hornet noise of the dive-bombers.[31]

Pte Reg Protheroe, 150 Field Ambulance, made his way to the beach at Bray Dunes:

The CO says to us 'right lads you're on your own, make your way to Dunkirk', we walked through villages that were choc-a-block with smashed up vehicles to hold up the German advance, we walked along a railway embankment that led to the beaches at Bray Dunes, it was night when we got there. In the distance we could see Dunkirk ablaze and I said 'I'm not going there'. Out to sea I could see the silhouettes of lots of ships but they didn't seem to be moving, when daylight came I found out why, they'd all been bombed and some were laid on their sides. Gerry planes came over but we were lucky as it was a really dull day and the clouds were real low, we walked down the beach to the water's edge, there was an officer in charge and he says to us 'what's your reference number?', I say 'we haven't got one', he says 'go to that office up there and get one'. Of course my mate says 'don't be daft he's putting us off, stand here'. We stood on the edge of the water and within 10 minutes there was hundreds behind us, the same officer came to us a few minutes after and said 'right

---

31  Manuscript sent to author by Wilfred Gilson (Hull, 1994).

we'll have you lot off now'. There were about 10 of us that couldn't swim so we got hold of each-others hands and walked out as far as we could to a rowing boat, we all piled into it and got took to HMS Codrington.[32]

Sergeant James McGarey, MM, 8th DLI:

We were told that once we got onto the beach we had to keep moving, even if you're dive-bombed and there is casualties just keep moving. There was drowned men, equipment, packs and rations that had been washed ashore lying around. I could see the odd boat out to sea, one was a hospital ship. It's funny but it never occurred to me that I might not get home safe, even though there was any number of dead lying on the beach. I remember at the time me and Dicky Moore had a touch of dysentery, you were supposed to keep moving but we had to stop and drop our slacks by this boat at the edge of the water. Why what you were passing, with having dysentery, was nearly all blood. Of course when we got home it was all in the papers about the blood stained beaches of Dunkirk. Dicky Moore says to me 'that must be were you and me were Jimmy, behind that boat.[33]

Lance Corporal Joss Little, 8th DLI:

We got through Bethune and down into Dunkirk as Gerry hadn't closed in by then, I says 'right lads we have to move on down to the beach', we'd just got onto it when the Stukas came screaming down machine gunning along the beach. Why none of the lads was hit, more through good luck than good management. Anyway I got the lads into the water and we'd been in there for a couple of hours when this military policeman comes along and shouts 'away lads get yourselves back on the beach'. I says 'what? with them up there machine- gunning the beach'. He says 'they cannot hit you man, the bullets just scatter round you'. I says 'aye why they've only got to hit yer once.[34]

Pte Roy Walker, 5th Battalion East Yorkshire Regiment, was detailed to bury the dead:

We tried waiting in the water up to our waists but gave up after a while, we then found a ship's raft and tried to row out, but as fast as we rowed out the tide pushed us back in. We then walked back to Dunkirk, shells were falling all the time and one dropped right in front of us and killed two lads. The sergeant major on the pier head said 'will you carry these lads, put them in a shell

Pte Roy Walker, 5th Battalion East Yorkshire Regiment.

---

32  Taped interview with author, James Nash (Hull, 1992).
33  G. Purdon, *From Coalfield to Battlefield* (Durham: County Durham Springboard Media Project, 1995), p. 62.
34  Ibid, p. 56.

hole and cover them with a blanket', which we did. He said 'give me the identity discs and you can have anything of use in their packs'. This was my worst experience throughout the whole war, maybe it was because I was so young and inexperienced I don't know. We had no air-cover, all we got was these Stukas coming at us none stop.[35]

Corporal Albert Snowdon, 5th Battalion Green Howards:

We got to the Mole and reached the place the boats were leaving from, the harbour master says 'no more boats tonight lads', so we walked onto the beach and bedded down. When I woke up next morning I was on my own, I thought this is a bonny kettle-o-fish. Nowt to eat and nowt to drink. The sun was blazing and Stukas were flying over us, I walked about all day and couldn't find my unit, it was chaos. I finally found an RP [Regimental Police] post and who should be there but our MO [Medical Officer] he said 'you aught to be in England now', when I finally got home I'd been reported missing in company orders.[36]

Corporal Sid Atkinson, 4th Battalion East Yorkshire Regiment:

The Stukas used to come screaming over and shooting, we got hidden among the sand dunes but there must have been a lot killed as they was all in big lines that went into the sea. Our officer says 'come on' and about 30 of us walked into the sea with all our gear on. We got so far and saw this little boat coming towards us, this chap in the boat came up to the side, he was terrifically strong, and said 'you don't want that' and with a knife ripped all our gear off, me rifle went and everything and he pulled us up like cherries out of the water.[37]

Corporal Anthony Rhodes, Royal Engineers:

Towards early morning great queues formed to go to the waters' edge and about four in the morning, out of the darkness, we saw boats coming in. Where they came in there was a little nucleus of men at the head of the water, and a great queue running from the sand dunes behind, perhaps a quarter of a mile long. Nobody told us what to do, but it seemed the decent thing to get into the queue and not to try to jump it. At the head of each little nucleus there was a naval officer, there must have been 10 or 12 of these queues and when we were half way up our queue the bombing started again. One man ran out of place to the head of the queue when he saw a boat coming. The naval officer turned on him and I heard him say 'go back to the place you've come from or I'll shoot you'. He said it very loudly for everybody to hear, that man went back with his tail between his legs.[38]

Mr John Osborne, civilian boat owner, picked up a number of French and British troops, leaving Dunkirk on 1 June:

35  Taped interview with author. Roy Walker (Scarborough, 1995).
36  Ibid, with Albert Snowdon (Beverley, 1994).
37  Ibid, with Sid Atkinson (Hull, 1996).
38  Ibid, with Anthony Rhodes (1999).

> As soon as we approached the beach a crowd of French soldiers, with all their equipment, rushed into the water and climbed on board before we had a chance to turn the boat around. The tide was turning and we became stuck on a sandbank, with great difficulty we persuaded the Frenchmen to get out of the boat and we were then able to turn it round so preventing it from capsizing. At one point I was nearly up to my neck in water keeping the bow of the boat pointing out to sea, still in my interview suit. We transferred our load eventually to a waiting craft and made one or two more trips, dawn was approaching and it was now our turn to make the return journey and get on our way before daylight. All this time we were so preoccupied with what we had been doing that we were hardly aware of all the activity going on around us. There were aircraft overhead all the time, friend and foe, continual bombing of the town, harbour and beaches by the Germans. Ships were being sunk and survivors rescued. All around the town and harbour of Dunkirk fires were blazing with a heavy pall of smoke hanging over it all. From much further off shore British ships were bombarding the German positions. We eventually left the beaches just before dawn on 1st June, I spent most of the return journey in the engine room of our little craft, trying to get warm and dry.[39]

Soldiers on the shore drove and pushed vehicles out into the sea to make a long causeways which men could walk over in deep water to get to the small boats, in this way heavily laden vessels, when loaded with men, would not touch the bottom and have to be pushed off the sand banks and out to sea. This was a cumbersome method but it worked.

Pte Arthur Chester helped with this essential task:

> We helped to make a pontoon with three ton wagons, we drove them out to sea until we was forced to abandon them, we made a causeway with planks so people could walk out on the canvas tops, that's how we got a lot of the wounded away. It got to the stage when it was every man for himself, time was running out and there was going to be no more boats. We got orders to line up and march out into the sea and we still had our equipment, rifles and helmets. We marched out and I was picked up by this little snibby [boat] and a few of us was hauled on deck, I was bomb happy, shell shocked, from then on, I can't recollect much more.[40]

Colour Sergeant Wilfred Gilson, 4th Battalion East Yorkshire Regiment:

> I was taken in an ambulance driven by Captain Parkinson of the Army Medical Corps, as we approached the town of Dunkirk it looked as though it was all ablaze, smoke rose into the sky in great big columns. The captain turned his vehicle around and headed back along the beaches, six French soldiers waved us down and ordered us out which we did and blow me if they didn't jump in and drive off leaving us stranded. We were there nearly all day and just after tea we got to the water along the pier made with lorries and small boats began picking us up. We were taken onto the Crested Eagle, it was armed with four heavy

---

39  Manuscript sent to author by Norman Hardy (Hull, 1994).
40  Taped interview with author, Arthur Chester (Hull, 1993).

A causeway of vehicles that was used to evacuate the wounded from the beaches at high tide. Taken by a German photographer on 4 June 1940 after the British had left.

machine-guns. There were all sorts of boats, big ones, little ones, destroyers and wot-not. We raised anchor about ten-o-clock and crossed the Channel, I fell asleep and woke up about six in the morning at Sheerness.[41]

Lt Bob Stafford, 4th Battalion East Yorkshire Regiment:

At Bray Dunes we dug-in for protection, there was a lot of action going on along the beach. There were thousands of French and British troops milling about all waiting to get on boats, the Germans were shelling the area and mortar bombs kept thudding around us. Along with CQMS Jagger and 14 other boys we got onto the Mole at Dunkirk and into a small boat that took us out of the harbour to an old tramp steamer. All the while being shelled by the Germans, French casualties on the beach were very bad but we could do nothing for them.[42]

Pte Sidney Nuttall, Royal Army Ordnance Corps:

We were getting shot up on the beaches at Bray Dunes, but luckily most of the dive bombing was done on the ships. I did see a dive bomber shot down by infantry using rifles.

41  Ibid, with Wilfred Gilson (Hull, 1989).
42  Ibid, with Bob Stafford (Hull, 1994).

The pilot made a mistake and instead of diving from the stern of the destroyer to the nose and carrying on up the coast, he arrived from the sea and finished up over the coast. There were thousands of men lying in the dunes and everybody started firing their rifles. We saw a piece come off the plane and it veered off and went into the ground well behind the town, then we saw the smoke coming up from where it crashed.[43]

151 Brigade, and many of 150 Brigade, marched along the beaches to Dunkirk, German aircraft swooped down on the defenceless troops but casualties from this activity remained relatively light. On one occasion two Stukas were on the home run after bombing Dunkirk Quay when they swooped low over the 6th DLI, throwing two grenades as they did so.

Pte Bert Davies, 6th DLI, was feeling the strain of battle:

All you could see was men, a lot of them had great-coats on although it was hot in June, I couldn't see us getting away on a ship as there were too many men. It looked as though we would become prisoners or get killed, there was a rumour that went round saying our division was selected as a suicide division, how true it was I didn't know at the time. Durham's again that was the thing, Durham's again, are there no other regiments taking part in this battle?[44]

Major Peter J Jeffries, 6th DLI, remembers when he finally reached the Mole:

About nine or 10 o' clock on 31st May we reached the Dunkirk Mole and the scene was extraordinary. The start of the Mole was one mass of troops, I moved forward to find out what we were to do. There was a small body of staff officers at the base of the Mole, sending out runners to bring groups of men forward to queue up at the Mole. We hoped that at the end of the Mole there would be boats to take us off and we realised as we shuffled forwards that this was the case. The Mole was shelled spasmodically but I never saw a shell hit it, one or two men had been killed close to the mole and you could see them lying

British troops waiting on the Mole at Dunkirk, 31 May 1940.

---

43  Ibid, with Sydney Nutall (1998).
44  Ibid, with Bert Davies (Durham, 1996).

there, but on the whole casualties on the Mole seemed light. Finally we got to the head of the queue and there was no boat, but about 50 yards out in the gloom I could see a boat approaching and sure enough a Royal Navy minesweeper eventually drew up alongside, threw down a gangplank and we marched on board.[45]

Pte Jack Toomey, DLI, approached Dunkirk and watched as German dive-bombers attacked the docks area:

> As dawn came up we found the main Dunkirk road and what a jam it was, after about 10 hours of stopping and starting, diving into ditches and back into the lorries we got near Dunkirk. Here we had to dash through a barrage of shrapnel so we slammed the old bus into top gear and went flat out down the road. We got to the outskirts of Dunkirk and stopped on a raised road with a canal on either-side and nice big trees sheltering us from the air. We got out and looked up, there were about 70 bombers, German naturally as we hadn't seen one of our planes for three weeks, knocking the hell out of the docks or what was left of them. From there we went to the beaches and they were black with troops waiting to go aboard only there were no boats.
>
> The following day dawn broke and we saw the most welcome sight of all, about a dozen destroyers off the beaches and more coming up, boats of all shapes and sizes, barges, skylarks, life-boats and yachts. Fortunately the day was cloudy and misty, the bombers only came once and as they came low beneath the clouds the navy let them have it, they slung up everything. I was scrounging for a drink of water and all I could get was champagne and wine, on this morning I had a drink of vin blanc and had to sit down, I was drunk as a lord. The last time I had anything to eat was about three days off and on an empty stomach the wine had a devastating effect.
>
> That evening we went aboard after making dash after dash up the jetty to dodge shrapnel, Gerry had got close enough to shell us with his light artillery. We got aboard and started off, there were about 800 of us on one small destroyer. The navy rallied round and dished out cocoa, tins of bully and loaves of new bread, this was the first grub some of us had for nearly four days and the first bread we had for a fortnight. When we were an hours run from Dover and thought we were safe a bomber came down and slammed three bombs at us, he missed us by six feet and put all the lights out downstairs. We got to Dover at 02:00 a.m. and climbed aboard a train, we were still scared to light cigarettes as a light on the beach meant a hail of bombs and we just dozed. At Reading we got out and shambled to the road outside, it was about 08:00 a.m. and people just going out to work stopped and stared, we must have looked a mob, none of us had shaved or washed for a week. Our uniform was ripped and torn and stained with blood and oil, I had no equipment bar a tin hat, a gas mask and a revolver I picked up from somewhere stuck in my map pocket. One or two old dears took one look at us and burst into tears, I don't blame them. I frightened myself when I looked in the mirror.[46]

---

45 H. Moses, *The Faithful Sixth* (Durham: County Durham Books, 1995), p. 148.
46 Manuscript sent to author by Jack Toomey (Durham, 1989).

When troops arrived at Dunkirk many large fires were burning and the port and beaches were being heavily shelled and bombed, units dispersed to await their turn to be taken off the Mole.

Pte Thomas Maher, 8th Bn DLI, will never forget the hellish nights as the troops tried to evacuate the wounded and the bravery of the nurses caring for them under fire:

British troops on the Mole at Dunkirk scramble aboard a waiting destroyer, 31 May 1940.

> The sergeant said 'It'll be the same thing again tonight, we're gonna get as many wounded out as we can soon as it gets dark'. This wasn't far from Dunkirk where you could see the sky was blood red. There wasn't just a few ambulances this time there was hundreds, we drove on into Dunkirk itself, a few of us got hit and the trucks were burning in the road. There were lines and lines of infantry, the RP's were directing them onto the beaches and the ambulances down to the docks, well there was men as far as the eye could see. There was a hospital ship there called the St David, we were getting all the stretchers out and lined up at the dock and the boat crews was taking them onboard. There were two nurses there and I'll never forget them, because by then they were shelling us all the time. The other side of the docks was being bombed and the beaches were getting it, well these lads were wounded and they were screaming like hell and these two nurses, one was an oldish woman and the other a young lass, was just walking among the stretchers saying 'alright lads we'll get you out'. Eventually we all got onto a boat and I was in the saloon were they gave us hot cocoa, we'd had no sleep for days and this lad says 'don't take your boots off', because when you've had them on for days and you've been on the march and take them off, your feet's that swollen they won't go back on again" Well that was it, I can hardly remember another thing.[47]

Mrs Rose Lyons from Hull was serving in the ATS and remembers the fear she and her comrades felt and the terrible sights as they were bombed and shelled:

---

47   G. Purdon, *From Coalfield to Battlefield* (Durham: County Durham Springboard Media Project, 1995), p.77.

I worked at No5 General Hospital, they took us from there to Vitre and we were cooking for the doctors and nurses, there was a lot of bombing and shelling as we moved from place to place. At Dunkirk the planes flew so low as they bombed us you could see the flames from their engine exhausts. I was crouched down and was so frightened as they bombed us that I clenched my teeth so hard I broke them all, they gave us rubber pieces to put in our mouths but it was too late by then. We finally got billeted on the promenade, the hospital had been a casino, on the top was a big red cross so they could see it was a hospital and we never got hit. I saw a hospital ship get blown up while I was there on night duty, we had nowhere to go so we volunteered to stay on at night and help the nurses out, the ship was right out at sea and we could see the big red cross on its side, they knew what they were bombing but it made no difference. I wouldn't have missed the experience for anything, but we were all very scared and saw some terrible things.[48]

French and British troops lined up at the Mole waiting to be evacuated and although the majority of the men remained calm the officers present kept discipline in any way they saw fit. At one point French stragglers besieged the Mole in a panic stricken effort to get away:

Lance Corporal William Ridley, 9th DLI:

Mrs Rose Lyon. (ATS)

> We moved to the Mole and we were stepping over dead Guardsmen and what have you. There was holes in the boards where Gerry had shelled it. These were made passable by placing planks over them. A company of French Poilus come and practically pushed us off the thing. Dunkirk had the smell of death, it was the stink of blood and cordite.[49]

Lance Corporal Joss Little, 8th DLI, helped load the wounded onto the boats and got something to eat for the first time in days:

> This military policeman told us to get away along the pier to get a boat there, we were standing at the end when this long ambulance train pulled in and we were helping to get the stretchers off. The lad I took along was a sergeant; I says 'why what's happened to yer?' He says 'I've caught a Blighty shrapnel wound in both me legs, they're getting out what they can

---

48   Taped interview with author, Rose Lyons (Hull, 1989).
49   Ibid, with William Ridley (Durham, 1993).

but there's some to come out yet' I says 'away man the best place for thee is in the hospital'. Why we were gannin along and there was this bloody great crowd of Frenchies, they'd be coming over to Blighty to join the Free French, anyhow we couldn't get through them. I had the stretcher handles and I was shouting 'sil vous plait, sil vous plait'. Well I got sick of shouting sil vous plait at the finish and me mates did as well. There was two or three Tommies standin around and they still had their rifles and that, so I says 'fix yer bayonets lads and just give them Frenchies a prod so we can get through'. So on gans the bayonets, great long ones, anyhow that did the trick. We got them on the boat and this doctor was stood on deck, he was a Major, he asked us to look after the wounded and see if there was owt they wanted and that. Why there was a bit of a canteen on the boat, tea and sandwiches and that kind of thing, the sailor was a Gateshead bloke, he says 'any of you want owt to eat?' I said 'I could eat a scabby horse between two mattresses'. You

British troops wading out to a waiting ship, Dunkirk, 30th May 1940.

could have jam or ham sandwiches and they were massive, I says to him 'hey it's a doorstep this lad'. So I got some for the lads I was looking after and took them big pots of tea, smashing', why I got them sat up and fed, some couldn't sit up like or use their arms. When I'd had mine and took back all the pots and that I went to the back of the boat for a smoke, by then Gerry was shelling the harbour and one of our boats was sending shells back inland you know. Anyway they hit our boat, I shoved one of the crew down as I fell and landed on top of a pile of rope. A bit of shrapnel caught me on the side of the head, I didn't feel owt but a few minutes after the blood was pouring down my face. So I ended up with this bloody great bandage on my head and my tin hat was perched on top of it like a monkey on a mangle. So anyhow the boat reversed out of the harbour, she was a Southern Railways steamer, and got away.[50]

A high explosive shell fell among the milling Frenchmen on the Mole and many of them were killed, the living took no notice and pressed forward filling the gap in the queue that they had left. In the early hours the order went out, no more ships, and the remaining troops of the 50th Division left the Mole to return to their previous positions. Men were in a great rush to get under cover as the port was now under heavy shell-fire.

50  G. Purdon, *From Coalfield to Battlefield* (Durham: County Durham Springboard Media Project, 1995), p.78.

British dead and wrecked vehicles litter the streets of Dunkirk, 1 June 1940.

Pte John Thompson, 5th Battalion Green Howards:

> Everybody turned and ran off the Mole because they started shelling us real heavy, when we got to the end of the pier they dropped a shell among us like, some men dropped and some didn't. I always remember one thing I saw on the big rocks as you enter the pier, there was a German dispatch rider, they'd shot his chest away.[51]

The next night came and the evacuation got under way again with officers taking the various units onto the Mole in an agreed order, once again the French stragglers appeared but found their way to the pier barred by troops from the 50th Division with fixed bayonets.

Pte John Thompson:

> We returned the next day and stood at the pier end with fixed bayonets, our line went quite a way along the beach and down to the waters' edge. Some of the poor French lads were rather panic stricken, they'd been rushing onto boats they shouldn't have been on.[52]

Major Cheeseman, Royal Artillery:

> Discipline and morale were high and the feeling of us all was one of resentment that we had not been able to have a proper go at Gerry. The men's behaviour as they waited at Dunkirk was wonderful and it made me very proud.[53]

---

51  Taped interview with author, John Thompson (Beverley, 1995).
52  Ibid, with John Thompson (Beverley, 1995).
53  Ibid, with Mr Cheeseman (1994).

British troops on a destroyer crossing the English Chanel, 30 May 1940.

Signaller Alfred Baldwin, 65th Field Regiment, Royal Artillery:

> Some people came along in the evening shouting '65th Field, 65th Field' so we joined them. We walked along the beach with them pushing Paddy on a bike as he was wounded, until we reached the foot of the Mole. By this time the air-raids had stopped, but artillery fire was coming in pretty heavily and there was lots of machine-gun fire from the west end of the town. At the bottom of the land end of the Mole there were lots of rocks and boulders so we couldn't push the bike any further. I got Paddy in a fireman's lift across my shoulder and clambered over the rocks. He was moaning like buggery, not about the pain, but because I insisted on carrying a rifle I had found. I was determined I wasn't going to let it go and he was moaning like mad about this, I was telling him to effing shut up. We clambered on to the land end of the Mole and there were shells dropping all around. A couple of boats were burning out at sea and there were fires all over the town with smoke and shouting in the dark, the noise was horrendous. We sat on the end of the Mole looking out to sea, on the right hand side was a very low wall and we crouched down behind this. Somebody lit a fag and as the match flared there was a great shout of 'put that light out!' Very shortly after that the Mole was hit by a shell. Then a shout went up 'wounded and injured first' I thought we qualified for that so I picked up old Paddy, slung him over my shoulder again, and went off along the mole. It was a very black night and there was all

this noise and confusion all around, yet I never felt any sense of fear, I don't think I was registering what was happening. We came to a gap in the Mole which was about 10 feet across and over it was laid a couple of planks. There was a naval chap standing at the land end of these planks, he said 'take a run at it mate' so I went back a few steps and ran at these planks. With the weight of one man they might well have been alright, but with two they were sagging pretty badly by the time I got to the middle. I think I would have fallen off had it not been for a couple of navy blokes on the far end who just grabbed hold of me and dragged me on by my battle-dress. I remember them shouting to me 'not much further now' I staggered on with Paddy still on my back and I think I'd have gone right off the end of the Mole but for two officers who stopped me and took Paddy off my shoulder, I then went up the gangway onto the ship. They carried Paddy up and sat us down on the deck which was pretty crowded, they wanted us to go down below but I wanted to stay on deck. I felt instinctively that if we were going to be bombed or shot at I would stand a better chance on deck, so we tucked ourselves into a corner out of the way. I must have gone to sleep because I don't remember the boat leaving the dock, but I do remember the next morning that we woke up and could see the coastline of England.[54]

Captain Stephen Holloway, Royal Engineers, was made a prisoner of war:

During a heavy bombing raid I went down flat on the beach to escape the missiles. Eventually I came to, having either been knocked out by the blast or just collapsed from sheer exhaustion. I came to as dawn was breaking and there was not a soul in sight on the beach, I realised I had been left for dead.[55]

German troops enter the burning ruins of Dunkirk after the British had left, 3 June 1940.

54  Ibid, with Alfred Baldwin (1998).
55  Ibid, with Stephen Holloway at the Veteran's re-union (Hull, 1993).

On the night of 2 June the last troops left the Mole at Dunkirk, they were tired and thoroughly worn out and many could barely summon up the energy to board the vessels that awaited them. By the light from hundreds of burning fires in Dunkirk and to the sound of ear splitting explosions they got away at last.

Sergeant George Denis Elliot, 6th DLI:

> I've never been so exhausted, our time came and we came to that famous pier, I was that tired I couldn't climb over the ships side and I was dropping between the pier and the side of the ship. A big sailor grabbed me and pulled me onboard, I moved from there like a zombie to one of the lower decks, I went into a corner and knew no more until another sailor woke me up. He said 'are you going back?' I said 'back where'? I was at Dover and didn't even know it.[56]

Lt Ian R English, 8th DLI, MC and bar:

> On Saturday we were told we must be ready to make a counter-attack, we waited for orders but by the evening the idea was abandoned and we were to march along the beach to Dunkirk. There was a lot of confusion when we first got there, a lot of troops milling around and no order as far as we could see. Then we got orders to go out that night to the Mole. It was very dark apart from the fires from burning oil tanks. French troops were also coming out and they were very anxious that they got on ships as well, they kept shouting 'Anglais a la droit' so we kept to the right of the gangway. Very soon a destroyer came in and we were told to jump aboard, which everybody did. Within a few minutes the ship was full and off we went.[57]

Lt Ian R English, MC and bar, 8th Battalion Durham Light Infantry.

Sergeant James McGarey, MM, 8th DLI:

> We went into Dunkirk itself and it was blazing, there was gear all over, lorries and that. For days they'd been burning tyres, smashing up vehicles and blowing them up, stacks of brand new stuff. Then we were back on the beach, there was a lot of officers and things were well organised around the pier, there was no panic and I saw nobody trying to rush their turn. We got on HMS Windsor and it was packed, the sailors were giving us tea and bread, it was lovely, and I went to sleep. They could have sunk that boat and I wouldn't have known as we'd had so little sleep in the last three weeks.[58]

---

56  Ibid, with George Denis Elliot (Durham, 1993).
57  Manuscript sent to author by Ian R English (Durham, 1989).
58  G. Purdon, *From Coalfield to Battlefield* (Durham: County Durham Springboard Media Project, 1995), p.43.

Pte Bert Davies, 6th DLI:

> On the night 1st/2nd June we were ordered to get our sections together and quickly and quietly march to get aboard ships waiting at the Mole. Not knowing where we were going and after a struggle we got aboard, packing in tightly. When we eventually got underway I remember a sailor came to me and said 'here's a mug of cocoa and a slice of bread and butter mate' it was just like nectar, I'll never forget it. After that I just slumped down and fell fast asleep too tired to worry about anything.[59]

British troops on board a destroyer arrive on the south coast of England, 1 June 1940.

Lt Allan Elton Young, Royal Engineers:

> We decided to round up our men who must be somewhere on the beach, so we started at one end and worked our way along. We gradually collected our two sections and they formed a group of some 70 men. I then did some reconnoitring and found that groups were being evacuated from the Mole by British destroyers, I decided we should join the queue there. This was being organised by an officer who sat in a little slit trench surrounded by groups of men, each of which had been given a number, and as room on the Mole became available he would call the numbers to move up the Mole in order. This was quite under control and disciplined, with everybody waiting their turn. We joined the queue but then

---

59 Taped interview with author, Bert Davies (Hull, 1994).

the organising officer got up and joined what I suppose was his unit and marched off up the Mole. Nothing happened for a bit so I moved forward and took his place as I thought somebody had to do it. I was only a 2nd Lieutenant but I had my gas cape on so there was no way anyone could tell my rank. As other groups came up I allocated them numbers and told them where to sit. Destroyers were coming and going and the groups gradually moved forward. Eventually the time came for our group to move forward so I, as my predecessor had done, got up from my little slit trench, re-joined my group and moved forward. We got on to the Mole and soon after that the shelling became worse, some shells landed on the Mole in the middle of one of the parties. The Mole wasn't straight, there was an angle in it, there had been an officer at the angle directing the groups onto the boats as they arrived and he had become a casualty. Again I went forward and took on the job of the man directing units onto the boats, shouting to them to get moving at the double when there was a boat in and telling them to lie low as the boat pulled out. I did this for a bit until again my unit got to the front and I joined them on a destroyer which took us back to England.[60]

Ships continued to sail to and from Dunkirk, the French Navy and merchant ships played an important role in the evacuation and suffered the same heavy casualties as the Royal Navy. In the final hours, as the BEF got away, it was the French who held the perimeter and kept the Germans at bay. On Monday 3 June one last desperate effort was to be made during the night to rescue the French rear-guard troops who had fought so bravely against enormous odds, these exhausted Frenchmen skilfully disengaged from the enemy and made their way to the docks where the ships were waiting for them. It was at this point the final tragedy of Dunkirk was played out, in the cellars and ruins of Dunkirk there had been hiding an estimated 40,000 French troops who had avoided the battle, they flooded onto the beaches and Mole. That final effort at evacuation saved 26,175 men, but few of them had fought in the rear-guard for whom the ships were intended, they could only watch the packed ships leave the harbour and wait to be taken into captivity.

When all seemed lost for the British Expeditionary Force Hitler's personal intervention saved the day, after his panzer divisions had overrun Northern France and had cut the British army off from its base he ordered a halt as they prepared to sweep into Dunkirk. This was the only remaining port of escape left for the BEF, at that time the bulk of the British forces were many miles distant from the port but Hitler held up his tank columns for three whole days. The reasons for this are complex and lie beyond the bounds of this study, but his actions kept intact the British forces when nothing else could save them. By making their escape possible he allowed them to re-group in England to carry on the fight and to defend the coast line against invasion, this battered and defeated army would alone carry hope into achievement. The British people were aware the BEF had only narrowly escaped but were totally ignorant of the causes of their defeat and so the myth began to take root of the Miracle of Dunkirk.

When British troops got home to England they were given hot drinks and food by the Red Cross and the Salvation Army, crowds waited for them on the quayside but many men were too far gone to care. The aftermath of Dunkirk meant a reunion for three Newcastle brothers; Lt Colonel Roland Wood commanding the 4th Northumberland Fusiliers, Second Lt Kenneth Wood commanding a DLI anti-tank Platoon and Captain George L Wood 6th DLI.

---

60  Manuscript sent to author by Alan Elton (1993).

The Green Howards arrive on the south coast, 1 June 1940. On the left with dog is CSM Jack Verity, 7th Battalion Green Howards.

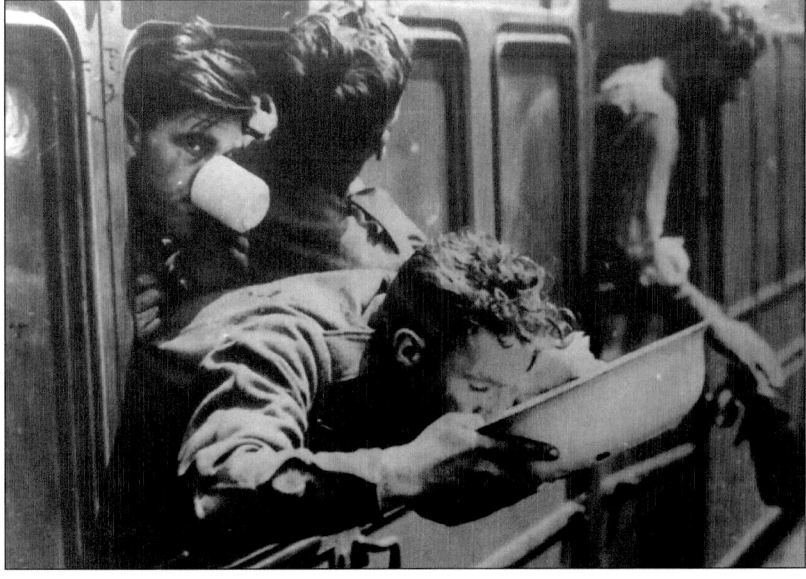

Worn out and tired British troops board a train on the south coast that will take them to their assembly areas for refitting and rest.

Captain George L Wood, DSO, MC and bar, 6th DLI:

> I don't remember what ship took us home, I just went to sleep, I think it was at Southend we landed but we were all so tired nothing seemed to matter anymore, people were cheering and waving flags, it was amazing. We had come home feeling ashamed, defeated and totally beaten. Yet there was everyone cheering and shouting as if it was the return of the conquering hero.[61]

Captain Wood was not alone in his feelings of shame and some men could not face the crowds, wanting only to get away.

Lance Corporal William Ridley, 9th DLI:

> When we gets to Dover seemingly we'd been bombed but I never heard owt, the boat I was on started to turn round and I thought 'Christ we're going back again' tears began to fill my eyes at the thought of it, but seemingly they always come in backwards when they come into Dover. When we got off the boat we boarded a train and sat on the floor because we were so ashamed, absolutely and utterly ashamed, I've never been proud of the fact I was at Dunkirk.[62]

Lt Colonel Peter John Jeffries, 6th DLI:

> We felt we'd done rather well to get back and still to be a co-ordinated unit, we were marvellously relieved of course to be back alive, I don't think we felt we were a defeated army at that time, but later of course one began to wonder about it a bit. I think the general mood in England was that it was a great thing to have got its divisions back.[63]

From the English ports the remnants of the 50th Division was directed to a large camp near Knutsford to get itself in working order, most men got a short leave and returned home to see their families, even in their home towns they were treated like heroes.

Sergeant Les Hilton, 4th Battalion East Yorkshire Regiment:

> Wives and mothers were waiting outside our camp for news of the men posted as missing and they had little idea of what we had been through or where we had been over the past few weeks. Women asked us questions about their missing husbands, questions we couldn't answer. They would stare intently into our faces to see if we were concealing anything from them but what could we say.[64]

Lt Ian R English, MC and bar, 8th DLI:

> In England the reception was amazing. We were put on a train and wherever we stopped people came up with coffee and cigarettes. We had evidence from this tremendous euphoria,

---

61 Newspaper cutting sent to author by John H Clark (Durham, 1996).
62 Taped interview with author, William Ridley at the Veteran's re-union (Hull, 1993).
63 Newspaper cutting sent to author by George Denis Elliot (Durham, 1992).
64 Taped interview with author, Les Hilton (Hull, 1989).

quite unfounded, that we were some sort of heroes and had won some sort of victory. It was obvious that we had been thoroughly beaten.[65]

Sergeant Max Hearst was puzzled at the attention he received from the civilian population:

> What I can't understand even to this day is why we were treated like bloody heroes, to me it was a major defeat, every street end had its flags out: 'welcome home our victorious lads' victorious? I got home and my elder brother who worked in the ship yards in Hull was taking me round all the pubs and everyone was buying us beer all night. It was amazing. They had no idea of the terrible beating we had just taken.[66]

Sergeant Arthur Chester, 4th Battalion East Yorkshire Regiment.

For other soldiers and their families it was time to count the cost as fathers, sons and other loved ones were found to be among the fallen, for them it was a time of great sorrow and numerous homes in every county went into mourning. Sergeant Arthur Chester, 4th Battalion East Yorkshire Regiment, had lost his brother John at Arras and his parents had no idea:

> My brother John and me were in the same company of the same battalion and I hadn't seen him since before the fight at Arras, we got separated. Just before we went on leave I went looking for him, I goes over to this sergeant and says 'hello sergeant have you seen my brother John Chester?' I could tell by his reaction as he stood there what had happened, he said 'don't you know? he was snipered at Arras' that was upsetting for me. So we got this leave, my parents had two sons in the war and didn't know where they were, you can imagine the state my mother was in. I came home and can remember walking down Moorhouse Road in Hull, that's where I lived at that time, my dad was stood on a stool outside washing the windows and saw me coming with my rifle slung over my shoulder. My heart was full because, well how was I going to tell my mother? When I got into the house I broke down. Naturally mother said 'where's John?' I couldn't bottle it up no more, it had to come out. She had a nervous do after that and was in a bad way.[67]

Pte John Chester, 4th Battalion East Yorkshire Regiment. Killed in action at Arras, May 1940.

65  Manuscript sent to author by Ian R English (Durham, 1989).
66  Taped interview with author, Max Hearst (Hull, 1994).
67  Ibid, with Arthur Chester (Hull, 1989).

After their short leave the men of the 50th Division began to return to their various assembly camps where the badly battered and depleted battalions began once again to take on their old forms, there were many gaps in the ranks that would have to be filled by new blood.

Pte Jim Betts was posted to the 4th Battalion East Yorkshire Regiment as a replacement:

> I was on my way to France to join the East York's and the next we heard of was the retreat and the evacuation at Dunkirk, it was quite a blow I can tell you. We were rushed back to our base camps and slept under canvas until we joined the 4th East York's down south. They'd no kit, no gear, nothing, some of the poor devils were in a bit of a state and were a bit down, but moral wasn't too bad. Most of them were from Hull but when I joined them so did a lot of men from Bradford and Bristol.[68]

Pte Norman Hardy was also a replacement and was put out because the men who had been at Dunkirk were given preferential treatment:

> We made up the numbers in the 4th East York's, they had just come back from Dunkirk you know. They was alright but Dunkirks is Dunkirks, if there was any extra kit being issued the Dunkirks got it first, every time something came up it was the Dunkirks who got it and we was left on the shelf sort of thing. Eventually we got over it but it was a bit of a bind at first, we resented it a bit and thought it was a bit rough.[69]

Corporal James Nash had served with the Royal Army Service Corps in Belgium and France as part of the 50th Division:

> I was in a bad way when I got back to England and felt very dejected and miserable, it took about 10 days for my morale to start to increase. But once the danger had passed I appreciated what had happened and how lucky I was to be alive. When I was alone I had a damned good weep on many occasions I don't mind telling you.[70]

Sergeant Arthur Chester, 4th Battalion East Yorkshire Regiment, returned from leave and was on parade at Blandford Camp when the Regimental Sergeant Major looked them up and down and with a few well-chosen words brought the men firmly back down to earth:

> During my short leave I was a hero for the day, I recall going to the Priory Pub in Hull with my dad, everybody wanted to ask me about Dunkirk and the BEF. Once we got to Blandford Camp the RSM got us on parade and told us in a way only an RSM can: 'right you lot, you've finished being heroes, now let's get down to some real soldiering.[71]

68 Ibid, with Jim Betts (Hull, 1988).
69 Ibid, with Norman Hardy (Hull, 1994).
70 Ibid, with James Nash (1992).
71 Ibid, with Arthur Chester (Hull, 1989).

# 9

## The 50th at Bay

In the latter part of June 1940 the 50th Division grew in numbers as new recruits came in, its ranks were further swelled by the inclusion of 69 Brigade into the divisional structure, this infantry brigade consisted of the 5th Battalion East Yorkshire Regiment and the 6th and 7th Battalions of the Green Howards, who had also just returned from France. Towards the end of June the whole division moved to the south coast to take on coastal defensive duties in a sector that ranged from Lyme Regis to Christchurch.

Sergeant Arthur Chester:

> We were re-organised and re-equipped with a new battle dress and all that kind of thing, we got plenty of foot slogging and training. There was the scare of invasion, if Hitler had started the invasion straight after Dunkirk he could have walked onto this island. We was rushed down to Poole in Dorset where we dug in along the coast waiting for the invasion, we was there quite a while until the invasion scare died down.[1]

Heavy artillery and anti-tank guns were virtually none existent and artillery men found themselves formed into rifle platoons, but even in this department weaponry was in short supply and men had to patrol the beaches armed only with wooden sticks.

Pte Ralph Hymer, 8th DLI, recalls the lack of weapons among the platoons:

> We went to Weymouth and when we got there we only had one rifle between seven men, fat lot of use that would be, we used to just roam up and down the beach night and day in all weathers. We were only armed with pointed sticks, if Gerry had come across the channel he'd have died laughing at us.[2]

---

1  Taped interview with author, Arthur Chester (Hull, 1993).
2  Ibid, with Ralph Hymer (Durham, 1991).

Major William I Watson, DSO, MC, 6th DLI, found the Durham accent of his men to be a problem at first:

> Everyone liked helping the Home Guard, at one meeting at Hele, having offered to provide instructors for the village of Cadbury, I was told it would be no good sending one of the fellows there as the inhabitants would never understand what he was saying and he would never understand what they were talking about. But despite being so foreign the instructors got on very well.[3]

Twenty-five poorly equipped divisions guarded the south coast as Hitler and his generals decided what to do next, on July 16th Hitler issued his Fuhrer Directive No 16 on preparations for a landing operation against England. The problems to be overcome in such an undertaking were formidable but Hitler insisted it must go ahead before the winter storms made it impossible, it was given the code name Operation Sea Lion.

In July the supply of weapons slowly began to improve for the 50th Division, a few bren-guns and bren-carriers arrived but by the end of the month there were still not enough to arm every company. The search was on for weaponry and many field guns that were called into service had seen action in other wars and were well passed their sell by date.

Major William I Watson remembers one old gun that was put into service with the 6th DLI:

> Today the gun was fired, this gun has given a great deal of amusement to us. A naval 4 inch gun from one of the old ships and one of a pair. Within two weeks it was mounted on a large diesel oil motor chassis, armoured round the driver and completely fitted out and handed over to 65th Anti-tank Regiment, with 50 gallons of fuel, stretchers and fire extinguishers. The site for the gun on the front was chosen by the general, it was the garage of an old woman, so without delay the garage was dismantled and rebuilt around the gun. The old lady was very upset and rightly so as she was convinced her house would be blown to bits, to which one and all concurred. But a generals word is law, today therefore two half charged rounds were fired. The results: round one, two slates dislodged off main roof, an ominous crack in wall appears, coal-house roof almost blown off and doors blown in, round two, 20 slates dislodged off main roof, crack in wall made very much larger, coal-house demolished, doors blown to bits and plaster off ceilings of five rooms.[4]

On the south coast of England thousands of concrete gun emplacements were hurriedly constructed, gun-pits were dug and barbed wire obstacles erected. During that memorable midsummer of 1940, with the ever present threat of invasion in the air, men had to be constantly on the alert, flashing lights or the sounds of gun-fire in the darkness over the Channel meant the inevitable 'Stand-to'. Air raid alarms would sound night and day as the bombers of the Luftwaffe made their way to Portland and throughout the daylight hours the troops had a grand-stand view of the Battle of Britain in the sky above them as Hitler tried to wipe the RAF from the skies. If Operation Sea Lion had any hope of success this task would have to be completed by

---

3   H. Moses, *The Faithful Sixth* (Durham: County Durham Books, 1995), p. 152.
4   Ibid, p. 156.

the Luftwaffe. Men who witnessed the dog-fights in those clear summer skies looked on with interested excitement as Spitfires and Hurricanes dived into massed enemy fighter and bomber formations, vapour trails criss-crossed the skies and blazing aircraft fell to earth in a life and death struggle played out on a grand scale.

Pte Reg Protheroe, 150 Field Ambulance, watched the battle above him with interest:

> We had a lovely view of the Battle of Britain, both sides were coming down like nine-pins all around us, we watched as hundreds of German bombers came over in perfect formation, the Spitfires didn't hesitate and dived in among them. It boosted our moral up quite a bit to see Gerry wasn't getting it all his own way now for a change.[5]

Throughout the summer the battalions of the 50th Division laboured on the coastal defences and relieved each other as they took their turn in divisional reserve. Men who had fought throughout the campaign in Belgium and France still lived in mortal fear of air attacks and they all knew what it was to be on the receiving end of unopposed dive-bomber attacks. However the much feared Stukas did not now have it their own way and these slow aircraft were easy pickings for the faster and more manoeuvrable English fighters. None-the-less when any plane flew low, as they had done over Dunkirk, the reaction of the veterans was instant and instinctive.

Pte Reg Protheroe:

> We were in a field and there was a battle going on over our heads, bits of shrapnel and things was dropping all around us. We were near Leamington Spa and it was a lovely day to be in the outdoors. An English fighter came roaring over us real low down with a loud roar and every man that had been at Dunkirk went flat on his face in the grass, it was a pure gut reaction. I always remember that because the civvies were all standing and looked at us as though we'd gone mad.[6]

Pte Jack Toomey, DLI, still felt the impulse for self-preservation:

> We went to Bournemouth to be re-equipped, one day three Spitfires roared overhead just above the pier and over the beach, I was on the beach lying flat on my face before you could say scarper. I just couldn't help it, it was a self-preservation instinct or something.[7]

Major William I Watson had a strange task for his men, meant to frighten the enemy:

> Shallow mock posts were dug in the shingle into which were placed plaster representatives of a fully equipped soldier from the bust upwards, the face being an excellent likeness of Mr Neville Chamberlain the former Prime Minister. All in the hope that the enemy would at any rate be deceived by numbers.[8]

---

5    Taped interview with author, Reg Protheroe (Hull, 1993).
6    Ibid, Reg Protheroe (Hull, 1993).
7    Manuscript sent to author by Jack Toomey (Durham, 1989).
8    H. Moses, *The Faithful Sixth* (Durham: County Durham Books, 1995), p. 153.

By September the threat of invasion was still very real and on the night of the first of that month the code-word 'Cromwell' was received at Divisional Head-quarters, this was the invasion alarm the BEF had been waiting for. British troops along the whole length of the south coast moved to action stations and prepared for the enemy assault, this was a nerve wracking time as men peered out to sea expecting to see barges full of German soldiers approaching. The 50th Division stood to their arms for 11 days and nights. By 15 September the weather was becoming too bad for a landing in force and the following day the weather broke as high seas pounded the coastal defences, on the 18th the men stood down. Hitler had lost his chance.

Early in October divisional exercises were carried out in the Dorchester area, the weather was bad and it poured with rain for the duration of the scheme. Not long after this event the whole division moved to the bleak moors of Somerset and Devon as orders were received to mobilise for overseas service. The quartermaster's stores began to fill up with tropical kit instead of the usual great coats and battle-dress. Christmas saw men going on embarkation leave, but on their return they found their departure date had been postponed and the New Year found the 50th training hard in the most miserable weather conditions as the moors were lashed by icy winds and driving blizzards across the bleak landscape.

By the Spring of 1941 the division was in good fighting order and fully equipped, much weeding out had been done among the ranks as each battalion was knocked into shape and a new confidence spread among the men. Herbert Glenton was with 150 Brigade at that time and remembers an air of professionalism about his unit he had not known before:

> We became much more professional for the first time, we had a new brigadier, they sacked the colonel and gave us professional soldiers. They made real soldiers out of us, other regular army personnel came to us and in the months spent in England we became a very professional unit. All NCOs went on courses and if they were not good enough they were thrown out, we lost quite a few officers the same way. When we moved out east we were as good as any brigade in the British army.[9]

By 21 April 1941 the first elements of the 50th Division were on the move to their port of embarkation, Liverpool, they were the various components of 150 Brigade plus advanced divisional headquarters. In unseasonable heat they marched from the railway station to the docks burdened with their kit and weapons.

Pte William Gleave, 4th Battalion Green Howards, recalls the kindness of the people of Liverpool as they marched down the streets to the docks:

> The citizens of Liverpool gathered on their doorsteps and on the pavements in large numbers to wish us God's speed and gave us a touching send off, cigarettes and other little gifts being pressed into our hands as we passed by encumbered by our sun helmets, kit bags and our other gear.[10]

---

9   Taped interview with author, Herbert Glenton (1995).
10  Manuscript sent to author by William Gleave (1996).

The ships that awaited them and were to carry the greater part of the brigade were the Empress of Russia and the Empress of Asia. The Empress of Russia carried the party from Divisional HQ, 150 Brigade HQ, the 4th Battalion East Yorkshire Regiment and 232nd Field Company, Royal Engineers. The Empress of Asia carried the 72nd Field Regiment Royal Artillery, the 5th Battalion Green Howards and 150 Field Ambulance. Once men and equipment had been loaded both ships moved into mid-river and dropped anchor, the men spent this time getting settled into their new home. As the ships up anchored and set sail for the Clyde their rails were packed with khaki clad figures who watched the shore line slip away into the darkness, many of these young men had experienced battle and wondered like Private Gleave 'would I ever see it again?'. As the shoreline slowly receded astern the troops gradually went below decks as thoughts turned to more immediate matters such as the next meal time. These had to be staggered as there were so many men on board.

Sergeant Arthur Chester, 4th Battalion East Yorkshire Regiment:

> We went down to Liverpool and embarked on the Empress of Russia, Lord Haw-Haw announced the news of our convoy on the radio. He knew all about our movements and what divisions were present and he said we would never get to our destination. That journey to the Middle East took us six weeks, you've never seen such a convoy, loads and loads of ships, it was massive. The journey was terrible.[11]

At night men had some difficulty in becoming accustomed to their sleeping accommodation, which were hammocks. These were so numerous that their edges touched and if a man wanted to go to the toilet at night a great amount of skill was needed to get out of and back into bed without causing discomfort to others. As the ships entered the Clyde the sight that awaited them was impressive in the extreme, a great armada of various vessels had been gathered to form a convoy and as the two old liners took up their positions for the journey no man could fail to be impressed by this great gathering heaving up and down on the tidal swell.

Pte William Gleave felt a new feeling of pride as the great fleet set sail:

> Dozens of ships spread across the river from destroyers to the battle-cruiser Repulse, with about a dozen ocean going liners thrown in for good measure, plus a good number of merchant ships. The sense of taking part in great events was uppermost in my mind as I surveyed this great fleet, a feeling which was magnified next day when the ships had entered the open sea and taken their allotted stations in the convoy. The sight of 14 destroyers spread out in a great fan across the front of the fleet with a dozen or more large troop ships forming the core of the convoy and the Repulse in the centre of this core, never had we felt more important.[12]

Pte William Gleave, 4th Battalion Green Howards.

11  Taped interview with author, Arthur Chester (Hull, 1992).
12  Manuscript sent to author by William Gleave (1996).

On the evening of 23 April 1941 the convoy moved out into the open sea heading for the Atlantic and it was not long before the troops felt the miseries of sea sickness as the great ships swayed from side to side. It would be many days before the next port was reached and the men of 150 Brigade settled down to a routine of training, inspections and physical exercise. Men had a lot of time on their hands and kit was scrubbed, blancoed and scrubbed again, this was repeated numerous times on the voyage and became a thorough nuisance. Men were never short of ideas when it came to finding shortcuts when cleaning their equipment, but not all of them worked out.

Pte William Gleave, 4th Battalion Green Howards, discovered a new and quicker way of cleaning his kit:

> Tying my kit to a long length of substantial cord and throwing the lot over the side of the ship it commenced to bounce along the surface of the waves and the resulting scouring action stripped all the blanco and dirt off with commendable speed. This trick rapidly spread, but some of the pieces of cord used were not up to the job and inevitably some individuals lost the whole of their webbing. The result was an epidemic of winning items of webbing which had been laid on the deck to dry, nobody wanted to pay for missing gear.[13]

The troops were packed into their quarters like cattle and the air in the lower decks could at times be cut with a knife. The remainder of the 50th Division sailed at the end of April and in early May, 150 Brigade in the leading ships arrived at Freetown on 16 May where the ships took on coal and provisions. The so called bum-boats came along side to trade with the troops and the natives of Freetown were only too keen to get their hands on any spare kit in exchange for goods. Others dived for any coins the troops cared to throw into the water and entertained the appreciative Tommies with their skill at diving and swimming, very few men got ashore in Freetown and three days later the ships up anchored and continued along their journey.

The men's misery was aggravated as it became hotter, deck sports were organised to relieve the boredom and the bull, boxing in particular was very popular and enjoyed by all. Arms training commenced when the ships were far out to sea and for some it was to prove a near fatal experience.

Pte William Gleave:

> A soldier called Billington and myself were talking away during a break when suddenly there was a single shot from a bren-gun, the round missed my back by about three inches, it nicked his left elbow and shot past the ear of the ships look-out. This worthy got quite excited and lost no time in reporting the incident. It turned out one of our training squad had been messing about with the bren and he was duly installed in the ship's brig without delay.[14]

---

13   Ibid, by William Gleave (1996).
14   Ibid, by William Gleave (1996).

Corporal Scriven, 8th DLI, remembers the day his ship crossed the Equator:

> As the troop ships crossed the Equator the time honoured ceremony of 'crossing the line' was to be performed, many of the 8th Battalion thought this a fine opportunity to have some fun at the expense of RSM Spike Jennings who it was anticipated would be the star attraction on the day in question. But Spike was a wiley old soldier and swore he had already crossed the line as a member of the 1st Battalion when sailing from China to Singapore and as there were no members of the 1st Battalion present to contradict him he got off the hook. Many doubted the 1st Battalion had sailed that far south but nobody was brave enough to call him a liar, Spike said 'that's my story and I'm sticking to it', it would have been a brave or foolish man who told him otherwise.[15]

The glorious sunshine and calm seas the men had been enjoying was not to last and a week after rounding the Cape the convoy ran into an unusually fierce storm, the likes of which had not been seen in that area for many years. The great ships were tossed about like corks as enormous waves broke over the decks, making it imperative that men stayed below to prevent them being washed overboard. In the living quarters anything loose was thrown about making meal times virtually impossible, the storm dispersed the convoy and the Empress of Asia was severely damaged and listing badly as it limped into Cape Town. It was here that many of the ships stokers deserted and the job had to be taken on by the men of 150 Brigade in the fiery heat of the Red Sea.

On 27 May the rest of the convoy docked at Durban and the men at last felt solid earth beneath their feet, a very pleasant four days was spent here and the troops found the people friendly. On June 1st the convoy continued its journey in calmer seas and arrived at Port Tewfick, near Suez, where the troops disembarked on 13th of that month. The Empress of Asia did not dock at Tewfick until 23 June, with the rest of the 50th Division arriving in late June and early July.

150 Brigade was at this time taken from the division and sent for duty in the Western Desert and Divisional HQ moved to Mena to plan the then unknown positions at Alamein, later moving to Cyprus in July 1941 and being joined first by 151 Brigade and later 150 and 69 Brigades. During the summer Greece had been evacuated and that bastion of the eastern Mediterranean, Crete, had been captured by the Germans. This greatly increased the importance of Cyprus as a stepping stone to Palestine and Syria. The 50th Division began their labours to put the island into a state of readiness.

Sergeant Arthur Chester's company was being taken to Cyprus on HMS Sheffield when they came under fire from the air:

> We was messed about in transit areas for a while then they moved us to Cyprus on HMS Sheffield, a destroyer. We was attacked by Italian high level bombers, they was after us alright, bombs splashed all around the ship. The pom-poms, anti-aircraft guns, was going like mad and they knocked one of them down, we could see the air crew was in the water and the captain announced over the Tannoy 'no survivors, no survivors, it's their water let them swim in it', and we left them there.[16]

---

15  Manuscript sent to author by Mr Scriven (Durham, 1997).
16  Taped interview with author, Arthur Chester (Hull, 1993).

Once on the island camps were set up and routines developed to meet the new conditions of this most pleasant posting, the brigades took up their defensive positions, each one being many miles from the next. Men laboured under the hot sun constructing trench systems, numerous strong points and an aerodrome.

Sergeant Arthur Chester:

> Dummy guns made of wooden posts was placed all around the coast, we gets billeted near Famagusta, they didn't have an aerodrome so we had to build one, we used to dawdle down to it each day. As soon as there was an air raid the Cypriot workers was off on their horse drawn carts as if they was in the Grand National.[17]

In their time off men could travel in the liberty truck to the coastal towns and villages, swimming in the clear blue waters was a treat not to be missed and in the local establishments good wine and fresh fruit were in plentiful supply, though overindulgence of either resulted in gippy-tummy. Cafes served traditional English food such as egg and chips and most of the troops sought out a photographer in order to send a memento of their visit home. The posting at Cyprus left most men with pleasant memories.

Pte Kilgallon, 9th DLI:

> Cyprus was a very pleasant place to be, it was nice and sunny, we worked of course, but overall it was a good experience. We helped build defence positions around this big aerodrome but the weather was lovely and we thoroughly enjoyed it.[18]

Pte Harry Forth, 5th Battalion East Yorkshire Regiment:

> I can only remember being bombed on one day and the rest of the time it was quiet, I called it a holiday compared to what we had been through in France, it was the best time I had out yonder.[19]

Lt Douglas King, 4th Battalion East Yorkshire Regiment:

> Cyprus was really very nice and at one point I took a patrol to the finger of the island to see if there were any U-Boats about. The most pleasant thing about that was the beautiful smell of the countryside. We had three months in Cyprus which was very pleasant indeed.[20]

Pte Kilgallon, 9th Battalion Durham Light Infantry.

17  Ibid, with Arthur Chester (Hull, 1993).
18  Ibid, with Mr Kilgallon (Durham, 1992).
19  Ibid, with Harry Forth (Cottingham, 1992).
20  Ibid, with Douglas King (Hull, 1994).

Pte Reg Protheroe, 150 Field Ambulance, knew his brother was on Cyprus and went looking for him:

> When I was at Famagusta somebody said 'do you want to go to Nicosia with this patient? You can go and see your brother at 149 Brigade', I got to 149 and said to them 'is Charlie Protheroe here?' they said 'oh no he's gone to see his brother at Famagusta', I thought well bugger me. We were on our way back when we decided to relieve ourselves at the side of the road, an ambulance was coming the other way and who should be on it but my brother. We found each other after all that messin' about.[21]

For a few however their stay on the island was to be memorable for other, not so pleasant, reasons. It was here the division suffered casualties, some of them resulting in loss of life. Battle training was going on apace in between working duties. Pte Ralph Hymer, 8th DLI, was on grenade throwing practice using live grenades.

> We were on a range practising grenade throwing, the trench we were in had a bend at the far end of it and there was a big bank in front of us to throw the grenade over. Lt Ward was in charge and there was a regular sergeant called Self. There was me and another private and it was our turn to have a go, we picked up a grenade each and pulled out the pins, the private with me threw his grenade but it hit the bank and rolled back into our trench. I saw this happen and threw my grenade as fast as I could over the bank and ran like blazes to get round the end of the trench. Sergeant Self jumped up onto the bank to escape the first grenade but mine exploded and got him in the legs, the officer was killed and the other Private lost a lung. I was on the firing party when we buried poor Lt Ward.[22]

Disease also took its toll of troops not yet used to such a hot climate, part of 150 Brigade had to be isolated from other divisional troops as an epidemic raged among them. Pte Herbert Glenton was with the 4th Battalion East Yorkshire Regiment when men began to be struck down with diphtheria:

> We stayed in Cyprus for three months and I would say it was one of the unhappiest three months we had, we had no billets, my company, A Company, was in an orchard of fig trees with little bivouacs. We got a diphtheria epidemic and it started in our company, the first to get it was Private Wright. We were not allowed near any of the rest of the battalion, it being contagious. It was not to happy a time really.[23]

The reunited 50th Division remained in Cyprus until 3 November 1941 when the task of defending the island was handed over to the 5th Indian Division and with it all the divisional transport and many weapons. The divisional transport had seen no action, handing it over to receive God knows what was a source of complaint for all ranks. Once it had left the island the division concentrated in the area of Haifa with the intention of heading for Palestine and then

---

21  Ibid, with Reg Protheroe (Hull, 1992).
22  Ibid, with Ralph Hymer (Durham, 1991).
23  Ibid, with Herbert Glenton (1995).

on to Iraq to fight side by side with the Russians in the Caucasus, they took over the transport and weapons of the 5th Indian Division and their worst fears were realised as much of the weaponry had been thoroughly worn out and most of the transport was unserviceable.

The next German thrust was forecast to come south east into Persia, by at least 10 armoured divisions, via the corridor of level country to the east of the Caspian. The 50th was detailed to help hold them in check and so it became increasingly important to get the troops to the predicted theatre of operations as soon as possible. With this grim thought in mind the brigades and attached arms laboured to re-equip themselves, normal procedures would have meant a delay in the set plans and so it was decided that 150 Brigade would be stripped of its stores and transport in order to make 69 Brigade and 151 Brigade mobile. After a period of hectic activity the two mobile brigades moved out across the desert via Baghdad to Kirkuk in Iraq. 150 Brigade was intended to re-join the division at a later date but owing to the fast changing circumstances of the time found itself separated from its mother unit once again.

On the morning of 12 November 1941, 69 and 151 Brigades began their journey and made an impressive sight as they moved across the Transjordan desert in desert formation, the countryside was now a desolate desert of rocky ground and local herdsmen with their camels looked on amazed at this display of military might on the move. On the 14th the ground changed to a hard flat terrain and the columns opened up into arrow head formation as they spread out across the desert. On the 16th the Euphrates was reached and camps set up, the next day was spent getting men and machines clean and in working order.

On 18 November the two brigades crossed the Euphrates and entered Baghdad, the population here was known to be hostile and so it proved, as the long columns of vehicles moved through Baghdad's main streets the civilians made inverted V signs, spit and threw the odd stone. Kirkuk was reached on 19 November after an unpleasant journey over bad roads and with a sandstorm blowing, weariness from this long journey was beginning to show on the troops faces. Soon after their arrival the Caucasian project was cancelled, the division however stayed here for some time preparing defensive positions, the weather was very bad, cold with torrential rain and life in the thick mud was very hard and even more so when the temperature plummeted. The weather in the first few days of 1942 continued to deteriorate as the temperature dropped to below freezing. Biting winds blew drifts of heavy snow across the landscape and keeping warm in such conditions was not easy.

Major William I Watson, 6th DLI, recalled the terrible conditions the troops had to endure:

> So when darkness fell, apart from the sentries who kept their lonely vigil in company with the howling jackals, all troops, dressed in as many cloths as possible and huddled together for warmth under their blankets, fell asleep in their tents while their sodden boots froze, until the cold dawn broke on the following day. Later, as if to increase the discomfort, this intense cold was followed by a thaw accompanied by torrential rain, which converted the whole camp into a sea of mud and ruined much of the digging operations.[24]

24  H. Moses, *The Faithful Sixth* (Durham: County Durham Books, 1995), p. 163.

Pte Herbert Thompson, 4th Battalion East Yorkshire Regiment:

> In 1941 we had three solid days of torrential rain and it seemed the desert was very similar to what I had been told about the Great War. In our box the trenches flooded and tanks and vehicles became bogged down, we were up to our knees in mud and water and any movement became nigh impossible. It was all mud and blather and it made us bloody miserable, it got so bad we were issued with a rum ration.[25]

In January 1942 the division, minus 150 Brigade, was ordered to the Baalbek area of Syria to relieve the 6th Australian Division, as soon as 69 Brigade arrived they began a period of hard labour as they worked to construct defensive positions intended to hold up the expected German thrust through that area against the tragic background of the fall of Singapore. 151 Brigade never reached Syria and at the end of January was ordered to go direct to the Western Desert to join 150 Brigade, and as the situation regarding Syria had improved 69 Brigade was ordered to do the same. British fortunes were at very low ebb as the 50th Division moved into this new theatre of operations, before them lay many trials and tragedies.

---

25  Taped interview with author, Herbert Thompson (Beverley, 1991).

## 10

## The Western Desert. 150 Brigade, December 1941 to March 1942

When the bulk of 50th Division left Haifa 150 Brigade was left behind with orders to follow on when the transport situation permitted, however on 19 November 1941 the Eighth Army launched a major offensive and 150 Brigade was ordered west to join them. The move from Haifa took place on 30 November and 1 December, personnel by rail and the ordnance of 72nd Field Regiment and transport by road. The Brigade destination was Bagush, desert training continued apace here for three weeks and invaluable help was given in this activity by the officers of the 7th Indian Division and the 2nd New Zealand Division as they rested from their heavy battles at Sidi-Rezegh and Bel-Hamed.

On 22 December the brigade was ordered to Bir Thalata, but before they left the divisional reconnaissance unit, 4th Battalion Royal Northumberland Fusiliers, was taken from them never to re-join the division, this unit would be decimated at Knightsbridge in the spring of the following year. The Bir Thalata area was bleak at this time of year, by day there were frequent sand storms and at night white frosts. Its featureless hard bedrock was the perfect place for the desert rail-head where the main army dumps were situated.

Pte William Gleave and his comrades in 4th Battalion Green Howards had to dig into the hard bedrock:

> We had a dismal Christmas, the everlasting grit in our food and drink was another trial that no-one enjoyed at this time and probably aggravated gippy tummy, which I for one was very prone to. When we were ordered to dig our bivvies in, spades were useless and on borrowing picks for the job found these were very little improvement. Swinging the pick overhead to bring it down produced a loud clang, the pick would rebound like a live thing and the wielder received a tingling shock through both hands, damn this for a game of soldiers was my thought as I struggled on. At the end of the week I had still only managed to make an oblong hole about five or six inches deep with a very uneven bottom, barely sufficient to lie down in, in fact I never did finish that hole to requirements, just stuck a small tent over the top with lumps of rock to anchor it as it was impossible to use tent pegs. Christmas came and went with very little to mark its passing, but this was only to be expected in the circumstances.[1]

---

1    Manuscript sent to author by William Gleave (1996).

At this time a troop carrying company of the Royal Army Service Corps joined 150 Brigade making all units mobile at last, the general feeling among the men and officers was that it could not now be long before the brigade was sent into action. On 5 January the 72nd Regiment, Royal Artillery, was ordered to Tobruk and from there to join units investing the German Garrison of 800 men still holding out at Halfaya. This small German force capitulated on 17 January 1942. The enemy troops at Halfaya and Sollum had resisted the British for two months during which time they had been bombarded from land, sea and air.

Sergeant Arthur Chester, 4th Battalion East Yorkshire Regiment, commented on the German garrison:

> Then we moved back to the desert all white legged, the old soldiers that were already out there were brown and shouted comments about our lack of sun-tans. We was taking over the 4th Indian Divisions positions, they was at Hell-Fire Pass [Halfaya Pass] and there was a hell of a battle going on there, that was the first time I saw our lads get really stuck in at Hell-Fire Pass, our first desert battle. We was on the winning side, we really gave them some stick. The Germans in this area got everything thrown at them but held out as long as they could, they was heroes.[2]

Major General Ramsden, the divisional commander, flew from Iraq and visited the brigade with orders that they were to re-join the rest of the 50th Division in Iraq. No sooner was the brigade ready to move when counter orders arrived with instructions to be ready to move west within four hours.

Lt Colonel W E Bush, DSO, MC, OBE, 5th Battalion Green Howards, was informed that the Eighth Army was in retreat:

> No sooner were we keyed up for the move when the order was reversed and we had four hours notice to move west, on 25th January 1942, Burns Day, the brigade moved to Bir Harmat in four columns, one composed of 72nd Field Regiment, RA, 232nd Field Company, RE and 150 Field Ambulance, the others each of one battalion. A deterioration of the situation at Benghazi had set in and strong enemy forces were compelling our forward units to give ground. This journey to Bir Harmat involved a desert drive of some 120 miles and it so happened that a very bad sand storm, accompanied by rain, blew most of the time and it will live in the memories of those who took part as a most exhausting experience. After a 12 hour halt at Bir Harmat the brigade was on its way again along 'F' route to the area of Tengeder, which was on the left or desert flank of the Eighth Army. By now Benghazi had been evacuated and the whole army was falling back towards Mechili, Timimi and Gazala.[3]

It was at Bir Harmat that the brigade received its first anti-tank guns, these were eight captured German 50mm guns taken in earlier battles. The brigade then pushed on a further 60 miles to the area of Garet El Auda, this was the southernmost limit of the line which the British and

---

2 Taped interview with author, Arthur Chester (Hull, 1992).
3 Manuscript sent to author by W E Bush (1992).

Allied Forces were temporarily holding and through which the main body of the Eighth Army was falling back as it gave ground to Rommel's offensive.

The 4th Battalion Green Howards, along with 285th Battery, 72nd Field Regiment, Royal Artillery, was sent 15 miles west to hold a position in the area of Bir Tengeder, to their front the tanks and armoured cars of the Royals and 4th South African Regiment patrolled the open plains and every day units of the Eighth Army fell back through their positions on their way east. Many of these units had made long detours through the desert to avoid the German forces that had cut them off. During the hours of daylight the brigade sent out patrols far and wide, often picking up remnants of British units as they fell back.

Lt Colonel W E Bush, DSO, MC, OBE:

> Patrols consisting of a troop of field artillery, infantry in trucks and carriers were sent out in all directions. To Lt Hugh Haigh of 285th Battery, RA, goes the honour of capturing the first prisoner, as he collected a German warrant officer who had apparently lost himself in the desert. I understand he had a few delicacies in the shape of wine, cigars and food on board, which were quite rightly legitimate prizes of war. Major H D Whitehead, MC, with a patrol from the 5th Battalion Green Howards was instrumental in collecting and leading in a column of our own troops who had made their way out of Benghazi when that place had been cut off from the east by the enemy, they had made a remarkable desert march of several hundred miles to join the main forces. This column was led by Lt Colonel Evans, DSO, of the Royal Sussex Regiment and consisted of his own battalion and Field and Anti-tank Artillery. The anti-tank guns were claimed by 150 Brigade and the rest of the column was directed to the main force nearer the coast.[4]

Pte John Thompson, 5th Battalion Green Howards, was out on patrol:

> We went so far forward we were only 1,000 yards from Gerry and we could see him clearly, the officer says 'while they're knocking about we'll give them something warm for breakfast'. So we radioed back to the artillery, it wasn't long before shells came screaming over us on their way to Gerry, one dropped about 20 yards in front of us but the rest was on target. After that we whipped round and cleared off.[5]

By 2 February the rear-guard task at Bir Tengeder had been completed and 150 Brigade began to pull back to Bir Hakeim, this position was the left flank of the Gazala Line upon which the Eighth Army was to make a stand. The brigade at once set to work constructing an all-round defensive position, mine fields were laid, barbed wire entanglements erected and infantry and gunners dug in as fast as they could. To the south light armour patrolled the open flank while the nearest troops to the north were the 201st Guards Brigade 15 miles away. On 15 February 150 Brigade was on the move again northwards to relieve the Free French at Bir Geff, who in turn moved to Bir Hacheim. 150 Brigade had not been in their new position long when on their right 69 Brigade and 151 Brigade took over the line and relieved the 4th Indian Division. The

---

4   Ibid, by W E Bush (1992).
5   Taped interview with author, John Thompson (Beverley, 1994).

Men of 150 Brigade look out over no-man's land from their slit trench, wondering when Rommel will make his next move, April 1942.

50th Division was back together again and at this time was given the dubious honour of being the only British infantry division in contact with the enemy anywhere in the world.

The general situation in the Gazala area at this time was as a direct result of the fighting during the winter, on 15 November 1941 the Eighth Army had launched Operation Crusader with the objective of engaging and destroying the Axis armour, cutting off the strong positions at Bardia and Sollum along the Egyptian/Cyrenaican frontier, relieving Tobruk and forcing the enemy forces to leave Cyrenaica completely. At first all went well with Crusader but on the third day of the attack Rommel launched his panzers into the battle and forced the British armoured thrust to halt around Sidi-Rezegh south east of Tobruk, there followed three weeks of continuous bitter fighting in which both sides suffered heavy losses.

The heavy fighting continued until early December when Tobruk was relieved and Rommel made a rapid and skilful retreat to the Agedabia area 100 miles south of Benghazi where the British pursuit was brought to a halt. At this point the 1st Armoured Division was moved to the forward area and the badly mauled armoured units that had been in action for so long were withdrawn for a rest and re-fit. By the third week of January Rommel was able to re-new the fight and joined battle with the British forces again, finding the British positions only lightly held the Axis forces broke through and pressed home their advantage rapidly. The situation deteriorated quickly, so much so that the British Commander, Ritchie, decided to evacuate Benghazi and the British forces streamed back to the Gazala Line. In his usual style Rommel followed hard on the heels of the Eighth Army until the situation stabilised at Gazala where both sides faced each other and began piling up supplies and reinforcements for the battles to come.

150 Brigade sat tight in their positions in the Gazala Line and during the lull in the fighting a few lucky men were allowed to go on leave to Alexandria and had to draw lots as to who went and who stayed. Pte Joe Kneeshaw, 5th Battalion Green Howards, drew a card and held his breath:

> We were in the Gazala Line and there was very little happening at that time, we were told there was leave going for four men from our company but we would all have to draw lots to see who went. This corporal got out a pack of cards and we were told to pick one and hold it to our chests and not to look at it under any circumstances, anyone who did was out of the running. Those holding an ace would get the leave, when I was allowed to look I had an ace, at last leave. That was how I survived the disaster at Gazala.[6]

Pte Joe Kneeshaw, 5th Battalion Green Howards.

This was a very active time for all elements of the 50th Division as they enclosed themselves in their fortress like boxes that were surrounded by vast mine fields, each box carefully covered to give all round defence. All positions were dug flush with the ground with no parapet and were very difficult to spot, anti-tank guns were in short supply and enough stores of food and water were stockpiled to stand a three week siege. The dead of other battles had been buried in this area and although they could not be seen their presence was all too obvious as Pte William Gleave found out:

> In the previous campaign a number of Indian troops had been killed and buried nearby, when the wind was in a certain direction the rotten smell of decomposing bodies would be carried down to us. Whoever had done the burying had not gone down very far and had made a bad job of it, they were dug up and reburied, not a pleasant job.[7]

Even though the men were in the front line certain overzealous officers insisted that the men do physical training to keep fit.

Pte Ralph Hymer, 8th DLI:

> We were made to do PT in the early morning while it was still cool enough, we all thought it was bloody ridiculous in our present situation being so close to the enemy. Gerry would spot any above ground activity and of course he spotted us and lobbed a couple of shells

---

6 Ibid, with Joe Kneeshaw (Market Weighton, 2017).
7 Manuscript sent to author by William Gleave (1996).

over each time he saw us, we all scattered back into our trenches swearing and cursing at the bright spark who made us do it.[8]

Sergeant Max Hearst, 5th Battalion East Yorkshire Regiment:

> We was in a front line position dug in like they was in the First World War and every now and then we got the Gerry recce planes over, a bit later you'd hear a distant boom so you'd get your head down, with that a few shells would come over. Everybody had to read part two orders, all companies will assemble for PT at 07:30 a.m. hours. You can just imagine, we was in a wadi and every silly bugger was there, hup two three, hup two three. Gerry must have thought it was his bloody birthday, a gaggle of planes came over strafing, you can picture it, a full battalion of men running and diving for cover, which silly fucker sorted this lot out. As it happened we had no casualties but this was more luck than good management.[9]

Another seemingly pointless activity as far as the troops were concerned was the clearing up of litter at the front. Pte Ron Railton, 5th Battalion Green Howards, recalled one such activity for the whole of his company:

> Every now and again we'd be formed in line, the company that is, and marched over an area and we had to pick up all the rubbish, this caused a lot of grousing. I often used to say to my mates that if anybody asks me what I got my medal for I'll say for picking up ruddy paper.[10]

The mine-fields surrounding each box had to be regularly expanded and the infantry were required to guard the sappers as they undertook this perilous work. Captain Douglas King took out one such party in the dark:

> Our positions were surrounded by enormous mine-marshes and one night I had the job of giving cover to a mine laying party with an RE officer in charge, they were working well and had worked a long time to cover the designated area. Suddenly there was a great explosion that lit up the area and nearly made me jump out of my skin, at first I thought Gerry was mortaring us but the RE chap told me one of his men had been setting the detonator of a mine when it went off blowing him to pieces and wounding two others.[11]

The division began to take its own casualties and the battalion cemeteries began to grow, each one situated near the various boxes. Lt Colonel W E Bush, DSO, MC, OBE, 5th Battalion Green Howards, witnessed the deaths of two popular officers:

> Captain Will Speke, MC, 72nd Field Regiment, RA, was unfortunately killed when his truck ran over a mine in the Temrad area. He was a very popular and efficient officer who

---

8 Taped interview with author, Ralph Hymer (Durham, 1992).
9 Ibid, with Max Hearst (Hull, 1989).
10 Ibid, with Ron Railton (Beverley, 1993).
11 Ibid, with Douglas King (Hull, 1992).

served with the brigade in France in 1940 where he won the Military Cross. He was buried with military honours in the brigade cemetery at Bir Geff. Another loss sustained by the gunners was Lt Pilly who was also killed by the explosion of a mine under his carrier on April 21st.[12]

The boxes being held by the brigades of the 50th Division were meant to be secure bases, able to hold out even in the event of an enemy breakthrough and giving the armoured forces a point of manoeuvre. Rommel was to take full advantage of this static form of defence and was to seize the initiative from the outset.

---

12   Manuscript sent to the author by W E Bush (1992).

**11**

## Operation Full Size: 20, 21 and 22 March 1942

In March 1942, 151 Brigade and 150 Brigade were to take part in large scale diversionary raids upon Tmimi and Martuba airfields, the two most important forward enemy air bases, with the intention of drawing away the Luftwaffe's attention from a sea going convoy en-route for the besieged island of Malta. Two columns were to operate against the air-fields while a third was to take up a covering position around Bir Temrad to cover the assembly of the Tmimi column. A column of the 1st Armoured Division was to draw the attention of enemy troops at Mechili and the Royal Air Force was to bomb both air-fields at dawn and at 6:00 p.m. on the 21st. This was the only support the column could expect to receive during the action.

Brigadier John Sebastian Nichols, DSO, commander of 151 Brigade, and future commander of the 50th Division, was in charge of the whole operation and would accompany the Tmimi column who were supported by tanks. The second column, preparing to attack Martuba, was led by Lt Colonel D S Norman, awarded the DSO for this operation, CO, 4th Battalion East Yorkshire Regiment. It is the latter column that shall be followed in detail, its make-up was as follows:

> One Platoon of the 3rd South African Reconnaissance Battalion. Armoured cars.
> 285th Battery, Royal Artillery, Major Clapham.
> One Battery 95th Anti-tank Regiment, Major Allen. 2 pounder and 18 pounder guns.
> One Battery Light Anti-aircraft Regiment.
> One section 232 Field Coy, Royal Engineers, Lt Cowton.
> C Coy, 4th Battalion East Yorkshire Regiment, Major Huddleston.
> Carrier Platoon 4th Battalion East Yorkshire Regiment.
> Battle patrol, 4th Battalion East Yorkshire Regiment, Lt Murphy.
> One Platoon, machine-guns of the 4th Battalion Cheshire Regiment, Lt Forgan.
> Medical and ambulance units.

On 19 March the situation changed somewhat as Ras El Eleba was taken by the Axis forces and an enemy post established there, this important feature was on the direct route chosen for the advance of the columns and it was imperative the German and Italian forces did not get advanced notice of the coming raid. A pre-emptive strike was to be delivered and the feature retaken before the columns approached it. A subsidiary column was formed to perform this task that consisted of:

> One Platoon of the East Yorkshire Regiment.
> One troop of the 286th Battery, Royal Artillery.
> One troop of the 95th Anti-tank Regiment, Royal Artillery.

On 20 March the columns moved out of the mine-field gaps in 150 and 151 Brigades front and by 3:00 p.m. had gathered in dead ground five miles south-east of Ras El Eleba, the attack on this position took place at 7:00 p.m. and it fell only after a sharp fight. As the main body of the columns passed within two miles of this feature the sharp crackle of continuous small arms fire could be heard clearly and the large flashes of larger explosions lit up the night sky. The troops in their trucks and carriers bounced along in the dark as they continued their dusty and difficult journey through the desert and as the sounds of gunfire receded behind them each man was left alone with his own thoughts.

Sergeant Bob Gibson, MM, 151 Brigade Provost Company, moved out before the columns to mark their route through the desert:

> I had the job of marking the route for that convoy with lamps, all I had to do was lay them out in the desert and pick them up on the way back. We were well ahead of the convoy on the way out and would be behind it on the way in, it was the way in I didn't look forward to. We laid Hurricane Lamps out in four gallon flimsies, petrol tins, with one side cut out and placed upside down over the lamps, these would face in the direction of the convoy and so couldn't be seen by Gerry.[1]

The Martuba column consisted of more than 200 vehicles and the terrain they had to travel over was rock strewn and full of pit falls, the men were caked in sand and dust as the column moved through the darkness to its destination.

Pte John Thompson, 5th Battalion Green Howards:

> We followed up at the rear of all these vehicles and found ourselves in a continuous dust cloud, it got everywhere and was a bloody nuisance, the one good thing was the truck wireless, it was playing The White Cliffs of Dover by Vera Lynn, it made me feel home sick for a time but the thought of what the new day might bring soon stopped that.[2]

The column reached Martuba before noon on 21 March and the infantry dismounted and took up their positions as the gunners of 285 Battery trained their sights on their targets. At noon there was an ear splitting roar as the artillery opened fire on the aerodrome with salvos of eight guns at a time, a number of Italian working parties had been taken by surprise by the arrival of the column and a few prisoners were taken, but because of the precarious position the taking of prisoners was not encouraged. Almost immediately the German artillery began to return fire on

---

1   Taped interview with author, Bob Gibson (Hull, 1991).
2   Ibid, with John Thompson (Beverley, 1994).

the British causing their first casualties, in the skies above two spotter planes appeared as they searched for the British gun positions. It did not take them long to get the information they needed and to relay it back to their base, shortly after a squadron of fighters and dive bombers roared out of the sky and strafed and bombed continuously the British positions, returning to their bases only to re-arm and re-fuel before taking off again and returning to the fight.

Lt Colonel W E Bush, DSO, MC, OBE:

> From 1:00 p.m. to 6:30 p.m. the enemy kept up continuous air attacks employing both fighters and dive-bombers, there being four separate attacks by 21 planes of the latter each time. In addition up to 20 fighters were in the air continuously, squadrons being seen to take off and relieve squadrons in the air. All the damage was done by the fighters using their canon shells against vehicles, soon the area presented a scene of chaos as burning vehicles exploded and burnt fiercely. Unfortunately for us the first to be hit was the anti-aircraft ammunition wagons, three going up in flames almost at once. This seriously affected the amount of anti-aircraft defence we could put up and only one enemy air-craft was shot down. In addition to this the number nine set, with which contact was maintained with the outside world, was hit and none of the other sets were strong enough to regain touch.[3]

Sergeant Arthur Chester, 4th Battalion East Yorkshire Regiment, witnessed the only aircraft to be shot down:

> I spent the biggest part of my time with my face in the sand, straf, straf, straf all the bloody time, we was getting knocked to hell out of it and the noise! Stukas screamed down on us, fighters machine gunned us and their bullets cracked over our heads and blew up the lorries. Bombs exploded around us and our own artillery and anti-aircraft guns kept blasting away through all of this. Casualties was laid all around, well we got one plane at least and it came over us so fast and low it lifted us off the ground and crashed in the rear. We went to it and there was this bloody big fat Itie whose parachute had stuck fast, he was all broken up but still had his slippers on.[4]

The British positions presented a view of desolation and burning vehicles littered the blackened scorched sand, the air raids ceased at 6:30 p.m. The raid had served its purpose of drawing the enemies' attention away from the Malta convoy and it got through safely. During the hours of daylight no move on land had been made against the column though German armour could be seen patrolling not more than 3,000 yards away.

Orders were received that there was to be no withdrawal until 7:00 p.m. and a small party left in daylight to mark the route with specially designed lamps over the difficult terrain. 40 vehicles had been destroyed in the air-raids, this caused great problems with the anti-tank and anti-aircraft guns as these needed to be towed back to the Gazala Line. When darkness fell there was no moon for the men to work by as troops laboured man-handling guns and equipment to waiting transports, some lorries towed two borfor guns as well as being loaded up with men and

---

3  Manuscript sent to author by W E Bush (1992).
4  Taped interview with author, Arthur Chester (Hull, 1992).

equipment. At mid-night on 21/22 March the heavily laden column moved off at a slow pace into the darkness. Some guns that could not be taken back were disabled and abandoned.

Pte Norman Hardy, 4th Battalion East Yorkshire Regiment, was glad to leave the battle-field:

> We were glad to leave that lousy place, lots of kit had to be left behind and we buried the dead as best we could in the night, the lack of a moon was a blessing for us as it hid our activities from the enemy and made the dead less visible as we put them underground. Two 25 pounders had to be left behind and the gunnery people were most upset about this, I think they were more upset about losing their precious guns than losing the men. Anyway under cover of darkness we move out of that place and good bloody riddance.[5]

Pte Norman Hardy, 4th Battalion East Yorkshire Regiment.

Progress was slow on the return journey, it was hot and dirty, a speed of not more than one mile per hour was maintained up until dawn when the column opened out into daylight formation at 6:00 a.m. on 22 March and the speed of the column increased to four miles per hour. At 7:00 a.m. two enemy spotter planes were seen in the sky, by now all men realised what this meant and awaited the inevitable air attack. At 9:00 a.m. a large formation of fighters and dive-bombers came into view and lost no time in fanning out into attack formation, the fighters came in low and sprayed the slow moving vehicles with canon shells to be followed by the Stukas howl as they came down vertically to release their bombs. A few wagons were hit and two anti-tank guns were blown to bits making the rear wheels of the transports that towed them jump up into the air.

Sergeant Herbert Glenton, 4th Battalion East Yorkshire Regiment:

> There was hell on, bombs exploded near our vehicles and showered us with sand and bloody big rocks, we were in a right old state as the sand got everywhere and clogged everything up. The canon shells hit with one hell of a metallic bang, it frightened the life out of us. One platoon from my company came back with half its men wounded or killed, men I'd known before the war.[6]

This attack however was not allowed to continue unopposed and a squadron of Kittyhawk fighters appeared and soon put an end to it. The column was left unmolested for the rest of the journey under the protection of the Desert Air Force and as the vehicles began the last part of their journey ambulance units from 150 Brigade were travelling out to meet them.

Captain Douglas King, 4th Battalion East Yorkshire Regiment, led one such unit but could not find the returning column:

---

5   Ibid, with Norman Hardy (Hull, 1996).
6   Ibid, with Herbert Glenton (1993).

The blazing airfield at Martuba after the raid, 22 March 1942.

I had to take these ambulances to a certain point out in the desert to meet the convoy as it returned and help with the wounded, after a while we got lost and did not know where we were, it was night time and as navigating the desert was bad enough in daylight we decided to sleep in the trucks until dawn in the hope of getting our bearings. As dawn broke I scanned the desert with my binoculars and saw the convoy moving towards us in the distance, what a relief, there were quite a few casualties for us to care for so we loaded our trucks with them and headed back to our lines. Various aircraft flew over us but none of them attacked us as we were marked with the red cross.[7]

By 11:00 a.m. both columns had got safely back behind the advanced British units and were back in their brigade areas by late afternoon. Casualties for the Martuba raid had been 15 killed and over 40 wounded. Equipment lost or destroyed was two 25 pounders, two Borfors Guns, two anti-tank guns and 50 assorted vehicles. The mission had lasted three days and the weary soldiers at last returned to their own lines to take up normal duties. Rest was out of the question as soon the 50th Division would be at the sharp end of events with one of its brigades fighting for its life, darker days were to come.

7   Ibid, with Douglas King (Hull, 1992).

Captain Bob Stafford, 4th Battalion East Yorkshire Regiment, was glad to be back among friends:

> It was a welcome view as our own lines came into sight and we moved through the gaps in our mine-fields to our positions and familiar faces, after what we had been through a hot meal and a laugh and a joke with friends was a great tonic and it soon raised our spirits. We beat a hasty retreat to the Gazala Line as it soon became obvious that things were hotting up.[8]

---

8 Ibid, with Bob Stafford (Hull, 1992).

# 12

## Disaster at Sidi Muftah: The destruction of 150 Brigade, 26 May to 1 June 1942

> The Blue
> Give me a brew can and let me go far away up in the Blue,
> sit in a laager and talk of the days of Benghazi and Mersa Matruh,
> sand in my teeth, sand in my hair, free from all worry, far from all care,
> and no redcap to check me for the clobber I wear, far away up in the Blue.[1]

Before continuing with the events of May 1942 it may be useful to the reader to have a description of the terrain over which the armies of both sides would fight and the problems this caused. The landscape is one of sharp contrasts and despite popular belief the desert is by no means made up of soft sand, there are grey plateaux's of rubble and rocks the size of footballs and endless plains of brown pebbles with flat topped hills of black and white rock at intervals. For miles without end the surface of the desert is flat and hard which will give way to soft sand without any warning, vehicles on the move churn this choking white dusty material up and can be seen for miles from the air. Steep escarpments stretch for hundreds of miles and then fall away in a series of terraces to a vast depression of shimmering sand dunes that go out to the farthest horizon, the climate is hostile to human life and the prevailing wind, though mild enough in summer, is cold at night. Turbulence was frequent and extreme and would cause winds to be whipped up to storm strength, blowing through camps at hurricane force and uprooting tents that were only held in place by pegs that had been sunk into the few inches of top soil that covered the solid rock beneath. The troops of both sides knew it as a bitterly cold wind that would penetrate even the thickest clothing and would chill a man to the bone very quickly. In the summer the winds travelling from the south would be super-heated by the endless sand seas of the interior and would whip across the desert at high temperatures, these are the dreaded Khamsin winds or sand storms which drive clouds of sand and dust before them of incredible density and can reach hundreds of feet in height, moving across the desert these looked like walls of sand.

---

1  Sent to the author by William Gleave, 4th Battalion Green Howards

Rommel and his generals plan the next move at Gazala, May 1942.

Major William I Watson, DSO, MC, 6th Battalion DLI:

> After a sultry morning the fierce Khamsin wind would blow and a huge grey cloud of sand towering into the sky would roll up from the west blotting out the sun and covering everything with a thick layer of dust. It was then that the sand choked the men, their weapons and vehicles and so charged the latter with that strange phenomenon, static electricity, to touch any vehicle produced an instant shock. It was then too that the atmosphere became so depressing that every soldier moved as listless automatons but mostly lay in their dugouts or posts hiding their faces until the storm passed.[2]

From the coastal road in the north which skirts the Mediterranean there were no roads of any kind in 1942, apart from the ancient tracks of the interior such as the Trigh Capuzzo and the Trigh el Abd [the way of the slaves]. South of the coastal road there are no towns and the names on the maps represent maybe an old disused fort, or a water hole known as a Bir in Arabic, or even a pile of boulders marking a caravan route. And so in this hostile and barren land the opposing armies faced each other and prepared for the next round of a life and death struggle that would decide the fate of thousands of men and eventually the outcome of the war.

---

2   H. Moses, *The Faithful Sixth* (Durham: County Durham Books, 1995), p. 165.

On 21 April 1942, 150 Brigade handed over the Bir Geff position to a brigade from the 1st South African Division and took up new positions at Got el Auleb, here they continued with the usual activities of digging trenches and gun pits. The Auleb defensive box was so far from the other boxes that in the event of an attack it could not expect support from the other brigades, this box that was to be held by 150 Brigade is known at times as the Auleb box or the Sidi Mufta box, either name is applicable as they are the names of features closest to or within the position. 69 Brigade was six miles away to the north and 10 miles to the south the Free French were at Bir Hacheim. The men holding the Gazala Line found themselves dug in as their fathers had been during the Great War and this was no easy thing to do in the hard rock of the desert, once in position the new features on the landscape had to be camouflaged and made as comfortable as possible for their occupants.

Intermittent shelling and bombing raids added to the dangers of a soldiers life, when a Storch spotter plane was seen overhead it usually meant a barrage and men would seek cover below ground, the dull boom of artillery would be heard in the distance and as men crouched low in their trenches the whistle of shells would be heard followed by the crump of explosions on the unlucky recipients. Another form of aggressive activity experienced by all the battalions in the line was Jock Columns, these hit and run raids were intended to either gather information or to attack a specific target and a full strength column would be made up of:

A company of infantry
Two detachments of three inch mortars
A battery of 25 pounder field guns
A battery of two pounder anti-tank guns
A platoon of Vickers machine-gunners
A troop of Borfors anti-aircraft guns and some medical personnel

Jock Columns and patrols were a regular feature of life in the front line and were often dangerous affairs.

Lance Corporal William Ridley, 9th DLI, was waiting to go out with a patrol that was cancelled:

We went through the mine-field gap and out into the desert and formed up, first it was on, then it was off, then it was on, then it was off again. It got to about noon and we was still there, Gerry was only 20 miles away, they buggered us about and somebody said 'right it's cancelled'. The trucks faced about to go back into the box, I was battle wise by this time and used to sit with my legs over the side of the truck and I was always watching the skies. I saw this gaggle of Stukas, I says 'Andy, Stukas', he says 'why they're away man'. I says 'aye but the buggers'll be back', I saw them come back and he says 'gerroff, no stay on'. Well by the time he'd said gerroff I was off, an RASC man had seen them too and he was runnin' along-side the truck and I landed on top of him, I could feel his fear, his panic. I grabbed hold of him and he was struggling like hell, I said 'lie still, lie still' but couldn't hold him you know and then the world came to an end. For a good five minutes they knocked, oh god, I had this terrible feeling I was going to be hit in the backside, the wheel I was laid against was punctured by a piece of flying shrapnel. Anyway I didn't move for a while, then I lifted my head and it was pitch black night and all I could see was the flames, they'd got the ambulances. I jumps up and the first thing I thinks of is the RASC lad, he'd got 15 yards past the truck and had got a belly full and was holding his entrails in with both hands. I dashed back to the truck and sorted my lads out and found one was covered in blood like, but it wasn't his, it was the sergeants who'd had his legs blown off. All the lads was there except the sergeant, one man was wandering around so I gets hold of him, his eyes, they had no pupils they was up in his head you know. I slapped him five or six times hard, slapped him backwards and forwards like shouting his name. I was belting his face and at the finish his eyes came down. There was this RP [Regimental Police] and he was panicking and shouting 'give us me tin hat, give us me tin hat'. So I was that mad I hit him with it, he went out like a light. That was the last I saw of him and I haven't seen him from that day to this. Then I thought about the poor bugger at the back of the truck, this lad had both fists in his guts so we carried him in, half way back he just stretched out and died. We carried another lad in who'd been hit in the testicles and they were like size five footballs, another of me mates had his leg blown off. One lad had done the daft thing you should never do, he'd got underneath a truck and the truck got hit, the petrol tank blew up and he crawled out through the flames. I saw him three months later in hospital and he was lying in bed naked, you could tell where his puttees and pants had been but the rest of him was all crisp. He'd lost the soft parts of his nose, ear lobes and lips. We lost a lot of good lads there.[3]

Lt Patrick Leslie Rome, MC, 6th DLI, was out on a fighting patrol when they came upon a German position:

Two of the patrol went forward to investigate two dark objects, one man returned to say that two light machine-guns were mounted in a small trench with two men fast asleep. We decided to capture the two men as no other section positions could be seen in the vicinity. Visibility was about 20 yards. On approaching the position the soldiers in the trench awoke and stood up, myself and one other rank were by this time five yards from the trench. The nearest German soldier repeated twice what appeared to be a question and sounded like 'hoo yah'. He then screamed loudly and I gave the order for the patrol to open fire, a grenade was thrown into the trench and I fired three shots at point blank range with my revolver. One Sapper who was also armed with a revolver opened fire as did one of the rifles close behind me, when the grenade had burst the screaming from the trench ceased and one of the light machine-guns was blown into the air. By this time many automatic weapons had opened fire and a green verey light went up from the centre of the mound.[4]

Sergeant Max Hearst, 5th Battalion East Yorkshire Regiment:

One day we was out on a jock column and we saw an enemy column moving through the desert, Captain Bilton was watching it through his field glasses for some time and told us it was an unarmed Italian convoy. At the time we said 'Ooh good show' as it sounded like an easy target. We made a B line for them and captured the lot, I got myself two huge cans of

3 Taped interview with author, William Ridley (Durham, 1993).
4 Manuscript sent to author by P L Rome (1990).

water which was scarce, with that we got set upon by the Germans who had been in close support and we hadn't seen them. They beat us up really badly and we took quite a few casualties and so we went hell for leather back to our positions at Gazala.[5]

Pte James Coglan, MM, 6th DLI, was in a truck that was caught in enemy fire:

The officer said 'retire' so I got into the wagon and all of a sudden I saw the end of the truck go up in flames, so I dived off and there were lads getting off the portee and running towards us. The officer called after me 'leave them, leave them', and I shouted back 'I'm going back for them'. So I went back for them and got two men off the portee, one had his back ripped open. I was out in the open and Gerry wasn't half giving me some hammer, I didn't think I would get back, I thought I'd had it. But I got them off and got back.[6]

Pte Jim Betts, 4th Battalion East Yorkshire Regiment, was out on a fighting patrol when the officer in charge lost his sense of direction:

It was decided a fighting patrol would be sent out at night to see if we could get any prisoners for intelligence purposes and I ended up being part of that patrol. We were well out when we ran into an Itie patrol in the dark, they opened up and so did we, one lad was stood up firing his bren gun and I told him to get under cover, he said 'not likely I'm enjoying this' I thought sooner you than me mate because tracer rounds were flying all around us. Don't know if we knocked them out or they just withdrew but it went quiet eventually. This young officer was with us and he was studying his compass, he said 'right this is the way back men, follow me'. Well a few of us knew he was wrong and we began to tell him so and he threatened to shoot us for disobeying orders, we said we're not going to end up prisoners so to hell with your compass we're going this way. So there we were in the middle of the desert at night arguing about the direction of our own lines. After a while flares shot into the sky, I asked him whose lights they were? He had to admit they were German lights coming from the direction he wanted to take us, so we went our way and got back safe. The next day he came to see us all and apologised for his mistake and asked how we knew the way back, 'Just look at the stars' we said. It must have taken a lot of guts to admit he was wrong, but he went up in our estimation because he did.[7]

The troops of the Eighth Army settled down to their routines and looked across the open desert in the direction of the Africa Corp wondering when the next blow would fall, and as usual Rommel decided the issue and struck first. The German and Italian forces were to deliver a preemptive strike which was to lead to the capture of Tobruk followed by an advance upon the Nile Delta. Malta was a thorn in the side of the Axis forces and their convoys could be attacked from its air-fields with ease, it would have to be eliminated. The German High Command authorised Rommel to launch an attack on Tobruk but added that he was to halt at the Egyptian frontier to allow maximum support to be given to the Malta undertaking. During May the Africa Corps

---

5   Taped interview with author, Max Hearst (Hull, 1993_).
6   H. Moses, *The Faithful Sixth* (Durham: County Durham Books, 1995), p.169.
7   Taped interview with author, Jim Betts (Hull, 1989).

was replenished by the arrival of new tanks, men, vehicles and essential supplies to swell their badly depleted ranks. For the new offensive Rommel had at his disposal some 90,000 men backed up by 560 tanks, 332 of which were German. The Luftwaffe provided 480 aircraft, Italian and German. The British forces at Gazala consisted of 100,000 men of the Eighth Army and 849 tanks, 167 of them the new Grants. Although Ritchie outnumbered Rommel on the ground, the air balance had swung heavily in the latter's favour, for the Desert Air Force had only 190 serviceable air-craft, most of them Kitty-hawks and Hurricanes, somewhat inferior to the new German Me 109F.

Once it had girded itself for battle the might of the Africa Corps moved *en masse* into no man's land and officers were taken on secret reconnaissance missions to familiarise themselves with the ground they would have to fight over. The German and Italian artillery began slowly to reduce the number of shells fired on the Gazala Line so as not to arouse suspicion, in order to build up stocks for the coming battle. Rommel's battle plan was for a diversionary attack to be launched upon the northern Gazala sector by the X and XX1 Italian Corps, this force was to be known as Cruwell and was to attack on the afternoon of 26 May, it was intended to hide the main thrust and to convince the British that the main German forces were in the northern sector where British observers would have seen numbers of tanks assembling and great clouds of dust being churned up as they clattered and roared about. But as the sun set the Panzer units in the north slipped away to join Rommel's flanking movement leaving only one Italian tank battalion, the dust being churned up now looked like massive numbers of tanks but was in effect air-craft engines with propellers fixed to lorry chassis that were slowly circling in the desert. The main body however would be concentrated in a second mobile group that comprised of the Africa Corps and the Italian motorised XX Corps led by Rommel which would sweep round behind Eighth Army's southern flank. On 26 May at 5:00 p.m. the code name Venice was sent to all Axis units and unknown to the British the battle for the Gazala Line had begun.

Lt Colonel W E Bush, DSO, MC, 5th Battalion Green Howards, saw the Italian diversionary force attacking but was surprised when they did not follow through:

> On the morning of the 26th May the enemy remained quiet and made no reply to our harassing fire which was continued until 2:30 p.m. at this hour our column, which was due for relief, stopped firing and commenced a withdrawal so as to hand over the front to the column from 69 Brigade. Suddenly the enemy came to life and under cover of artillery fire

A German half-track tows a large artillery piece into position, May 1942.

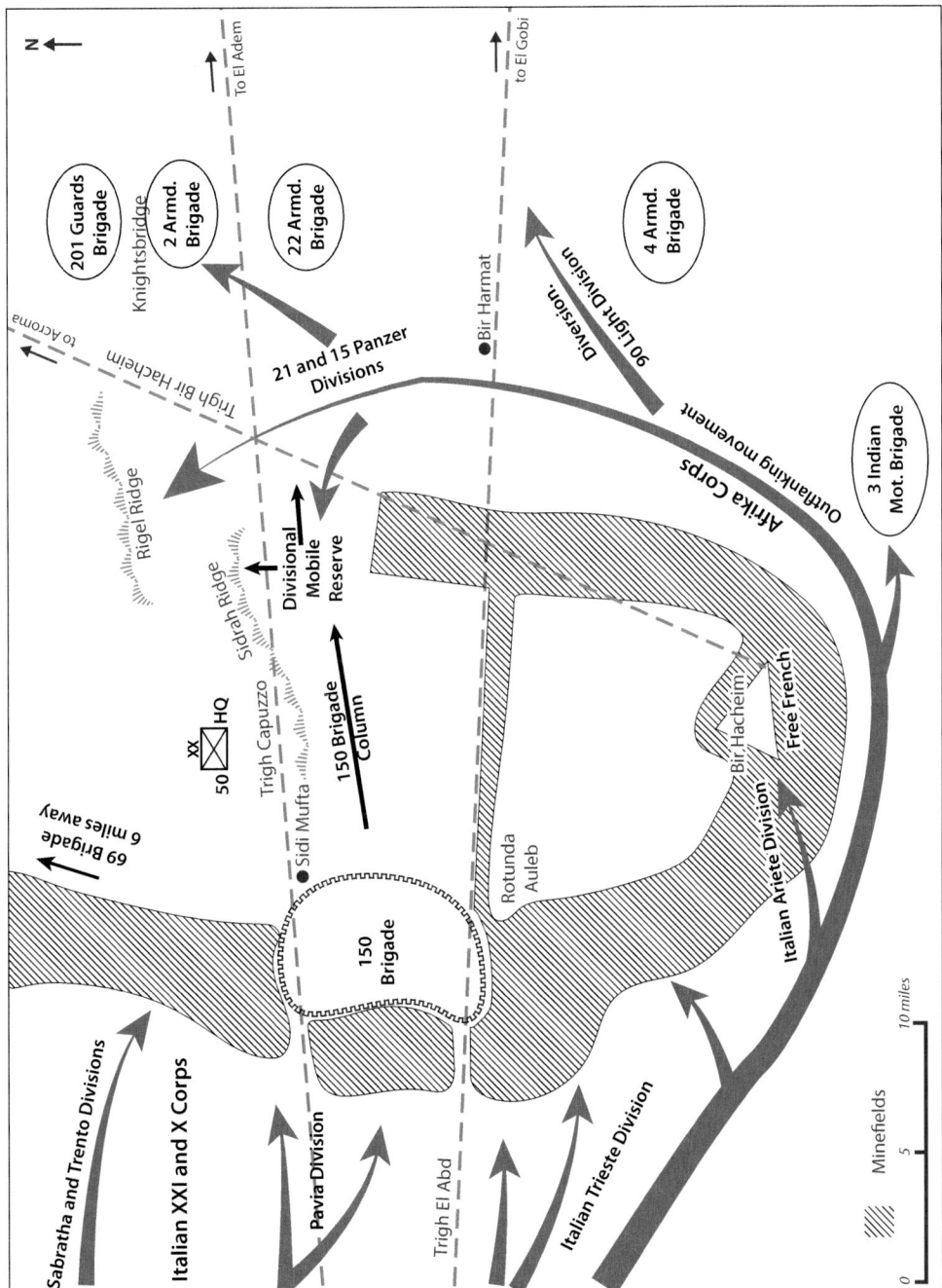

Map 6 Rommel's forces advance and outflank the British line, 27/28 May 1942.

advanced with tanks and armoured cars. The withdrawal of our troops proceeded to plan, the battalion leap-frogging its troops and replying to enemy fire. For some unknown reason the enemy advance stopped short at Barrel 13 and our column was able to withdraw into the main positions unmolested by enemy ground forces. It was however bombed by six Stukas when passing through the gap in the mine-field.[8]

Major D'arcy Mander, DSO, 4th Battalion Green Howards, had the same experience:

> We were due to hand over to another Jock Column from 69 Brigade on the 26th and that morning the enemy were strangely quiet. At 2:30 p.m. we stopped firing and were preparing to move quietly back to base when suddenly the desert erupted into life and it seemed to us that the entire Africa Corps were advancing towards us under the cover of artillery fire. We withdrew fairly smartly but in good order, each troop leap-frogging its way back and thus providing continuous support for the column as we were chased back to our mine-field. However when they came into range of the field and medium artillery of the main 50th Division positions the enemy attack was not pressed home, although an air strike by six Stukas of the Luftwaffe was indeed pressed warmly home as we filtered our way back through the mine-field.[9]

The weak attacks by the Cruwell Group produced little reaction from the British as the outflanking forces, with brilliant moonlight to aid them, moved on their pre-set course to Bir Hacheim in the south. The advanced guards of the 15th Panzer Division moved ahead of the main body, behind them followed the boxes of the Panzer Regiments with artillery, engineers, motorised infantry and anti-tank units on the flanks and in the centre was the Hump, the thousands of trucks of the supply echelons. In between the massed tanks of the 21st Panzer Division on the left and the 15th Panzer Division on the right marched corps headquarters led by Rommel. This mass of vehicles and men covered an area of 11 square miles and must have been an impressive sight as the might of the German and Italian forces thundered towards the British left flank in a cloud of sand and dust.

British armoured car patrols met this awesome force en-route and withdrew quickly signalling news of this movement to Eighth Army Headquarters as they did so. On 27 May at 3:30 a.m. this great mass of armour halted just south of Bir Hacheim after marching 32 miles by compass bearing throughout the night. Here they took up attack formation, re-fuelled and prepared for the next move forward. Eighth Army dismissed the movement of this outflanking group as a feint intended to draw attention away from the centre and the north. Ritchie had suggested as early as 20 May that Rommel's most likely line of attack would be along the Trigh Capuzzo on 50th Divisions front. Auchinleck went on to add that a flanking attack was not out of the question, he advised Ritchie to concentrate his armoured forces on the Trigh Capuzzo and that the armoured divisions should be kept intact and not committed to the battle piecemeal. Unfortunately for the British Ritchie and his divisional commanders paid little attention to the latter part of Auchinleck's advice.

---

8   Manuscript sent to author by W E Bush (1992).
9   Ibid, by W E Bush (1992).

By dawn on 27 May the German 90th Light Division on the German right flank was already on its way to El Adem, on its left was the 15th Panzer Division, on the left flank of the 15th Panzer Division was the 21st Panzer Division and on their left was the Italian Ariete Division, the advance behind the British Gazala Line had begun. So far Rommel's battle plan had worked well but from here on things started to go drastically wrong, his intelligence staff had provided a fatally incomplete account of the enemy's positions and strength. To the south of Bir Hacheim a box held by the 3rd Indian Motorised Brigade was struck by the left flank of the Axis forces, its existence being unknown to Rommel. The Indian Brigade sent a desperate message to Eighth Army 'the whole of the bloody Africa Corps is drawn up in front of us like a bloody review', for over an hour the Indian troops held off the Ariete Division and two battalions of the 21st Panzer Division, but then the 5th Panzer Regiment launched a fierce attack against the under armed defenders and the Axis forces rolled over the doomed position at approximately 6:30 a.m.

The Italian Ariete Division then came up against the Free French at Bir Hacheim and a French column commanded by Major Amiel was operating well forward under orders of the 7th Armoured Brigade. Amiel reported the movement of large numbers of tanks around Rotunda Segnali and as darkness fell on the 26th radio messages flooded in confirming Amiel's information. The Frenchmen sat in their positions that night and listened to the rumble and roar of numerous tank engines as Rommel's forces churned their way southward, to the north the Gazala Line was lit up with parachute flares and flashes of gun-fire. On the morning of 27 May the French Brigade was under attack and put up a fierce resistance, halting the Ariete Division in its tracks, the Italian attack was launched with great panache as their tanks smashed through the British mine-fields. The French anti-tank gunners took a steady toll of the enemy tanks as they advanced but six tanks broke into their position firing at anything that moved, most of these tanks were knocked out by the French 75's firing over open sights, others became victim to Borfors anti-aircraft guns and the tough French Legionnaires finished the job by scrambling over the tank hulks firing revolvers through the observation slits and dropping grenades into the turrets.

French anti-tank gunners in action at Bir Hacheim, 27 May 1942.

In the centre the 15th Panzer Division came upon the 4th Armoured Brigade in the process of deploying, the 8th Hussars were cut to pieces and the 3rd Battalion Royal Tank Regiment lost many of its Grants. The Axis forces that were to sweep behind the British Line began to slow down as British armoured assaults smashed into them. The addition of two new weapons took the Africa Corps by surprise, the new Grant tanks and the six pounder anti-tank guns. These enabled the British to engage the enemy at a greater distance than normal and gave them more lethal fire-power against Axis armour. The battle raged continuously to the rear of the British boxes and Rommel's valuable store of petrol was fast being used up, no fresh supplies could get through and the attack was being starved to death.

Lt Bill Close, MC and bar, 3rd Battalion Royal Tank Regiment, saw an ominous sight to his front and it seemed to be drawing ever closer:

> The Africa Corps was never a pretty sight and seen through binoculars at 3,000 yards range it looked positively evil. A long wall of dust was extended ahead of us with dark objects visible in it, the mysterious shadows in the murk didn't look friendly. Jim Hutton, the squadron leader, asked if they might be friendly as the other regiments in the brigade were supposed to be on our flanks, but the CO said they weren't. The daily heat haze was developing making observation very difficult, but it could not hide the fact that only a panzer group moved in such a deliberate fashion extended over a broad front, speed carefully regulated to aid command and control and to save fuel. When we got to within 2,000 yards or so the images became sharp and I realised that it was the Africa Corps going about its business. Jim reported the enemy strength, 'I say again 200 tanks', I thought he might be mistaken and started to count them myself. There seemed to be 20 in the front rank and similar lines at 200 yard intervals stretching into the distance behind them, they were coming on faster than I had thought at first glance. The CO ordered us to send a troop to the left to look out for the 8th Hussars and the rest of us, the light squadron, got smartly out of the line of fire to cover the battalion's right.[10]

Lt Robert Watt, 3rd Battalion Royal Tank Regiment, was waiting out in the open when the heavier Grant tanks came up behind him. Their new armaments gave the enemy a shock as they engaged them at much longer ranges than they had been able to before:

> There just ahead of us was a cloud of dust coming in our direction, this was it, the whole bloody German army coming straight for us and here we sat out in the open, 16 light tanks [Honeys] with 37mm pop-guns with 100 enemy tanks charging towards us hell bent on driving us into the ground. The rest of the regiment came up behind us, hull down, and as the range closed the COs voice came through loud and clear 'open fire and throw everything you have at them including any spare bully'. Their new 75mm guns caused chaos among the advancing panzers, it was almost as if they were unaware of our presence or the power of our guns until a few of their tanks started to burn. Enemy tanks started milling around as if out of control and the infantry went to ground. But within minutes the enemy

---

10   W. Close, *Tank Commander* (Barnsley: Pen and Sword, 2013), p. 63.

column had stopped and sent a salvo of armour piercing shells flying in our direction with high explosive screaming overhead.[11]

Sergeant Buck Kite, MC and bar, 3rd Battalion Royal Tank Regiment, was relaxing with his crew and did not expect to see the enemy for a while:

> None of us felt we would meet the enemy for some time and many commanders like myself were sitting on their turrets, the drivers had their flaps open and the crew were passing round biscuits plastered with jam or bully beef. We pulled up an incline and over the horizon came this mass of vehicles, I was wondering who the devil they could be when the CO's voice came over the wireless 'that is the enemy'. I'd been so engrossed by the sight that I hadn't noticed a motor-cyclist about 50 yards away, it was only when he spun round and roared off I saw he was a Gerry dispatch rider. My heart sank as the enemy soft skinned vehicles began to pull back leaving upwards of 90 tanks coming toward us, when they were about 1,000 yards away there were flashes all along their front rank and a hail of shells all going one way screamed around us. We still hadn't received the order to open fire and waiting for it was pure agony, we were still moving slowly forward and at least three of our number had been hit and were in flames by the time it came.[12]

Sergeant Buck Kite, MC and bar, 3rd Battalion Royal Tank Regiment.

Lt Bill Close, MC and bar, 3rd Battalion Royal Tank Regiment, watched as the German armour came on in their usual confident manner, only to receive a shock as the new Grant tanks opened fire on them:

> The 15th Panzer Division cannot have been expecting the reception it received having seen the light squadron first it may even have assumed that the others, seen through the haze, were also equipped with light Honey tanks. They certainly slowed down to fire at a range which would normally be beyond the effective reach of our 37mm guns, perhaps hoping that we would oblige them by closing and suffering the usual consequences. Instead 3rd RTR's heavy squadrons halted along a low ridge and opened fire with sponson and turret guns, simultaneously delivering the quantity of shot equal to four conventional squadrons of the one cannon per tank variety. The Panzers slewed to a halt with fragments of metal flying from them as they were hit. Instead of the sharp crack of two pounder shells on German metal there was a noisy rending of metal as heavy shot ripped through armour plate at 1,200 yards and smashed off pieces at 1,500.[13]

11   Interview with author, R Watt (1989).
12   R. J. Icks, *Famous Tank Battle* (Northamptonshire: Profile Publications, 1973), p. 79.
13   W. Close, *Tank Commander* (Barnsley: Pen and Sword, 2013), p.69.

A British Grant Tank passing a knocked out Italian tank.

Captain Robert James Crisp, DSO, MC, 3rd Battalion Royal Tank Regiment, was in the light squadron fitted out with Honey tanks. These were no match for the German anti-tank gunners and soon fell victim to the superior fire power of the enemy:

> Suddenly there was a fearful bang and simultaneously I was drenched from head to foot in an astonishing cascade of cold water. For a moment or two I was physically and mentally paralysed, I just could not believe that anything like that could happen. Then the realisation came swiftly and terribly, the water tins on the back of the tank had been hit, it could mean only one thing. As I looked backwards I was already giving the order to the gunner to traverse the turret as fast as he bloody well could. In one comprehensive flash I saw it all and the fear leapt up in me. Not 50 yards away a 50mm anti-tank gun pointed straight at the Honey light tank I was in, pointed straight between my eyes. Beyond it were other guns and then as the dust drifted over the scarp the sight I had dreaded most, a number of motionless Honeys and the huddled black bereted men crouched on the sand or stretched out in the agony of death. It took less than a second for the whole scene and its awful meaning to register in my mind, I could see the German gunners slamming the next shell into the breach as the turret whirled. In the same moment I saw the puff of smoke from the anti-tank gun and felt and heard the strike on the armour plating. I looked down into the turret, a foot or two below me the gunner was staring at his hand, over which a dark red stain was slowly spreading. Then he gave a scream and fell grovelling on the floor. In the top right hand corner of the turret a jagged hole gaped and through it, like some macabre peep show, I could see the anti-tank gun being reloaded. I knew that in a few seconds I would be dead. Twice I felt the Honey shudder and the second time more water came

pouring in. My mind leapt about trying to find some way to stay alive and I suddenly saw a slim chance. If the tank could move at all we could drop over the edge of the escarpment where we would be out of sight of those blasted anti-tank guns. I could see them framed in that jagged hole, the gunners working feverishly, their faces strained and vicious. I said urgently into the mike 'driver advance, over the edge quick!' I felt the gears engage and for a split second the world stood still, then the engine revved and the Honey heaved forward and dropped with a violent crash over the escarpment. In the turret we were hurled about like corks and then the bouncing stopped and we rode smoothly down the slope. We were out of sight of the guns on top of the escarpment and with a great rush of unbelief I knew we were going to get away with it. So much had happened and I had looked closely into the valley of the shadow that I found it difficult to return to reality, I just could not fully absorb the situation. My thoughts went out to the rest of the squadron, where were they? What had happened to them? Were they all dead? It was something I had to find out. We were chugging along casually through the deserted silence of the wadi, it was uncanny after the tumult and terror just behind us and the thought kept on intruding that we were no longer on earth, that we were driving in some ghost tank on another level of existence, that we were all dead. When I put the mouthpiece to my lips I was half prepared to hear no voice come out. The unreality persisted when the Honey swung right in response to my order and moved slowly up the slope to the crest.

    As soon as my eyes were above the lip of the escarpment we halted and the full picture of horror burst in on me immediately. 500 yards away, like a projection on a cinema screen, lay the battle-field. My eyes lifted to the tall black columns of smoke leaning slightly in the wind, and followed them down to the Honeys gasping smoke. Four of my tanks were blazing infernos, three others just sat there sad and abandoned. A line of German anti-tank guns with their crews still manning them lined the top of the drop and the whole scene was silhouetted sharply against the yellow clouds of dust which rose in a thick fog from the wadi bank. I said wearily over the intercom 'ok Whaley, there's nothing we can do, let's go back'. We followed the wadi southwards as it grew shallower, eventually disgorging us unobtrusively on to the plateau over which we had charged so bravely, when? Ten minutes ago? an hour ago? today? yesterday? How many lives ago? My wrist watch was staring me in the face as we paused on the rim of the depression. The hands pointed to 17 minutes past one, 17 minutes.[14]

Oberleutnant Herbert W Schmidt, Artillery Regiment, 90th Light Division, commanded a battery of anti-tank guns, the British Grant tanks attacked and rolled over his position:

I held my fire but the companies on the right let rip with the 50mm Pak guns, I saw some of their shells bounce harmlessly off the British Grants. On the other hand the enemies replying fire was grim, his shell bursts among our infantry were particularly deadly. Now a shiver went through me, from out of the dip emerged rank after rank of the new tanks, a good 60 in all, they came at us with every muzzle blazing. I got my right gun in action and it stopped one tank, several others were burning but the bulk of them came on relentlessly.

---

14  Manuscript sent to author by Herbert Thompson (Beverley, 1994).

What was wrong with my left gun I wondered, it was silent its muzzle drooping to the ground, I leapt from my trench despite the stuff whistling all round and raced to the gun. Two of the crew were sprawled on the ground dead, the breach of the gun was shattered. The loader lay beside a wheel bleeding from a machine-gun bullet to the chest 'water, water' he gasped. A fresh salvo burst beside the gun, tanks were obviously attacking at point blank range. To stop there meant death, I dropped prone and tried to cradle the head of the wounded man in my arms. He shook his head at me, 'I'll carry you to my trench there's water there' I shouted in his ear. He shook his head again and to my consternation he heaved himself to his feet and half stumbled half ran to my slit trench, now British tanks were right on top of the front lines in the sector to my right. I scrambled back towards my trench, Muller was not there, and I dragged the wounded gunner half way into the hole with me. My Italian water bottle was half full of coffee and I thrust it into the man's shaking hand, he drank greedily and then sagged back, dead, his legs dangled in the hole, his torso lay twisted on the rim of it. Shell bursts were now erupting all around, was I alone here now? As I wondered this a reply came from behind where Sergeant Webber was firing my third gun, he pumped out shell after shell but there was little help in his valour. 12 tanks swung at us to neutralise this menace, their guns blazed insistently at us and they came straight on. I dropped my glasses and rolled to the bottom of my trench where Muller had spread a blanket, I dragged it over myself in ineffectual protection. The toes of the dead man's boots dangled six inches from my eyes. The earth trembled and my throat was like sandpaper, this then was the end, my fiancé would be told 'It is with deep regret that I have to inform you …….' She would read I died a hero's death for the Fatherland and what would it mean? That I was just a mess in the sand at an unidentified spot in the sand near an unimportant point in the desert. A tank crunched at the edge of my trench and I heard an English voice calling, was it a man in a tank or an infantryman following up with a fixed bayonet? A blanket is not much good against a bayonet. The minutes crawled by and I now heard German voices, the British were rounding up prisoners. Firing had ceased and I heard the tanks rolling off towards the south, silence descended on the battlefield and still I lay there like a sleeping man. When I lifted my head the sky had dimmed from its brassy afternoon glare, evening was coming. I saw no sign of life until I was startled by a figure that burst like a jack-in the-box from a slit trench some way back, it was my man Muller, he had an anguished look on his face, 'are you well *Oberleutnant*'? He called to me and added oddly 'I am not'. It was good to be alive.[15]

Sergeant Buck Kite, MC and bar, remembers his Grant tank taking hit after hit as he tried to reverse out of action:

My gunners and loaders didn't need any advice from me, they could see all they needed through their periscopes and sights. While they loaded and fired I crouched in the turret trying to weigh things up. My troop officer's tank on my left began to back out of the line in some sort of trouble and the tank on either side was burning furiously. We were being hit by all sorts of things and although it was suicide to put your head outside it was impossible

---

15   Manuscript sent to author by H Wernaman, Africa Corps Veteran (Germany, 1989).

to see a thing inside. The air was stinking and thick with cordite fumes from the two guns going hammer and tongs and our eyes were red rimmed and streaming, you could taste the explosive.

Now and again there would be a terrific thud and the interior filled with dust and sparks as the tank rocked on its bogies. Despite the noise and smoke we were scoring hits. We were using ammunition at a tremendous rate and I was relieved when the CO came on air and ordered us to reverse slowly while continuing to engage. We'd edged back about 30 yards when I felt a tap on my beret, a bailed out crew member from another tank shouted in my ear that they needed morphia for a badly wounded man they had dragged onto the back of my tank. I had just got it when there was a heavier than usual crash and the 75 gunner said he couldn't fire any longer as the gun was damaged. We hadn't gone another 50 yards when there was a terrific thump and bits of metal and sparks flew about the inside and the tank stalled. Someone shouted 'Chalkie's been hit, his flaps been blown off and there's a bloody great hole in the front of the tank'. We'd barely backed another 50 yards when a solid shot smashed into the engine at the rear without touching anyone, but although there was a nasty smell like seized bearings there were no flames and the boys on the back were able to get down with their casualty while we lifted out Chalkie, a nightmare job as he was in great pain and we had to give him morphia too. While we were doing this I glanced around and saw the enemy tanks were slowly moving forward again and that our remaining tanks, about six in all, were still engaging them with every gun fit to fire. The rest of the Grants were either burning or standing abandoned.[16]

The 8th Hussars met the Africa Corps as it swept around Bir Hacheim, their light Honey tanks were no match for the heavier Panzers and they were cut up badly:

Major J W Hackett, Officer Commanding C Squadron, 8th Hussars:

I got C Squadron on the move very quickly, they were a handy lot. We went up a slope in this typically undulating desert country and as I reached the top of this rise the commanding officer said to me over the radio 'report to me when you first see them'. I came over the top and there in front of me was the whole bloody German army, as far as I could see and coming my way. I replied to the colonel's transmission 'am engaging them, out'. I put up a black flag to say attack, in those days wireless was not too reliable and like a mug I forgot to take it down again. Any tank flying a flag is of course a control element and attracts fire, so I attracted all the fire there was. I suppose my tank was the first in the Eighth Army to be knocked out that day, which was about three minutes after putting up the black flag. I got burnt, quite badly as it turned out.[17]

Corporal Harold Harper, 8th Hussars:

We had only gone 600 or 700 yards when we heard a garbled message from the commander's radio which immediately told us something was wrong. Captain Birkin jumped out

---

16  Ibid, by P Jackson (1992).
17  R. J. Icks, *Famous Tank Battle* (Northamptonshire: Profile Publications, 1973), p.179.

and dashed across to the armoured car and I followed him. I've never seen anything like it in my life, Major Garry Birkin, Captain Ivor Birkin's brother, lay flat on the floor obviously dead. I went to the back and opened up the doors of the armoured car. Apparently an armour-piercing shell had gone clean through the middle of the battery commander as he was standing in the turret and then chopped the heads off the two radio operators. All you could see was the two lads, their hands still holding their mouth pieces although their heads had rolled onto the floor. I returned to my own vehicle but decided I must go back and pick up Captain Birkin who was in a very distraught state having just seen his brother killed.[18]

The 3rd RTR and the 8th Hussars were driven back with heavy losses, the Germans brought forward a battery of the dreaded 88's and their deadly fire drove off the surviving British tanks. This combined with Panzer attacks from flank and front made the 4th Armoured Brigade's position untenable and it fell back upon El Adem later in the day.

Lt Bill Close, MC, 3rd Battalion Royal Tank Regiment, came under fire from the advancing panzers:

> I felt a tremendous crash on my tank followed by a yell from below to bail out, we had become a broadside target for a number of enemy panzers that had crept closer, almost unseen in the murk and dust. An armour piercing shot had penetrated the front plate, slightly wounding Lance Corporal Colclough the driver. When I checked the tank after bailing out I was surprised to find we had been hit five times without being penetrated.[19]

The reaction to Rommel's assault on the morning of the 27th by Eighth Army was sluggish and uncoordinated and even as the attack rolled in some would still hold the view that the main assault would come in the north. Lt Parry was with a mobile repair shop in the south of the British Line and his radio operator had difficulty raising Regimental Headquarters, he was told to search other bands. A message came on the set loud and clear and not in code, it was from an officer in the south sending a message to XXX Corps HQ at El Adem, the officer stated:

> There is a cloud of dust to the south and it has the appearance of a military formation. Through the haze I can now see tanks, difficult to identify but possibly Mk 1V's.[20]

The reply to this news came from a very bored sounding individual who kept repeating 'there are no troops to your south'. Undeterred the young officer in the south continued:

> I am counting [panzer] Mk 1V's, there is no doubt repeat no doubt that this is a large German force. Mk 1Vs number over 30, there are also Mk 111s and a large number of motorised infantry. This could be, I repeat, could be the Africa Corps moving toward El Adem.[21]

18  Manuscript sent to author by Harold Craig (Bridlington, 1992).
19  W. Close, *Tank Commander* (Barnsley: Pen and Sword, 2013), p.73.
20  C. E. Lucas-Philips, *Alamein* (London: Heinemann, 1962), p. 203.
21  Ibid, p. 204.

Still XXX Corps refused to believe this report and repeated a number of times 'there are no enemy forces in your area'. The sender of the bad news of this unexpected thrust continued with his message to the bitter end:

> I have been spotted by the enemy and have come under fire [the explosions from incoming shells could be heard in the background]. It is undoubtedly the Africa Corps moving at speed towards El Adem, I am under fire and [message ends].[22]

The broadcast ended abruptly as fierce tank battles raged to the east behind the Gazala Line for most of the day, still the Panzers pressed forward against the British counter attacks.

Lt John Michael Gregson Halstead, Queen's Bays, was in the thick of it as shells screamed around his tank. The excitement of battle did not last long as he became a target for the German anti-tank gunners:

Lt John Michael Gregson Halstead, Queen's Bays.

> The mirage is clear now and I can see what to shoot at and get Swire, my gunner, onto some guns and lorries. Gerry opens up on us now and then anti-tank shells whip past us with sharp cracks. They keep so low on the ground that their flight can be seen by the swirl of sand just below the projectile, very uncomfortable feeling that one may come inside at any moment. What a change from range practices, a very satisfying target in front of us and once more we are in the real thing, rather like an important football match after weeks of practice games. I glance along the line on either side but all is well, no tanks stopped yet. I give a cheer on the internal communications set, which probably blasted Swire's and Wilson's ears, when I see one of his shots blow up a full petrol lorry. Gun firing well and line rolling slowly on to the Gerry line, then a terrific crash and a cloud of smoke inside the tank and driver Wilson reels sideways. An anti-tank shell has come through the front. We are stopped now and without another thought I nipped out of the top and thought of getting Wilson out and away while the going was good. Loader Mounsey came out the side door, then a shell landed nearby and made a nasty mess of him, the poor chap lay screaming on the ground, his legs almost in ribbons. I could do nothing so I turned for Morphia to Bradley who was out behind the tank, but that was the last thing I did. I felt a great blow on the face and fell to the ground unable to see or do anything but wave a hand feebly in the air. There was no pain, I just felt helpless. A few minutes later a tank pulled up beside me and I felt someone picking me up,

---

22   Ibid, p. 204.

one foot hurt very much and I could just see with one eye the end of my left boot removed and a gory mess there instead. The pain became too much for me then.[23]

150 Field Ambulance mobile dressing station was stationed to the rear of 150 Brigades position, one and three quarter miles to the north west of the Knightsbridge Cross Roads, never dreaming they would see the enemy behind their own lines. On the morning of 27 May the noise from the tank battles that raged south and east of their positions became louder as the British armour fell back.

Pte James Keith Killby, 150 Field Ambulance, was taken aback to find German tanks in the medical compound:

> From the early morning of the 27th we knew something was in the air, at about midday the noises of battle became too loud to be ignored and we joked it was our lads on manoeuvres. In the next two or three hours it steadily increased in intensity, but whatever it was it was hidden from us behind this big escarpment. Then there seemed to be a pause and a number of tanks appeared which was a heartening sight until the turret of the leading tank was opened revealing a German head. That really shook us, how could they have got here? Our CO went up to a tank and spoke to the German officer as though speaking to a rider in Rotten Row, that restored our equilibrium. A German officer inspected the operating theatre while we were all rounded up and searched, but as there were casualties to be dealt with some of the orderlies and MOs were allowed to return to the theatre. Soon the tank column left saying they would be in Tobruk by evening. Numerous tank columns followed them during the day and each time we got rounded up, but once they understood we were a hospital they seemed to treat us with more respect. They gave us some of their wounded and we did all we could for them and put them in the tents that were our wards, by nightfall we had been left free again, but only to stay where we were as all our trucks had been taken early in the proceedings. Next day was comparatively quiet though whenever a vehicle came into the camp we were not sure whether it would be British or German and the opposite side fired on it. Whenever a German unit came in we took them over to their own wounded who spoke well of us.[24]

During the afternoon of the 27th there arose a crisis for the Africa Corps, the effort of beating down the British tank attacks used up valuable supplies of petrol, no fresh supplies were getting through as the French at Bir Hacheim and British tank units had intercepted and destroyed many of Rommel's supply columns, the attack was being starved to death.

Trooper James Palmer, Royal Tank Regiment, took part in the complete destruction of a large Italian supply column, the unremitting violence and the screams of the dying left an indelible mark upon his conscience:

> An Italian supply column came along escorted by light tanks at each side, like destroyers escorting a convoy. We moved down the side of the column firing as fast as we could,

---

23 Manuscript sent to author by M Halstead (1991).
24 Ibid, by J K Kilby (1992).

trucks burst into flames and within minutes the road was blocked with burning lorries. The Italians were in a complete panic with men jumping out of their trucks and firing blindly at anything, machine-guns spluttered and we could hear the pinging of bullets hitting the side of our tank. The air inside was filled with cordite and smoke, all the gunners were firing as fast as they could load and there was no need to select targets as each one we aimed at was a hit. Anti-tank guns were manhandled out of the column and fired at us at point blank range, men were throwing grenades at us as we moved down the column and the Italian tanks were scattered all around us firing away. Everything was burning and there were the horrible sounds of men screaming and dying, tanks were hit and their ammunition exploded, some of the crews scrambled out of the blaze seeking shelter. The air was full of the whine of bullets as hot metal and shrapnel came raining down, smoke swirled around and the sound of explosions rent the air, the noise of battle was unbelievable. All the convoy was burning, all their tanks were hit or abandoned and what was left of the Italian infantry was lying at the side of the road waving white flags. The wounded and maimed were screaming and dying. For two hours we had gone berserk, shooting, killing and burning and now we were dazed and confused and sickened. This kind of carnage must surely scar the minds of all those tank crews involved and I know that my soul will be damned for having been a part of it.[25]

Erwin Rommel was very worried at his lack of success in defeating the British forces behind the Gazala Line, he wrote in his diary:

There was also a British surprise awaiting us here, one which was not to our advantage, the new Grant tank, which was used in this battle for the first time on African soil. Tank after tank was shattered in the fire of the tank guns. Finally we succeeded in throwing the British back to the Trigh el Abd, although at the cost of heavy casualties. The British however soon came back to the attack. When at around mid-day I and my staff attempted to get through to the 90th Light Division at El Adem, our column was attacked by British tanks and we were forced to turn back. In the afternoon heavy tank fighting flared up south of the Trigh Capuzzo, 1st British Armoured Division joined in the battle, its powerful armoured units attacking mainly from the north-east. The British armour, under heavy artillery cover, poured there fire into the columns and panzer units of the Africa Corps, which were visible for miles. Fire and black smoke welled up from lorries and tank losses. Many of our columns broke into confusion and fled away to the south-west, out of the British artillery fire. Looking back on the first days fighting it was clear that our plan to overrun the British forces behind the Gazala Line had not succeeded. The principal cause was our underestimate of the strength of the British armoured divisions, the advent of the new American tanks had torn great holes in our ranks and our entire force now stood in heavy and destructive combat with a superior enemy. I will not deny I was seriously worried that evening.[26]

---

25   Ibid, by J Palmer (1993).
26   B. Liddle-Hart, *The Rommel Papers* (London: Capo Press, 1953), p. 302.

Colonel Alwin Wolz, Flak Commander, saw Rommel in the middle of this chaotic situation:

> In the midst of this avalanche I caught site of some Flak 88s, we raced over to them and suddenly found Rommel there, completely hemmed in by panicking troops. He angrily rebuked me that my flak was to blame for all this because it was not shooting back. I managed to stop three 88s and then the other half of the Heavy Flak Battery of the Corps Combat Group. The armada of enemy tanks was closing in and only 1,500 yards away, 20, 30, 40 big tanks, ahead of them was the Africa Corps supply trucks fleeing, all quite defenceless to tank attack. In the midst of this chaos was Rommel, the HQ of the Africa Corps, regiments, signals trucks, in short the entire muscle and nerve centre of the combat divisions up front.[27]

At 5:15 a.m. on 28 May the 15th and 21st Panzer Divisions were ordered to advance to Acroma and el Tamar respectively. The 15th however was unable to carry out these orders because of an acute shortage of tank and artillery ammunition and fuel, plus it had only 29 working tanks, one infantry battalion had been destroyed and the artillery regiments had suffered heavy loss. The 21st Panzer Division attacked alone and captured el Tamar by 9:00 a.m. cutting a destructive swathe through the British units it encountered. The 21st halted on the heights of point 219 after destroying a British column code named Stopcol, crushing an armoured attack by 8th Battalion Royal Tank Regiment and taking out the box at Commonwealth Keep. Rommel's supply situation was now critical and at last light on the 28th the Africa Corps was still surrounded with strong British forces moving along the Trigh Capuzzo towards the trapped German divisions. The 28th was a day of wasted opportunities for the British as Eighth Army had expected the Axis forces to maintain their northward progress and had been gathering their strength to take them in flank. However the continuing inactivity of the British units allowed Rommel to continue gapping the mine-fields to his rear and to seek out routes for his supply columns to use the following day. At the end of the day on 28th General Ritchie was confident that the tide of battle was swinging in his favour, he knew Rommel was trapped against the British mine-fields and expected the Axis attack to wither and die during the next few days. If Ritchie had pressed home his advantage by using the Eighth Army's superiority in numbers the Africa Corps could have been crushed.

All day on 29 May the British armour was locked in battle with the Axis forces, Rommel's supply situation was now so dire, he was within 24 hours of being forced to sue for peace because of his acute lack of water, fuel and ammunition. He now decided to concentrate his efforts on opening up a supply route through the mine-fields just north of the box held by 150 Brigade and the sappers of the Italian Trieste Division had already cleared a gap. The attacking Axis forces then withdrew into a defensive crescent held on the outer perimeter by large numbers of 88mm anti-aircraft guns, the British armoured forces threw themselves at this tempting target and were hurled back each time with grievous losses. It seemed to British eyes at this time that the situation for Rommel was hopeless but the German commander had other ideas. He saw the situation as a bridgehead from which his forces could burst forth when supplies came through.

---

27  Manuscript sent to author by H Wernaman, Africa Corps Veteran (Germany, 1989).

150 Field Ambulance Mobile Dressing Station found itself in the path of the panzers as they withdrew into their defensive perimeter to await supplies and refit. Pte James Keith Killby, 150 Field Ambulance, found the same German unit that had visited them earlier on their way to Tobruk was back again as they pulled back:

> Soon after daybreak next morning we found Gerry all around us, it was the same column in the camp that had been with us earlier but he did not explain why he was not in Tobruk. Gerry's columns stretched a long way either side of us and he was not there for the protection of the Red Cross but because strategy demanded it. We were agreeably surprised to find that if we pointed out that a vehicle or gun was parked beside a ward it was usually moved and if we found a German soldier going through our kit and explained we had been working for German wounded he put it back. From dawn till after dark we were attending to German wounded. In the wards and throughout the entire camp German and British doctors and orderlies were working side by side attending to the German wounded who came in an endless stream throughout the day. One minute we would find ourselves in a German tank helping out the wounded, then clearing away others who tried to take our water which we needed for ourselves and the patients. But in that too the German doctors more than helped and at times individuals gave us food and water from their own diminishing supply. As we had heard a great deal about German toughness we were glad to find that he was ducking as shells flew overhead long after we had given it up as too much like hard work. The minor casualties were treated in a large tent by the orderlies, the more serious in the operating theatre where a strange scene was being enacted. German officers were constantly in and out while our orderlies and doctors worked with the German men and doctors and seldom were there less than two others being attended to in the operating theatre, the theatre was merely a big tent dug deep in the ground. One or two British wounded appeared, we never quite knew from where, but we found a German doctor attending to one of them. We did our best with our limited German vocabulary of a dozen words or so, to find out the needs of the wounded, while our doctors and the German doctors managed to work together with the aid of French and at one time quite an energetic discussion on the beauties of Scotland was carried on in the three languages. During these hectic 12 hours, when through the endless work that had to be done we never noticed the noise of shells flying overhead and bursting near, two things stood out. First that given the opportunity and the right job British and German can work together. But what was even more satisfying was to see the attitude of contempt of the German doctor's change to open admiration once they saw our doctors at work.[28]

At 6:00 a.m. on 29 May detachments of the Africa Corps and 5th Panzer Regiment were sent to open up a supply route to the west of Sidi Muftah and ran headlong into the strongly defended box held by 150 Brigade who had recently been reinforced by 1st Army Tank Brigade HQ, 44th Battalion Royal Tank Regiment and one squadron of 42nd Battalion Royal Tank Regiment, 30 tanks in all. The Germans had no idea this position existed which dominated the two minefield gaps but it was obvious that without its destruction the supply situation could not be totally

---

28  Ibid, by J K Kilby (1992).

alleviated. South of the battle-field over 1,000 German trucks full of supplies were unable to get through because of the attacking British forces, Rommel personally led out a column in the direction of the Ariete Division to find and guide in these vital supplies that would be essential in maintaining his forces while they attacked 150 Brigade.

Rommel's interpreter, Wilfried Armbruster, was with Rommel when he personally guided a column of supplies back to his beleaguered units:

> I drove off with the C in C and we piloted the supply column up behind Ariete's line heading for the Africa Corps, tanks were again attacking us in flank and Rommel ordered them to be encircled. We found Westphal again and took him along with us. Ariete fell back slightly and again there was chaos. Shelling began again and Schneider was injured standing next to me. Rommel then led the whole lot right up to the Africa Corps, it was a fantastic drive, we were being shot at the whole time but everything came off terrifically.[29]

The Africa Corps was now back in business and a desperate battle for survival was about to begin with the troops of 150 Brigade. During the days that followed Rommel's position was attacked continuously by the Eighth Army and the RAF rained bombs and machine-gun fire upon the Axis forces, this maelstrom of fire and steel was known to the Germans as the Hexenkessel and to the British as the Devil's Cauldron. The men in 150 Brigade box could see little of events taking place but the terrific noise of battle could be heard clearly, slowly the sounds of battle drew closer as the German panzers moved toward the rear of the Gazala Line.

Major Gerald Percival Jackson, MC, Royal Tank Regiment:

> We ended up in the area popularly known as the Devil's Cauldron, one could see why, the place was covered with derelict British, Italian and German tanks, vehicles, guns and needless to say numerous dead bodies, which in the heat of the summer gave off a pungent sweet scented smell and they were covered in thousands of black flies. No doubt the same flies that seemed to appear from now on to share our bully and biscuits. It was the first time I had seen Grant tanks brewing up and it was not a pretty sight, the crews were virtually sitting on a petrol tank of 100 gallons of aviation gasoline and a large quantity of high explosive shells, all of which were highly inflammable. Sometimes when they were hit the whole lot would explode and the turret, weighing several tons, could be seen being blown off high into the air.[30]

Lt Robert Watt, 3rd Battalion Royal Tank Regiment, looked out over the Devil's Cauldron and although he was now a battle hardened veteran he was shocked by what he saw:

> I carefully approached the ridge above the Cauldron and moved to a position of observation, I scanned the area and it gave me the creeps. Accustomed as I was to battle-field wreckage I was shocked at what I saw, this was indeed the Devil's Cauldron. The valley in front of me vanished to the horizon to the north and south and was littered with an unimaginable

---

29  S. W. Mitcham *Rommel's Desert War* (USA: Stackpole Books, 2007), p. 202.
30  Interview with author, G P Jackson (1994).

# Disaster at Sidi Muftah: The destruction of 150 Brigade, 26 May to 1 June 1942   179

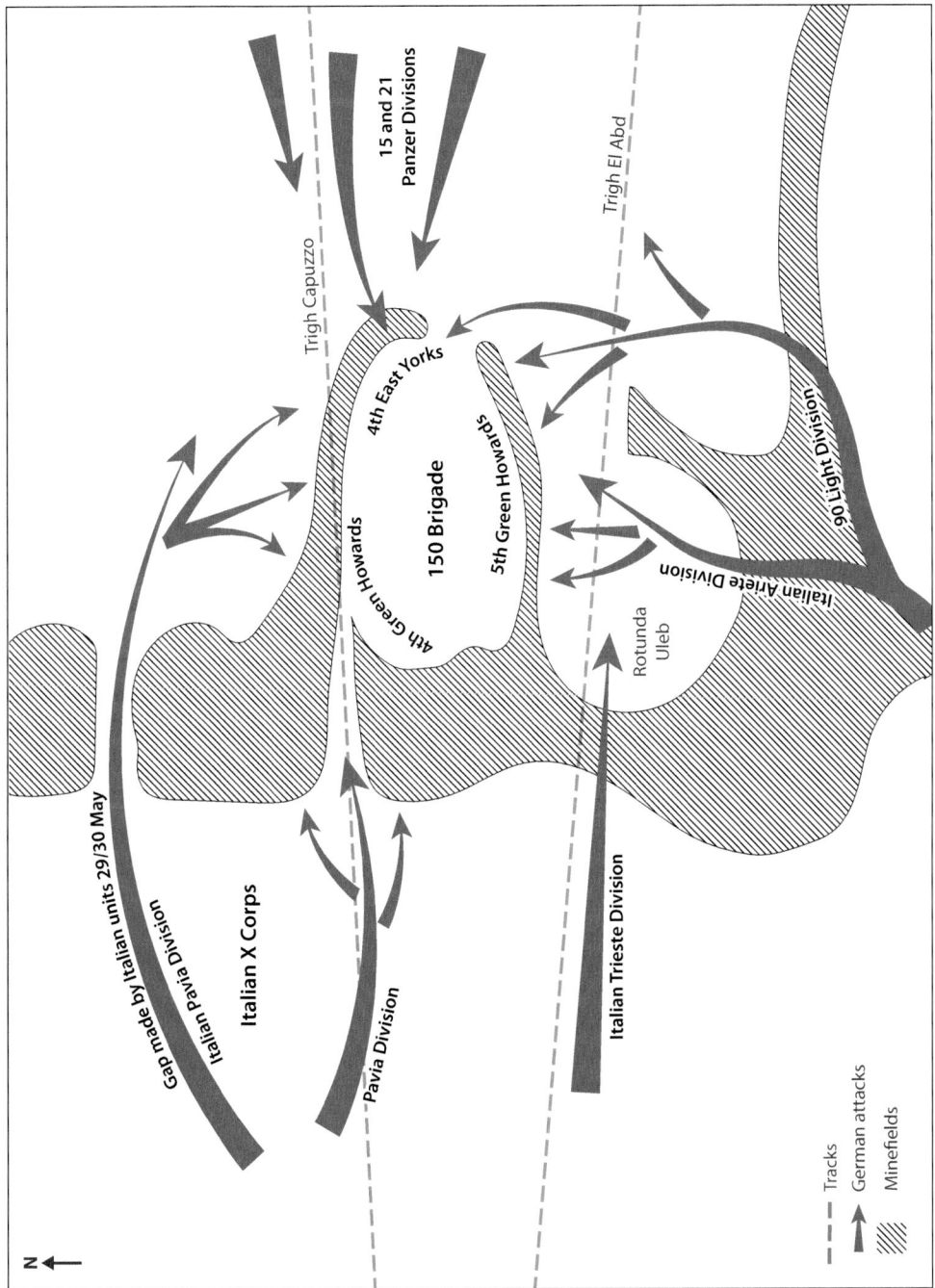

Map 7   Rommel's forces turn upon 150 Brigade at Sidi Muftah, 29/30 May 1942.

mass of debris, the whole area was a confusion of burnt out vehicles, trenches, barbed wire, clothing and equipment, with a few bodies lying around like bundles of discarded rags. What a pathetic shambles. In the heat of the desert sun a cold hand gripped my heart and I shuddered.[31]

The Eighth Army Headquarters took Rommel's withdrawal as a sign he was leaving the field, German vehicles rushing through the mine-field gaps were thought to be proof of this. Their optimism was misplaced however as they were supply vehicles returning to get fresh materials. For the men of 150 Brigade the prospect of an imminent attack meant their first major action in the desert.

Sergeant Arthur Chester, 4th Battalion East Yorkshire Regiment, sat in his slit trench on the outer perimeter of the box held by 150 Brigade and although he could see very little of the events taking place he knew by the noise of battle that the enemy must be very close:

> The ground all around us was shaking and trembling because of the large numbers of tanks moving around in our rear, we were that close to them. Nothing could be seen for all the dust and muck that was being kicked up but the sound put the wind up us all.[32]

Pte William Gleave, 4th Battalion Green Howards:

> I was a runner at Brigade HQ and as such was one of the first individuals to know that the anticipated battle had at last commenced, it was with mixed feelings of excitement, fear and a sense of adventure that I realised our brigade was at last, after months in the desert, about to take part in a real full-sized shooting war. Everyone at times like this has thoughts about their personal fortunes at the commencement of a battle and I was no exception.[33]

On 28 May the German and Italian forces began to blunder into the rear of 150 Brigade's position and the men of the East Yorkshire Regiment and the Green Howards took their first prisoners, the enemy pushed forward constantly from the east and the desert seemed to be full of Axis vehicles of every description.

Lt Colonel W E Bush, DSO, MC, OBE, 5th Battalion Green Howards, could hear the sound of battle to his rear and saw the first German tanks as they ran into a British mine-field:

> The noise of battle was now heard due east or in rear of our position, the standing patrol of the 5th Green Howards at Barrel 9 on the Trigh el Abd could plainly see large numbers of vehicles and gun flashes that went on all day. The standing patrol of the 4th Battalion East Yorkshire Regiment, two miles east of Rotunda Metifel, was forced to withdraw as the enemy was advancing in strength. The first enemy contact with our main position was made by 12 tanks which drove onto the mine-fields about one and a half miles south of the Auleb gap. They were immediately engaged by artillery fire as they were a long way from any infantry posts and out of small arms range. The enemy crews realising their plight quitted

---

31  Interview with author, R Watt (1989).
32  Taped interview with author, Arthur Chester (Hull, 1991).
33  Manuscript sent to author by William Gleave (1996).

their tanks and withdrew before they could be captured. A party of sappers completed the destruction of these tanks.[34]

Major D'Arcy Mander, DSO, 4th Battalion Green Howards, was sent through the mine-field with a patrol to find out what was going on to his front:

> I was sent with a three inch mortar team right through the mine-fields to see what was going on at the far side and to stir things up a bit, when we arrived we shot up a large concentration of vehicles, drawing down upon ourselves an avalanche of artillery and machine-gun fire. I remember directing operations from a ridge and seeing a bit of wire right under my nose, which under investigation proved to be one of our own anti-personnel mines. If I had gone another yard I would have detonated it, it went off anyway when a large shell exploded in front of me and I commenced my withdrawal airborne by the force of the explosion. We all managed to get back although I recall having to carry the three inch mortar barrel all the way back as we had one or two wounded in our little battle.[35]

150 Brigade's advanced troops on the outer perimeter had to withdraw in the face of this assault as artillery duels and tank battles raged in the Devil's Cauldron, one troop of the 287th Battery, 124th Field Regiment, Royal Artillery, was lost with its supporting tanks during one of the ongoing actions and any survivors that were able withdrew to 69 Brigades box.

Major Harold Ian Bransom, DSO, 124th Field Regiment, Royal Artillery, recalled the end of his unit as the Germans advanced:

> The reserve had been sat for two weeks waiting for anyone who might come round the flank, when they did it was an incredible sight, the Africa Corps came into view with their tanks and vehicles massed together in one enormous column. You didn't know where to put the shells it was so big, it was rather like throwing stones into the crowd at St James's Park. We were firing point blank over open sights but they went straight over our positions and didn't stop.[36]

Major Peter William Rainier, 232nd Field Company, Royal Engineers:

> For days that Cauldron was the scene of terrific fighting, black columns of smoke rose from scores of knocked out tanks brewing up. Shapeless red patches that had once been fighting men lay in the sand where the cruel tank treads had ground them down. There was the smell of the burning flesh of tank crews trapped in their seething vehicles. Planes swooped, engines roared and bombs burst, the noise of their explosions barely heard above the clamour of the milling tanks and the staccato whang of the guns.[37]

---

34  Ibid, by W E Bush (1992).
35  Ibid, by W E Bush (1992).
36  Ibid, by H I Bransom (Norfolk, 1990).
37  Ibid, by P W Rainier (1991).

Picture by Cpt Cyril Mount, Royal Artillery. Camouflaged British Artillery position in action, Western Desert 1942.

Twenty three-ton lorries left 150 Brigade box and headed for Tobruk to pick up badly needed supplies of ammunition for the artillery. They never made it back and fell victim to the marauding panzer columns. The shortage of shells for the guns of the Royal Artillery was now serious and each gun was restricted to 25 rounds a day. On the evening of 28 May the troops of 150 Brigade were told to expect an attack upon their rear from the direction of the Devil's Cauldron. The whole defensive position was tightened up and any troops on patrol outside the box were quickly drawn in, new positions were prepared, existing ones strengthened and extra mines laid to close up the exit and entrance gaps in the mine-fields.

On the morning of 29 May small arms fire and mortar bombs took a steady toll of the British defenders, enemy shell-fire was not so intense but by mid-day German tanks and motorised infantry could be seen massing in preparation for an attack. To the front of the Capuzzo Gap the German artillery laid down a thick smoke screen and under cover of this German Mk 1V and Italian M13 tanks moved forward with infantry following. The 72nd Field Regiment, Royal Artillery, laid down an inferno of fire upon the advancing German and Italian units forcing the infantry to wheel north. The tanks pressed on and ran straight into the British mine-field where their tracks and wheels were blown off, the crews bailed out with lightning speed and abandoned them. That night a patrol from the 4th Battalion East Yorkshire Regiment went out and disabled them by setting them on fire.

Pte Herbert Thompson, 4th Battalion East Yorkshire Regiment, was on the patrol that went out into the minefield to immobilise the German and Italian tanks:

> As we moved out of the box in darkness the sounds of battle in the distance was loud and frightening, we expected to come across Gerry troops at any moment and were on full alert. The lights from explosions flickered on the horizon and I held my rifle tight with one up the spout, safety catch off. As we moved through the gap the dark shapes of tanks loomed up before us, silhouetted by the fires in the distant sky. It soon became obvious nobody was around so the lads dropped grenades and fired flare guns into the turrets, they were soon ablaze. As we returned to the box the tank ammunition and petrol tanks started to explode and lit us up good and proper, but we were not fired on, I was so glad to get back.[38]

The enemy forces advanced cautiously over the Rotunda Ualeb, the position just vacated by the 4th Battalion East Yorkshire Regiment to shorten the defensive front. With sufficient ammunition the brigade artillery could have stopped any advance in daylight over this area, however because of the rationing of artillery shells only selected targets could be singled out, this shortcoming cannot have been lost on such a formidable enemy. The drivers and spare men of the medium battery Battle-axe and the 72nd Field Regiment Royal Artillery were pressed into an infantry role and held a section of the front. The enemy artillery was now in position and began to lay down a series of creeping barrages that swept back and forth over the whole area held by 150 Brigade, air activity increased and Stuka dive bombers screamed out of the sky to unload their bombs onto the beleaguered Tommies below. The anti-aircraft teams in the box blazed away while their ammunition lasted. One of the German aircraft that flew over the box held by 150 Brigade was carrying the Commander of the Africa Corps, General Cruwell, his Storch spotter plane was hit a number of times and was forced to come down in the box. The troops on the ground were not in the mood for pleasantries as the disgruntled blood covered officer soon found out.

Pte William Gleave, 4th Battalion Green Howards:

> General Cruwell was shot down over the 4th Green Howards area, according to the version I heard the general was doubled back to our lines with rifle and bayonet in rear, also he was relieved of his Iron Cross and his gold signet ring, about which loss he complained in indignant terms to our brigadier. I saw a gold signet ring inset with a black stone with gold initials worn by Private Brooks, 4th Green Howards, and was told this was the General's ring.[39]

Major D'Arcy Mander, 4th Battalion Green Howards, was responsible for carrying out preliminary interrogations of prisoners in order to establish what units faced the positions held by 150 Brigade. The identity of this prestigious new captive was as yet unknown and the bedraggled looking and blood soaked individual was brought before Major Mander who treated him as he would any other Private soldier, at first:

---

38 Taped interview with author, Herbert Thompson (Beverley, 1994).
39 Manuscript sent to author by William Gleave (1996).

They found the pilot had been killed and brought in the passenger who was covered in the pilot's blood, he was brought to me in a dug-out at Battalion Headquarters and the interrogation went something like this: Me, in German [aggressive voice] 'Sit down! pay-book'. All German soldiers carry their pay-book [A mine of information] on them at all times. Reading from his pay-book I continue: 'So you are an officer eh? Second Lieutenant? Lieutenant? Captain? Major? Lt Colonel?' [from now on in a less ferocious voice] 'Colonel? Major General? Lt General?' Then it dawned on me who I was addressing and I quickly changed my tune: 'I am sorry I spoke to you so roughly General Cruwell I had no idea who you were, are you alright? Can we clean you up a bit? is there anything I can do for you?' Lt General Cruwell was the commander of Rommel's Africa Corps and was quite a prize, he told me he would be alright if he could have a wash and said there was something I could do for him. He informed me he was wearing the Knights Cross of the Iron Cross, [the German equivalent of the VC] when captured and that one of our chaps had taken it and he would very much like it back. A few words with the sergeant of the party produced the decoration which I handed back to the general. He was then consigned to the care and hospitality of Brigadier Haydon, our brigade commander, who arranged for his onward journey to GHQ in a tank.[40]

Lt General Cruwell, Africa Corps Commander, left his own account of the moment his plane was shot down:

I took off at 8:30 a.m. in my Fieseler Storch, my pilot did not have the right map ready. The OC Luftwaffe Africa, General Von Waldau, gave him precise directions, make for Segnali and then turn due east. It was soon clear to me that we were still flying directly into the sun. The pilot reassured me and said we could not possibly miss the flares. But then the worst happened and we were over the British lines. We were flying at about 500 feet and came under machine-gun fire, the first burst hit us in the tail, the second riddled the engine and the third killed the pilot. He slumped back dead in his seat. As though by a miracle the machine did not crash but flattened out and made a perfect crash landing, smashing the undercarriage to pieces. The fuselage cracked and splintered around me but to my good fortune the door did not jam. I was in the foremost line of the box held by 150 Brigade, the British soldiers rushed up and took me prisoner.[41]

General Ludwig Cruwell, OC Africa Corps, May 1942.

---

40  Manuscript sent to author by W E Bush (1992).
41  C. E. Lucas-Philips, *Alamein* (London: Heinemann, 1962), p. 274.

On the night of 29/30 May patrols were out constantly seeking information about the enemy's movements, battle patrols went out to snatch prisoners and to harass any working parties that were lifting mines and preparing positions for the coming battle.

Lt Colonel W E Bush, DSO, MC, OBE, 5th Battalion Green Howards, received optimistic reports about a fast retreating enemy, though what he saw on the ground did not seem to back up this view:

> The 30th May, while we were hard pressed and in the words of one company commander spent the day plugging holes, the reports from higher command on the wireless were of a most optimistic tone. During the night orders were received for a tank sortie to be prepared to leave the box to harass the retreating enemy, Desert Air Force reports came in to the effect that 1,500 enemy motor-transport were stopped for lack of petrol in the Cauldron area. It was said that the gap in the mine-field, which the enemy had now completed between our box and 69 Brigade, was like a starting gate with enemy motor-transport jockeying for position to get away. Officer commanding 5th Green Howards was ordered to send an officers patrol to contact the Free French at Bir Hackeim with a request for them to co-operate in harassing the retreating enemy in their area. Captain H Huntrod, with a section of carriers and a two pounder anti-tank gun, could not at first find a gap to get through after two attempts to find a gap in the enemy line on our southern front, they succeeded at about 8:00 a.m. He reached Bir Hackeim but was unable to return, he and his party took part in the fighting of this gallant force when it cut its way out on 11th June, Captain Huntrod and the party were unfortunately captured when operating with the rear-guard of the Free French.[42]

With the dawn on 30th came the enemy in force upon point 174 which was held by 232nd Field Company, Royal Engineers. After a fierce fight the position fell to the 5th Panzer Regiment before 9:00 a.m. The tanks in the Auleb box launched a counter attack under cover of a heavy smoke screen preceded by an artillery bombardment but failed to dislodge the enemy. From point 174 the enemy had good observation over a large part of the defended area and could now direct his own artillery more accurately. Throughout the day on the 30th the German units probed the British defences, numerous vicious actions were fought as the enemy tanks and infantry sought a weak point that they could exploit.

Pte John Thompson, 5th Battalion Green Howards:

> They came down on our position just after dawn, tanks advanced with infantry coming up behind them. Our artillery bashed them and the machine-gunners kept up a terrific fire on them and they were forced to go back. Someone came over to us and said 'Gerry's broken in, fix your bayonets and follow me'. We all ran forward ready for business but by then Gerry was pulling back leaving burning tanks and his dead.[43]

---

42  Manuscript sent to author by W E Bush (1992).
43  Taped interview with author, John Thompson (Beverley, 1994).

Oberleutnant Walter Dorn, Tank Commander, 15th Panzer Division, moved forward with his unit into a hail of anti-tank fire but could not locate his tormentors:

> There is heavy fire coming from the right with puffs of smoke appearing in front and muzzle flashes on the left. Where are these well camouflaged anti-tank gun positions hiding? There is little time for thought and as I feverishly seek out the enemy gunners a small cloud of dust and smoke breaks out on the lead tank that was a hit. The tank commander falls out of the turret, bounces off the hull, flops onto the sand and lies there. Another two men appear and take shelter behind their tank and the wounded tank commander drags himself along the ground and joins them. With a violent thud and without any warning a heavy metallic blow strikes my tank and in the crew compartment a shower of sparks fills the place. The driver below sits with his head falling forward and blood running down his face, It's time to get out, the wounded gunner has the presence of mind to traverse the turret to one side so that the hatches are facing away from the enemy fire. I shout to the driver to get out but he does not move, he's probably dead. Machine gun bullets fly all around us as we fall out of the hatch but our luck holds and we cower behind the tank.[44]

150 Brigade Headquarters was out of touch with 50th Division Headquarters at last light on the 30th and the morning of 31 May, the only entry for that day in the divisional war diary states:

> 09:00 hrs 150 Br'de out of tel comm. 12:00 hrs enemy attack developed from east and NE. with approx' 20 tanks. [Rest of message corrupt].[45]

On the night of 30/31 May British patrols continued to harass the enemy on all fronts in an attempt to prevent the lifting of mines under-cover of darkness, Captain Douglas King of the 4th Battalion East Yorkshire Regiment led one such patrol:

> As we crossed no-man's land every nerve was on edge, the landscape presented a scene that would have done any horror film proud. Flares climbed in the sky and cast eerie shadows that moved about as they fell to earth and played merry hell with our vision, tracer skipped low over the ground in all directions as enemy machine-gunners fired on fixed lines. Add to this the ominous black and smoking shapes of knocked out tanks and lorries and the broken bodies of the dead and you will have some idea of the fear that gripped us all. We were out to observe, our orders were not to attack and as we approached point 174 a mass of tanks could be made out in the darkness, we lay still and listened for a while and watched any movement, then we slipped away and reported what we had seen.[46]

The Capuzzo Gap was now in constant use by the Axis forces and reinforcements and supplies poured through, 150 Brigade now faced a greatly strengthened enemy while their own situation grew worse and because of the desperate shortage of shells very little ammunition could be spared to harass the stream of enemy supply columns getting through. At 8:00 a.m. on 31

---

44   Manuscript sent to author by H Wernaman, Africa Corps veteran (Germany, 1989).
45   J. Lucas, *Panzer Army Africa* (London: Purnell, 1977), p. 76.
46   Taped interview with author, Douglas King (Hull, 1992).

May heavy shell-fire descended upon and swept over the beleaguered British box indicating that there would soon be a general assault, it was obvious from the large calibre of some of the duds that landed in the area that the enemy had brought up his large ordnance. At 10:00 a.m. the enemy attacked the north-east corner of the box held by the 4th Battalion East Yorkshire Regiment, solid armour piercing shot screamed above the heads of the defenders, fired by the German tanks as they advanced with their infantry hunched behind them to get some protection from the British machine-gun and rifle fire. The defending artillery and mortar crews poured a withering fire into the enemy ranks, slowly using up their precious ammunition, the shrieking air was thick with smoke, dust and fumes as the noise of battle reached a terrifying crescendo.

Sergeant Arthur Chester, 4th Battalion East Yorkshire Regiment, was in his slit trench when the German tanks broke into his position:

> The ground shook beneath us as there was that many tanks moving to our front, I was given a case of six sticky bombs, they was like maracas, you was supposed to be a hero and as the tanks came up you would stick these things on the side. It wasn't as easy as it sounded with a dirty big tank coming up to your position and stuff flying about all over the place. Some of the lads that tried to do it got crushed under the tanks tracks, some tanks ran over the trenches and spun round on one track while the men were still in it, we could hear their screams as they ground them into the earth. Artillery and mortar shells dropped all around us, shells whistled over-head, each one seemed to be closer than the last, we expected the next one to be right on us they was coming that fast.[47]

In the afternoon of the 30th and during the night of 30th/31st Rommel himself moved up with the forward companies to reconnoitre the possibilities of an attack on the Auleb box and detailed units of the 90th Light Division, the 21st Panzer Division and the Italian Trieste Division for an assault on the box the next morning. The attack went in under the watchful eye of Rommel, he commented in his diary:

> German and Italian units fought their way forward yard by yard against the toughest British opposition imaginable. The defence was conducted with considerable skill and, as usual, the British fought to the last round. They also brought a new 57mm anti-tank gun into use [six pounder] in this action. Nevertheless by the time evening came we had penetrated a substantial distance into the British positions.[48]

The German attacking force began to make headway and some of the defending forward units were overrun in the melee, the defenders were given no respite and at noon on 31st another attack was launched on the south-east corner of the box, also held by the hard pressed 4th Battalion East Yorkshire Regiment. In this sector there was no mine-field to deter the attackers who advanced in armoured carriers. A ferocious barrage came down upon the defenders just before the attack went in scoring many direct hits on Royal Artillery gun-pits. Bofors anti-aircraft

---

47  Ibid, Arthur Chester (Hull, 1992).
48  B. Liddle-Hart, *The Other Side of the Hill* (London: Pan Books, 1983), p. 98.

guns were used to good effect by the defenders in an anti-tank role against the German armour but were soon targeted by the German forward observation officers who directed their own artillery onto them, knocking them out one by one. Gaps in the defensive line were beginning to appear and frantic efforts were made to plug these, staff from the 4th Battalion East Yorkshire Regimental HQ were armed and rushed to the front with orders to hold the line while the battalion reserve was brought forward. Casualties were mounting under the relentless pressure of enemy attacks and the ammunition situation was now very serious indeed.

Pte Herbert Thompson, 4th Battalion East Yorkshire Regiment, watched the carnage around him and knew that the end was near:

> 25 pounders fired over our heads over open sights into the oncoming tanks, Stukas roared down on us, the noise was horrifying. The Germans looked tired like us, war weary and unshaven. We had a medical unit in the middle of the box, it was heavily shelled and dive bombed. The dead were a pitiful sight to see. Some of the sections in our company had already been captured by now and we were out on a limb and didn't know what was going on. The artillery was still firing and the Germans were still shelling, it was perfect hell upon earth. I wonder now how we survived, we thought well who's next?[49]

Pte Herbert Thompson, 4th Battalion East Yorkshire Regiment.

Pte Chittock, MM, 150 Field Ambulance, was collecting the wounded of both sides in no-man's land:

> We were in no-man's land and it was rough, we were getting men out of tanks, one chap was shot dead standing beside me, I thought you live again. We went out to pick up any casualties, German or ours, as we picked them up they used to pull a tank across our front and one at each side of us to give us some protection, we pulled the ambulance in and picked up the wounded. All the time there was plenty of shit flying about, we hardly got any sleep, I don't remember sleeping. We finished up in no-man's land advanced dressing station. The British tanks and artillery was firing one way over us and the Gerries was firing the other way. We had quite a few casualties and hadn't time to dress them up, but we made them as comfortable as we could.[50]

Pte William Gleave, 4th Battalion Green Howards, sat amid an inferno of explosions as shells and bombs rained down on his position:

---

49 Taped interview with author, Herbert Thompson (Beverley, 1994).
50 Ibid, with Alfred Chittock (1989).

Disaster at Sidi Muftah: The destruction of 150 Brigade, 26 May to 1 June 1942   189

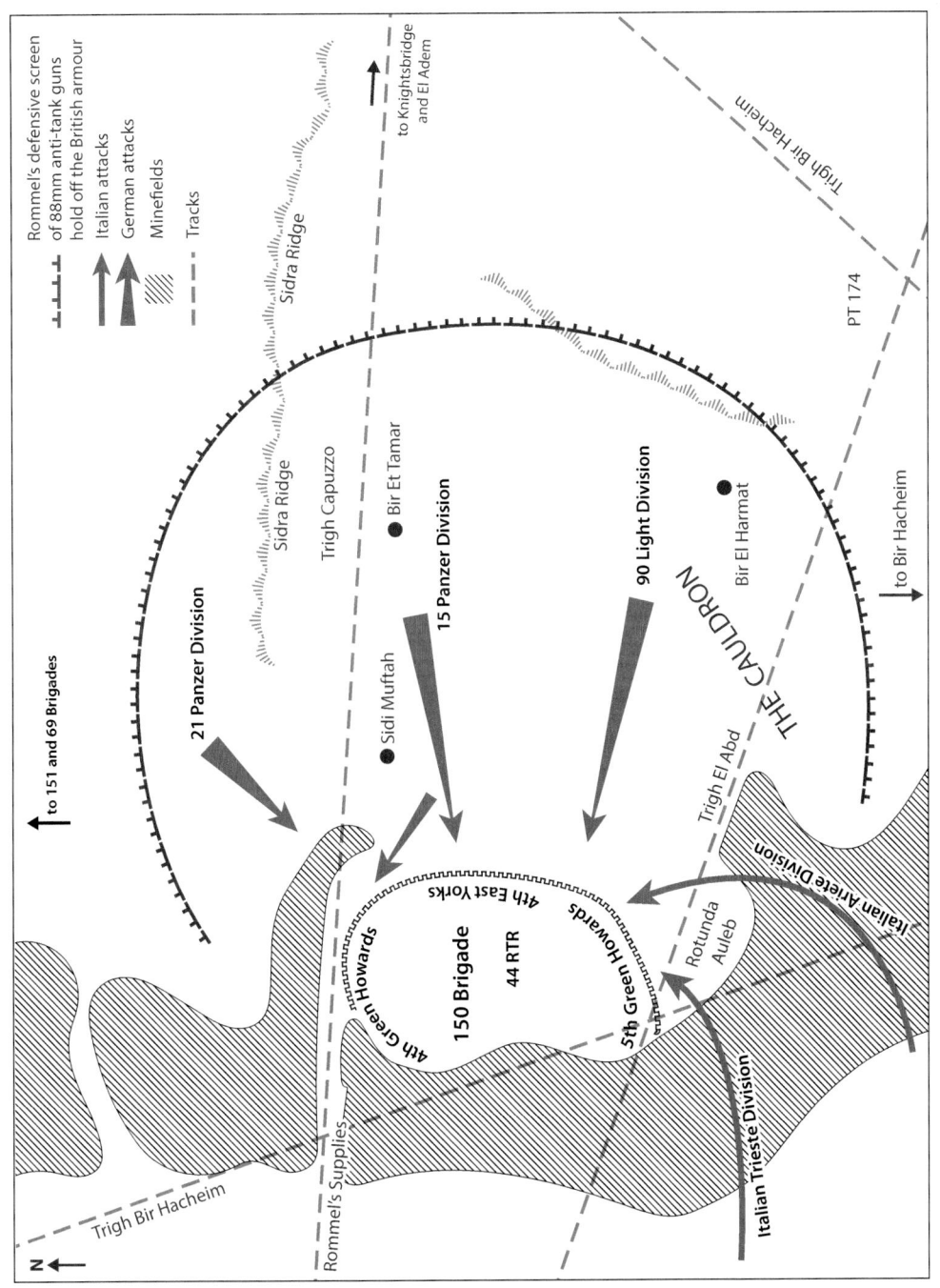

Map 8  The destruction of 150 Brigade, 1 June 1942.

All our time was now spent in slit trenches as far as possible when off duty, but in the gruelling sun being subjected to the everlasting pounding of the enemy's creeping barrage as it probed back and forth are not pleasant conditions. The climax being reached when a shell made a direct hit on three 44 gallon water drums stacked close to my trench, the drums disappeared in a terrific detonation as the trench sides collapsed in on top of me filling my mouth, nose and ears with choking sand. My misery was however tempered by the fact that I was still in one piece. Tanks, vehicles and guns were now being destroyed by enemy shell-fire and spirals of black belching smoke could be seen rising in the sky from various parts of the box. The medium guns in particular were unfortunate in that they were singled out for special attention in the shape of an attack by a formation of Stukas. These ominous looking planes descended on the unfortunate battery during a lull in the shelling, arranged presumably to let them get on with their job. Having a grandstand view of this attack made me thankful that we were not on the receiving end.[51]

Signaller Roy Lee, Battle-axe Battery, Royal Artillery:

> Coming at us we had artillery shells shooting air-burst rapid-fire and machine-gun fire, the German armour and German vehicles got right up to our position, they were in full view mind, vehicles and tanks all around us, palls of acrid smoke, the smell of human flesh roasting and burning. The first taste of hell but not the last.[52]

For Battle-axe Medium Battery the situation was deteriorating rapidly, the enemy was so close that the gunners were being hit by small arms fire and casualties in the unit mounted steadily. Anything that moved was shelled and as vehicles attempted to take away the wounded to the dressing station they came under heavy shell-fire, many of them receiving direct hits killing all on board. On the southern sector Italian and German sappers began picking up mines and two German tanks shielded them from the heavy machine-gun fire coming from the British line. British tanks arrived on the scene and the sappers and tanks were driven off. D Company, 5th Battalion Green Howards, was not attacked on the 31st, they had been hit the day before but the violence of the counter attack the enemy received had made them more cautious. However shelling in this area continued all day and the slightest movement brought down a hail of machine-gun and artillery fire.

Pte Ron Railton, 5th Battalion Green Howards, volunteered to be a runner and lived to regret his hasty decision:

> Runners were needed and they wanted volunteers, well I volunteered but I'll never volunteer no more. If anybody was frightened I was. The officer says to me 'go straight across to HQ and give them this message'. Off I went with this battle going on all round me, the Gerry tanks was firing at us and the Bofors guns were blasting at them and I had to go in between them to get through, when I got there I was absolutely buggered. The sergeant at HQ said 'you'd better stop here mate' but I told him I wanted to go back to the lads.

---

51 Manuscript sent to author by William Gleave (1996).
52 Interview with author, R Lee (Hull, 1993).

So I sets off and these ruddy Stukas came over and dropped their bombs, well the explosions, it made me cringe, I dropped to the earth and if there'd been a stone near I'd have got under the bloody thing I'll tell you.[53]

Pte John Thompson, 5th Battalion Green Howards:

There was Gerry tanks all over the place, one got really close to us and was hit by our anti-tank gunners, it went up with a great boom and burnt fiercely for ages with its ammunition going off like a fire-work display, the crew stood no chance of getting out as it brewed up. Later when the fire had died down we looked into the burnt out turret and the driver was still sat at the controls, he was like a little old shrivelled up man and burnt black.[54]

Panzergrenadiers await the order to move off, May 1942.

At 4:00 p.m. after the British positions had been shelled and dive-bombed since dawn the German troops launched an attack from the north on the front held by 4th Green Howards. Heavy machine-gun fire raked the British line, 20mm guns on mobile platforms plastered the trenches and as gaps were made through the mine-fields the German sappers marked them with white tape under the cover of this hail of fire. German tanks and infantry poured through the gaps and a ferocious fight ensued, the violent momentum of the assault overran a machine-gun section of the 2nd Cheshire's who fought to the last, more German infantry came through the mine-fields and overran the Green Howards out-posts in hand to hand fighting and heavy casualties were now being taken on both sides.

Sergeant David Monk, 4th Battalion Green Howards, was in action day and night, when he did get permission to sleep he found the enemy streaming through the mine-field to his front:

I was the sergeant of a battle patrol, a platoon of volunteers who towards the latter days of the break-through at Gazala were constantly in action against the Germans and Italians. By day we manned the defences and at night it was our job to probe the defences of the enemy, bag a prisoner and return with whatever information we could gather. 150 Brigade was entrenched behind the mine-fields and my battalion, the 4th Green Howards, were told that a prisoner was required for interrogation. That night we put on our desert boots,

---

53  Taped interview with author, Ron Railton (Beverley, 1995).
54  Ibid, with John Thompson (Beverley, 1994).

donned our camouflaged night-shirts, checked our arms and set forth. We managed to return with a prisoner as dawn broke and handed him over to intelligence, we couldn't get any rest yet and were kept busy while the afternoon and were then told to catch up on some sleep and retire for a well-earned rest, shell-fire was constant at this time but we were so tired we only wanted to get our heads down. Imagine our surprise when we found the enemy armour immediately to our front and about to break through the mine-field, Guy Fawkes Night was nothing compared with what followed. Shells were thrown at us in increasing numbers and machine-guns chattered constantly keeping us in our trenches and for good measure we received a dose of Stuka dive bombing. I am proud to say the 4th Green Howards stood firm and repulsed all attacks, when the enemy had withdrawn he left nine burning tanks, a staff car and many dead bodies on our front.[55]

Pte William Gleave, 4th Battalion Green Howards:

A message had to be taken to the defence platoon's position that was at the rear of the box, they had four German anti-tank guns that had been captured previously and had them facing to the east in case of an attack on the rear of the box where there was no mine-field. As I approached the position to deliver my message I was just in time to witness a shot from one of the anti-tank guns score a bulls-eye on the turret of an Italian M-34 tank which was one of several probing the defences. Almost everyone seemed to be below ground level at that time because of the barrage of solid AP shot [armour piercing shot] being fired by enemy tanks which were plainly in view. I lost no time in lying down to hand down my message to the platoon commander in his trench. On the signature being obtained the return to the brigade signals tent was done at the double amid falling AP [armour piercing] shot.[56]

The enemy withdrew having had enough for now. Under heavy fire Captain Paul Watson, 4th Battalion Green Howards, led his carrier section into the gap in the mine-field made by the enemy and re-laid the mines, for this brave and selfless act he was awarded the DSO. As night fell on 31 May the British troops in the box were completely exhausted by their efforts to hold the enemy at bay, they could look forward to neither rest nor fresh resources and water was in short supply. While the brave defenders at Auleb fought a desperate holding action on the 31st a number of attempts to reach them with fresh supplies had been made though none got through, they were all were intercepted by the marauding panzers. No co-ordinated corps attack was launched against the Axis forces and the British armour had continued to expend its energy against Rommel's defensive screen of 88s in piecemeal fashion. Rommel recorded in his diary:

However in spite of the precarious situation and the difficult problems that faced us I looked forward that evening full of hope to what the battle might bring. For Ritchie had thrown his armour into the battle piecemeal and had thus given us the chance of engaging them on each separate occasion with just about enough of our own tanks. This dispersal of the British armoured brigades was incomprehensible. In my view the sacrifice of the 7th

---

55   Ibid, with D Monk (Hull, 1992).
56   Manuscript sent to author by William Gleave (1996).

Armoured Division south of Bir el Harmat served no strategical or tactical purpose whatsoever, for it was all the same to the British whether my armour was engaged there or on the Trigh Capuzzo, where the rest of the British armour entered the battle. The principal aim of the British should have been to have brought all the armour they had into action at one and the same time. They should never have allowed themselves to be duped into dividing their forces before the battle or during our feint against the Gazala Line.[57]

The men of 150 Brigade fighting and dying in the box deserved better than this, as late as 3:50 p.m. on the 31st Eighth Army still seemed unaware of 150 Brigades true situation and continued to send optimistic messages, but as the day drew to a close the tone of the commanders changed as it became evident that all was not well, Ritchie sent the following signal to Auchinleck:

Vital to success to maintain 150 Bde position hence enemy attacks on them. They have done wonderful work and are short of ammunition. Trying to get to them still by land from north and south by air. 50 Div report best of their belief gaps [in mine-fields] were closed last night.[58]

The strain began to show as Eighth Army commanders argued and bickered over the air, these conversations were picked up by British tank units. Lt Colonel Harold Peter Pyman, 7th Armoured Division Headquarters, recalled:

It was the only occasion during World War Two that I heard divisional and brigade commanders tearing each other asunder over the wireless in the heat of battle. No good can come of such behaviour, whatever hard words may have to be said in private conference after an event.[59]

Brigadier Haydon, Commanding Officer 150 Brigade, called a conference at 10:00 p.m. on 31 May in the 4th East Yorkshire Regiment's Headquarters and gave orders for all units to organise themselves as best they could and to prepare for the morning. He told his officers that relief was not out of the question but that it must arrive by dawn before the Germans renew the attack. Men, water and ammunition were in short supply and it was with heavy hearts that unit commanders went out into the night to organise their men and to prepare their positions. Flares lit up the night sky and across no-man's land could be heard the rumble and roar of tanks and vehicles on the move as the enemy massed his forces for one last great effort to overcome the British box.

Shortly after mid-night 50th Division Headquarters sent a signal to X111 Corps, it was in turn sent to Eighth Army Headquarters and was passed straight to Ritchie the army commander at 1:55 a.m. 1 June. This was the first note of real alarm and read as follows:

Situation 150 Brigade serious, enemy penetrating area … demand support first light.[60]

---

57  B. Liddle-Hart, *The Other Side of the Hill* (London: Pan Books, 1983), p. 107.
58  I. S. O. Playfair, *The Middle East and the Mediterranean* (London: HMSO, 1960), p. 382.
59  Manuscript sent to author by H P Pyman (1994).
60  Ibid, by W E Bush (1992).

Rommel offered Brigadier Haydon the chance to surrender his position but his offer was rejected, the epic and heroic stand made by the men of 150 Brigade was an irksome and serious diversion to his plans and he ordered an assault for the next day of massive proportions in order to eliminate this stubborn resistance. At dawn the Luftwaffe was to launch the heaviest possible aerial attack on the defenders at Auleb, this was to be followed by a massed tank and infantry assault on the defences. As dawn broke on the 1st June 1942 the sky was a dirty grey, tired and unshaven the British troops sat in their prepared positions and looked across no-man's land. To the north the sounds of a tank battle could be heard clearly and as the first rays of the sun lit up the landscape the German forces were unleashed.

Leutnant Wolf, Panzer, Panzer Grenadier Regiment, 21st Panzer Division, advanced through the British mine-fields with his company and received a hot reception from the defenders:

> Everything depended upon a good take off position and a quick break-through at the greatest possible speed, no zig-zagging, straight at the enemy was the drill. At the first light of dawn a salvo from the artillery gave the signal for the attack. On the left 9th Company, 10th Company on the right and battalion staff in the centre, in this order we advanced in vehicles at 40 mph across the mile and a half stretch to the British positions. Each company was accompanied by a sapper section to deal with the barbed wire and the mines. Once off our transport the 10th Company succeeded in breaking through the mine-field in the first rush, but number 9 was caught up in the middle of it. The massed fire from the box was concentrated on the men and their vehicles, Captain Reissmann roared to me, his aid; 'Wolfe, hurry over to the 9th and tell the men they must get out of the mines. To lie there is worse than to attack'. The Tommie's were entrenched in solid well camouflaged positions and they sat tight. I made it to the 9th but was hit by a shell splinter in my shoulder, as I fell I was caught by Sergeant Major Friedrich. I gave him the orders and a section of sappers and volunteers was gathered, a small lane was cleared through the mine-field and the company was through.[61]

The concentration of the whole effort of the Africa Corps to take out the box at Auleb/Sidi Muftah dominated the 1 June. At 7:30 a.m. 30 Panzer, from 15th Panzer Division, and a battalion of the 104th Regiment, together with the Corps Battle Group struck down from the north. While from the south came the 90th Light Division and from the south east elements of the Trieste Division attacked. British patrols out in no-man's land saw this mass of men and machines advancing and beat a hasty retreat back to their own lines.

Sergeant Herbert Glenton, 4th Battalion East Yorkshire Regiment, was out on patrol and was surprised to come across the German and Italian forces as they massed for the assault:

> We left the box with a couple of sections in the early hours of 1st June when it was still dark, an officer called Westerdale was in charge. We came short of a big deep gully and halted, then we advanced on foot to the edge of this cliff and looked over the edge. There stretching out before us was what looked like the whole of Rommel's bloody army, tanks, troops and everything. We shot back to the truck and went hell for leather for the box, being fired on

---

61  Manuscript sent to author by H Wernaman, Africa Corps veteran (Germany, 1989).

British troops take cover behind a knocked out vehicle in the Gazala Line, May 1942.

as we did. From then on there was all hell let loose, our artillery fired into the advancing enemy over open sights.[62]

Enemy tanks and infantry launched a determined assault against the outer perimeter, overrunning many posts with the first shock. Stuka dive-bombers fell out of the sky with a piercing howl and dropped their deadly loads on the desperately tired defenders. It was no easy task for the attacking force as it beat its way through the outer defences, the British troops resisted resolutely.

Pte John Thompson, 5th Battalion Green Howards, was in the outer perimeter defences when he knew the game was up:

> Stukas came and bombed us, their artillery shelled us and our guns fired until they had nothing left. I was in the trenches with C Company and stuff was flying everywhere, the next thing we saw was a caterpillar tracked vehicle with a gun on it coming towards us. Gerry marched some of our lads they had taken prisoner across our front so we couldn't fire you see. I had a Thompson sub-machine gun, I stripped it and slung the parts far and wide, I made sure they wouldn't use that again.[63]

Only 13 tanks of 44th Battalion Royal Tank Regiment were left, five of them moved toward the perimeter in a south-easterly direction amid a hail of shot and shell. As they approached the

---

62  Taped interview with author, Herbert Glenton (1993).
63  Ibid, with John Thompson (Beverley, 1994).

enemy the barrage of noise abated and for a brief moment a great silence hung over this stricken field, the only noise being heard was the roar of the tank engines and the creaking of their tracks as these armoured vehicles approached the enemy anti-tank gun lines to fight an unequal duel.

Major Williamson, 44th Battalion Royal Tank Regiment:

> After going forward for about 400 yards the enemy guns came to life and we found ourselves under heavy anti-tank fire. We made for two pimples about 600 yards away, on arrival at these pimples, which afforded us no protection as we were being fired on from two sides. Major Green came up on air to say he was hit and out of action and that the remainder were to carry on.[64]

Major Williamson fought on until his was the only tank left and he then made his way to Brigade Headquarters and took up a defensive position in the area. Brigadier Haydon saw that the northern sector was crumbling and in full knowledge that no early relief was possible decided to make a break for it rather than be taken prisoner. He took an armoured car and met two tanks at a secret gap in the western mine-field, the brigadier got out of his vehicle to talk to Major Williamson who commanded one of the tanks. Shelling was by now very heavy and one dropped near the group and Haydon fell, Major Williamson went to his aid but found he had been killed, hit in the chest. The situation in the box deteriorated rapidly and at 150 Brigade Headquarters documents were being destroyed. Many artillery positions had fired their last shells and spiked their guns. Those that were able continued to engage the enemy firing at point blank range into the advancing panzers and infantry.

Major Elliot, 451st Battery, Royal Artillery, saw the Germans bringing up large calibre guns and his position came under heavy fire from more than one direction:

> Our position was on the eastern flank of the 5th Green Howards and was very exposed. We got to our gun-pits as the sky began to turn grey, the guns were half in action when a quad came dashing back through the mist pursued by about 12 Mark 1V tanks. They fanned out, took hull down position, and having encircled the four guns opened fire from all directions. Guns, ammunition trailers and quads were all hit and loose boxes of ammunition in the pits caught fire. After 25 minutes the enemy brought up mobile guns on tank chassis and a battery of 50 millimetre anti-aircraft guns on mobile platforms. They then proceeded to open up with everything they had and Mk 1Vs advanced with infantry on foot and on the tanks. The volume of fire was tremendous and concentrated on our position.[65]

Major Elliot's position fell shortly after and this was to be the story throughout the box. Still the enemy met opposition, for as long as the British possessed ammunition they would resist. Just before noon German tanks and armoured vehicles continued to break through more of the shrinking defensive perimeter, self-propelled guns and machine-guns were brought up and under a hail of fire the enemy swept into this dying outpost. The sheer desperation of the situation propelled Rommel into an act of bravery, some would say reckless foolishness for a

---

64   Manuscript sent to the author by Mr Williamson (1991).
65   Ibid, by Mr Elliot (1992).

commander, and he placed himself at the head of one of the leading companies and led it into the battle and onto its objective.

Captain Bob Stafford, 4th Battalion East Yorkshire Regiment, resisted as long as he had ammunition, but it eventually ran out and there was no hope of escape:

> I kept firing for as long as I had ammunition thinking we could still escape. I suggested to Major Watson we could get out this way and that way, but every time we stuck our heads up machine-guns opened up a terrific fire on us. German anti-tank guns were firing at very close range and he finally wore us down. We were running very short of ammunition by noon and eventually we ran out completely, unable to get away all we could do was to sit and wait until he picked us up.[66]

Sergeant Herbert Glenton, 4th Battalion East Yorkshire Regiment, commanded an anti-tank gun, the position he was in became isolated as the German armour pressed forward. It was not long before resistance became futile:

> He had big tanks and long armoured vehicles with guns mounted on the back of them. I was commanding a two pounder anti-tank gun as part of the brigade reserve, two trucks came across our front from the back of a big escarpment 200 yards away and things then started to happen. We opened fire and knocked out both trucks, Gerry had an accurate four inch mortar and he started dropping these things all around us. We could see his tanks all over the top of the escarpment, we fired on them but I don't know if we hit any, suddenly it became obvious that our own artillery was firing smoke, they had nothing else left. In our position we were cut off from everything, if we could hold out long enough to make him withdraw we had a chance of survival, if we couldn't we were dead ducks. When he saw our artillery had nothing but smoke to stop him that's when he came in, we were attacked from left and right, my men were in a hole and the next thing I knew there was a terrific crash when a shell scored a direct hit on our gun leaving it a heap of twisted metal. All we had left then was rifles and a bren gun, at one point I saw a German tank crash straight through a hospital tent. One tank came straight for us, a fella next to me said 'what shall we do?' I said 'there's nothing we can do, just hope he stops before he gets to us'. He stopped 20 yards in front of our position and a tank man opened his turret and shouted to us in English 'come out'. So I said come on lads we've had a go and unless you want to die this is it.[67]

Sergeant Arthur Chester, 4th Battalion East Yorkshire Regiment, had to surrender in the heat of battle and was shocked when he saw what was left of his once proud 150 Brigade:

> Our trench was under constant attack as the Gerry armour rolled in, shells and bullets flew in every direction. Our orders was to hang on as long as possible as there is a column trying to reach us, I think that columns still in the desert. This one tank came belting at us, his six pounder gun pointing right down, he could have blasted us right out the ground. He

---

66   Taped interview with author, Bob Stafford (Hull, 1992).
67   Ibid, with Herbert Glenton (1993).

stopped short of our trench and we were expecting the gun to go off at any second. The turret opened and the commander popped out of the tank and waved two pistols at us, 'out, out' he shouted. We climbed out with our hands up and had to run as there was this tank battle still going on all around us, we was still in the thick of it. We got the shock of our lives when we saw where we had run to, we saw what was left of the brigade sat on the ground, tattered, torn and captured.[68]

Pte William Gleave, 4th Battalion Green Howards, was told it was every man for himself:

> I was a runner and left my slit trench to return to the signals dug-out, shell-fire swept the area constantly as I did so and I frequently dived to earth as they exploded close to me. However my luck held and I approached the dug-out but no signs of life were visible. From my left a square dark shape emerged from the sandy gloom, because of the noise of battle I had not heard its approach and with visions of being machine-gunned I dived once more to the floor and pressed myself into the sand and earth. Another shell seemed to make a bee-line in my direction, the shell detonated and shrapnel sang overhead. I jumped up to check on the tank and with relief saw it was a Valentine, it must be about the last one left surely and it seemed to be reversing out of action. I finally arrived at brigade signals dug-out and pushed the sand flap to one side, I climbed down and was very surprised to find the place filled by 12 or 13 men. I wondered why the signals sergeant hadn't chased them all out to their own slit trenches, I didn't have to ask how things were. Nobody seemed to be saying much, everybody was serious as things were so bad. My fellow orderly was present in the dug-out nursing a wound, I knew Jimmy wasn't going to do any more message carrying. It was about an hour afterwards that the phone rang to be answered by the signals sergeant, after several seconds he put down the receiver, again with an odd expression on his face he said 'that's it lads, everything has to be destroyed, all papers burned. Gerry has broken through, when you've finished here its every man for himself'. Even though everybody had been expecting those words for some time it still came as a shock to hear them spoken. I wondered how my old friends in the 4th Green Howards had fared and I'll bet there are some familiar faces missing by now.[69]

Major D'arcy Mander, DSO, 4th Battalion Green Howards, was checking on his platoon positions when the end came:

> About nine o' clock that morning Brigadier Bill Haydon was killed, he was a fighting soldier of the old school who had led from the front. The last words I heard from him after I got back with my jock column were 'here we bloody are and here we bloody stay, Nolens bloody volens'. With shot and shell flying about from almost every point of the compass I made my way on foot to B Company HQ, I found the Company Sergeant Major in a state of collapse and, before setting out to visit the platoons in my command, I laid my revolver, field glasses and a box of grenades in the Company Command Post. Guided by

---

68   Ibid, with Arthur Chester (Hull, 1989).
69   Manuscript sent to author by William Gleave (1996).

an orderly I set out to look round Company HQ. Hardly had I commenced this task before we were attacked from the rear by the usual full panoply of Germans, with infantry on foot escorting various fighting vehicles, one of which was a four barrelled anti-aircraft cannon, probably 20mm calibre. I shouted to my orderly 'down', we both dived into slit trenches, I cursing because I had no weapon, when my orderly called out 'shall I fire Sir'? But the answer came from the Germans as the barrels of the Pom-Pom were depressed and we were treated to a fusillade of explosive cannon shells and a hail of stones and splinters rained down on us. Having arrived only minutes earlier I dived under some rubbish and heard the Germans calling 'come out Major Mander, come out Major Mander'. I was soon discovered and ignominiously hauled out, Company HQ and the three platoons, which were spread out over a front of 2,000 to 3,000 yards and which I had not even had time to visit, were winkled out one after another.

At the time of our capture food, water and ammunition in the 150 Brigade box was pretty low and the men had suffered from being pinned in their slit trenches through the heat of the day on very short rations. I shouted to them to collect and take with them all the food and water they could lay their hands on but was roughly silenced by a German officer who indicated forcefully that he was the one giving the orders and that I could shut up or I would be shot, I shut.[70]

Major A H G Dobson, MC, 232nd Field Company, Royal Engineers, watched the last act being played out and tried to make his escape:

They mopped up 150 Brigade, all the guns had been lost or were out of ammunition and the few tanks we had were all out of action. It was just the foot soldier sitting in a hole in the ground with a bren-gun and he hadn't really much hope by that stage. I remember the sapper commander on the phone saying 'I can see the tanks coming now, they are only 50 yards away and I don't think I shall be telephoning much more'. That was the end of his particular unit and this went on all the way round. Eventually the Brigade Commander [Brigadier Haydon] was killed shortly afterwards in the last German attack. As far as 150 Brigade was concerned the war was over and it really became sauve qui peut, every man for himself. I went off with four or five others in a scout car. We hoped we might manage to drive through the mine-field and we got a long way before there was the usual explosion and the wheel was blown off. We just sat there hoping we hadn't been seen, but we had and we were shelled, it was very unpleasant. That night we set off to walk back towards what we hoped was our lines, but after a long nights walking we ran into a German LOC [lines of communication] unit who, praise them, were very good to us.[71]

---

70  D. Mander, *Mander's March on Rome* (Gloucestershire: Sutton Publishing, 1987), p. 95.
71  Manuscript sent to author by A H D Robinson (1994).

**13**

## Aftermath

---

Between 1:00 p.m. and 2:00 p.m. on 1 June 1942 the Auleb box fell to the Axis forces who then moved in to round up what was left of 150 Brigade, many of whom sat in their trenches out of water and ammunition and suffering severe dehydration waiting to be taken into captivity. Others made desperate attempts to escape into the mine-fields where they would wait until nightfall and then try to find a way to their own lines, most of these were captured and a very small number got away. Sgt Davis of the 4th Battalion Royal Northumberland Fusiliers jumped on a passing lorry, only to be badly wounded when the enemy saw it and shelled them, after which he was picked up by a German patrol and taken prisoner. The men of 150 Field Ambulance, who's position had been occupied by Panzer units in the rear of 150 Brigade, found themselves left alone as the German tanks made their way to the struggle for the box at Auleb.

The men of 150 Field Ambulance in the Gazala Line, May 1942. Seated centre is James Keith Kilby.

Pte James Keith Killby, 150 Field Ambulance, had been working with German medics and got on with them very well as they cared for the wounded of both sides:

> Before the German tank units and medical staff moved out that night many scenes took place that I think would not have pleased Hitler, especially when one Gerry rendered God Save the King on a mouth organ. On two things the Germans and our lads soon found they were agreed, the desert and the Italians, but what they said is unprintable. We were struck by the extreme youth of so many of the Germans, so it seemed that one quarter of some of the units were 20 or under. All that night the German columns were milling around our camp until about 3:00 a.m. when a long line of tanks and vehicles started to stream westward and for an hour or more our position resembled Hyde Park Corner. They took all the wounded they could with them, some were reluctant to go and the more serious cases they left with us. On the evening of the 2nd June news was brought from the Guards Brigade by Reverend R Lunt, Chaplin to the Coldstream Guards, that 150 Brigade had been taken and we were ordered to evacuate the Mobile Dressing Station, wounded and all. Had a meal of German sausage and coffee followed by a wash, including our feet. We marched out at 10:45 p.m. by moonlight and were guided through the mine-fields to the box held by the Guards at Knightsbridge.[1]

Pte William Gleave, 4th Battalion Green Howards, and his comrades tried to escape through the mine-field only to find German troops waiting for them on the other side:

> The lads slipped away to continue their walk through the mine-field, still heading roughly west, a short time later the trip wire of the mine-field came into view. But to our disgust as we approached the wire we saw several Africa Corps troops waiting on the other side of the wire and already having seen us. The situation did not seem to offer any possibility of escape so as they beckoned to the lads to come out of the mine-field with their hands up, I took the bolt out of my rifle and slung it away, to be followed a few seconds later by the rifle which I threw in the opposite direction. The proximity of the enemy troops gave me an unreal feeling as though it was a bad dream, the reality of the situation was impressed on me however by the sight of a red, white and black swastika flag draped over the bonnet of a nearby Volkswagen. We were not searched by the Germans but just kept waiting until some of their vehicles drove up and we were motioned to climb aboard these and shortly driven away.[2]

The brave troops of 150 Brigade had fought for days an isolated and unsupported battle against the might of Rommel's forces. The British, Italian and German wounded were tended by the medical staff of both sides as the prisoners were herded to the rear. Africa Corps soldiers took pity on the defeated foe and shared with them their precious water, a rare commodity on that sweltering day in the desert.

---

1  Manuscript sent to author by James Keith Kilby (1991).
2  Ibid, by William Gleave (1996).

The Auleb box, 2 June 1942. In the background the men of 150 Brigade queue up for water.

Sergeant Arthur Chester, 4th Battalion East Yorkshire Regiment:

> We dare not move as everyone was trigger happy, we were not sure whether we would be prisoners or gun fodder, none of us had water and some blokes couldn't put their tongues back into their mouths they was so swollen and dry. Some peoples morale was lower than others, we was all frightened, we didn't know if we would be shot as we had heard all about German brutality. Some of the Germans was good to us and gave us their water bottles. The Italians took our rings, watches or socks and boots for a drink, the Italian soldiers was badly equipped. When the German troops saw the Italians behaving like that they belted them, they didn't like the Italians. I was covered in blood blisters, it was caused through bits of shrapnel that had hit me and my face was all pitted through shell blast, but I never felt it while much later.[3]

Towards the end of the battle bullets still flew around and Pte Herbert Thompson, 4th Battalion East Yorkshire Regiment, saw one man take a stray bullet even though the main fighting was over. And as they were being marched into captivity the Desert Air Force attacked them, not being able to distinguish friend from foe:

---

3   Taped interview with author. Arthur Chester (Hull, 1991).

> We were stood about not knowing what to do when a stray bullet cut Cpl Harry Binks jugular vein, we knew he was dying but had no medical facilities, they'd been blown apart. We put field dressings on his neck but he slowly faded and died, poor old Sergeant Shilitoe nursed him to his death and was covered in his blood. We were very badly bombed by our own side the same day we got captured, we dived for cover and watched the melee that was going on, the only way to identify the dead was by their pay books, they were so badly smashed, it was awful. One man was completely gone below the belt, he was still alive but not for long poor sod.[4]

Sergeant Herbert Glenton, 4th Battalion East Yorkshire Regiment, was marched into captivity through the German units and caught a sight of Rommel:

> I was walked off the battle-field with others and as we made it behind this big escarpment, well, I'll never forget that sight, massed German armour, guns and infantry as far as I could see, just going about their business. As we were marched through this mass of men and machines I noticed there was a flurry of activity among the Germans about 100 yards in front of us as though something different was happening, the troops suddenly jumped to attention and who should it be other than Rommel himself. He came over to us and said through his interpreter 'don't be ashamed, if you had held us up much longer we would have had to pull back, I have ordered water to be brought up for you, good luck'. The Germans told us we were unlucky as all prisoners on this front were to be handed over to the Italians and we said 'isn't that good'? They said 'no they'll starve you and they're no more soldiers than your wife is.[5]

Rommel always led from the front and although his tactics were at times reckless, driving his own superiors into fits of rage and despair, he inspired his own men and commanders by example and held the respect of the troops from both sides. When the box fell Rommel was there and his seemingly chivalrous actions towards many of the defeated Tommies left an everlasting impression upon the men of 150 Brigade. Rommel moved around the now quiet battle-field that was littered with the dead of both armies, burnt out tanks and vehicles and all the debris of war. He asked to meet Brigadier Haydon only to find he had been killed along with many other good men. The survivors who saw or met Rommel that day speak of it with great pride when they look back upon that historic moment.

Pte Ron Railton, 5th Battalion Green Howards:

> Rommel came over to our big group as we sat on the floor and spoke to us through an interpreter, we was in a terrible state but I recall it clearly, he was stood up in an open top car when he addressed us. He said 'you needn't tell us your regiment, we know', that's the only bit I can remember but it's all a bit hazy, then he drove off to another group. He was a bloody toff was Rommel you know.[6]

---

4   Ibid, with Herbert Thompson (Beverley, 1994).
5   Ibid, with Herbert Glenton (1993).
6   Ibid, with Ron Railton (Beverley, 1996).

Captain Bob Stafford, 4th Battalion East Yorkshire Regiment:

> Major Watson and myself were taken in front of General Rommel, speaking to him through his interpreter, he said we had put up a stout defence which I suppose was a kind of compliment, I recall not being in the mood for pleasantries at the time as I was in such a state. He wished us good luck and departed.[7]

Pte Alfred Chittock, MM, 150 Field Ambulance:

> We was in the bag by dinnertime, we got rounded up and marched off the battle-field and were forced to sit on the floor in the blazing sun, the heat was unbearable and some of the Gerries came over and gave us a drink of water from their own canteens, water never tasted so good. I looked round at the lads near me and they were in a terrible state, I must have looked the same. I saw a car drive up to our group, which was quite big by then, an officer was standing up in it and someone said 'look its Rommel' and it was. He spoke to some of our officers, though I was too far away from him to hear anything, I'll never forget my first sight of the Desert Fox.[8]

Lt Terry Gorman, Royal Tank Regiment, was in a bad way as he and his comrades marched through the desert under a blazing sun, drastic measures were called for if they were to survive:

> Harry was hit, I put my arm round his waist and pulled him back into the tank, he was dead and the back of his head was a bloody mess, its contents slowly emptying onto my shirt. As I cradled him in my arms a huge Gerry stood over me, rifle aimed at my head. 'Englisher' he shouted, I looked him right in the eyes, time to die I thought. Suddenly the fierce blue eyes seemed to soften and his aim relaxed, 'Rous', he spoke calmly and jerked a thumb behind him. I left poor Harry where he lay 'you are now prisoners of the 3rd Reich' announced a German officer to a bedraggled group of us, we were told to walk towards the Axis Lines, there was to be no water and no transport. I staggered along in a dream, we could not keep together as a group and I found myself alone, my tin helmet offered little protection against the blazing sun and I was in a bad way. Suddenly above and in front of me I could see a huge cup and saucer brimming over with freshly brewed tea, it was one of my Aunt Polly's cups and she made a great cuppa, if only I could reach it. I must have collapsed, when I opened my eyes the huge unshaven face of a German soldier replaced Aunt Polly's cup. He held me up with one arm and was trying to pour some foul black liquid into my mouth. 'Café' he intoned 'café' I spluttered and managed to get to my feet, they had no water to spare but gave me a little more coffee and a tube of cheese and pointed me in the right direction.
>
> A little further along I came across three of our lads resting, they were despondent as we had no water and no protection against the sun. A voice called out 'good morning gentlemen', I turned round to be met by a bedraggled tankie officer like me of the Royal

---

7 Ibid, with Bob Stafford (Hull, 1994).
8 Ibid, with Alfred Chittock (1992).

Tank Regiment, his name was Captain Lloyd Ledger. He said 'If we stay here we'll die, we have to get up and walk and try to flag down some transport', 'now piss into this' he produced a dirty tizer bottle from his pocket which had a small amount of liquid swimming around the bottom. I looked at him in amazement, he continued 'If we're going to get out of this we'll need fluid'. I don't know how we did it but each of us in turn made our contribution until there must have been half a pint in the bottle. 'For God's sake don't drink the stuff" he urged 'Rinse your mouth out and spit it back into the bottle'. This we did at regular intervals as we resumed out trek, that bottle of piss was the difference between life and death. Later we ran into some Italian Fiat trucks bound for Durna and as we bounced along it dawned on me that I was a Prisoner of War.[9]

Pte William Gleave, 4th Battalion Green Howards, was being taken into captivity by a rather panicky German anti-tank unit:

I was being taken by an anti-tank unit to the transports that would take us into captivity when the cry went up 'tanks, tanks!' The anti-tank gunners drove off the track, set up their guns and parked the lorries carrying the prisoners behind the guns. A few minutes later an eight wheeled armoured car approached the scene, inside of which was a standing figure. I studied the man in it, I had a feeling his features were familiar to me. It was Rommel himself, I watched this legendary soldier closely, Rommel did not appear to be in a good frame of mind and commenced a tirade which would have done any British sergeant major proud. The anti-tank unit's senior officer stamped to rigid attention several yards in front of the armoured car where Rommel proceeded to give him the works in a loud raucous voice. I turned to one of the panzer grenadiers who had sat himself down at my side and nodding towards the Africa Corps Commander I said 'Rommel?' The soldier gave a delighted grin and exclaimed 'Ya, Ya'.[10]

The anti-tank crew prepared their guns to move and the column sped off to meet another group of lorries where they offloaded their prisoners and disappeared into the blue. The new transports, some of which were captured British trucks, moved off in another direction and presently approached a group of stationary lorries and an Italian tank. Pte Gleave remembers:

The lorry I was on, a three tonner, was an Eighth Army vehicle, its original owners having been 1st Armoured Division whose Rhino Divisional sign it still sported. After travelling a little while ahead of us I spotted a small group of stationary lorries, also an Italian tank which was in the centre of the group. As our lorry was about to pass this gathering it slowed down and I, sat fairly high up, was able to get a good view. The side hatch and the turret of the tank was open, while on the ground stretched out alongside it was the figure of a big man who's chest and head were covered over with a tent half. One could just see his group of medal ribbons, but this only confirmed what I already knew. The dead officer was Brigadier Haydon our Brigade Commander and as I was one of the runners who had

---

9   Ibid, with Terry Gorman (1993).
10  Manuscript sent to author by William Gleave (1996).

seen him daily and had been in his office many times, especially before I had been posted to Advanced HQ, I recognised him immediately.[11]

Water and food were in short supply and added to this discomfort was the intense heat as the sun beat down mercilessly on the captured troops as they were driven to their destination, the Port of Tripoli. At the port the prisoners of war were taken onboard large merchant ships, the voyage to Italy only added to their suffering and all men who experienced this misery hold bitter memories of their callous treatment at the hands of their Italian tormentors.

Sergeant Arthur Chester, 4th Battalion East Yorkshire Regiment:

> At Tripoli we were put into a big tramp steamer and at that time we were in such a bad way we were just passed caring. A lot of the lads had dysentery and desert sores so morale was low to say the least. The Italians was taking the mickey out of us, laughing at us, they was real brave soldiers then. We were all kept in the dark cargo hold with the hatches shut, with dysentery and all things like that, the blokes couldn't control themselves without messing themselves and just had to do it were they were in the dark hold of the ship. We said to the Ities 'you'll never get us there, the Royal Navy's waiting for you'. The Italians all had life jackets on.[12]

Sergeant Herbert Glenton, 4th Battalion East Yorkshire Regiment:

> The Germans took us back so far and then handed us over to the Italians who moved us along the coast to Tripoli in civilian trucks, it took us three days I think. They sorted 300 of us out and put us on this German cargo ship, put us in the dark hold and battened down the hatches. That was a shocking journey as there were men with dysentery and men with untended wounds down there in the darkness. The journey seemed endless in that dark space with all sorts of smells and the groans of suffering men down there, I shall never forget that.[13]

The story of 150 Brigade ends here, but for each individual survivor their story had another three years to go before liberation. Most spent this time in a prisoner of war camp, others like Captain Douglas King and Major D'arcy Mander escaped and eventually found their own lines. A few escaped captivity in Italy and fought with the Italian partisans against the Germans, Sergeant Arthur Chester was one such brave soul. These individual stories lie beyond the bounds of this study but the men of 150 Brigade have a proud record by anyone's standards and their war service speaks for itself within these pages.

By 28 May 1942 Rommel had rashly spread out his own units across the desert in a wild gamble at Gazala and by noon that day was out of touch with many of those units and facing imminent defeat. On the 29th he was desperately short of supplies and with a tank strength of little better than 50 percent was forced to withdraw. He chose to occupy a position to the north of Bir Hacheim near Sidi Muftah, soon to be known as the Devil's Cauldron, and did

---

11  Ibid, by William Gleave (1996).
12  Taped interview with author, Arthur Chester (Hull, 1991).
13  Ibid, with Herbert Glenton (1996).

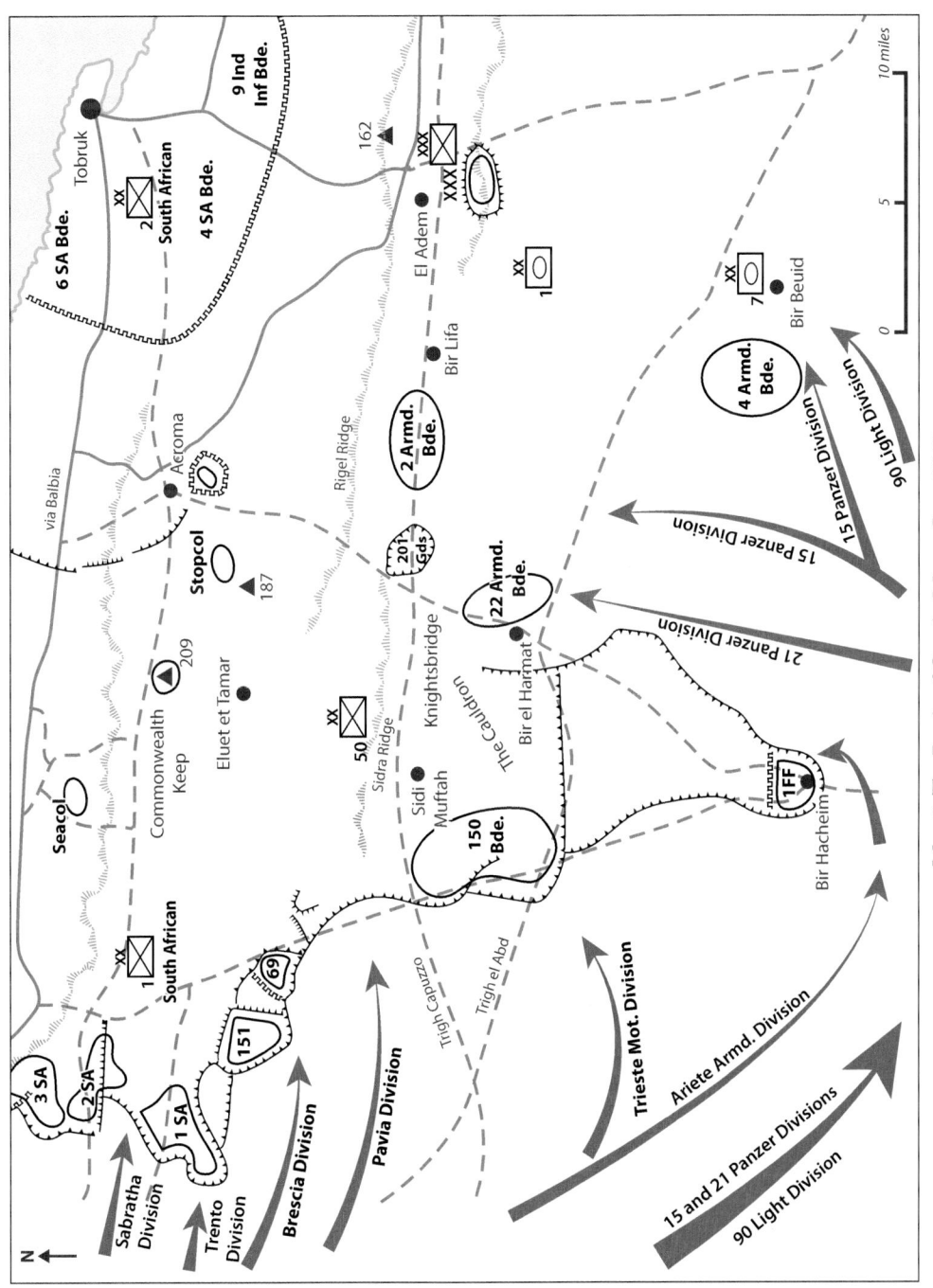

Map 9 The Battle of Gazala, May to June 1942.

so while being totally oblivious to the fact that the ground to the west was strongly fortified by 150 Brigade, cutting him off from his badly needed supplies. This was the moment for Ritchie to attack in strength with all available forces against an opponent in dire-straights. He needed to support 150 Brigade urgently and prevent Rommel opening up supply lines through the British mine-fields and focus a crushing air and artillery bombardment upon the Cauldron as a preliminary to a massed infantry and tank attack. The systems of ground and air co-ordination in the forefront of the battlefield were still badly underdeveloped by the British. The Luftwaffe, superbly handled by Kesselring, were making life very difficult for the Desert Air Force. With Auchinleck's encouragement the Eighth Army had rescinded the traditional function of command by breaking down its forces into brigade groups co-ordinated by divisions in a loose framework of control overseen by corps and army head-quarters. This effectively eliminated any possibility of achieving rapid concentration of effort. In no department was this dilution of effort more fatal than in the artillery, whose units were spread evenly around the battle-field, most being employed in batteries of eight guns, sometimes in regiments of 24 guns and rarely by divisions of 72 guns. A corps artillery effort could have brought massive and crushing fire power down upon the enemy with its several hundred guns controlled by telephone as in 1918, now even easier to arrange with the new radio networks available. Fully aware that Rommel's forces were suffering from shortages of water and supplies and that Rommel was within 24 hours of having to surrender, Ritchie dallied and failed to capitalize on his advantageous position. The British forces enjoyed a tank superiority of between 500 and 250 tanks and a still greater superiority in artillery power, senior British commanders believed that come what may Rommel's forces would be beaten as a result of their isolation. Possibly this is the reason why they indulged themselves in long drawn out discussions as to the best course of action to take, always feeling that time was on their side. It seems beyond belief that from the moment Rommel backed his forces into the Cauldron a whole week passed before a fully co-ordinated corps attack was launched, unless one draws the conclusion that the upper levels of Eighth Army's leadership was unworthy of the brave men under their command.

# 14

## The Gazala Gallop

The destruction of 150 Brigade allowed the German and Italian forces to have free passage through the mine-fields for their supply columns to the area known as the Devil's Cauldron, during the first few days of June Rommel strengthened and re-supplied his tired units and it was now only a matter of time before the Axis Forces were strong enough to go on the offensive. The first British counter attack, Operation Aberdeen, got underway on 5th June and was an unmitigated disaster. Rommel was prepared for the British attack which was poorly organised with tanks and infantry operating independently of each other. The German screen of 88mm anti-tank guns took a heavy toll of the British tanks.

Lt H Fitzjohn, 22nd Armoured Brigade, took part in an attack on a screen of 88s and was met with a storm of fire:

> We advanced at first light under cover of a smoke screen in a Matilda heavy [tank] and when we got through the smoke we found ourselves in the middle of a mine-field which no one knew was there. Sited all along the front were dug in 88mm guns which started potting off our tanks like a shooting gallery. As we tried to get passed the mine-field the best part of the 21st Panzer Division came round our right flank and started belting away at us. We didn't know what was happening, in the next tank to me was our troop leader, Lt Coulton, he got his head blown off. The Panzers came on and we heard their 75mm and 50mm shells banging into our right hand side. The first shell that hit us showered me with aluminium paint from the inside of the tank. Then a shot came and smashed my periscope, but the shell had twisted the casing around it and I couldn't pull the broken prism out. I was in a horrible position, should I open up and repair the damage or should I wait. Then we had another big bang and the intercom went dead. Now I was driving blind, it was absolute chaos. Suddenly we were hit in the turret and it was jammed, the tank was useless. I was told to turn around and away we came. As we were coming back out I opened my driver's hatch as I knew it was comparatively safe and my heart sank to my boots, for as far as the eye could see were Matildas on fire or knocked out. I passed one and there was our squadron leader laid out on the side of it. When we got back there was a roll call and there were 12 of us left out of 70 that went in.[1]

---

1  Manuscript sent to author by B Leonard (1995).

Rommel sat fast in the Cauldron as the British expended their energy attacking his outer perimeter of anti-tank guns in piece meal fashion. The failure of Operation Aberdeen was the signal for the Axis Forces to break out of the Cauldron and on the afternoon of 5 June the tanks of the 21st Panzer Division smashed a path through the British in the direction of Knightsbridge. 15th Panzer Division advanced south through Bir el Harmat. The British forces were now fighting desperately to hold the marauding panzers back from overwhelming the entire Gazala position. With the destruction of the British armour virtually complete Rommel could now turn his attention to the Free French defensive box at Bir Hacheim.

The Free French at Bir Hacheim had held out for many days against concerted attacks from the air and on land, the Luftwaffe flew 1,300 sorties against the French position in 10 days, the Germans and Italian commanders had given them the chance to surrender on numerous occasions but still they fought on. Repeatedly the Axis forces attacked with artillery, tanks and infantry. Before the French positions lay hundreds of enemy dead and smoking black tank hulks. Squadrons of Stukas rained down bombs on the brave Frenchmen and the Africa Corps launched fresh assaults. With each attack the defenders numbers dwindled as the outer perimeter was nibbled away by the German and Italian infantry. On 9 June the enemy broke into the French position and ugly hand to hand fighting ensued amid the roar and rumble of this ferocious battle as the Frenchmen repulsed their foes one last time. On the night of 9th it became obvious that the position could not be held much longer and on 10 June the French garrison was ordered to withdraw rather than allow it to be destroyed like 150 Brigade. They left behind them a scene of utter desolation strewn with hundreds of dead from both sides and wrecked tanks and armoured cars burning in the blackened sand. This had been an epic stand and a great feat of arms, of the 3,600 men who originally held the position only 2,700 returned to safety.

Rommel commented on his Free French opponents:

> After our summons to surrender had been rejected the attack opened about mid-day. The Italian Trieste Division from the north east and the German 90th Light Division from the south east advanced against the fortifications, field positions and mine-fields of the French defenders. With our preliminary barrage there began a battle of extraordinary severity which was to last 10 whole days. I frequently took over command of the assault forces myself and seldom in Africa was I given such a hard fought struggle. The French fought in a skilfully planned system of field positions, small defence works, slit trenches, small pill boxes, machine-gun and anti-tank gun nests, all surrounded by dense mine-fields. It was a particularly difficult task to clear lanes through the mine-fields in the face of the French fire. Superhuman feats were performed by the sappers who suffered heavy casualties. During the first few days of our attack on Bir Hacheim the mass of the British forces kept astonishingly quiet.[2]

The 12 June was a day of disaster for the Eighth Army and was to be a turning point in the Gazala battle as two German divisions smashed the British armoured reserve destroying 120 armoured vehicles. On the morning of the 13th Rommel edged his units forward towards Knightsbridge boldly pushing his anti-tank guns between his advancing tanks and using the

---

2   B Liddle-Hart, *The Rommel Papers* (London: Da Capo Press, 1953), p. 280.

Top left: Soldiers of the French Foreign Legion pause for a bite to eat during a lull in the fighting. Bir Hacheim. May 1942. Top right: Colonel Amilakvari, left, commander of the 13th Regiment, Foreign Legion, in conference with his battalion commander Puchios, right, and other officers. Bir Hacheim. May 1942. Colonel Amilakvari would be killed at Alamein on 24th October 1942. Bottom left: Smiling French survivors of Bir Hacheim heading for Alamein, June 1942. Bottom right: Troops of the French Foreign Legion going out on patrol at Bir Hacheim. May 1942.

The Devil's Cauldron. Knocked out tanks and vehicles litter the landscape, June 1942.

tanks as bait to lure the British armour closer. The Axis troops took full advantage of the dust and haze to give them cover, coming to grips with the British in a position of distinct advantage. The sharp crack of anti-tank fire from the 88s filled the air as stricken British tanks burst into flames or were forced back while taking numerous hits from German tanks and guns. In the latter half of the day the box on Rigel Ridge fell and the Guards were forced to abandon Knightsbridge after fighting continuously for almost a fortnight. By the end of the day on 13 June only 50 cruiser and 20 infantry tanks were left to the Eighth Army, forcing the armoured brigades to withdraw, leaving behind them many hundreds of tanks that could have been recovered and put back into service.

Brigadier Harold Ian Bransom, DSO, 124th Field Regiment, Royal Artillery, saw the carnage as tank after tank took hits:

> As the sun came up the most frightful battle started, we were being heavily shelled and machine gunned and our tanks were brewing up all around. Our leading tanks reached the mine-field below the ridge and were being absolutely shot out of the ground. We were trying to set up our guns behind them to cover them but we couldn't see what we were firing at. After three hours we fired smoke so that the remnants of our tanks could get out, they withdrew and reformed. It seemed obvious that the Bosche was going to put in a counter attack so we put down as much protective fire as we could.[3]

---

3   Manuscript sent to author by H I Bransom (1994).

During all of this the remaining two brigades of the 50th Division, with the South Africans on their right, sat tight in their defensive boxes as the battle raged around them and aggressive patrols from both boxes were out continuously harassing the enemy. Water was rationed and men not required for patrols or manual work kept below ground in their slit trenches. As Rommel rounded Bir Hacheim on 27 May Cruwell Group made feeble attempts to draw the British attention to the predicted attack area in the centre and shelled the British boxes constantly. Any Italian units that attempted to close with 69 Brigade and 151 Brigade were soon dealt with.

Pte Kilgallon, 9th DLI:

> The Italians attacked our position, we opened fire and scattered them, a lot of them were hit and our stretcher bearers tried to bring the wounded in but snipers shot the stretcher bearers even though it was obvious what they were doing, we said sod that leave them to rot. One lad I was with got shot clean through the wrist.[4]

Raids from both boxes did great damage to enemy supply columns and numerous actions were fought adding to Rommel's already acute shortages of water, fuel and ammunition. As the men of 151 and 69 Brigades went about their business they had no way of knowing that the terrific noise of battle in the distance was the death throes of 150 Brigade.

Pte John H Clark, 8th DLI:

> A mile or so away there was a German convoy passing, these passed every day with supplies and we launched snatch raids to destroy or capture their precious cargoes. When we attacked our carrier and mortar platoons would have the job of cutting out a certain number of vehicles you see, we always captured quite a few vehicles but never without a fight, we killed quite a lot of their men and lost a few of our own unfortunately. In one such raid Lt Robinson was standing up in his carrier and got a small anti-tank shell right through his body. In the distance we could hear a continuous rumble night and day but we had no way of knowing it was 150 Brigade fighting for their lives.[5]

69 Brigade was closer to the 150 Brigade box and the ferocity of the battle for the doomed position could be seen and heard clearly.

Pte Harry Forth, MID, 5th Battalion East Yorkshire Regiment:

> Gerry was battering the box held by 150 Brigade with intense fire, we were too far away to support them but the noise of battle was terrific. At night we could see the gun flashes lighting up the sky, they never seemed to stop. 88mm and tank shells flew over us with a whistle or a crack, there were that many we felt the next one must get us. Gerry overran the 4th Battalion we found out later, that was a knock back.[6]

---

4   Taped interview with author, Mr Kilgallon (Durham, 1996).
5   Ibid, with John H Clark (Durham, 1992).
6   Ibid, with Harry Forth (Cottingham, 1989).

With the loss of 150 Brigade and the Free French position at Bir Hacheim, the abandoning of Knightsbridge and the destruction of the British armour, the victory so confidently predicted by Ritchie at the end of May had turned to sour defeat. Little if any of this news was known to the remnants of the 50th Division, officers and men of both 69 and 151 Brigades still waited for the face to face conflict they confidently expected would come. During this bleak period the 50th Division continued to carry out harassing raids on the enemy columns that swept through the mine-field gaps daily and caused the Axis Forces as much trouble as possible. In the air Stuka squadrons were very aggressive and circled the divisional sector all day working in relays, any movement brought them screaming out of the skies to drop their deadly load with frightening precision. As the Axis Forces became stronger both boxes came in for regular heavy attacks from artillery and from the air, the men in 69 Brigades box swore they could set their watches by the artillery barrages and just before the expected volley they would go to ground.

Pte Harry Forth, 5th Battalion East Yorkshire Regiment, and his wife Rene.

Sergeant Max Hearst, 5th Battalion East Yorkshire Regiment:

> One bloke, during the middle of a barrage of high explosive shells, stayed above ground to watch a 25 pounder gun team at work, well there was an old saying, if you hear it coming it aint got yer name on it, well we heard it coming and it got him. Above the explosions we heard the shout 'stretcher bearer!' so we had to go. When we got there we couldn't find a mark on him and thought it was blast that killed him and had to carry him under shell-fire to the medical tent which was at the other side of the Wadi. He was laid out and a medic noticed a small amount of blood in one eye, he had been hit by a thin sliver of steel from an exploding shell. When we got back to our second in command he said 'you lads did damned well, I'm recommending you both be mentioned in despatches'. That same day we carried him across. Our padre was a brave man, he would hear the shout for stretcher bearers and he would go out with them, we lost him that day as well.[7]

Gunner Harry Wood, 74th Field Regiment, Royal Artillery, was in the box held by 69 Brigade:

> It was a quiet night near us but a tank battle was raging in the distance, we were issued with solid steel shot for tank penetration but hadn't fired a round yet. It was a quiet night on guard when I heard movement in front of the guns just before dawn. An NCO on the

---

7   Ibid, with Max Hearst (Hull, 1992).

next gun told me to challenge them and like a fool I stood up in full view and shouted 'halt, who goes there'. To my surprise six men put their hands up and came forward, they were a patrol of the Queen's Regiment that had lost their way back after a night patrol and were relieved to find our lines again. Here I learned a valuable lesson, to stay under cover when making a challenge as this wasn't the barracks back in Blighty. We moved nearer the front the next day and started shelling the enemy. The ground was very rocky and digging was impossible, only the scooping out of a few inches of sand was possible. Still we felt better slamming shells into the breech and keeping busy. Tank transporters were bringing back damaged tanks from the battle ahead and ambulances trundled backwards and forwards with the wounded. In the afternoon we had a Stuka raid and as they peeled off out of the sun the ack-ack opened up from all angles, I glanced up from a prime position and clearly saw the swastikas on their tails and the bombs being released directly above my head. The target was bren-carriers and vehicles nearby and as stones and shrapnel dropped on us like rain it was evident the raid had been a success. Sergeant Robson was now showing signs of extreme nervousness, a pity really because we had a good gun area and I knew that he knew his gun drill back to front, but the screaming of the Stukas had unnerved him, who knows what memories they brought back.[8]

On 14 June, faced with the prospect of utter defeat, Ritchie, the commander of the Eighth Army ordered a withdrawal from the Gazala Line. To the undefeated brigades still holding out this was a bitter blow.

Major William I Watson, DSO, MC, 6th DLI, was in 151 Brigades mess when a grim faced young officer entered the room and said 'you'll not be so happy when you hear what I've got to say'. He brought news of the order to retire:

This was a knockout blow! Everyone was completely stunned at the news. Here was a brigade that had been waiting for over three months to meet the Axis Forces face to face and longing for the moment to introduce itself in no uncertain manner. Now it was required to carry out what seemed to most of its members as another Dunkirk. It was unbelievable and seemed a dismal end to the hopes that had been running so high.[9]

For the troops still in the Gazala Line the danger of encirclement was very real indeed, for Rommel was now re-organising his tired forces for an advance on Tobruk. The South African forces to the north made good their escape on the night of 13/14 June, but for the two remaining brigades of the 50th Division a withdrawal was not so straight forward. Conventional withdrawal was impossible as the coast road and the desert immediately to the south of it were adequate only for the South African's now on the move. If the 50th Division moved to the east it would come up against large formations of German armoured forces and so a bold plan was devised that envisioned a break out to the west through the Italian Sabratha, Trento, Brescia and Pavia Infantry Divisions. Forcing a way through and turning south across the enemies lines of communications, then to turn eastward in a wide arc around Bir Hacheim, heading

8   Manuscript sent to author by H Wood (1989).
9   H Moses, *The Faithful Sixth* (Durham: County Durham Books, 1995), p. 201.

for the frontier at Fort Maddelena some 120 miles from Hacheim. This audacious plan was a great gamble as it was by no means certain that the division would emerge from its battle with an entrenched enemy in a condition to carry on the fight, nor was it certain that those who did would survive the long journey without having to fight further desperate encounters in the desert wastes.

Each brigade was to force its own bridgehead through the enemy lines to their front, allowing the main body to pass through these in a series of small columns, giving some of them a better chance of success if others were checked. Any equipment not required to enable the division to fight or maintain it on its long journey was jettisoned. All items that had to be abandoned were disposed of carefully as there could be no large scale demolitions or fires in case they should give notice to the enemy of the impending withdrawal. On the afternoon of 14 June a Khamsin blew masking the additional activities in the divisional area. Stores and spare equipment of all kinds were destroyed, booby trapped or buried.

The Khamsin abated by 6:00 p.m. and enemy artillery fire increased, however daylight was fading and observation became impossible, the artillery fire ceased as darkness fell. On 69 Brigades front the 5th Battalion East Yorkshire Regiment attacked the enemy in two waves forcing a breach in the Italian lines, the going was not easy and the troops came up against stiff resistance from the Italian infantry.

Pte Harry Forth, MID, 5th Battalion East Yorkshire Regiment, was in the vanguard when his luck ran out:

> Our truck was hit by anti-tank fire and exploded. The whole lot went up in a sheet of flame. One lad was sat in the corner of the back of the truck and we tried to get him off but he just sat there stunned, we tried to get him off but it was just impossible. Me and three other chaps got laid down behind a Valentine tank that had been hit, the flames from our truck, and others around us that had been hit, lit up the area and the enemy artillery homed in on us.[10]

The night air was rent with explosions and the rattle of machine-gun fire, tracer bullets skipped across the landscape in the darkness and blazing vehicles of all kinds lit up the scene. Sergeant Max Hearst was one of the men who lay behind the knocked out tank with Private Forth and remembers this disturbing incident clearly 50 years on:

> The order came to dismount, before we'd cleared the vehicle Gerry got the range and quite a number of vehicles got hit including ours, the thing burst into flames. One lad had been hit, not enough to kill him but he couldn't move and was still on the truck. I'll never forget that, I used to wake up for years after the war hearing his screams. He was stuck on the truck in the flames and burnt to death. I could still hear the screams in my ears when we advanced.[11]

---

10  Taped interview with author, Harry Forth (Cottingham, 1989).
11  Ibid, with Max Hearst (Hull, 1992).

The going was to be just as tough on 151 Brigade front as the 8th DLI forced their own bridgehead through the enemy lines, the Italian troops to their front had been reinforced by German units. The sight of the burning vehicles of the 5th Battalion East Yorkshire Regiment was clearly visible as the Durham's watched salvo after salvo of enemy shells straddled the Yorkshiremen's column. D Company, 8th DLI, led by their commander Major Harold Sidney Sell, MC, had been lifting mines as the light faded and once darkness fell they rushed through the gap they had made. Major Sell remembers:

> We went in vehicles and almost got to the enemy positions before they realised what had happened. My truck was hit by an anti-tank shell and blown to pieces, but I was lucky as both myself and the driver were alright. Then we went through their dug-outs with grenades and tommy-guns and cleared the whole lot out and with my batman using his bayonet with deadly skill I joined in the fighting. We overran the Germans with our Marmon Herrington armoured cars and shot up all their machine-gun positions, they were eliminated as were the Italians. We now took up defensive positions on either side of the gap we had made then the whole of the 8th and 6th Battalions went through. The trouble started afterwards because Joss Percy [CO 9th DLI] came to the conclusion, after hearing the noise of battle, that we'd been destroyed. So he turned his battalion the other way and forced his way back to Tobruk and on to Mersa-Matruh. At the time I was having a council of war with my officers wondering what the hell to do next, we didn't know what they were doing and couldn't reach them on the radio as it had been destroyed by gunfire. We stuck it out until dawn, by that time the Germans had rallied their troops and we were being pretty heavily pounded and suffering casualties. I said to my men 'that's it lets get out' so we broke out into the desert and swept round the old Free French position at Bir Hacheim, being shot up as we did so by the Germans. When I got passed the mine-fields I had three armoured cars, myself and two other blokes, that was all. The rest of the company had been wiped out or taken prisoner.[12]

Major William I Watson, DSO, MC, 6th DLI, made it through the enemy lines and out into the open desert though not without incident:

> Prompt at 8:00 a.m. the 8th Battalion did their attack and then we started to go through their gap which was the width of the column. As we advanced the enemy began to realise what was happening and they started shelling us, the truck with the CO on went up on a mine killing the driver. This held up my column and we were now being shot at. To add to our difficulties the armoured car in my column went up on a mine, somehow we managed to crawl passed the armoured car without going up on a mine ourselves. When we were out I said to my chaps 'If you stick to my tail I'll do my best to get you through'. It was a fearfully nasty experience driving across the German positions along the Trigh Capuzzo. We saw the German bivouacs and camp fires. We drove for 30 miles into the desert and I went on for another five to make sure we were really clear. By now all sorts of vehicles from other columns were tacking on to me. I remember a great big German three tonner lorry was

---

12   J Thompson, *Desert Victory* (London: Ebury Press, 2012), p. 181.

bearing down on us in the dark and we were just going to put a shot into it when we heard a lot of Geordie voices inside, they were men from the 8th Battalion and had captured it when making their escape.[13]

Lance Corporal William Ridley was with the 9th DLI as they headed in the other direction for the coast road:

> They decided to withdraw through the front line of the bloody Italians and Germans, fantastic, who thought that fucking gem up? We went up to the front and passed through a pathway through the mine-field, it was like Guy Fawkes night, everything was going up and there was tracers flying all over the place. Italians was running at the side of our trucks and firing and what have you. An ammunition dump went up, talk about Guy Fawkes, it was a terrific sight. We were stuck in this truck in the middle of a mine-field and there was one lad called Bluey Smith, he was panicking and he took short, well you know how fear loosens the anus. The lads said 'hang your arse over the bloody side of the truck, you're not doing it in here'. Bluey was hanging his rear end over the tail board of the truck and for once in my life when we say the shit was flying, it was.[14]

Pte Thomas Collier, Royal Army Service Corps, drove his truck at speed through the enemy positions:

> We went out through the Italian lines and drove over their tents, I don't remember if anyone was in them. I do remember it was a clear moon-lit night and we kept course by following the Milky Way. The signals lorry was tuned to the forces radio and we could hear 'Rose of England' being broadcast live from a concert at the Royal Albert Hall, this gave us all a boost to carry on and to this day I get emotional when I hear that song.[15]

Major William I Watson, DSO, MC, 6th DLI:

> 69 Brigades column was to the east and moving in the same direction as us and it was virtually impossible to tell friend from foe as the Germans were using so many of our captured vehicles. The battalion experienced very heavy anti-tank fire and had to pass through a veritable cross-fire of projectiles that went hissing passed us into the night. Trucks and other vehicles were going up in flames. The carrier platoon under Captain Caldwell and Lieutenant Boys-Stone respectively, working as a screen on either flank, were by now inexorably involved in this hopeless melee. It was not long before Captain Caldwell's carrier was ablaze from a direct hit. Sergeant Hall, seeing what had happened, drove up to his aid in his carrier but before he reached the scene his carrier was also hit. He and his crew jumped out but before he could get away the carrier received another hit and burst into flames and Sergeant Hall himself was seriously wounded in the leg. Efforts were made to get him to safety but it was impossible, by now the battalion had faded away in the dark with the result

---

13 H Moses, *The Faithful Sixth* (Durham: County Durham Books, 1995), p. 207.
14 Taped interview with author, William Ridley at the Veteran's re-union (Hull, 1993).
15 Manuscript sent to author by T Collier (1992).

that Captain Caldwell and the others were taken prisoner. On the other flank Lieutenant Boys-Stone servant was killed in the act of firing his Bren-gun from the back of his carrier, but despite this the carrier closed with an enemy anti-tank gun and crushed one of the crew before pulling out into the darkness once more. Amongst the trucks that were hit was that of Major Ferens who was bringing up the rear of the column, with the result that both he and the occupants were all slightly wounded.[16]

The retreat that was christened by the troops The Gazala Gallop now began in earnest as the divisional troops raced through the Italian and German lines and out into the blue. Many vehicles were shot from under them leaving stranded men to wait in the desert in the hope of being picked up by following vehicles, tanks or armoured cars, Pte Harry Forth, Sergeant Max Hearst and their comrades scrambled onto another truck and roared through an Italian encampment and took them completely by surprise.

Pte Harry Forth remembers:

> We entered the Italian lines without a challenge and ran right through the centre of all these tents, they were just waking up and didn't know what hit them. All I had was a bren-gun, I just had to let go at them, knocked two of them over while they were shaking their blankets. We got through there safely and shot off into the blue. After half a day or so the truck just gave out, we smashed it up and moved off on foot. We marched for four days at night as spotter planes were out looking for stragglers throughout the day. The heat was terrible.[17]

As a stretcher bearer Sergeant Ken Rutherford, 5th Battalion East Yorkshire Regiment, remembers being told to make the wounded as comfortable as possible and to leave them behind as the enemy would be able to give them the proper care and treatment they would need. The truck he was travelling in came under heavy machine-gun fire and the men had to dismount as casualties were increasing:

> The chap in front of me got back on the truck and I was the last, I got my foot on the top of the rear wheel when the driver took off and I was thrown to the ground and left. Trucks were blazing all around the area and machine-gun bullets were flying about, I panicked as my rifle was on the truck, I had nothing. I lay down and waited, standing up at the first thing I heard approaching. Unfortunately for me it was a tank which I clambered onto and thought well at least I'm safe now. We came across the truck that left me, it had been shot up pretty badly and most of the men on it killed, there's fate for you. The tank eventually lost a track and we began to walk, an old ambulance came along and we travelled with them until that burned out. By that time there was a decent crowd of us, my section started off with 23 men, now there was only seven of us left.[18]

---

16  H Moses, *The Faithful Sixth* (Durham: County Durham Books, 1995), p. 177.
17  Taped interview with author, Harry Forth (Cottingham, 1989).
18  Ibid, with Ken Rutherford (Hull, 1993).

There followed a nightmare journey, on foot or by transport, across country in an area unknown to the troops and crawling with the enemy. A number of vehicles ran straight over precipices as they rushed forward in the darkness, others ran headlong into enemy formations too strong to get through and were taken prisoner or killed, but many forced a passage through and flew out into the desert. Many vehicles were destroyed by mines or enemy artillery fire and some simply broke down leaving the unlucky passengers to walk and risk being picked up by enemy patrols. However this seemingly foolhardy plan of escape worked and slowly but surely the troops filtered through the desert to the frontier.

Lt E H G Moss, 50th Division Intelligence Officer, gives a detailed and eloquent description of his journey to freedom:

> It was a black night with brilliant stars but not a wisp of moon, we started grinding and jolting off through the darkness at four or five miles per hour, nose to tail, with every now and then strange unexplained halts while we looked and listened and wondered what was happening. My own truck was spluttering and I had continually to ask for a push from the three tonner behind me to get it started again. After a couple of miles we came over a small rise and suddenly saw a glow of flames in front of us, a few tracer bullets came singing past, then the column came to a standstill and we sat and waited, a long line of black vehicles with a few men talking in low voices here and there, not a cigarette end showing. In front of us on a low ridge three or four vehicles were burning and there seemed to be something moving against the glow of the flames and lit up smoke. Intermittently tracer bullets, red, green, purple and the occasional anti-tank shell cracked past, they were all over our heads. Now and again there came the bigger crash of a shell somewhere beside us.
>
> On the left we could see other fires in the distance, nothing moved for some time, it was a curiously beautiful scene with little fireworks singing past us and over our heads, the dots of blazes of smoking light ahead of us and the long dark column of vehicles, all drowned in a glittering night. After half an hour or so the firing was still going on and it looked as if we would be risking disaster for the whole column to go straight forward in a crocodile, each vehicle coming over the ridge in turn and being silhouetted against the glow, but it was no good standing still. Soon we saw some trucks moving on in front of us past the fires apparently without hurt. We did not realise what a smoke screen had been created round there and presently we began to move ourselves.
>
> We safely ran the gauntlet past the first ridge, after that we past more burning trucks and carriers and our column lost one or two vehicles on mines or from anti-tank shells, but as we went on our way the firing gradually died down and we had no desperate adventures. The night wore on and we kept grinding southwards huddled in our greatcoats as it grew colder and colder. The extreme darkness was a strain on the drivers as there were many patches of rough going and obstacles reared up suddenly in the night. In the south, as the morning broke, it found us split up into small scattered parties, each making its own way to the wire. It had been an exceptionally cold night and I remember the sun coming up yellow and egg shaped through layers of mist, which hung in all the hollows and stretched out like a streaky sea to the horizon.
>
> We were now a small group of 20 or 30 vehicles crossing a smooth undulating desert, there were one or two alarms of enemy tanks as we went round Bir Hacheim. We stopped and sent on two armoured cars that were with our party but nothing was found.

> By the middle of the morning we were well beyond Bir Hacheim and we swung round south east, the desert was now completely brown, bare and trackless. The ground became gradually more broken and the going varied from sandy patches to patches of stony ground or of small black sharp edged pebbles, but never a bird or beast or tyre mark, only the continual shimmering mirage which closed in on us as the sun climbed higher and the heat grew. That was the hottest day I ever knew, there was no stir of wind and when we made a long halt in the middle of the day the heat came down in a flattening blaze which made one want to wriggle and twist for a moment of relief, one of the men on my truck had sun-stroke. There were some of us I suppose who were missing after it all and will never be accounted for, these poor souls met their deaths in the lonely desert. The next morning, after another very cold and dewy night, we set off again, by 08:00 a.m. we had met the wire a couple of miles south of Fort Madalena and then, coming out of a fold in the ground, we saw the fort itself. A small white stone ruin on the top of a low rise in the desert, not much to look at but it had a well with plenty of fresh, cold water and I have seldom been so glad to see a place.[19]

Pte Thomas Collier, Royal Army Service Corps, was deeply affected by his experiences during the retreat:

> We were bombed by Stukas and machine-gunned by their Messerschmitt 109 escorts as we moved through the desert. A single plane came in at 400 feet and everybody opened fire on it, the pilot dipped his wings to show that he was one of ours but regretfully by then we had shot him down. He bailed out but his parachute didn't open because he was so low. He hit the deck and bounced along for about 30 feet, sadly he was killed, a 19 year old pilot. It took us ages to get over that. After one bombing raid I got out from under the truck and couldn't believe my eyes, an enormous bomb had landed nose down just 10 feet from the vehicle and hadn't exploded, that bomb just didn't have my name on it. I said to my driver Jock 'let's get out of here'. An officer came back to find us and said that many of the wagons that were full of troops had taken direct hits and the scene was disastrous, we followed what was left of the convoy. At one point we passed a Bofors gunner with his head sliced completely off, after seeing that I looked neither to the left or right, trying just to focus on the road ahead.[20]

Colonel Joss Percy's 9th DLI was now heading north to the coast and had located a pass a mile east of the one used by the rest of 151 Brigade, as they descended they were attacked by Stukas, knocking out vehicles and inflicting numerous casualties on the men. The other two columns of the 9th DLI pressed on and crossed into rough dune territory near the coast and converged as they approached the beach, this terrain would suit the infantry if they came to action. Rear guards of the South African Division were also using the same route and as this combined force reached M'Rassus water point a total of between 300 and 400 vehicles was on the scene. The head of the column was heavily engaged with enemy ground troops supported by tanks and artillery on the escarpment, Colonel Percy ordered an immediate attack by such forces as could

---

19 Manuscript sent to author by E G H Moss (1994).
20 Taped interview with author, T Collier (1992).

be rallied on the spot. Other troops were alerted to be ready for action as soon as possible and anti-tank units were deployed on the flanks to protect the stationary column. Major Slight drew together any troops in the immediate vicinity and amid a ferocious hail of bullets led his men forward to the attack. The actions of this brave officer enabled the column to reach the Tobruk perimeter and was to earn him a DSO.

Pte Kilgallon, 9th DLI, was with a column that was being held up by a German gun at an important point on the coast road:

> We came to this place just outside Tobruk, there was wagons burning and dead bodies laid everywhere. On this one corner tanks and vehicles were stood burning, you couldn't get by. This German gun position had the corner controlled and this fella came to me and said 'you know about the gun, just come with me'. So off we went and we looked over the top of this rise and saw a small oasis. This German gun was in there controlling this particular turnoff. He said 'can you put some smoke bombs down there?' I said 'of course I can'. He said 'put some smoke down there and I'll go straight across it and run the buggers over with the bren-carrier'. We fired our mortar and put 20 smoke bombs across and he went in with two carriers and run straight over them and came back with about 20 prisoners. I'll always remember these Germans, they were laughing at us saying 'you bloody fools you're surrounded'. I didn't understand the situation then and they were taken away in a wagon.[21]

South African armoured cars joined in the fighting as they patrolled the area and 25 pounders engaged the enemy at close range, prisoners were herded to the rear. The way to Tobruk was now open and Colonel Percy gave the order to advance, no sooner had this been done when seven German tanks appeared on the scene and attacked the vulnerable transports and infantry that were packed tightly together presenting a tempting target. The infantrymen looked on with interest as the anti-tank gunners sprang into action.

Lance Corporal William Ridley, 9th DLI:

> After a long march in the sweltering heat we ended up outside of Tobruk, we were on the coast road near to the sea and when the lads got to the Med they went straight in the water with their cloths on to cool off. The anti-tank gunners took their togs off and went into the sea in the nuddie. After a while the shout went up 'tank attack, tank attack'. Of course they dashed out of the water with nothing on and jumped onto the red hot gunner's metal seats, you've never seen such a comedy act in your life. There was Mk111s on the horizon, our lads had a side view of them and knocked three of them out even in the nuddie. I'll bet they had some blisters on their bums that night.[22]

Lance Sergeant J E Turnbull, 74th Field Regiment, Royal Artillery, came into action with his unit and saw clear targets in the form of German tanks:

---

21   Ibid, with Mr Kilgallon (Durham, 1989).
22   Ibid. William Ridley. Veteran's re-union. Hull 1993.

We limbered up and started to move forward, soon all three guns were subjected to intense machine-gun fire, standing on the front wing of the quad [towing vehicle] I could hear bullets whistling around us and occasionally there was a splash and a column of spray in the sea on our left as something bigger and better passed us by and landed in a watery grave. In front the troop commander and gun position officer were making the gun platforms and waving us into action with the utmost urgency. Everybody rose to the occasion and we dropped the trails and ran the guns onto their platforms at lightning speed. Limbers were moved up and ammunition prepared. The target for our gun was pointed out to me by the troop commander and we cracked off straight away. After three perfect rounds we were ordered onto a fresh target and proceeded to immobilise another tank 700 yards away. All this time there was an intense barrage of small arms, armour piercing and high explosive fire aimed at us.

The ammunition numbers [ammunition carriers] were working like Trojans bringing ammunition across 300 yards of open ground to the gun. Our ammunition limber was hit and caught fire and on looking behind me I found that our quad was also blazing merrily. Three of our men were wounded and we recruited the services of an ammunition number from the next gun and were able to carry on firing. High explosive shells were still bursting over and around us and he became a casualty almost straight away. By now the ammunition position was becoming serious since some cordite charges had been burnt on the limber and the supply on the burning vehicles was blowing up. It was found impractical to move any of the other ammunition limbers on the position since any movement subjected them to fresh shelling. However the opposition found things a little too warm for them and when we had fired our last complete rounds the enemy tank force had been put out of action and we were free to push on. According to our troop commander our troop destroyed or immobilise six enemy tanks and probably accounted for four more. Our losses were one burnt out quad, one limber destroyed and one gun with a wheel blown off. We had one man killed and 15 wounded.[23]

The different elements of the 50th Division had made their way to the frontier from many directions and even though they had successfully broken out of the Gazala Line the division had suffered a very severe blow. The work of collecting the columns and vehicles scattered over 100 miles of desert was a tremendous effort. Before the breakout the divisional transport was on its last legs, now what was left of it was in an appalling state. The trials of the 50th Division were far from over and the lack of kit and equipment, jettisoned before their flight from the Gazala Line, was to be keenly felt before much longer. The men of the 50th Division gathered together and rested for a few days in the area known as the Kennels near Bir Thalata, it was known for sure that the Eighth Army was streaming back to the frontier pursued by the victorious panzers though details of events were scarce. Nothing was known of the fate of the garrison at Tobruk, it was generally assumed that they would hold out as they had done before. When it arrived the news of the fall of Tobruk hit the troops like a thunderbolt and was considered to be a disaster of the first magnitude. Rommel was jubilant as 1,400 tons of petrol, 2,000 vehicles and 5,000 tons of food fell into his hands. 31,000 British troops were marched into captivity.

23   Manuscript sent to author by J E Turnbull. 1994.

Meanwhile men were still fighting and dying as British units carried out desperate rear-guard actions seeking to hold back the re-supplied units of Panzer Army Africa. The remnants of the 50th Division was ordered to the area of Mersa Matruh to re-organise, on the night of the 22/23 June the 10th Indian Division withdrew through their ranks and on the following day German advanced guards came into contact with the 50th who fell back steadily and in good order harassing the enemy as they went by shelling his forward units. Anything that could be used by the enemy was destroyed and a trail of carnage and destruction was left by the retreating British. On the afternoon of 23 June a black pall of smoke rose into the sky above the village of Sidi-Birani as the British store of supplies that could not be got away in time, was reduced to ashes. Engineers worked themselves to a standstill as they blew up communications facilities and water points, it was no easy task in the short time available to put out of action the elaborate systems built up by the Eighth Army to maintain itself in this hostile wilderness. The British rear-guard units approached the area of Mersa-Matruh and what was left of the 50th Division was brought together once more and disposed in a defensive position south east of Matruh with the 10th Indian Division garrisoning the port. The Axis units came on at a terrific rate, despite the fact that their lines of communication were stretched to breaking point, their tanks were nearing the end of their endurance and their air cover was difficult to maintain as the bases in Cyrenaica were left further behind.

On the evening of 25 June the German advanced guards made contact with the hastily prepared defences of Mersa Matruh and it was at this point that Auchinleck took over personal command of the Eighth Army. He knew that if the Eighth Army made a last stand at Mersa Matruh they could be defeated and destroyed. He told his corps commanders his aim was:

> To keep all troops fluid and mobile and to strike at the enemy from all sides. Armour not to be committed unless very favourable opportunity presents its self. At all costs, and even if ground has to be given up, I intend to keep the Eighth Army in being and to give no hostage to fortune in the shape of mobile troops holding localities which can easily be isolated.[24]

---

24   C E Lucas. *Alamein*. [London. Heinemann 1962] p.291.

15

## Mersa Matruh, 26 to 29 June 1942

The enemy would now be fought over the large stretch of land between the meridian of Mersa-Matruh and the El Alamein gap. Ritchie's plans for the defence of Mersa Matruh had been hurriedly compiled between 22 and 24 June. The 10th Indian Division would garrison Matruh with the two remaining brigades of the 50th Division 16 kilometres to the south east around Gerawala. Inland the 5th Indian Division would be positioned around Sidi Hamza, the New Zealand Division eight kilometres to the rear at Minqar Qaim and the 1st Armoured Division, now containing both of 7th Armoured Divisions armoured brigades, in the open desert 16 kilometres to the south-west. Each division was now to be reorganised into battle groups, the new tactics proposed were unpractised and the Eighth Army was now facing a bewildering number of changes. It found itself with a new commander, it was withdrawing before a victorious enemy and no sooner had it prepared to fight one type of battle when it was ordered to fight another. In the midst of all this turmoil it was told to change its organisation and tactics, but before these things could be done Rommel decided the issue as usual and attacked.

By this stage Rommel's Italian intelligence services had broken the American diplomatic cypher and he had been provided with detailed information of the plans and condition of the Eighth Army. Colonel Bonner F Fellers, military attaché in the American Embassy in Cairo, was sending detailed reports back to Washington which was intercepted by the Italians. On 16 June 1942 Fellers reported the full extent of British tank losses and remaining forces, so providing Rommel with the intelligence that encouraged him to press his tired and worn out forces on even further, taking the biggest risk of his career. His intention was drive the British out of Egypt completely.

The German forces before Mersa Matruh were brought to a halt but the main armoured units struck on past the allied flank bypassing the 10th Indian Division and the two weakened battalions of the 50th Division. They continued to press the main body of the Eighth Army as it fell back to the Alamein position. By 27 June the Germans had cut the road east of Mersa Matruh and the two divisions found themselves isolated. Once more the two battalions of the 50th Division, already worn out by weeks of fighting, were called upon to wage a heavy defensive battle. The German and Italian troops were equally tired but with the heady scent of victory in their nostrils and the example shown by their seemingly tireless commander, they fought on and on, with the mirages of Cairo and Alexandria before them. Rommel's order of the day, issued after the fall of Tobruk, made more demands on his troops, but they carried out his orders no matter how tired they were for they knew Rommel spared no-one, least of all himself. Rommel roused his tired troops for one last final effort to defeat the Eighth Army:

> We have taken in all 45,000 prisoners and destroyed or captured more than 1,000 armoured fighting vehicles and nearly 400 guns. During the long and hard struggle you have dealt the enemy blow after blow. Now for the complete destruction of the enemy. During the days to come I shall call upon you for one more great effort to bring us to this final goal.[1]

On the night of 26 June 1942 the 9th Battalion DLI hurried to its allotted post on some raised ground 16 miles south east of Mersa Matruh, it stood on the left of 151 Brigade and on its own left flank was the open desert with the New Zealand Division some miles beyond that. As darkness fell the companies deployed placing one anti-tank team with its gun to their front, two young gunners, Pte Adam Wakenshaw and Pte Eric Mohn, were as we shall see fated to stand out in the battle about to start. The hard rock desert floor made digging impossible and in the distance the men could hear the panzer units busily engaging scattered Indian patrols.

The moon slowly rose in a clear sky illuminating the landscape with a pale light as the men settled down to get what rest they could and the sentries peered out into the open desert. The night was full of ominous distant sounds that made the men uneasy, to the west could be heard the crump of explosions and the crackle of small arms fire as the Indian Division fought for its life. From above came the purr of aircraft engines followed by the explosions of distant bombs. To the battalions immediate front an enormous Albacore flare hung in the sky suspended by its parachute giving the landscape an eerie brilliance. As it fell to earth and faded shadows moved in all directions and eyes strained to adjust to the darkness once more. The dark indistinct shapes of enemy tanks and vehicles could be observed in the distance to the Durham's front, anxious men watched with strained faces as the enemy troops dismounted and after a while moved off. Once more the silence of the night enveloped the Tommies and the desert around them.

When the German and Italian units finally attacked the defenders of Mersa Matruh 151 Brigade found itself in the path of the German 90th Light Division and elements of the 21st Panzer Division, heavy close quarter fighting ensued in a desperate struggle for survival. The 9th DLI stood to arms an hour before dawn on the 27th and almost at once the dim light was broken by the flashes from the muzzles of German guns as the enemy artillery softened up the Durham's positions before the main assault. In the grey light of dawn tanks and self-propelled guns mounted on tank chassis crawled slowly towards the Durham's positions, they halted at a distance and turned their fire onto a battery of 74th Field Regiment who returned the fire with their 25 pounder guns, explosions rent the air as the two sides slugged it out.

The battery position was to the north of 9th DLI and was isolated to such an extent it could not be supported by other units and before it was light the Germans overran the gunners. They then directed their attention to the 9th DLI whose anti-tank gunners crouched low behind their two pounder guns for protection, they watched as the dark shapes of tanks and self-propelled guns from 21st Panzer Division formed a crescent around them and began to close with them. Between these vehicles could be seen running the small figures of the 90th Light's Panzer Grenadiers. Sighting the DLI's four anti-tank guns the enemy gunners began to plaster them

---

1     B Liddle-Hart, *The Rommel Papers* (London: Da Capo Press, 1953), p. 280.

with high explosive while standing off at a safe distance, the highly trained gun teams made no reply and held their fire waiting for the German armour to close within killing range. Casualties were now being taken by the Durham's as shells burst all around them sending splinters of steel and shrapnel screaming through the air. Still the gunners held their nerve and sat tight amid this inferno of shell-fire, the panzers closed very cautiously and as they came within 400 yards of the anti-tank teams the two pounders sprang to life. The gunners worked feverishly firing shot after shot and shells tore into the German soft skinned vehicles, several of them going up in flames.

Pte Adam Wakenshaw and Pte Eric Mohn had been first into action and had knocked out a German gun tractor by putting a shell through the engine. The enemy tanks halted and began to pour their fire onto the anti-tank gun positions while Panzer Grenadiers dropped mortar bombs upon them at a terrific rate. Mohn and Wakenshaw's gun was hit in this hail of fire, the crew being seriously wounded and Wakenshaw's left arm blown off above the elbow. He and Mohn lay semi-conscious amid the carnage as shells continued to explode around them, as their senses slowly returned Wakenshaw and Mohn struggled to rise to their knees, from a trench to the rear a sergeant major shouted 'come on Wakenshaw it's time to go'. Perhaps he did not hear him, but he took no notice. No one else but Mohn and Wakenshaw could be seen alive in the company area and the sergeant major shouted out again 'look out for that armoured car on the left, come on we must go'. With one last extraordinary effort and despite the intense fire all around them Wakenshaw and Mohn crawled back to their position behind the gun and together they continued to engage the enemy, Mohn aiming the gun with Wakenshaw loading the shells awkwardly with one arm. The pair scored hit after hit as they laboured to keep the gun in action, but after five rounds a German shell exploded along-side of the gun and killed Eric Mohn. The force of the blast wounded Wakenshaw again and threw him several yards away from his position, in a daze he dragged himself back to his gun and single handed tried to carry on the fight as best he could. As he placed one more round into the breach and was about to fire the enemy scored a direct hit on the ammunition, the resulting explosion destroyed the gun and killed Wakenshaw.

Pte Adam Wakenshaw, 9th Battalion Durham Light Infantry.

For his actions at Mersa Matruh Pte Adam Wakenshaw was awarded the Victoria Cross. Pte Eric Mohn was not recommended for a medal.

The assault rolled in on the 9th DLI with continuing ferocity by the 90th Light and fierce hand to hand fighting lasted for some hours, but the Germans kept renewing their attacks and slowly but surely the isolated companies were worn down and their resistance began to lessen. The Durham's had made the Germans pay a heavy price, every yard of ground yielded was defended doggedly by these north countrymen and it took the Germans two hours to overrun the position. The 8th DLI was attacked from the south west at 5:30 p.m. by captured Stuart tanks which were driven off after a sharp fight, inflicting heavy casualties on the Germans. The

6th Battalion was attacked by self-propelled guns and armoured cars and fought a two hour running battle.

Major Harold Sidney Sell, MC, 8th DLI, saw the new six pounder anti-tank guns come into action at Mersa Matruh:

> We were all on the escarpment near Mersa Matruh, enemy patrols were probing around throwing grenades, with us shooting back at them. That night we were being shot at by German six wheeled armoured cars. We had just been issued with new six pounder anti-tank guns. Nobody knew how to fire them but one of the gun crews decided to stalk an armoured car. They pulled the gun to where they could see the armoured car, opened the breach and focused on the car down the barrel. They quickly put a round in and fired, as it was only 100 yards away, they blew it to smithereens.[2]

Captain Richard Ellison Ovenden, MC, 6th DLI:

> Shortly after 6:30 p.m. I was called to the head of the wadi, in which I had established my headquarters, by a report of armoured cars and saw approaching on my left flank two self-propelling guns, a bren-carrier and other vehicles, including armoured cars. They were flying our pennants and gave an indefinite recognition signal. Covered by my men, they approached slowly to about 150 yards when I recognised them as German and at about that time they put up their hands shouting 'don't shoot'. They were signalled to get out of their vehicles and the leading gunner started to do so with his hands still in the air. Suddenly he jumped back into his turret and fired, scoring a direct hit on a two pounder gun near me killing the two gunners and putting the gun out of action. My two left hand platoons were shot up by two self-propelling guns and were forced to surrender. Shortly after this one of those guns was hit and put out of action but the remaining one compelled the surrender of the forward section of my right centre platoon also. By this time an enemy ammunition wagon was burning fiercely and two armoured cars appeared to have been hit. The regimental sergeant major worked round to the right a bit and finding the two pounder anti-tank gun there deserted got it into action and hit the remaining enemy gun which caught fire. He also put the enemy commander's staff car out of action and killed the officer. [RSM Page was awarded the Military Cross for his bravery].
>
> A small party of enemy infantry then debussed from a semi-tracked vehicle but this was hit and the men dispersed by fire. One vehicle that had been set on fire was cleverly recovered by the enemy at about this time, I believe this to have been an armoured car, and it was uncanny to see the plume of smoke moving away from our position. Lieutenant Stanley was the officer i/c troop carrying transport attached to us and kept one bren-gun mounted on a truck for A/A defence, this I was keeping in reserve. After my two left hand platoons had capitulated I shouted to him to cover my left flank. He immediately rushed his gun to a somewhat exposed but very advantageous fire position and kept up a very accurate fire for the remainder of the action using armour piercing bullets. After about 10 minutes firing the firing-pin of his gun broke and the gun was useless. Without hesitation he went forward

---

2   Manuscript sent to author by William Ridley (Durham, 1996).

across bullet swept ground and brought back an abandoned gun and continued firing although continually fired upon by both machine gun and cannon. His general bearing was in the highest tradition and his action undoubtedly saved my left flank from being turned. [Lt T G Stanley, RASC, was awarded the Military Cross for his bravery].[3]

Pte George S Richardson, 6th DLI, was near Major Ovenden during this action:

There were two wadis stretching downhill from the escarpment. To the right of us in one wadi was the Company Sergeant Major and Company Quartermaster Sergeant Andel with the cookhouse staff and other battalion HQ staff, about 25 in all. In the other wadi was Regimental Sergeant Major Page, about eight of us from the signal platoon and some others from HQ company, drivers and buglers, about 30 of us. One officer, Major Ovenden, was with Regimental Sergeant Major Page, it was about 1:00 p.m. and we had constructed heaped blocks of rock about two feet high to give rifle cover for firing posts. We'd all been issued with armour piercing rifle bullets and some tracer and we also had our bren-gun. Suddenly Regimental Sergeant Major Page spotted an approaching armoured car. At first, after giving a flag signal of recognition and receiving one in return he said 'I think it's South African'. But as it got closer he shouted 'Bosche! open fire'. We did. There were three armoured cars and one wagon load of infantry, the first armoured car got to within 100 yards when I fired and shouted 'got him' as one of the Germans slumped over his turret. My mate next to me, Herbert Latham from the signal platoon, said 'no you didn't I got him'. Lance Corporal Jimmy Sixsmith who was at the left side of us said 'shut up you both got one'. The German infantry dismounted and set up a spandau machine-gun about 300 yards away but lying on the open sand. We killed quite a few and just when we thought we were winning a burst of machine-gun fire hit the top of our rock cover and splattered splinters down Herbert Latham's back and through his battle-dress jacket. He said 'I've had it George', I started saying 'our father who art in heaven' and those around, including Herbert, carried on praying. There was a shout to stop firing and we watched Company Quartermaster Sergeant Andel and the cookhouse party all marching out with a few Germans. The Germans decided to break off the action and went away leaving behind two armoured cars, We had a chance to bandage up the wounded, including Herbert, who had lots of pebble rash on his back but nothing serious. As dusk came it was quiet out front, Regimental Sergeant Major Page, who had a wound in one leg, went out to examine the armoured cars and found some maps and that we had been fighting a section of the 21st Panzer Division.[4]

When it became obvious the brigade position was now hopeless such men as were left were ordered to withdraw, many however ended up in German hands.

Pte Kilgallon, 9th DLI:

All hell broke loose when we were in this wadi, shells were roaring over the top of us right, left and centre. This captain shouted at us 'every man for himself, get out'. I broke the gun

---

3   H Moses, *The Faithful Sixth* (Durham: County Durham Books, 1995), p. 188.
4   Ibid, p. 189.

up and got everybody on the carrier, this other officer came along and said 'hang on' and we all went back to our slit trench. I heard these voices and said 'hey! these are bloody Germans'. We were sodding terrified, they waved their guns at us so we ran forward and became prisoners, we were herded to the rear with the battle still going on around us. Adam Wakenshaw was in the same company as me, he was a canny fella, I remember him saying 'that's the bloody life for me [as an anti-tank gunner] instead of marching I'll be riding' poor bugger.[5]

Lance Corporal William Ridley, 9th DLI, was hit during the battle:

We were on this ridge when Gerry came at us and we were surrounded, he was closing in for the kill when we got the order, every man for himself. I just stood up when bang! I got hit. There was a jet of blood spurting from my arm. There was one truck in the depression so I went there and the sergeant said 'what's the matter, where've you been hit?' because I was saturated with my own blood by this time. They threw me on the truck and the driver put his foot down and off we went like a bat out of hell with Gerry firing all sorts of stuff at us.[6]

The men of the 9th DLI were overcome after a vicious and bloody battle, but Wakenshaw, Mohn and his comrades had done better than they could ever know, their resolute action had stopped the enemy advance. The battalion, combined with the divisional artillery, had inflicted such grievous casualties on their attackers that the Germans were forced to withdraw from the ground they had captured and move to the rear to lick their wounds. During the evening the men of the 8th DLI went over the ground to pick up the personal belongings of the dead, the area was full of wreckage and the dead of both sides were strewn across the blackened sand. Among the detritus of war was found the charred and mutilated bodies of Pte Adam Wakenshaw and Pte Eric Mohn and not 200 yards away from their position the blackened burnt out hulk of a tank.

After the war Major Sell wrote of Adam Wakenshaw:

The army fulfilled his demands and I am sure he was happy, he accepted authority and his training produced the type of man who throughout our history has followed his appointed leaders to the end. To me Wakenshaw will remain as a person who, having no benefits from fortune or society or even by birth, nevertheless rose to spectacular heights of courage in war, which in peace might well have passed unnoticed in the daily fight against fortune, in which he would have been to the end an uncomplaining loser.[7]

On the night of the 27/28 June what was left of the 50th Division was ordered to attack southward along the enemy's lines of communication to create as much havoc as possible. As the troops formed up into several columns and began their move into the unknown the scene was lit by brilliant moonlight, the enemy was very close and it was not long before contact was made. The rattle of small arms and machine-gun fire from both sides filled the air and coloured tracer

---

5    Taped interview with author, Mr Kilgallon (Durham, 1992).
6    Ibid, with William Ridley (Durham, 1994).
7    Manuscript sent to author by Mr Kilgallon (Durham, 1992).

The battlefield grave of Pte Adam Wakenshaw, next to it is the anti-tank gun he and Mohn operated.

rounds cut through the darkness of the night as they skipped across the landscape, it was not long before the German artillery joined in and began to lay down an intense barrage on the slow moving vulnerable columns of vehicles. Bright flashes illuminated the area and many trucks burst into flames as they were hit, numerous men were killed or wounded in this bitter and confused action. The divisional columns disengaged themselves from the enemy and had made it back to their own positions near Mersa Matruh by dawn on 29 June, where things were now becoming desperate.

Sergeant Max Hearst, 5th Battalion East Yorkshire Regiment, was with the remnants of 69 Brigade 25 miles south of Mersa Matruh when the order to withdraw was given:

> A bloke says to me 'have you got any cigs yorkie?' so I gave him a packet and he gave me a bottle of beer, I'm laid there, beer and a fag, marvellous. With that a fluttering sound goes over our heads and this bloke was going to get up to see what it was. I says 'it's a bloody armour piercing shell'. Very cautiously we looked over the trench side and saw this line of armour and support vehicles with troops on them heading straight for us. With that there was a clank and a chuff of engines from behind us and three Honey tanks went out to meet the German attack, they were massively outnumbered but you had to admire their pluck. Honeys were just glorified bren-carriers and had no chance against the fire power the Gerries had, It wasn't long before they were knocked out and burning.[8]

Pte Roy Walker, 5th Battalion East Yorkshire Regiment, came under deadly friendly fire as his patrol moved forward to meet the enemy:

---

8  Taped interview with author, Max Hearst (Hull, 1992).

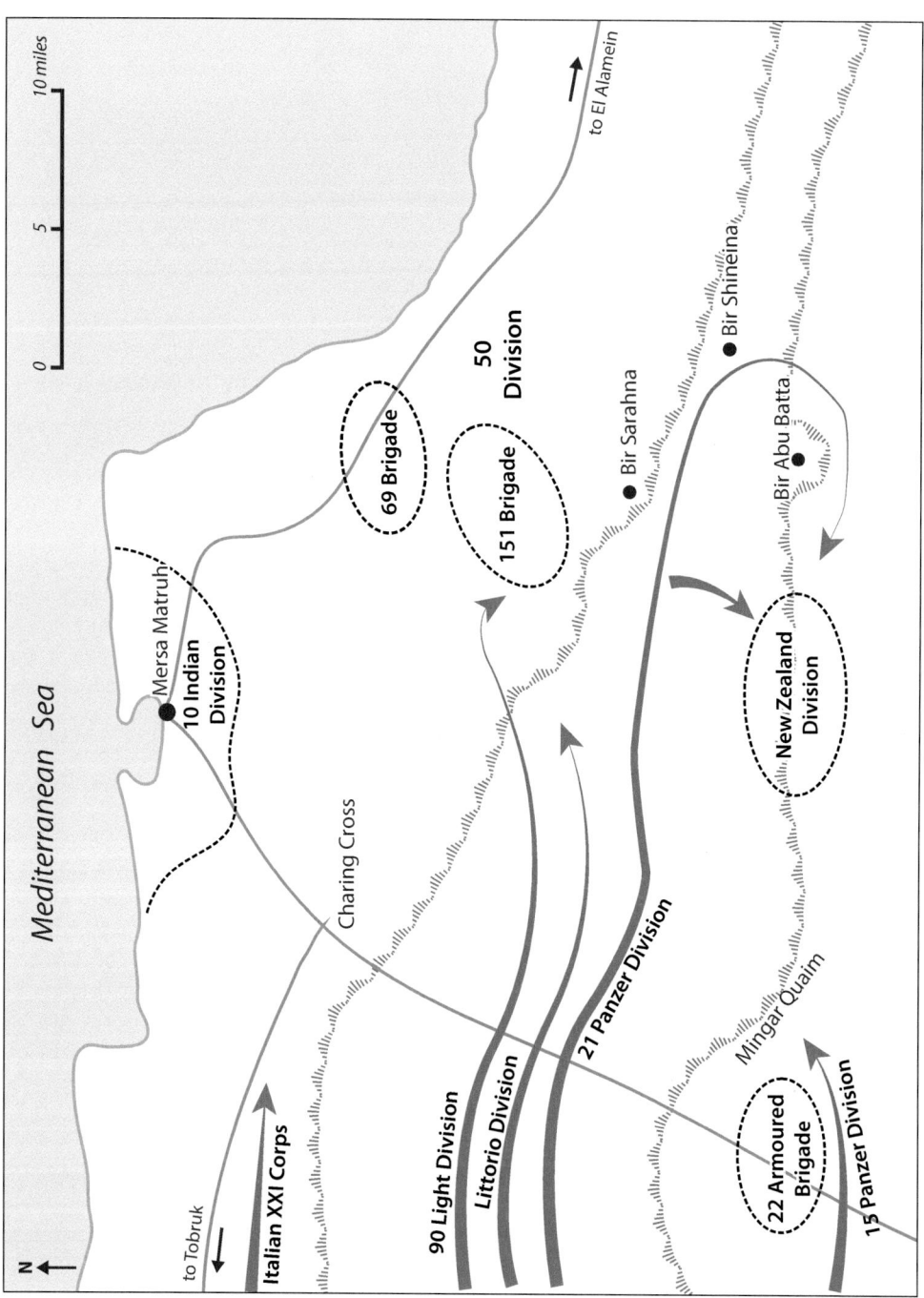

Map 10 The Battle of Mersa Matruh, 26/27 June 1942.

> The first night attack I went forward in failed, I went out in a 15cwt truck with a three inch mortar on it, we got too far forward and a Green Howards bren-carrier sprayed us with bullets killing Sergeant Attenborough, Corporal Key and another lad. The next attack I got in a three ton truck, Gerry was waiting and got a machine-gun trained on us. With the first burst he killed the driver and the truck almost turned over when it came to a stop. Shells were bursting all around and the flames lit up the whole area making us very visible to Gerry. In the confusion I got onto another 15cwt truck and as we sped off a German armoured car chased us firing as he did so, good job he was a bad shot.[9]

When the enemy realised the men of the 50th Division were trying to pull out they became ever bolder and raids were made into the divisional area by German armoured units and at one point Divisional HQ came under attack. The whole sector held by the 50th Division was now being swept by heavy concentrations of artillery fire and during the day of the 29th orders came from X Corps to break out. The plan was very similar to the one executed at Gazala, only this time the British troops were exhausted and alarmingly short of serviceable transport, the enemy was in close proximity and consisted not only of infantry but also of armour closely supported by artillery. The steep ravines that had to be negotiated made the ground unfavourable for escape and surprise was non-existent, the plains on the higher ground had to be reached if there was to be any hope of re-joining the Eighth Army and this ground was held by the Axis forces.

As the remnants of the 50th Division formed up for the breakout the basin they were gathering in was subjected to a steadily increasing volume of artillery fire and enemy infantry probed the thinly held defences looking for a possible weak point to exploit. Among the ranks of the 50th Division's rifle-men were now to be found batmen, cooks and orderlies, anyone who could hold a rifle was pressed into service as the 50th prepared to launch itself onto a desperate venture whose successful outcome was by no means certain. As dusk fell on the 29th the columns of all arms were formed up and ready to go, their orders were to take them through the ravines, out onto the plains, through the enemy positions and to swing east to join the remains of the Eighth Army.

The troops stood to their arms under a full moon that made them feel very exposed, eventually the enemy became aware that the outer defences were unmanned and before the columns could move off anti-tank shells began to score direct hits on the motionless vehicles and solid shot projectiles struck home with a loud clang. At last the columns began to move into the steep sided wadis, soft sand and rocks posed a problem in parts and valuable time was used up overcoming these obstacles, any column unlucky enough to be caught in the wadis at daybreak would be destroyed by the Germans at their leisure. Once on the plain enemy vehicles were in view but quite often made no aggressive moves, they were using many captured British vehicles themselves and seemed not to distinguish these British columns from their own.

Pte Ralph Hymer, 8th DLI, headed straight through a German camp on one lorry and was very nearly caught:

> The RASC came up and we dumped a lot of our gear, got into the back of the wagons and laid down flat. An officer said 'we'll go right through the German Lines and there is to

---

9   Ibid, with Roy Walker (Scarborough, 1989).

be no firing'. This interpreter got onto the front of the truck with the officer, it was bright moonlight and the convoy moved off. In the distance you could see the German camp, it was all tents and we were going smack through the middle of it. When the leading truck was challenged the interpreter told them we were a German column passing through. They were using our captured vehicles and had taken everything we had, I looked over the tailboard as we went through and there was Germans rushing about left and right grabbing rifles. We got so far through when the drivers put their foot down and went hell for leather, only the last three wagons got caught.[10]

Pte Douglas Welsford, Royal Army Service Corps, was trying to move his truck along roads choked with other vehicles:

With the first light came further bursts of shelling, some landing uncomfortably close, our company headquarters was ignorant of any orders and so took the initiative and moved out from Mersa. About 15 miles along the coastal road, with the sea so close it could be seen shimmering on our left, we were brought to a stop by vehicles blocking the road. On closer inspection other vehicles were seen among the sand dunes on the seaward side and on the road was a motley collection of transport of all types and sizes. An assortment of small and large trucks, some carrying infantry and some bren-carriers, intermingled with them but seemingly isolated from their normal command were limbers towing pieces of artillery. I had alighted from my vehicle and walked forward to acquaint myself as to what was happening, someone pointed out where the road rose and cut through the escarpment about half a mile away, it was just beyond this I was told that the Germans had cut the road. A bren-carrier was sent forward to reconnoitre the road and we watched as it trundled away getting smaller and smaller as it rose toward the escarpment and then to finally disappear. There was silence for a while and then we could hear a prolonged burst of gunfire, then silence again. We watched and waited but the carrier failed to reappear. It was then that shells began to land among us.[11]

Lance Corporal William Taylor, 5th Battalion East Yorkshire Regiment:

As dawn broke our first two three tonners went down a wadi, the Germans was on the other side and their machine-gunners opened up, both trucks burst into flames. We stopped at the entrance to one wadi where a Gerry anti-tank gun was firing down it, my section was told to go and silence it. We got behind some rocks and the German gunners could be seen clearly behind their gun, we let fly with our rifles and it went quiet, I don't know if we killed them or they ran away. It was

L/Cpl William Taylor, 5th Battalion East Yorkshire Regiment.

---

10   Ibid, with Ralph Hymer (Durham, 1992).
11   Manuscript sent to author by D Welsford (1988).

then that the bloody Stukas made an appearance and dive bombed us, it was bad when the bombs landed among the men, arms and legs were kicking about the ground. The noise of the dive bombers and the bombs exploding around us was horrible, everybody scattered.[12]

Captain Robert James Crisp, DSO, MC, 3rd Battalion Royal Tank Regiment, watched as a lorry hurtled over a steep escarpment:

Even as I watched a great lorry went plunging down the escarpment out of control, it struck some outcrop and leapt high into the air somersaulting to the bottom in a fantastic avalanche of earth, rock and scrub and odd shaped bundles of men integrated with jagged pieces of wood and metal.[13]

Sergeant Max Hearst, 5th Battalion East Yorkshire Regiment, headed through the open desert hoping to find safety:

They wouldn't let us on the first truck we tried to get on, four or five of us eventually got onto a 15cwt truck, Len Wheelbank was on our truck and he was mortally wounded, he died on the journey. We went right out into the blue, we ran the gauntlet two or three times still under fire. When it had quietened down a bit I lit a cig under a blanket, in the glow I could see my hand was covered in blood, a bloke said 'hey your wounded' I thought hell where? My rifle butt had been hit and when it splintered had made a deep scratch in my hand. Our truck drove all night and as day broke we saw we was on our own, we saw some movement in the distance and headed toward it hoping it was our blokes. Turns out they was, it was gunners setting up their 25 pounders in new positions, we set out for one team and when we got there they was all wogs [Indian troops]. Anyhow we travelled for three days before we got back to our own lines.[14]

Gunner Ted Smith, Royal Artillery, was taken prisoner as he and his comrades tried to make it to the open desert and never forgot the kindness shown to him by the Africa Corps soldiers he met:

We went in low gear but as we crossed the escarpment we came under heavy machine-gun fire at close range. I could see the muzzle flashes through the canvas and our truck stopped instantly, its engine riddled. We scrambled over the tailboard and five or six Germans were already on us and I heard 'hands up Tommy, for you the war is over'. I was rapidly searched by one infantryman who dropped the ammunition clips and a bren-gun magazine I was carrying on to the sand. In another pouch I had a few tubes of sweets taken from an abandoned canteen wagon near Mersa Matruh, he pulled these halfway out then dropped them back in the pouch. Heartened by his attitude I pointed to the back of our vehicle and made the gesture of putting on a coat, he nodded and I pulled out my greatcoat, a great asset as the nights were very cold.

12  Taped interview with author, William Taylor (Hull, 1990).
13  R Crisp, *Brazen Chariots* (London: Norton Paper Backs, 2005), p. 94.
14  Taped interview with author, Max Hearst (Hull, 1992).

My mate Jock and I were taken off but we had only gone a few yards when a German soldier called over to our guards and led us to where a badly wounded British sergeant was lying near a knocked out truck. Jock and I carried him for a short distance, but then we heard more of our trucks approaching and the Germans clearly wanted to get back to their posts. They indicated that we should leave the sergeant, but before doing so I covered him with my greatcoat.

From time to time in the next few hours there would be heavy firing as our vehicles tried to break through at various points. In what proved to be the last incident a staff car was shot up as it crashed through at high speed into the depression in which 20 or so prisoners had been gathered. All the occupants were killed and I took a senior officers sleeping roll, which proved a real boon over the next few months. The more distant firing died down and it was not long before I was asleep. As the years pass I sometimes think of the impeccable conduct of those Africa Corps soldiers who shot up our truck and took me prisoner. They were good soldiers and good men and I hope they survived the war.[15]

Pte Douglas Welsford, Royal Army Service Corps, was in a column that came under heavy fire before they broke free and headed out into the open desert:

For the break out we were organised into packets of vehicles, one thing we had in our favour was the moon, it was shedding just the right amount of light for the drivers to see the vehicle in front of them and for them to see where they were driving. Leaving the road the vehicles worked their way towards the escarpment, they were in a low gear and the noisy discordant sound of the engines was shattering the silence of the desert night. The object was to slip out unobserved but the noise that they were making must surely be heard in Berlin. After a while the tension left us, we had passed over the escarpment and were moving into the vastness of the desert, perhaps all was going to be well after all. The moon was giving just the right amount of light and enabled us to avoid the larger stones and boulders, but even so the ride was bumpy. Suddenly there was a rat-a-tat and crackle of small arms fire, at the same time shells were exploding somewhere in front of us. Crossing the sky from our right we saw the trajectory of tracer, balls of light bouncing across the sky, the front of the column was first to receive the barrage of fire and then we could feel it all around us. The whistle and shriek of the bullets and shells passing over and around us was frightening, subconsciously I put up my great coat collar for protection. For a short time the mind is in a state of stupor and then from the pandemonium comes the reality of what was happening, it was not possible to go forward, vehicles in front had stopped and were trying to extricate themselves. Without being told my driver had somehow managed, in the calamitous confusion, to turn the vehicle and swing out into the desert and we raced along bumping over the uneven ground, other vehicles that had come through unscathed were roaring along with us.[16]

15  Manuscript sent to author by T Smith (1993).
16  Ibid, by D Welsford (1988).

# Conclusion

Those lucky enough to make it to the open desert moved quickly to the Alamein Line with German armour in hot pursuit, some 50th Division troops had not received the late order to go to Alamein and had gone to Fuka instead only to find the Germans waiting to take them into captivity. What was left of the 50th Division gathered behind the Alamein position only to return to the front line on 1 July helping to defend Ruweisat Ridge. Rommel's victorious advance from Gazala did not now possess the necessary momentum to smash through the strong Alamein positions and his attempts to do so were frustrated. The first of his attacks came in daylight on 30 June when a column under the command of Hauptman Briel came up against the Alamein mine-field and a British barrage came down on them indicating that the first Battle of Alamein had begun.

On that day the much weakened Africa Corps had only 55 runners [operational tanks] but as ever Rommel was eager to push on, he knew that if he gave the British a breathing space they would improve their positions and build up their strength, but he also knew he had driven his exhausted troops hard. The Germans and Italians had fought without respite for five weeks and had long since passed the limits of human endurance, but still he was left with no other option than to ask them for one more gigantic effort. In his haste Rommel spent too little time on reconnaissance of the ground his troops would have to fight over and paid the price, his troops moved forward on 1 July at 3:00 a.m. 15th Panzer Division ran straight into a well defended brigade position of the 8th Indian Division at Deir el Shein, the fresh Indian units held off the 15th and elements of the 21st Panzers for a day, during which time the British armour arrived and chased the German units from the field. The 90th Light Division fared no better and its forward movement was halted amid a hail of flying steel and high explosive. This was a black day for the Panzer Army and it suffered heavy losses it could ill afford.

The next day the attack was resumed with the same results and air attacks by formations of Mitchell bombers in formation roared down upon the German units with terrifying precision. The 4th Armoured Division counter attacked and forced the 21st Panzer Division back along Ruweisat Ridge taking a heavy toll of the German armour in the process. On 2 and 3 July Stuka dive bombers pounded the British positions followed by German infantry assaults supported by tanks, only to be held by the British and driven back. To the south of the ridge came the main attack, this was fought to a standstill by the 1st Armoured Division, for all this effort and sacrifice by the troops of the Panzer Army it had only reached a point just nine miles east of Deir el Shein. Ferocious British counter attacks fell upon the Axis Forces and the New Zealanders overran parts of the Ariete Division, driving back units of the Brescia Division from the western end of the El Meirar Depression.

Rommel's attempt to breach the Alamein line by frontal assault had failed, the British in their well-prepared entrenched positions held out with resolution, the line they were defending was the last naturally strong position before the Nile and they were determined to stay put. That hot July saw a series of attacks as each side sought to gain the best tactical position for itself and most of Ruweisat Ridge passed into British hands. Rommel must have been aware that for the moment he had lost the initiative and on the 5 July the German and Italian units began to lay vast mine-fields and prepared defensive positions.

On 10 July the 9th Australian Division launched an attack on the coastal sector breaking the Italian Sabratha Division and capturing Tel el Eis Hill. Rommel moved the 21st Panzer Division to this sector in order to stop any further attacks by the British and as the German armour was now drawn to the coastal sector the British launched attacks in the central sector held by the Italian Pavia and Brescia Divisions. The situation for the Panzer Army was now growing desperate as its resources in both men and materials was slowly being ground down.

On 21 July the British offensive was renewed on Ruweisat Ridge in the hope of ejecting the Axis forces from the high ground they still held. The conflict was bitter in the extreme and the New Zealanders attacked at night losing 700 men. The 23rd Armoured Brigade, who were now at full strength, moved forward early on the 22 July and passed the New Zealand flank at speed, it soon found itself in a mine-field and their advance ground to a halt. The stranded tanks stood immobile, unable to move forward or back for fear of hitting a mine and were shot to pieces by the German armour and their supporting anti-tank gun teams. A total of 93 British tanks were destroyed in the space of 23 hours. A similar catastrophe occurred on 26 July and cost the British dearly.

At the end of July the battle was called off but the achievements of the Eighth Army were clearly visible, because of the disaster at Gazala they had been forced to retreat nearly 200 miles and at the end of that rout they had not only turned to meet the victorious Africa Corps but had taken the offensive against the marauding panzers. Under a blazing sun they had cleared most of Ruweisat Ridge of enemy forces in some of the fiercest actions yet seen. But now both sides were exhausted, each fell back behind their own defensive screens and began to build up their own forces for the inevitable coming offensive.

The two armies had fought each other to a standstill, some of Rommel's superiors argued that a withdrawal to the Libyan frontier would wrong foot the Eighth Army and shorten their lines of supply. The British vehicles, petrol and supplies captured at Tobruk and at Mersa Matruh had enabled the Africa Corps to advance to Alamein, but the petrol supplies left were now not enough for him to make a phased retreat in good order. Once Rommel's forces had been held they were trapped at Alamein, he had staked everything on breaking the Eighth Army and defeating the British in Egypt. Rommel had no choice but to hang on and to hope that he could somehow get fresh supplies of men and machines through but the Africa Corps was now 1,400 miles from its supply base. By the end of August the Luftwaffe had flown in supplies Rommel had listed as urgent, ammunition, tanks and guns, a considerable achievement for the logistic organisations of the Axis forces. But the army was still desperately short of fuel which would be needed to launch an attack. The British had been waging a successful air and naval campaign against Axis shipping which was to have a fatal effect on the Axis logistic chain. The Africa Corps was pinned before the British at Alamein, Rommel was increasingly ill through the strain of command and his hopes of an advance on Alexandria and victory had disappeared like a mirage.

# Conclusion

The first struggle for Alamein had ended and by late July the British commanders began to lay their plans and rebuild their badly mauled divisions. The future intentions of the Axis Forces had been predicted and the tactics for the coming battle discussed. The Eighth Army had suffered 50,000 casualties since their retreat from the Gazala Line and now the British stood at bay on the Alamein Line, in all of this the men of the 50th Division played their part. Behind the front new blood came into their ranks and all the various units were re-equipped.

The men of the 50th Division had come a long way since their mobilisation in 1939 and these once green recruits were now battle hardened veterans who had taken part in many of the most significant actions of the war so far. They had met the Wermacht in France and had fought Rommel for the first time at Arras on 21 May 1940, other actions were fought at Ypres and on the Dunkirk perimeter and at many smaller places in between. At Gazala they had lost 150 Brigade in its entirety and had fought their way out only to make another stand at Mersa Matruh, again they had to fight their way out, taking a VC and many other awards on the way. The majority of the division's horrendous casualties were inflicted during these two breakouts and were the result of five weeks of severe defensive fighting. Even after having retreated in such depressing circumstances, after having lost so many men and most of its equipment the division still played its part in the defence of Ruweisat Ridge. What was left of the 50th Northumbrian Division was not in good shape when it reached the Delta, the average strength of the only two infantry brigades remaining, 151 and 69 Brigades, was only 300 men each, less than half the original establishment and they had very little in the way of transport. The artillery had lost the 72nd Field Regiment at Gazala. All other units within the division had also suffered heavy losses. Since its formation in 1941 the Eighth Army had suffered 80,000 casualties and the battered Northumbrian Division had taken more than its fair share with 9,000 casualties. Now came a time of intensive training and consolidation as the Eighth Army prepared for the next round with the now battered and exhausted Panzer Army Africa, Rommel was now worn out with the stress of command and was not the man he was, his opposite number, Montgomery, was fresh to the fight and had resources coming in that he was amassing in preparation for the great battle that would take place in October and was to take its name from an insignificant little railway siding called El Alamein.

# Appendix I

## Order of Battle – 7th Panzer (Ghost) Division May 1940

---

25th Panzer Regiment
6th Panzer Grenadier Regiment
7th Panzer Grenadier Regiment
78th Panzer Artillery Regiment
7th Motorcycle Battalion
37th Panzer Reconnaissance Battalion
42nd Anti-tank Battalion
58th Panzer Engineer Battalion
83rd Panzer Signal Battalion

Formed at Gera in 1938 as the 2nd Light Division it originally included 66th Panzer Battalion and the 6th and 7th Mechanise Cavalry Regiments. It was converted into a Panzer Division in the winter of 1939-1940 and placed under the command of Major General Erwin Rommel.

# Appendix II

## Order of the Battle – 3rd SS Panzer Division, Totenkopf May 1940

3rd SS Panzer Regiment
15th SS Panzer Grenadier Regiment – Thule
6th SS Panzer Grenadier Regiment – Theodor Eicke
3rd SS Panzer Artillery Regiment
3rd SS Panzer Reconnaissance Battalion
3rd SS Anti-tank Battalion
3rd SS Panzer Engineer Battalion
3rd SS Panzer Signal Battalion
3rd SS Anti-aircraft Battalion
3rd SS Projector Battalion

# Appendix III

## Order of Battle – German 90th Light African Division

---

Organised as Africa Special Purposes Division from units already in Africa during August 1941. Re-titled 90th Light Division on 28 November 1941. Composed of infantry units only.

155th (motorised) Infantry Regiment
200th (motorised) Infantry Regiment
361st (motorised) Infantry Regiment Africa
200th Panzer Grenadier Regiment (motorised) Africa
Panzer Grenadier Regiment (motorised) Africa*

* This division was made up of many unusual units. The 361st Regiment consisted of many men who had served with the French Foreign Legion. The Panzer Grenadier Regiment was raised out of Special Unit No 288, one of whose battalions was composed of Arabs from the North African population.

# Appendix IV

## Order of Battle – 15th Panzer Division, sent to North Africa between April and June 1941

8th Panzer Regiment
15th (motorised) Infantry Brigade
115th (motorised) Infantry Regiment
8th (motorised) Machine-gun Battalion
15th (motorised) Motor Cycle Battalion
33rd (motorised) Reconnaissance Battalion
33rd Panzer Artillery Regiment
33rd Anti-tank Battalion
33rd Panzer Engineer Battalion
33rd Panzer Signals Battalion

# Appendix V

## Order of Battle – 21st Panzer Division (formerly 5th Light Division)

---

The 5th Light Division was first sent to North Africa during February 1941 and was re-titled as 21st Panzer Division on 1 October 1941.

5th Panzer Regiment
104th (motorised) Infantry Regiment
3rd (motorised) Reconnaissance Battalion
155th Panzer Artillery Regiment
39th Anti-tank Battalion
200th Panzer Engineer Battalion
20th Panzer Signals Battalion

# Appendix VI

## Order of Battle – Bir Hacheim. 1st Free French Brigade, May 1942

---

### Commanding Officer – Koenig

2nd and 3rd Battalions Foreign Legion – CO Lt Colonel Amilakvari (KIA Alamein)
2nd *Bataillion de Marche de l'Oubanghi Chari* – CO Lt Colonel de Roux (died in air crash) and Major Ameil
*Bataillion du Pacifique* – CO Lt Colonel Broche (KIA Bir Hacheim)
1st *Bataillion Infanterie de la Marine* – CO Major Savey
*Fusiliers Marins* – CO Lt Commander Amyot d'Inville (KIA Italy)
1st Artillery Regiment – CO Major Laurent-Champrosay (KIA Italy)
22nd North African Company – CO Captain Lequesne
2nd Anti-Tank Company – CO Captain Jacquin

Engineer and signals detachments and a large medical team completed Koenig's establishment.

# Appendix VII

## Order of Battle – 50th Division, May 1940

**CO Major General G Le Q Martel, DSO, MC**

**150 Infantry Brigade**
CO Brigadier C W Haydon, MC
4th Battalion East Yorkshire Regiment – CO Lt Colonel R H Martin
4th Battalion The Green Howards – CO Lt Colonel C N Littleboy, MC
5th Battalion The Green Howards – CO Lt Colonel W E Bush, MC

**151 Infantry Brigade**
CO Brigadier J A Churchill, MC, ADC
6th Battalion The Durham Light Infantry – CO Lt Colonel T H Miller, TD
8th Battalion The Durham Light Infantry – CO Lt Colonel C W Beart, MC
9th Battalion The Durham Light Infantry – CO Major J E S Percy, MC
4th Battalion the Royal Northumberland Fusiliers – CO Lt Colonel R Wood, TD

**25th Infantry Brigade**
CO Brigadier W H C Ramsden, DSO, MC
7th Battalion The Queen's Royal Regiment – CO Lt Colonel G A Pilleau
2nd Battalion The Essex Regiment – CO Lt Colonel A H Blest
1st Battalion The Royal Irish Fusiliers – CO Lt Colonel G H Gough, MC

**Royal Artillery**
CRA Brigadier C W Massey, MC
72nd Field Regiment – CO Lt Colonel R M Graham, MC
74th Field Regiment – CO Lt Colonel R T Edwards, AFC
65th Anti-tank Regiment – CO Lt Colonel K W Hervey

**Royal Engineers**
CRE Lt Colonel W H Spires (succeeded by Major Swam on 18 May)
235 Field Park – CO Captain N Pearson
232 Field Company – CO Major R W S Casebourne
Field Park Company – CO Major C W Pegler

**Royal Corps of Signals**
CO Lt Colonel T T J Sheffield, TD
No 1 Company – Captain Miner
No 2 Company – Major C C Fairweather
No 3 Company – Captain N I Bower

**Royal Army Service Corps**
Ammunition Company – Captain E E Bonner
Petrol Company – Captain V R Bonner
Supply Column – Major E Steele
3 Petrol sub-park – Captain C E Westmorland
11 Troop Carrying Company – Major W A Woolam
12 Troop Carrying Company – Major W R Bingham

**Royal Army Medical Corps**
149 Field Ambulance – Lt Colonel G G Drummond
150 Field Ambulance – Lt Colonel Morrison, MC
Hygiene Section – Captain N Baster
Bath Unit – 2nd Lt G M Cooper

## Appendix VIII

### Order of Battle – 150 Brigade, 26 May to 1 June 1942

4th Battalion the East Yorkshire Regiment
4th Battalion the Green Howards
5th Battalion the Green Howards
2nd Battalion the Cheshire Regiment, D Coy (machine-gunners)
72nd Field Regiment, Royal artillery
25th and 26th Medium Battery, 7th Medium Regiment, Royal Artillery
259th (Norfolk Yeomanry) Anti-tank Battery, Royal Artillery
81st and 25th Light Anti-aircraft Battery, Royal Artillery
232nd Field Company, Royal Engineers
Tactical HQ, 1st Army Tank Brigade
44th Battalion, Royal Tank Regiment
One squadron, 42nd Battalion Royal Tank Regiment

# Appendix IX

## Order of Battle – Panzer Army Africa

---

**(Axis forces in action at Gazala)**

**German Africa Corps**
15th Panzer Division
21st Panzer Division
90th Light Division

**X Italian Corps**
Brescia Infantry Division
Pavia Infantry Division

**XX Italian (motorised) Corps**
Ariete Armoured Division
Trieste Motorised Division

**XXI Italian Corps**
Trento Infantry Division
Sabratha Infantry Division

# Appendix X

## Order of Battle of Attacking Columns – Arras, 21 May 1940

---

**Right Hand Column**
8th Battalion Durham Light Infantry
7th Battalion Royal Tank Regiment
365th Battery 92nd Field Regiment Royal Artillery
260th Battery 65th Anti-Tank Regiment
151st Brigade Anti-Tank Platoon
4th Battalion Royal Northumberland Fusiliers, one Platoon scout-car

**Left Hand Column**
6th Battalion Durham Light Infantry
4th Battalion Royal Tank Regiment
368th Battery 92nd Field Regiment, Royal Artillery
206th Battery 65th Anti-tank Regiment
151st Brigade Anti-tank Platoon
4th Battalion RNF, one Coy motor-cycle and one Platoon scout-car

# Appendix XI

## 50th Division Gallantry Awards, France 1940

This list may well be incomplete but I have done my best to trace all awards during the many years that I worked on this manuscript.

| Name | Rank or Number | Unit | LG Date | Award |
|---|---|---|---|---|
| Alexander, W. J. | L/Cpl (4390374) | 4th Bn Green Howards | 11/07/40 | MM |
| Beart, C. W. (MC) | Lt Col | 8th DLI | | MID |
| Blackman, D. W. W. | 2/Lt | 6th DLI | | MC |
| Booth, J. R. | 2/Lt | 4th Bn Green Howards | 20/12/40 | MC |
| Boustead, J. | L/Cpl (4264667) | 6th DLI | 11/07/40 | MM |
| Bush, W. E. | Lt Col (MC) | 5th Bn Green Howards | 05/07/40 | DSO |
| Cant, J. | Cpl (4447343) | 6th DLI. | 11/07/40 | MM |
| Carr, P. | 2/Lt | 6th Bn Green Howards | | MC |
| Carruthers, J. | Sgt (4456094) | 8th DLI | 11/07/40 | DCM |
| Chrystal, F. | Pte (4271204) | 4th RNF | 11/07/40 | MM |
| Clare, V. H. | Cpl (7684623) | 50 Div Provost Coy | 11/07/40 | MM |
| Clark, R. | Pte (4273726) | 4th RNF | 20/12/40 | MM |
| Clarke, J. F. | Pte (6914308) | 4th RNF | 11/07/40 | MM |
| Claye, D. H. | 2/Lt | 8th DLI | | MID |
| Cowan, T. | Sgt (7350296) | 149th Fld Ambulance | 11/07/40 | MM |
| Cox, J. R. | L/Cpl (6006299) | 4th Bn East Yorks Rgt | KIA 30th May 1942 | MM |
| Cummins, R. L. | Cpt | 6th DLI | | MC |
| Curry, J. | CSM | 8th DLI | | MID |
| Dean, G. C. | Pte | 6th DLI | | MM |
| Duggan, T. F. | Revd | RACD Att 8th DLI | 20/12/40 | MC |
| Dumville, W. G. | Cpt | 5th Bn Green Howards | | MC |

251

| Name | Rank or Number | Unit | LG Date | Award |
| --- | --- | --- | --- | --- |
| English, I. R. | 2/Lt | 8th DLI | | MID |
| Fatherley, J. | Pte (4344670) | 4th East Yorks | 20/12/40 | MM |
| Fletcher, H. | Cpl | 8th DLI | | MID |
| Frankish, F. | S/Sgt (7348884) | 150th Fld Ambulance | 11/07/40 | DCM |
| Fulcher, A. L. | Pte (5830049) | 5th Green Howards | 11/07/40 | MM |
| Heslop, J. R. | Cpt | RAMC Att to 6th DLI | | MC |
| Iceton, G. E. | Pte (4457030) | 6th DLI | 11/07/40 | MM |
| Jackson, D. A. | Spr (1881970) | 505 Fld Coy RE | 22/10/40 | MM |
| Jickells, T. H. | Pte (4337800) | 4th Bn East Yorks Rgt | KIA 28th May 1940 | MID |
| Kemp, J. P. | A/CSM (4439323) | 9th DLI | 20/12/40 | DCM |
| Kirby, E. L. | 2/Lt | 4th Bn Green Howards | | MC |
| Laidler, R. | Pte | 6th Bn Green Howards | | MM |
| Latham, J. T. | Sgmn (2574424) | 150th Bde Signals | 11/07/40 | MM |
| Leinster, A. W. | Lt | 4th RNF | 20/12/40 | MC |
| Lightfoot, T. | RQMS | 8th DLI | | MID |
| Littleboy, C. N., MC. TD. | Lt Col | 4th Bn Green Howards | | DSO |
| Long, A | Sgt (854257) | 94th Fld Rgt RA | 11/07/40 | MM |
| Martin, R. H. | Lt Col | 4th Bn East Yorks Rgt | | MID |
| McLaren, R. S. | Major | 8th DLI | | MID |
| McLaren, R. S. | Lt Col | 8th DLI | | DSO |
| Minor, B. | Cpt | 50 Div Signals | 11/07/40 | MBE |
| Needham, J. R. | Pte (4389350) | 5th Bn Green Howards | 11/07/40 | MM |
| Owen, T. B. | Pte (4391132) | 5th Bn Green Howards | 11/07/40 | MM |
| Pallas, T. | Sgt | 6th DLI | | MM |
| Peacock, J. H. | L/Sgt (4390667) | 4th Bn Green Howards | 20/12/40 | MM |
| Pointer, R. L. | Bdr (861601) | 65th A/Tank Rgt RA | 20/12/40 | MM |
| Puddle, R. L. | Pte (4034240) | 6th DLI | 11/07/40 | MM. |
| Ramsden, W. H. C. | Bdr | 50th Division | 27/08/40 | CBE |
| Rice, R. | Pte (4344207) | 4th Bn East Yorks Rgt | Died 28th May 1940 | MID |
| Robson, T. L. | L/Bdr (895235) | 74th Fld Rgt RA | 20/12/40 | MM |
| Salmon, G. S. | L/Sgt (2217940) | 505th Fld Coy RE | 20/10/40 | DCM |
| Saul, W. W. | Pte (4444561) | 9th DLI | 20/12/40 | MM |
| Scuffham, A. | Pte (4389287) | 4th Bn Green Howards | 11/07/40 | MM |
| Sharman, F. W. M. | Lt | 4th Bn East Yorks Rgt | 20/12/40 | MC |

# Appendix XI

| Name | Rank or Number | Unit | LG Date | Award |
|---|---|---|---|---|
| Skorochod, A. | Sgt | French Military Mission – Att 8th DLI | | DCM |
| Steel, M. R. (DSO, MC) | Lt Col | 6th Bn Green Howards | | Bar to DSO |
| Temple, A. T. | | 8th DLI | | MID |
| Thompson, J. F. | Sgt (1023358) | 4th RNF | 11/07/40 | DCM |
| Tidball, G. K. | Pte (4344534) | 4th Bn East Yorks Rgt | POW May 1940 | MID |
| Underwood, W. | Gnr (908457) | 74th Fld Rgt RA | 20/12/40 | MM |
| Walker, A. | Pte (4386033) | 5th Bn Green Howards | | MM |
| Watson, G. H., MC. TD. | Major | 4th Bn East Yorks Rgt | POW May 1942 | MID |
| Whitehead, H. D. | Cpt | 5th Bn Green Howards | | MC |
| Wilson, C. | Pte (4273534) | 4th RNF | 11/07/40 | MM |
| Wood, G. L. | Cpt | 9th DLI | 20/12/40 | MC |

**Appendix XII**

**4270383 Private Adam Wakenshaw, VC. 9th Battalion Durham Light Infantry, 151st Brigade, 50th Northumbrian Division**

---

Adam Wakenshaw was born in Newcastle upon Tyne on 9 June 1914, the youngest of 13 children of Thomas and Mary Wakenshaw to survive childhood. Thomas was a labourer and the family struggled constantly against poverty and hardship in a very poor neighbourhood in Gateshead, Newcastle. Adam ran barefoot in the streets and sold newspapers to earn a few pence pocket money. At fourteen he left St Abysm's Roman Catholic School to work underground at St Elswick pit and tried unsuccessfully to join the army at the age of sixteen, his mother heard about this and promptly brought him home. He later worked at a tripe factory and as a builders labourer. In 1932 aged 18 years he married Dorothy Ann Douglas and by 1939 they had three children, John, Thomas and Lillian and resided at 16 Duke Street, Newcastle upon Tyne.

When the Second World War began in September 1939 Adam left his labouring job and joined the army serving in the 9th Battalion the Durham Light Infantry,151 (Durham) Brigade as part of the 50th Northumbrian Division. In time he found himself in the anti-tank platoon in which, without shining, he became a good and reliable gunner. Major Harry Sell commented on him; "He had that seemingly helpless mystification that grew out of distressed areas constantly harassed by well-meaning officials". In 1940 the British Expeditionary Force was Defeated and Adam saw action at Arras, Carvin, Ypres and on the Dunkirk perimeter. Though wounded he escaped back to England with his unit.

In February 1941 Adam's son John Wakenshaw was killed in a road accident near his home, his Father was given a few days compassionate leave to return home to Newcastle, this was to be the last time he and his wife would be together. In May 1942 the 50th Division found itself manning the Gazala Line as part of the Eighth Army holding back Rommel's victorious Africa Corps. On 26 May The German and Italian units attacked and outflanked the British units, 150 Brigade was overrun and the British armour smashed. The remaining two brigades of the 50th Division, 151st and 69th, became surrounded and had to break out into the desert and make a long detour back to their own lines. On 21 June Rommel's forces took Tobruk and pressed the British back towards Alexandria, the British units stopped at Mersa Matruh to make a stand in an attempt to gain time for the retreating Eighth Army. Before dawn on 27 June the German 90th Light Division moved against the 151st Durham Brigade, the first assault landed on the 9th DLI who were positioned on a small plateau about 17 miles south of Mersa Matruh. The ground here was flat and rocky with very little cover for the infantry, to their front on a gentle slope were stationed four two pounder anti-tank guns and their crews who waited patiently behind their guns for the enemy to come within range. Among one of these crews was Adam Wakenshaw.

At 0500 hours the German infantry attacked supported by tanks and artillery, during the advance a tracked vehicle towing a light gun came within range of Adam Wakenshaw's gun, the crew opened fire at once and sent a shell crashing through the vehicles engine stopping in dead. A German mobile gun advanced and fired at the anti-tank gun teams killing or seriously wounding all of the crews, with the anti-tank guns silenced the Durham infantry positions were now swept by intense mortar and artillery fire. The Germans moved forward to the knocked out tracked vehicle with the intention of bringing the light gun it was towing into action upon the Durham's positions that were only two hundred yards away. Adam Wakenshaw lay near his gun terribly wounded with his left arm blown off above the elbow, he saw what the Germans were doing and although he was still under a hail of fire crawled back to his gun. With the help of the gun aimer, Private Erick Mohn, who was also badly wounded, Private Wakenshaw loaded shells with his good arm and five more rounds were fired scoring direct hits on the tracked vehicle, setting it on fire and damaging the light gun. Then a German shell burst close by killing Private Mohn and the blast threw Wakenshaw away from his gun wounding him again in the process. The infantry looked on at the enfolding drama before them and with disbelief watched Wakenshaw drag his broken and bleeding body back to his gun, once in position he placed one more round in the breech and was preparing to fire when a direct hit on the ammunition box killed him and silenced his gun.

There was now nothing to hold up the German advance and by 0700 hours the three forward companies of the 9th DLI were surrounded and one by one overrun. On that day the 9th Battalion lost twenty men killed, over sixty wounded and three hundred taken prisoner. The Germans withdrew later to lick their wounds, during the evening men of the 8th Battalion searched the abandoned battle-field, behind a wrecked anti-tank gun the broken body of Adam Wakenshaw was found stretched out near the breach block beside the ruined ammunition box. The troops buried him in the hard ground where he had fallen. In 1943 Wakenshaw's body was re-buried in El Alamein War Cemetery, Egypt, with full military honours. In January 1945 the Egyptian Mail described the scene during a visit:

> In the centre of the cemetery was a two pounder anti-tank gun, painted with the familiar dun coloured camouflage of the Eighth Army, but now twisted and shell shattered. Against the shield rested a wreath of withered white roses and purple bougainvillaea. The ribbon fluttered and the dry petals rustled in the freshening wind. It was the gun served by Private Wakenshaw.

Later this gun was sent home to stand outside the regiment's depot at Brancepeth Castle near Durham City, today the gun manned by Private Wakenshaw VC and his comrades still bears the scars of that fierce fight and is now in the DLI Museum, Durham.

In his last letter home to his wife Adam wrote "Never mind Dolly when I get back from all this we'll have a better little home of our own," When he was killed his semi-crippled wife was left with Thomas aged seven, Lillian aged three and her 68 year old mother, they lived in a one room slum. In his home town a fund was set up to raise money for their journey to Buckingham Palace to pick up his medal. Men from the DLI gave up their clothing coupons to dress the children and on 3 March 1943 Thomas stood to attention as the King pinned the Victoria Cross on his chest with a few well-chosen words. Back home the kindly Geordies rallied around the family and they were re-housed in a better quality home. The Lord Mayor of Newcastle, Alderman Dixon, called on Mrs Wakenshaw to pay his respects and to express his sympathy upon her loss and told her steps were being taken to ensure that the family of such a brave soldier should not suffer as a result of his death. It was announced later that a shilling fund had been opened in the city to assist Mrs Wakenshaw and her family, civic chiefs and businessmen immediately came forward with subscriptions amounting to two hundred pounds which increased by the day. However nothing could console Dorothy Wakenshaw, two years later the children were taken into care and Dorothy died unable to come to terms with the life of a VC's widow. The medal that could have brought some measure of comfort for her, had she sold it, went to the Regimental Museum – she just gave it away. As soon as Thomas was old enough he joined the army in his Father's old regiment – the DLI.

Adam Wakenshaw was long remembered in the back streets and along the riverside of Newcastle for all the trouble he used to cause his mother. When he went off to the war old Mrs Wakenshaw told him bluntly she would not miss him. In his last letter to her he told her "I am sorry for all the trouble I have caused you by being a bit wild, you said you would not miss me when I went away, but you will miss me more than any of the others." When his mother read the story of his bravery she said "He was right when he said I should miss him, he was a wild lad but there was never any real harm in him."

The Headmaster of St Aloysius Roman Catholic School, Mr Joseph Dixon, commented on Adam; "I strongly deprecate to certain references to Adam as an urchin and a dead end kid, the phrases were entirely out of place, Adam was quite a normal lad, high spirited undoubtedly, but with little to distinguish him from others."

Major Sell of the DLI said of Adam Wakenshaw; "The army fulfilled his demands and I am sure he was happy. He accepted authority and his training produced the type of man who throughout our history has followed his appointed leaders to the end. To me Wakenshaw will remain as a person who, having no benefits from fortune or society or even by birth, nevertheless rose to heights of spectacular courage in war, which in peace might well have passed unnoticed in the daily fight against fortune, in which he would have been to the end an uncomplaining loser."

## Cathedral Church of St Mary

In the south side of St Mary's church, where Adam Wakenshaw was baptised and married, there is a two light memorial window. It replaced a window that was damaged by the bombing of Newcastle during the Second World War and was designed by the artist Cate Watkinson. It tells the story of Adam Wakenshaw from his humble beginnings in Newcastle to his death in the wastes of North Africa.

VC Citation, *London Gazette*, 11 September 1942

## Appendix XIII

**Numbers of British and Allied troops who were evacuated from Dunkirk and landed in England, 27 May to 4 June 1940:**

---

**From Dunkirk Harbour**
27 May – 7,669
28 May – 11,874
29 May – 33,558
30 May – 24,311
31 May – 45,072
1 June – 47,081
2 June – 19,561
3 June – 24,876
4 June – 25,553

Total – 239,555

**From the beaches**
28 May – 5,390
29 May – 13,752
30 May – 29,512
31 May – 22,942
1 June – 17,348
2 June – 6,695
3 June – 1,870
4 June – 622

Total – 98,671

Grand total – 338,226

## Appendix XIV

## 50th Division Honours and Awards 1941 to August 1942

A date before the award indicates when the award was won, a place name in brackets before the award indicates where the award was won. This list may well be incomplete but I have done my best to find as many awards as possible in the time left to me.

| Name | Rank | Unit | Award |
| --- | --- | --- | --- |
| Asquith, H. (781992) | L/Bdr | 74th Fld Rgt, RA | (Gazala) MM |
| Ayrton, T. G. | Sgt | 8th DLI | MID |
| Bainbridge, J. J. H. (76716) | Lt | 74th Fld Rgt, RA. Att. 151 Bde | 9 April 1942, MC |
| Bark, A. W. | L/Cpl | 8th DLI | MM |
| Beart, M. W., MC | Lt Col | 8th DLI | MID |
| Beatie, C. | Pte | 8th DLI | MM |
| Bellamy, D. (471352) | RQMS | 74th Fld Rgt, RA. Att. 151 Bde | (Mersa Matruh) MM |
| Brannigan, M. J. | CSM | 8th DLI | MM |
| Bray, P. E. | Lt | 5th Bn Green Howards | (Auleb-Gazala) MC |
| Broadley, F. (1536081) | Sgt | 25th LAA Rgt, RA. Att. 151 Bde | (Gazala) MM |
| Brown, J. | Pte | 8th DLI | MM |
| Brunton, F. H. | Major | 6th Bn Green Howards | (Gazala) MC |
| Burdett, W. (6895188) | Sgt | 5th Bn Green Howards | (Auleb-Gazala) MM |
| Burnett, C. A. (1877822) | L/Sgt | 505 Fld Coy, RE. Att. 6th DLI | (Gazala) MM |
| Burton | Cpl | 5th Bn East Yorks Rgt | (Mersa Matruh) MM |
| Cairns, A. | Sgt | 8th DLI | MM |
| Cairns, A., MM | Sgt | 8th DLI | DCM |
| Calvert, W. S. (156839) | Lt | 25th LAA Rgt, RA | 1 July 1942, MC |
| Capon, W. W. | Pte | 6th DLI | MM |
| Cass, R. (4390829) | L/Sgt | 4th Bn Green Howards | (Auleb-Gazala) DCM |
| Chapman, J. H. | Cpt | 6th DLI | MC |
| Charlton, W. | L/Cpl | 8th DLI | MM. |
| Coglan, J. E. | Pte | 6th DLI | MM |

| Name | Rank | Unit | Award |
|---|---|---|---|
| Cole, F. L. | Cpt | 6th DLI | MC |
| Cooke-Collis, E. C. | Lt Col | 6th Bn Green Howards | (Mersa Matruh) DSO |
| Crawford, W. | Sgt | 8th DLI | MM |
| Crawford, W., MM | Sgt | 8th DLI | Bar to MM |
| Crossling, J. P. (547888) | TSM | 25th LAA Rgt, RA. Att. 151 Bde | (Mersa Matruh) DCM |
| D'Auvergne, F. C. | Sgt | 6th DLI | MM |
| Daneale | Lt | 8th DLI | MID |
| Dash, G. (865431) | BSM | 124th Fld Rgt, RA. Att. 69 Bde | (Gazala) MM |
| Davies, L. L. J. (The Reverend) | Cpt | RACD Att. 6th DLI | (Mersa Matruh) MC |
| Davies, W. | Sgt | 6th DLI | MM |
| Denchfield, E. A. (5-51766) | Cpl | 8th DLI | (Gazala) MM |
| Dickinson, R. | Sgt | 8th DLI | MID |
| Dorman, R. A. | 2/Lt | 6th DLI | MC |
| Dougan, J. | Pte | 6th DLI | MM |
| Edwards, W. | L/Sgt | 5th Bn East Yorks Rgt | (Mersa Matruh) MM |
| English, I. R. | Cpt | 8th DLI | MC |
| English, I. R., MC | Cpt | 8th DLI | (Sidra Ridge) Bar to MC |
| Evans, V. | 2/Lt | 7th Bn Green Howards | (Gazala) MC |
| Exall, J. (4380801) | RSM | 4th Bn Green Howards | (Auleb-Gazala) MC |
| Fawkes, L. V. F. (58033) | Major | 74th Fld Rgt, RA. Att. 151 Bde | 9 April 1942, MC |
| Fearon, G. R. | Pte | 8th DLI | MM |
| Fennwick, T. | Cpt | 8th DLI | MID |
| Ferguson, K. (903011) | Sgt | 124th Fld Rgt, RA. Att. 69 Bde | (Gazala) MM |
| Fitzgerald, L. (1907696) | Dvr | 233 Fld Coy, RE | (Mersa Matruh) MM. |
| Foreman, D. J. (4753817) | Pte | 7th Bn Green Howards | (Sidra Ridge) MM |
| Fox, P. H. D. | Major | 5th Bn Green Howards | (Auleb-Gazala) DSO |
| Glasper, H. | Cpt | 8th DLI | MC |
| Goodchild, J. H. (151326) | Lt | 25th LAA Rgt, RA. Att. 151 Bde | (Gazala) MC |
| Goodwin, R. | Pte | 8th DLI | MID |
| Grey, R. M. | Sgt | 6th DLI | MM |
| Grimston, R. (56234) | Cpt | 74th Fld Rgt, RA. Att. 151 Bde | (Gazala) DSO |
| Gunn, A. | Sgt | 6th DLI | MM |
| Halliwell, W. S. (1476623) | Sgt | 25th LAA Rgt, RA. Att. 69 Bde | 1 July 1942, MM |
| Hart, S. | Cpl | 8th DLI | MM |
| Haseley, C. R. | Sgt | 6th DLI | DCM |
| Haseley, C. R., DCM | Sgt | 6th DLI | MM |
| Higgins, A. (4389360) | Sgt | 6th Bn Green Howards. | (Mersa Matruh) MM |

| Name | Rank | Unit | Award |
|---|---|---|---|
| Higginson, W. | Pte | 8th DLI | MM |
| Hill, G. | L/Sgt | 8th DLI | MM |
| Hogg, J. G. | CSM | 5th Bn East Yorks Rgt | (Mersa Matruh) MM |
| Holmes, B. (4440719) | Pte | 8th DLI | (Mersa Matruh) MM |
| Hudson, J. | Pte | 6th DLI | DCM |
| Hull, C. M. | Cpt | 6th Bn Green Howards | (Mersa Matruh) MC |
| Irvine, J. B. (52200) | Cpt | 74th Fld Rgt, RA. Att. 151 Bde | (Gazala) MC |
| Jackson, M. L. P. | Lt Col | 8th DLI Att. Green Howards | DSO |
| Jennings, A. | RSM | 8th DLI | DCM |
| Jordan, P. B. (5046992) | Pte | 9th DLI | 2 November 1942, MM |
| King, W. J. (1892085) | Spr | 233 Fld Coy, RE | (Mersa Matruh) MM. |
| Knowles, F. (799890) | BSM | 124th Fld Rgt, RA. Att. 69 Bde | (Gazala) MM |
| Lake, P. H. | Pte | 8th DLI | MID |
| Leng, J. (4380815) | Sgt | 5th Bn Green Howards | (Auleb-Gazala) DCM |
| Lewis, P. J. | Lt | 8th DLI | MC |
| Lightfoot, T. | RQMS | 8th DLI | MID |
| Lishman, S. | Cpl | 6th DLI | MM |
| Lucas, P. J. A. | Cpt | 8th DLI | MC |
| Macdonnel, F. E. A. | Lt Col | 7th Bn Green Howards | (Mersa Matruh) DSO |
| Malone, J. | Sgt | 8th DLI | MID |
| Mattock, T. A. | CSM | 5th Bn East Yorks Rgt | (Mersa Matruh) DCM |
| McDermott, I. (2651938) | Sgt | 8th DLI | (Gazala) MM. |
| McFarlane, J. O. | L/Cpl | 6th DLI | MM |
| McMahon, J. | A/RSM | 6th DLI | MM |
| Medway, E. C. | Lt | 9th DLI | 18 October 1942, MC |
| Michael, D. D. | Pte | 8th DLI | MM |
| Norman, D. S. | Lt Col | 4th Bn East Yorks Rgt | (Martuba raid) DSO |
| Oakes, E. T. | Lt | 124th Fld Rgt, RA | 13 May 1942, MC |
| Oliver, J. G. (4387081) | CSM (KIA 6 April 1943) | 6th Bn Green Howards | (Mersa Matruh) MM |
| Ovenden. | Cpt | 6th DLI | MC |
| Page, A. | RSM | 6th DLI | MC |
| Pearson, E. (4690698) | Sgt | 82nd LAA Bty, RA. Att 69 Bde | (1st July 42) MM |
| Pearson, E. (4690698) | Sgt | 25th LAA Rgt, RA. Att. 69 Bde | 1 July 1942, MM |
| Pearson, M. | Cpl | 8th DLI | MM |
| Penwill, D. J. | Cpt | 5th Bn East Yorks Rgt | (Mersa Matruh) MC |
| Peveller, J. | Cpl | 8th DLI | MID |
| Place, R. | Lt | 8th DLI | MC |
| Pluck, W. L. (4393084) | L/Sgt | 6th Bn Green Howards | (Mersa Matruh) MM |

| Name | Rank | Unit | Award |
| --- | --- | --- | --- |
| Prangell, W. H. (1099092) | Gnr | 74th Fld Rgt, RA. Att. 151 Bde | (Gazala) MM |
| Rae, G. C. (548029) | Sgt | 25th LAA Rgt, RA. Att. 151 Bde | (Gazala) MM |
| Ralph, R. T. (4397603) | Pte | 7th Bn Green Howards | (Sidra Ridge) MM |
| Ranson, J. | CSM. | 8th DLI | MM |
| Ranson, J. | CSM | 8th DLI | MID |
| Redpath, E. (721558) | BSM. | 74th Fld Rgt, RA. Att. 151 Bde | (Gazala) DCM |
| Reeves, G. K. (323359) | Bdr | 274th LAA Bty, RA. Att. 151 Bde | (Gazala) MM |
| Reeves, G. K. (323359) | Bdr | 25th LAA Rgt, RA. Att. 151 Bde | (Gazala) MM |
| Robbins, F. F. | Major | 5th Bn East Yorks Rgt (KIA 26 July 1942) | (Mersa Matruh) MC |
| Robinson, A. E. | Pte | 5th Bn East Yorks Rgt (KIA 25 October 1942) | (Gazala) MM |
| Robinson, H. | Pte | 5th Bn East Yorks Rgt | (Mersa Matruh) MM |
| Sell, H. | Major | 8th DLI | MC |
| Sell, H. | Major | 8th DLI | MID |
| Stansfield, T. W. G. | Lt Col. | 5th Bn East Yorks Rgt | (Mersa Matruh) DSO |
| Stansfield, T. W. G. (34918) | Lt Col | 5th Bn East Yorkshire Rgt | (Mersa Matruh) DSO |
| Swallow, T. M. | Pte | 8th DLI | MM |
| Tennant, T. E. | Sgt | 8th DLI | MID |
| Thompson, J. | Sgt | 8th DLI | MID |
| Thompson, J. (1616111) | Bdr | 25th LAA Rgt, RA. Att. 69 Bde | (Mersa Matruh) MM |
| Turnbull, J. E. (899232) | L/Sgt | 74th Fld Rgt, RA. Att. 151 Bde | (Gazala) MM |
| Turton, R. H. | Major | 50 Div HQ | (Gazala) MC |
| Usher, G. F. (4391050) | Sgt | 7th Bn Green Howards | (Gazala) MM |
| Wakenshaw, A. H. (4270383) | Pte (KIA 27 June 1942) | 9th DLI | (Mersa Matruh) VC |
| Watson, P. B. | Cpt | 4th Bn Green Howards | (Gazala) DSO |
| Watson. W. (4461442) | Cpl | 8th DLI | (Gazala) MM |
| Wilson, R. (1591121) | Gnr | 82nd LAA Bty, RA. Att. 69 Bde | (Gazala)MM |
| Wilson, R. (1591121) | Gnr | 25th LAA Rgt, RA. Att. 69 Bde | (Gazala) MM |
| Wood, G. E. | CSM | 8th DLI | MM |
| Wood, G. L. | Cpt | 6th DLI | Bar to MC |
| Wood, J. W. | Pte | 8th DLI | MM |

# Appendix XV

## The British Free Corps

---

Document given to British troops in POW camps by the German authorities asking them to join the struggle against Bolshevism by serving in the British Free Corps.

As a result of repeated applications from British subjects from all parts of the world wishing to take part in the common European struggle against Bolshevism authorisation has recently been given for the creation of a British volunteer unit.

The British Free Corps publishes herewith the following short statement of the aims and principles of the unit.

1. The British Free Corps is a thoroughly British volunteer unit, conceived and created by British subjects from all parts of the Empire who have taken up arms and pledged their lives in the common European struggle against Soviet Russia.

2. The British Free Corps condemns the war with Germany and the sacrifice of British blood in the interests of Jewry and international finance and regards this conflict as a fundamental betrayal of the British people and British imperial interests.

3. The British Free Corps desires the establishment of peace in Europe, the development of close friendly relations between England and Germany and the encouragement of mutual understanding and collaboration between the two great Germanic peoples.

4. The British Free Corps will neither make war against Britain or the British Crown, nor support any action or policy detrimental to the interests of the British people.

Published by the British Free Corps.

This document was given to the author by Herbert Thompson, 4th Bn East Yorkshire Rgt. Herbert was taken prisoner at Gazala, 1 June 1942, when 150 Bde was overrun.

# Appendix XVI

## Chronology of the War 3 September 1939 to 7 September 1942

**1939**

3 September – Great Britain declares war on Germany.

**1940**

10 May – Germany invades Holland, Belgium and Luxembourg. Allies move to the Dyle Line. Churchill becomes Prime Minister.
11 May – Eban Emael falls to German paratroopers. Rapid German advance in Holland.
12 May – The French dig in on west bank of the Meuse, leading German units reach Meuse. Allied lines of communication bombed by the Luftwaffe.
13 May – German forces cross the Meuse at Sedan and Dinant. British and French forces man the Dyle Line. Dutch withdraw to fortress Holland.
14 May – Rotterdam bombed. Allied aircraft bomb German floating bridges over the Meuse but fail to stop the Germans expanding their bridgehead.
15 May – Holland capitulates. Rommel's 7th Panzer Division breaks through at Philippville. Army Group B attacks the Allied forces holding the Dyle Line.
16 May – The Belgian government withdraws to Ostend. Gamelin orders the French and British forces to retreat from Belgium. German forces penetrate fifty miles into France.
17 May – Germans enter Brussels.
18 May – Germans take Antwerp. Panzers reach Amiens.
19 May – Weygand appointed commander in chief.
20 May – Rommel's 7th (Ghost) Panzer Division reaches Arras. Guderian's panzer formations arrive at Noyelles on the coast.
21 May – The British counterattack at Arras causing the German advance to falter and making Hitler and the German high command nervous.
22 May – Rommel restores the situation and the German forces press on to Boulogne and Calais.
24 May – Hitler gives the halt order – panzers not to cross the Aa Canal.
25 May – Boulogne taken, the Allies fall back on Dunkirk.

26 May – Calais surrenders. Hitler rescinds his halt order and unleashes the panzer forces. The British and French are forced back to a beach-head perimeter around Dunkirk. Operation Dynamo begins.

27 May – King Leopold of the Belgians is forced to sue for peace.

28 May – Belgium surrenders unconditionally.

29 May – Germans take Ostend and Ypres.

31 May – French defence of Lille ends. Lord Gort hands command of the BEF over to Alexander and returns to England. Churchill visits Paris.

1/2 June – Serious and heavy fighting around the Dunkirk perimeter, troops taken off the beaches and from the port of Dunkirk in naval and civilian ships.

3 June – End of Dunkirk evacuation. Germans bomb Paris.

4 June – Allies abandon Dunkirk.

5 June – The Battle of France begins.

9 June – German forces assault the French army who continue to fight it out.

10 June – Italy declares war on the United Kingdom.

11 June – German advance into central France continues, Rheims falls. Paris declared an open city.

12 June – Guderian launches his panzer divisions against Chalons sur Marne.

13 June – Churchill meets Reynaud for the last time.

14 June – Germans enter Paris. Maginot Line breached. De Gaulle flies to England. Germans take Verdun. Reynaud is left with no choice but to sue for peace.

16 June – Guderian's panzers are now on the Saone. Dijon falls. Large German forces cross the Rhine at Colmar. Reynaud resigns. Petain forms a new government and asks the Germans for peace terms.

17 June – Guderian's armoured units reach the Swiss border near Pontarlier.

18 June – De Gaulle's first broadcast from London. Rommel takes Cherbourg.

19 June – German forces reach the Loire. Brest and Nantes taken.

20 June – Germans enter Lyons. France asks Italy for an armistice.

21 June – Italians attack in the Alps and towards Menton on the Cote d'Azur. Hitler meets French delegation at Compiegne for surrender.

22 June – France accepts German terms and signs armistice. French forces surrender.

24 June – French sign armistice with Italians.

25 June – The Battle for France ends.

11 August – Italian troops attack British Somaliland.

15 August – British troops begin to evacuate Somaliland.

19 August – The British evacuation of Somaliland is completed.

13 September – The Italian Army crosses the frontier with Egypt and occupies Sollum.

17 September – Sidi Barrani is captured by the Italians.

12 November – The German Supreme Command issues instruction No 18 requesting that a force be raised to support the Italians in North Africa for the purpose of an attack upon Egypt.

6 December – The British Western Desert Force moves out to open a counteroffensive against the Italians.

9 December – The British offensive opens at 07:15 hours.

11 December – The British recapture Sidi Barrani.

17 December – The British counteroffensive recaptures Sollum.
23 December – A head count of prisoners shows that 35,949 Italians have been taken since the opening of the British offensive.

**1941**

5 January – General Berganzoli surrenders the town of Bardia.
22 January – The Australian Division enters Tobruk.
29 January – British troops re-enter Somaliland.
30 January – Derna falls to the British.
4 February – British 7th Armoured Division leaves Mechili to cut off the retreating Italians beyond Benghazi.
25 February – Italian Somaliland is occupied by the British.
27 February – The first patrols of the German Africa Corps clash with the British.
12 March – The newly arrived units of the Africa Corps parade in Tripoli.
24 March – The Africa Corps attacks and captures El Agheila.
31 March – The Germans strike at Mersah Brega.
3 April – Benghazi is captured by the Germans.
5 April – Addis Ababa, capital of Ethiopia, is captured from the Italians.
6 April – German forces invade Yugoslavia and Greece.
7 April – Derna falls to the Axis forces.
10 April – The British Army withdraws on Tobruk.
11 April – German armoured units cut the Tobruk – El Adem road. Two thousand British soldiers are taken prisoner, including three generals.
13 April – Tobruk is encircled and Bardia captured.
14 April – The German attacks on Tobruk are repulsed.
27 April – Part of the Africa Corps thrusts across the Libyan – Egyptian frontier and captures Halfaya Pass.
28 April – Sollum falls to German troops.
15 May – General Wavell opens Operation Brevity, a limited campaign to gain jumping off positions for a future and larger offensive.
16 May – The Duke of Aosta's forces surrender in Ethiopia. Rommel throws in a counterattack against the British.
27 May – British troops remaining in Halfaya Pass are driven out by German armoured units.
15 June – Wavell's major offensive against the Axis forces is launched – Operation Battleaxe.
22 June – The German army invades Russia.
1 July – Wavell is replaced by General Claude Auchinleck.
17 November – Lt Colonel Keyes leads a commando raid on what is believed to be Rommel's Head Quarters.
18 November – A new British offensive – Operation Crusader – opens.
19 November – Sidi Rezegh is captured by the Eighth Army.
20 November – Fighting continues around Sidi Rezegh.
21 November – The British garrison at Tobruk makes a sortie to link up with the forces in the Sidi Rezegh area.

22 November – The 21st Panzer Division attacks British armoured units.
23 November – The massed German armour defeats the piecemeal British tank attacks. New Zealand troops occupy Bardia.
24 November – Rommel sends a column over the Egyptian Frontier.
26 November – The commander of the Eighth Army, General Cunningham, is replaced by Ritchie. The British Tobruk garrison captures Duda and links up with the infantry force taking part in Operation Crusader.
29 November – Von Ravenstein is taken prisoner by the British.
30 November – During the day heavy German attacks are launched against the British corridor between Sidi Rezegh and Tobruk
6 December – There is heavy fighting south of Sidi Rezegh which lasts until 8th December.
13 December – Rommel launches a counterattack and opens a five day offensive battle.
17 December – The German offensive fails and Rommel's troops begin to withdraw from Gazala.
19 December – The Eighth Army recaptures Derna and Mechili.
23 December – The Eighth Army recapture Barce.
24 December – The Eighth Army captures Benghazi.

## 1942

2 January – Bardia is recaptured.
5 January – The Eighth Army's attack opens at Halfaya Pass.
6 January – Rommel attacks the Eighth Army from positions at Agedabia.
8 January – The Eighth Army drives back Rommel from Agedabia.
12 January – Sollum falls to the British.
17 January – The Eighth Army recaptures Halfaya Pass.
21 January – Rommel's offensive re-opens at El Agheila.
23 January – The Africa Corps recaptures Agedabia.
4 February – Derna falls to the Axis troops.
14 February – After a two week pause Rommel renews his offensive.
15 February – Singapore falls.
20 March – The 50th Division sends two columns on raids against Tmimi and Martuba Airfields. (Operation Full Size)
21 March – The two columns attack the airfields.
22 March – The 50th Division withdraws its columns and they head back to the Gazala Line.
26 May – The third German offensive opens, Rommel takes the Africa Corps on a wide flanking movement southward around Bir Hacheim on the left flank of the Gazala Line while Italian forces hold the attention of the 50th and 1st South African Divisions in the north.
27 May – Rommel's forces make first contact with Bir Hacheim, held by the Free French, at the southern end of the Gazala Line. The French repulse the Africa Corps attacks.
28 May – Rommel's plans begin to go wrong as supplies of ammunition, petrol, food and water dwindle and as British armoured units smash into his panzer divisions he backs up against the rear of the British line held by 150 Brigade. The presence of a strongly held brigade position at Auleb/Muftah comes as a great surprise to Rommel. This area would be known

as the Cauldron and Rommel placed numerous 88mm anti-tank guns in a crescent facing the British tank units who obligingly threw their tanks at them – the German gunners destroyed the British armoured brigades at their leisure. Supplies slowly filter through the British minefield gaps to the Africa Corps but 150 Brigade must be taken out if the Axis forces are to survive.

29 May – Rommel's forces attack 150 Brigade. General Cruwell's plane is shot down over 150 Brigades position and he is taken prisoner.

30 May – Rommel attacks 150 Brigade all day.

31 May – The attack on 150 Brigade continues while Rommel's defensive perimeter holds off the British armoured forces. The position of 150 Brigade is now desperate as they hold off vastly superior forces with no sign of relief or fresh supplies.

1 June – At dawn massed formations of Stukas rain bombs down on the worn out defenders of 150 Brigade, creeping barrages of artillery sweep back and forth across the box, then the position is attacked by massive panzer and infantry units with Rommel at their head. After fierce hand to hand fighting 150 Brigade is overrun by noon and Rommel can now re-supply the Africa Corps and renew his offensive. British counterattacks fail.

2/3 June – Rommel renews his offensive against Bir Hacheim, the Free French manning this position hold out against heavy air attacks, massed tank and infantry assaults and enormous concentrations of artillery fire in an epic action.

5 June – 21st Panzer Division breaks out of the Cauldron and makes for Knightsbridge.

10 June – The Free French holding Bir Hacheim are ordered to withdraw.

12 June – A great tank battle in the Knightsbridge area opens. Rigel Ridge and Knightsbridge fall.

13 June – At night the 1st South African Division begins its withdrawal from the Gazala Line along the coast road.

14 June – 151 and 69 Brigades, all that remained of the 50th Division, break out of the Gazala Line, with the enemy in their rear there was no hope of retreat so they attacked west through the Italian lines, turned south and rounded Bir Hacheim and then turned east and headed for the Egyptian frontier and their own lines. The whole of the Eighth Army was now in full retreat.

16 June – The Axis forces attack at Sidi Rezegh.

18 June – The Africa Corps opens its attacks on Tobruk.

20th June; Attacks on Tobruk continue.

21 June – Tobruk falls. Bardia is captured.

24 June – The victorious Panzer Army advances into Egypt.

25 June – Auchinleck takes command of Eighth Army.

27 June – The British make a stand at Mersa Matruh. The Axis forces attack the defending British units but are held.

27/28 June – At night the tired troops of the 50th Division are ordered to attack southwards across the enemy's lines of communication to destroy transports and disorganise supplies. In this confused operation at night the 50th took losses it could ill afford and on the 28th the attacking troops were back in their own positions at Mersa Matruh.

29 June – The British units at Mersa Mutruh find themselves surrounded and by the light of a full moon have to break through the Axis forces and out into the desert once more heading for the Alamein Line. Mersa Matruh falls.

1 July – Rommel's forces reach the Alamein Line.
2 July – The first Battle of Alamein begins.
3 July – Rommel breaks off the battle.
4 July – Eighth Army counter attacks along Ruweisat Ridge.
10 July – The Australians capture Tel El Eisa from the Italians.
23 July – Mussolini visits North Africa.
26 July – The British attacks are held and flung back by the Germans.
18 July – General Alexander to take over as Commander in Chief in the Middle East.
General Montgomery takes up his post as commander Eighth Army.
31 August – The Battle of Alam el Halfa opens.
3 September – The New Zealand Division mounts a drive in the Alam el Halfa sector to cut the German lines of communication.
7 September – The attack fails and Montgomery stops the battle – the Second Battle of Alamein.

# Bibliography

Atkin, R., *Pillar of Fire* (Hampshire: Sidgwick and Jackson, 1990)
Austin, J. C. [Gun Buster], *Return via Dunkirk* (London: Hodder and Stoughton, 1940)
Barnet, C., *The Desert Generals* (Australia: Allen and Unwin, 1960)
Battistelli, P. P., *Alamein* Gloucestershire: Spellmount, 2011)
Beckett, F. W., *Rommel, A Reappraisal* (Barnsley: Pen and Sword, 2013)
Bidwell, S., *Gunners at War* (London: Arrow Books, 1970)
Blyth, J., *Soldiering On* (London: Hutchinson, 1989)
Bradsey, S., *Atlas of World War Two Battle Plans* (Israel: Helicon Publishing, 2000)
Bush, G., *150 Brigade in the Middle East, June 1941 to June 1942* (Unpublished manuscript written in a German prisoner of war camp by officers of 150 Brigade who were captured at Gazala)
Carrel, P., *The Foxes of the Desert* (London: Macdonald, 1960)
Cheale, Bill, *Fighting Through from Dunkirk to Hamburg* (Barnsley: Pen and Sword, 2011)
Clay, E. W., *The Path of the 50th* (Aldershot: Gale and Polden, 1950)
Close, Bill, *Tank Commander* (Barnsley: Pen and Sword, 2013)
Crawford, R. J., *I was an Eighth Army Soldier* (London: Gollanz, 1944)
Crisp, R., *Brazen Chariots* (London: Norton Paperback, 2005)
Davidson, E., and D. Manning, *Chronology of World War Two* (London: Cassell, 1999)
Deighton, L., *Blitzkrieg* (London: Grafton Books, 1990)
Delaforce, P., *Churchill's Desert Rats* (Barnsley: Sutton Publishing, 2002)
Delaforce, P., *Monty's Northern Legions* (Barnsley: Sutton Publishing, 2004)
Doherty, R., *A Noble Crusade* (Gloucestershire: Spellmount, 1999)
Duncan, J. and G. Forty, *The Fall of France* (Kent: Guild Publishing, 1990)
Ellis, L. E., *The War in France and Flanders 1939 to 1940* (London: Crown Copyright, 1953)
Farrar-Hockley, A., *The War in the Desert* (London: Faber and Faber, 1969).
Halstead, M., *Shots in the Sand* (London: Gooday Publishing, 1990)
Holmes, R., *Bir Hacheim-Desert Citadel* (USA: Ballantine Books, 1972)
Icks, R. J., *Famous Tank Battles* (Northamptonshire: Profile Publications, 1973)
Irving, D., *The Trail of the Fox* (London: Weidenfield and Nicolson, 1977)
Kershaw, R., *Tank Men* (London: Hodder and Staughton, 2008)
Lewin, R., *Life and Death of the Africa Corps* (London: Crown Publishing, 1977)
Lewis, P. J. and I. R. English, *Into Battle with the Durhams* (Uckfield: Naval and Military Press, 1990)
Liddle Hart, B., *History of the Second World War* (London: Da Capo Press, 1999)
Liddle Hart, B., *The Other Side of the Hill* (London: Pan Books, 1983)

Liddle Hart, B., *The Rommel Papers* (London: Da Capo Press, 1953)
Lucas, J., *Panzer Army Africa* (London: Purnell, 1977)
Lucas, J., *War in the Desert* (London: Leventhal Ltd, 1982)
Lucas Philips, C. E., *Alamein* (London: Heinemann, 1962)
Lucas Philips, C. E., *Victoria Cross Battles* (London: Heinemann, 1973)
Macksey, K., *Military Errors of World War Two* (London: Arms and Armour Press, 1987)
Macksey, K., *Rommel, Battles and Campaigns* (London: Levental Ltd, 1979)
Mander, Darcy, *Mander's March on Rome* (Gloucestershire: Sutton Publishing, 1987)
Messenger, C., *The Art of Blitzkrieg* (London: Ian Allen Ltd, 1991)
Mitchellhill-Green, D., *With Rommel in the Desert* (Barnsley, Pen and Sword, 2017)
Mitcham, S. W., *Hitler's Legions* (London: Leo Cooper, 1985)
Mitcham, S. W., *Rommel's Desert War* (USA: Stackpole Books, 2007)
Moore, W., *Panzer Bait* (London: Leo Cooper, 1991)
Moses, H., *The Faithful Sixth* (Durham: County Durham Books, 1995)
Neillands, R., *The Eighth Army* (London: John Murray, 2004)
Nightingale, P. R., *The East Yorkshire Regiment in the War 1939-1945* (Howden: Mr Pye Books, 1952)
Olive, M. and R. Edwards, *Rommel's Desert Warriors* (USA: Stackpole Books, 2012)
Playfair, I. S. O., *The Mediterranean and the Middle East* (London: HMSO, 1960)
Purdon, G., *From Coalfield to Battlefield* (Durham: County Durham Springboard Media Project, 1995)
Quarry, B., *Encyclopaedia of the German Army* (London) P Stevens Ltd, 1989)
Rissik, D., *The DLI at War* (Durham: Brancepeth Castle, 1953)
Sadler, J., *El Alamein* (Gloucestershire: Amberley Press, 2012)
Samwell, H. P., *An Infantry Officer with the Eighth Army* (London: Blackwood, 1945)
Schmidt, H. W., *With Rommel in the Desert* (London: Constable, 1997)
Stewart, A., *Eighth Army's Greatest Victories* (London: Leo Cooper, 1999)
Sebag-Montefiore, H., *Dunkirk* (London: Penguin, 2007)
Synge, W. A. T., *The Story of the Green Howards 1939 to 1945* (Richmond: Green Howards, 1952)
Thompson, J., *Desert Victory* (London: Ebury Press, 2012)
Warner, P., *Alamein* (Barnsley: Kimber, 2007)
Whiting, C., *The Poor Bloody Infantry* (London: Spellmount, 2007)

# Glossary

| | | | |
|---|---|---|---|
| **A/A** | Anti-Aircraft. | **Coy** | Company. |
| **A/CSM** | Acting Company Sergeant Major. The 'A' before any rank means the rank has not been made permanent yet. | **Cpl** | Corporal. |
| | | **Cpt** | Captain. |
| | | **CQMS** | Company Quartermaster Sergeant. |
| | | **CSM** | Company Sergeant Major. |
| **AP** | Armour piercing shells. | **DCM** | Distinguished Conduct Medal. |
| **Armd Div** | Armoured Division. | | |
| **Att** | Attached, this can refer to a man who was in the Green Howards but was attached to the Durham Light Infantry. | **DLI** | Durham Light Infantry. |
| | | **DSO** | Distinguished Service Order. |
| | | **Fld Amb** | Field Ambulance. |
| | | **FDL** | Forward Defensive Line. |
| **Bar** | When a man won a gallantry medal for bravery and was awarded the same medal again, he would wear a silver bar on the ribbon of the first award, this would denote he had won it twice, i.e. Military Medal and Bar. | **Flimsey** | Petrol can. |
| | | **FOO** | Forward Observation Officer. |
| | | **FUP** | Forming up Place. |
| | | **GHQ** | General Head Quarters. |
| | | **Got** | Saucer-like depression in the desert, as in Got Auleb. |
| | | **Grant** | American heavy tank with a turret and sponson gun, supplied to the British tank units in May 1942 in the Western Desert. |
| **Bde** | Brigade. | | |
| **Bdr** | Bombardier, a Corporal in the Artillery. | | |
| **BEF** | British Expeditionary Force. | **Grey Hen** | Army earthenware Rum Jar marked SRD. |
| **Bir** | Place name, as in Bir Hacheim. | **HMS** | Her Majesty's Ship. |
| | | **Honey** | British Light Tank. |
| **Bn or Btn** | Battalion. | **HQ** | Head Quarters. |
| **Brewing up** | Making tea, or a tank that is burning fiercely with the crew still inside. | **Hrs** | Hours. |
| | | **Hull down** | This is when a tank takes up a firing position in a depression or behind a rise in the ground. In a |
| **Buckshee** | Going spare. | | |
| **CO** | Commanding Officer. | | |

| | | | |
|---|---|---|---|
| | defensive position holes would be dug into the ground so that the tanks could drive into them leaving only the turret above ground level, presenting the enemy with as small a target as possible yet being able to use its own gun to good effect. | PSM | Platoon Sergeant Major. |
| | | PT | Physical Training. |
| | | Pt | Point as seen on maps, high ground. |
| | | Pte | Private. |
| | | Poilus | Slang name given to French Soldiers by the French People, means 'The Hairy Ones'. The British Equivalent would be Tommy and the German Fritz. |
| In the bag | Taken prisoner. | | |
| Ind | Indian. | | |
| Inf Div | Infantry Division. | Pz Div | Panzer Division. |
| Jock Column | Mobile all-arms flying columns used to harass the enemy and retain the initiative. | Quad | Artillery towing vehicle. |
| | | RACD | Royal Army Church Deoartment. |
| | | RA | Royal Artillery. |
| Khamsin | Giant desert dust storm. | RAMC | Royal Army Medical Corps. |
| KIA | Killed in Action. | | |
| Lay Doggo | Feign death or lie low. | RAP | Regimental Aid Post. |
| LAA | Light Anti-aircraft. | RP | Regimental Police. |
| L/Cpl | Lance Corporal. | Recce | Reconnaissance. |
| L/Sgt | Lance Sergeant. | Revd | Reverend. |
| Lt | Lieutenant. | Rgt | Regiment. |
| Lt Div | Light Division. | RNF | Royal Northumberland Fusiliers. |
| Matilda | British heavy infantry support tank. | | |
| | | RP | Regimental Police. |
| MC | Military Cross. | RSM | Regimental Sergeant Major. |
| Mg | Machine-gun. | | |
| MID | Mention in despatches. | RTR | Royal Tank Regiment. |
| MM | Military Medal. | S Afr Bde | South African Brigade. |
| MO | Medical Officer. | Sgt | Sergeant. |
| Mot | Motorised. | S/Sgt | Staff Sergeant. |
| Naffi | Navy, Army and Air Force Institute which provided canteens and shops for British military personnel. | Sidi | Term of respect for a holy man, as in Sidi Muftah. |
| | | Sgmn | Signalman. |
| | | TD | Territorial Decoration. |
| NCO | Non Commissioned Officer. | The Blue | The Desert. |
| | | Trigh | Desert Track. |
| OKH | German High Command. | TSM | Troop Sergeant Major. |
| OP | Observation Post. | VC | Victoria Cross. |
| Osiers | Willow trees. | Wadi | Dried up river bed. |
| Pltn | Platoon. | Windy | To be frightened or unnerved. |
| POW | Prisoner of War. | | |
| Provost | Military Police. | | |

# Index

## PEOPLE

Amilakvari, Colonel xi, 211, 245
Atkinson, Corporal Sidney 32-33, 39, 88, 115
Auchinleck, Field Marshal Sir Claude 164, 193, 208, 224, 265, 267
Austin, Captain John Charles 65, 75, 83, 91, 102, 104

Baldwin, Alfred 124–125
Battiscombe, Major C R x, 93-94
Betts, Pte Jim 132, 161
Bransom, Major Harold Ian 181, 212
Bush, Lt Colonel W E 145–146, 149, 153, 162, 180, 185, 246

Caldwell, Captain 218–219
Cheeseman, Captain 89, 105, 123
Chester, Sergeant Arthur x, 24, 71–72, 74, 80, 93, 108, 116, 131–133, 137, 139–140, 145, 153, 180, 187, 197, 202, 206
Chittock, Pte Alfred 31, 42, 188, 204
Churchill, Brigadier J A 50, 65
Churchill, Winston 78, 88, 96, 246, 263–264
Clark, Major K A 67–68, 70
Clark, Pte John H x, 62, 213
Close, Lt Bill 166–167, 172
Collier, Pte Thomas 218, 221
Craig, Lt Thomas 50, 58
Crisp, Captain Robert James 168, 235
Cruwell, General Ludwig ii, 183–184, 267

Davies, Pte Bert 62, 118, 127
Davis, Sergeant Charles E 48, 64, 75, 200

Elliot, Sergeant George Denis ix, 38, 51, 86, 126
English, Lt Ian R x, 54, 65, 67, 97, 126, 130

Farthing, Captain 72, 74
Fort, Pte Bob 22, 44
Forth, Pte Harry xi, 140, 213–214, 216, 219
Franklyn, Major General 50, 78

Gibson, Sergeant Bob x, 29, 39, 92, 152
Gilson, Colour Sergeant Wilfred ix, 19–21, 30, 32, 38, 73-4, 116-117
Gleave, Pte William x, 136–138, 144, 148, 180, 183, 188, 192, 198, 201, 205
Glenton, Sergeant Herbert ix, 25–26, 72, 74, 85, 136, 141, 154, 194–195, 197, 203, 206
Gort, Lord 38, 49–50, 78–79, 264

Halstead, Lt John Michael Gregson xi, 173
Hardy, Pte Norman xi, 132, 154
Haydon, Brigadier Bill 85–86, 184, 193–194, 196, 198-199, 203, 205, 246
Hearst, Sergeant Max ix, 39–40, 43, 82, 92, 94, 101, 131, 149, 160, 214, 216, 219, 231, 235
Hilton, Sergeant Les 71, 84, 111, 130
Hitler, Adolf 34–36, 38, 78, 84, 128, 133–134, 136, 201, 263–264, 270
Holloway, Captain Stephen 111, 125
Howard, Sergeant Leonard 94, 99, 102, 111
Hymer, Pte Ralph 133, 141, 148, 233

Jackson, Pte Thomas W ix, 29, 61
Jeffries, Major Peter J ix, 42, 52, 63, 93, 97, 118, 130

Kilgallon, Pte x, 140, 213, 222, 229
Killby, Pte James Keith 174, 177, 201
King Leopold 88, 264
King, Captain Douglas x, 21, 25, 91–92, 140, 149, 154, 186, 206
King, Colonel John 52, 55-56
Kite, Sergeant Buck xi, 167, 170
Kneeshaw, Pte Joe x, xv, 105, 148

Ledger, Corporal George 101, 111
Little, Corporal Joss 22, 44, 89, 114, 121

Maher, Pte Thomas 22, 31, 46, 54–55, 60, 62, 82, 84, 120
Mander, Major D'arcy 164, 181, 183, 198–199, 206
Martel, General 44, 71, 82

McGarey, Sergeant James 21, 30–31, 61, 64, 66, 107, 114, 126
Miller, Lt Colonel Harry ix, 46, 52–53, 61
Mohn, Eric 226–227, 230
Mount, Captain Cyril xi, 182

Protheroe, Pte Reg ix, 27–28, 80, 113, 135, 141

Railton, Pte Ron 81, 149, 190, 203
Ridley, Corporal William 18, 33, 39, 64, 81, 83, 93, 121, 130, 159, 218, 222, 230
Ritchie, General Neil 147, 162, 164, 176, 192–193, 208, 214–215, 225, 266
Rommel, Field Marshal Erwin i–ii, ix–xii, 37, 49–50, 55, 57, 59–60, 77, 146–147, 150, 158, 161–166, 172, 174–176, 178–180, 184, 187, 192, 194, 196, 201, 203–206, 208–210, 213, 215, 223, 225–226, 237–240, 254, 263–270

Sell, Major Harold Sidney 217, 228, 230, 256
Snowdon, Corporal Albert x, 88, 115

Stafford, Captain Bob ix, 28–29, 40, 117, 156, 197, 204

Thompson, Pte Herbert xi, 143, 183, 188, 202
Thompson, Pte John ix, 29, 41, 84, 123, 146, 152, 185, 191, 195
Tidball, Pte Ken x, 24–25, 108–109
Toomey, Pte Jack 99, 119, 135

Vaux, Lt Peter 51, 60, 63, 67, 69

Wakenshaw, Pte Adam ii, viii, xi, 226–227, 230–231, 254–256, 261
Walker, Pte Roy x, 39–40, 114, 231
Watson, Major William I 134–135, 142, 158, 197, 204, 215, 217–218
Watt, Lt Robert 166, 178
Welsford, Pte Douglas 234, 236
Williams, Sergeant John 23, 28, 102
Wood, Captain George L x, 68, 104, 128, 130
Wood, Lt Colonel Roland 70, 128
Wright, Sergeant Major Thomas B ix, 19–20

## PLACES

Achicourt 55, 58–59, 61, 63, 67, 69, 75
Agedabia 147, 266
Albert Canal 33–34, 36–37
Alexandria ii, 148, 225, 238, 254
Amiens 32, 263
Ardenne 34, 36–37
Arras i, vii, ix–x, xii, 20–21, 36, 43–44, 49–51, 54–55, 57–61, 65, 67, 71–72, 74–78, 80, 86, 131, 239, 250, 254, 263
Arras-Doullens Road 54, 61
Auleb xi, 159, 180, 185, 187, 192, 194, 200, 202, 258–260, 266, 271

Bardia 147, 265–267
Beaurains 49, 60–61, 63, 68
Belgium ix, 17, 34–38, 40, 50, 80, 132, 135, 263–264
Benghazi 145–147, 157, 265–266
Bir el Harmat 193, 210
Bir Geff 146, 150, 159
Bir Hacheim ii, vii, xi, 146, 159, 164–165, 171, 174, 206, 210–211, 213–215, 217, 220–221, 245, 266–267, 269, 271
Bir Thalata 144, 223
Bock 40, 88
Bray Dunes 103, 105, 108, 113, 117
Bulskamp 97, 104

Cambrai 56, 78
Capuzzo Gap 182, 186
Carvin 67, 81–83, 254
Cherbourg 27–28, 264

Dainville 51–52
Dendre 38–39
Devil's Cauldron xi, 178, 181–182, 206, 209, 212
Duisans 54, 64–66
Dunkirk i, vii–viii, x, 40, 65, 74–75, 78–79, 83, 89, 91–93, 96–97, 99, 101–103, 105, 107–123, 125–126, 128, 130, 132–133, 135, 215, 239, 254, 257, 263–264, 269–270
Dyle River 34, 36–38, 263

Egypt 17, 225, 238, 255, 264, 267
El Adem 165, 172–173, 175, 265
El Alamein ii, xi, 139, 172, 184, 211, 224–225, 237–239, 245, 255, 267–270
Escaut 34, 39–40, 43

France i, viii–x, 17–18, 23, 26–29, 32, 34, 37–38, 52–53, 56, 78–79, 96, 128, 132–133, 135, 140, 150, 239, 251, 263–264, 269

Gateshead 18, 26, 122, 254
Gazala Line i–ii, xi, 146–148, 153, 156, 159, 162, 165, 173, 175, 178, 193, 195, 200, 215, 223, 239, 254, 266–267
Givenchy 60, 67, 75

Haifa 141, 144
Halfaya 145, 265–266
Holland 34, 36, 263

Iraq 142, 145

Khamsin 157–158, 216, 272
Knightsbridge 144, 174, 201, 210, 212, 214, 267

La Panne 100, 111
Lens 27, 75, 82–84
Lille 32–33, 40, 46, 81, 87, 264
Liverpool 136–137
Loos 32, 80
Luxembourg 37, 263

Maginot Line 37, 264
Malta 151, 153, 161
Maroeuil 65–66
Martuba xi, 151–152, 155, 260, 266
Mechili 145, 151, 265–266
Menin Gate i, 84–85, 88
Mersa Matruh ii, vii, xii, 157, 224–228, 231–232, 235, 238–239, 254, 258–261, 267
Meuse 35–37, 263
Middle East i, 137, 193, 268–270

Poperinge 86–87
Puchios xi, 211

Ras El Eleba 151–152

Ruweisat Ridge 237–239, 268

Sabratha 215, 238, 249
Scarpe River i, 44, 50, 71-72, 74, 81
Sidi-Rezegh 144, 147
Singapore 139, 143, 266
Sollum 145, 147, 264–266
Somme ix, 21, 49, 80
Syria 139, 143

Tmimi 151, 266
Tobruk 145, 147, 161, 174, 177, 182, 215, 217, 222–223, 225, 238, 254, 265–267
Trigh Capuzzo 158, 164, 175–176, 193, 217
Trigh el Abd 158, 175, 180

Vimy Ridge i, 44, 46, 48, 50, 65–66, 71, 75

Wailly 55, 57–58, 77
Wancourt 55, 57
Warlus 57, 59, 61, 63–66
Western Desert iii, vii, xi, 139, 143–144, 182, 264, 272

Ypres Salient 18, 84
Ypres i, 18, 21, 82, 84–88, 239, 254, 264

## MILITARY UNITS AND FORMATIONS

**Allied Forces**
1st Armoured Division 147, 151, 205, 225, 237
1st Army Tank Brigade 50, 177, 248
1st South African Division 159, 267
3rd Battalion Royal Tank Regiment xi, 166–168, 172, 178, 235
4th Armoured Brigade 166, 172
4th Battalion East Yorkshire Regiment ix–xi, 17–20, 24–25, 28–29, 32, 38, 40, 71–74, 80, 85, 87–88, 91–92, 108, 111, 115–117, 130–132, 137, 140–141, 143, 145, 151, 153–154, 156, 161, 180, 182–183, 186–188, 194, 197, 202–204, 206, 246
4th Battalion Green Howards x, 136–138, 144, 146, 157, 164, 180–181, 183, 188, 191–192, 198, 201, 205
4th Battalion Northumberland Fusiliers 36, 64
4th Battalion Royal Northumberland Fusiliers x, 26, 48, 50, 64, 67–70, 75, 144, 200, 250
4th Battalion Royal Tank Regiment 50–52, 53, 63, 67, 69, 250
5th Battalion East Yorkshire Regiment ix–xi, xv, 39–40, 114, 133, 140, 149, 160, 213–214, 216–217, 219, 231, 234–235
5th Battalion Green Howards ix–x, xv, 29, 41, 72–73, 81, 84, 87–88, 105, 115, 123, 137, 145–146, 148–149, 152, 162, 180, 185, 190–191, 195, 196, 203, 252
5th Division 49, 66, 97

5th Indian Division 141–142, 225
6th Battalion Durham Light Infantry 23, 28, 30, 38, 42, 46, 50, 55, 158
6th Battalion Green Howards x, 81, 103
6th Durham Light Infantry ix–x, 23, 28, 30, 38, 42, 46, 50, 52–53, 55, 57, 61–63, 67–68, 70, 81–82, 86, 93, 97, 102–103, 118, 126–128, 130, 134, 142, 158, 160–161, 215, 217–218, 228–229, 246, 250–252, 258–261
7th Armoured Division 192–193, 265
7th Battalion Royal Tank Regiment 50, 52, 55–58, 60, 69, 250
8th Battalion Durham Light Infantry 21–22, 29–30, 44, 46, 50, 54–55, 61–64, 66, 84, 86, 89, 97, 101, 107, 111, 114, 120–121, 126, 130, 133, 139, 141, 148, 213, 217, 227–228, 230, 233, 250–253, 258–261
8th Hussars 166, 171–172
9th Battalion Durham Light Infantry viii–xi, 18, 33, 39, 44, 51, 81, 83, 93–94, 104, 121, 130, 140, 159, 213, 217–218, 221–222, 226–227, 229–230, 252–255, 260–261
10th Indian Division 224–225
42nd Battalion Royal Tank Regiment 177, 248
44th Battalion Royal Tank Regiment 177, 195–196
50th Northumbrian Division i–iii, v, vii–viii, xiii, xv, 17–18, 24–27, 32–33, 36, 38–40, 43–44, 49–50, 61, 79–80, 82, 84, 86–87, 89, 94–95, 97,

101, 105, 108, 122–123, 130, 132–136, 138–139, 141–145, 147–148, 150–151, 155, 164, 186, 193, 213–215, 220, 223–225, 230, 233, 237, 239, 246, 251–252, 254, 258, 266–267, 269
69th Brigade 133, 142–143, 146, 159, 162, 164, 185, 213–214, 231
72nd Field Regiment 137, 144–146, 149, 182–183, 239, 246, 248
74th Field Regiment 89, 101, 105, 214, 222, 226, 246
90th Light Division 165, 169, 175, 187, 194, 210, 226, 237, 242, 249, 254
92nd Field Regiment 62, 250
95th Anti-tank Regiment 151–152
124th Field Regiment 181, 212
150th Brigade vii, x–xii, 32, 44, 71–72, 74, 81, 84–88, 97, 101, 105, 107, 118, 136–139, 141–148, 151, 154, 157, 159, 176–184, 186, 189, 191, 193–194, 196–197, 199–203, 206, 208–210, 213–214, 239, 248, 254, 266–267, 269
150th Field Ambulance ix, xi, 27–28, 31, 42, 80, 113, 135, 137, 141, 145, 174, 177, 188, 200–201, 204, 247
151st Brigade Provost Company x, 29, 32, 39, 44, 50, 71, 81, 85–86, 92, 97, 104–105, 107, 118, 139, 142–143, 146, 151–152, 213, 217, 221, 226
232nd Field Company 137, 145, 151 181, 185, 199, 248
285th Battery 146, 151-152
365th Battery 50, 250
368th Battery 50, 250

British Artillery xi, 77, 104, 175, 182
British Expeditionary Force (BEF) xii, 36, 38, 43, 47, 50, 64, 77-79, 88, 94, 96-97, 104, 128, 132, 136, 254, 264, 271

Cheshire Regiment 42, 151, 248

Desert Air Force 154, 162, 185, 202, 208

Eighth Army xiii, xv, 144–147, 161–162, 164–165, 171–172, 176, 178, 180, 193, 205, 208, 210, 212, 215, 223–226, 233, 238–239, 254–255, 265–270

Frankforce 74, 78
Free French i–ii, vii, 122, 146, 159, 165, 185, 210, 214, 217, 245, 266–267
French Army 38, 78–79, 264

French Foreign Legion xi, 211, 242, 245

New Zealand Division 144, 225–226, 268

Royal Air Force (RAF) 62, 97, 134, 151, 178
Royal Army Medical Corps 83, 116, 247, 273
Royal Army Service Corps 82, 132, 145, 218, 221, 234, 236, 247
Royal Artillery xi, 38, 50, 62, 65, 75, 83, 89, 91, 105, 109, 112, 123–124, 137, 145–146, 151–152, 181–183, 187, 190, 196, 212, 214, 222, 235, 246, 248, 250, 273
Royal Engineers 22, 44, 94, 99–100, 102, 111, 115, 125, 127, 137, 151, 181, 185, 199, 247–248
Royal Navy 109, 119, 128, 206

Territorial Army ix, 17–19, 21, 23, 74, 95

Welsh Guards 49, 72

Yeomanry 17, 248

**Axis Forces**
5th Panzer Regiment 165, 177, 185, 244
7th Panzer Division ix, 49, 52, 54, 57, 59–60, 263
15th Panzer Division vii, 164–167, 186, 194, 210, 237, 243, 249
21st Panzer Division vii, 164–165, 176, 187, 194, 209–210, 226, 229, 237–238, 244, 249, 266–267
25th Panzer Regiment 57, 240

Cruwell Group 164, 213

German 90th Light Division 165, 210, 226, 254
German High Command 35, 38, 78, 161, 263, 272

Italian Ariete Division 165, 178, 237
Italian Brescia Division 215, 237-238, 249
Italian Corps 162, 249
Italian Trieste Division 176, 187, 194, 210
Italian Trento Infantry 215, 249

Luftwaffe 35–36, 41–42, 81, 109, 134–135, 151, 162, 164, 184, 194, 208, 210, 238, 263

Panzer Army Africa vii, 186, 224, 239, 249, 270

SS Totenkopf Division i, x, 59-60, 77